SAMURAI DEEPER KYO

VOLUME 15

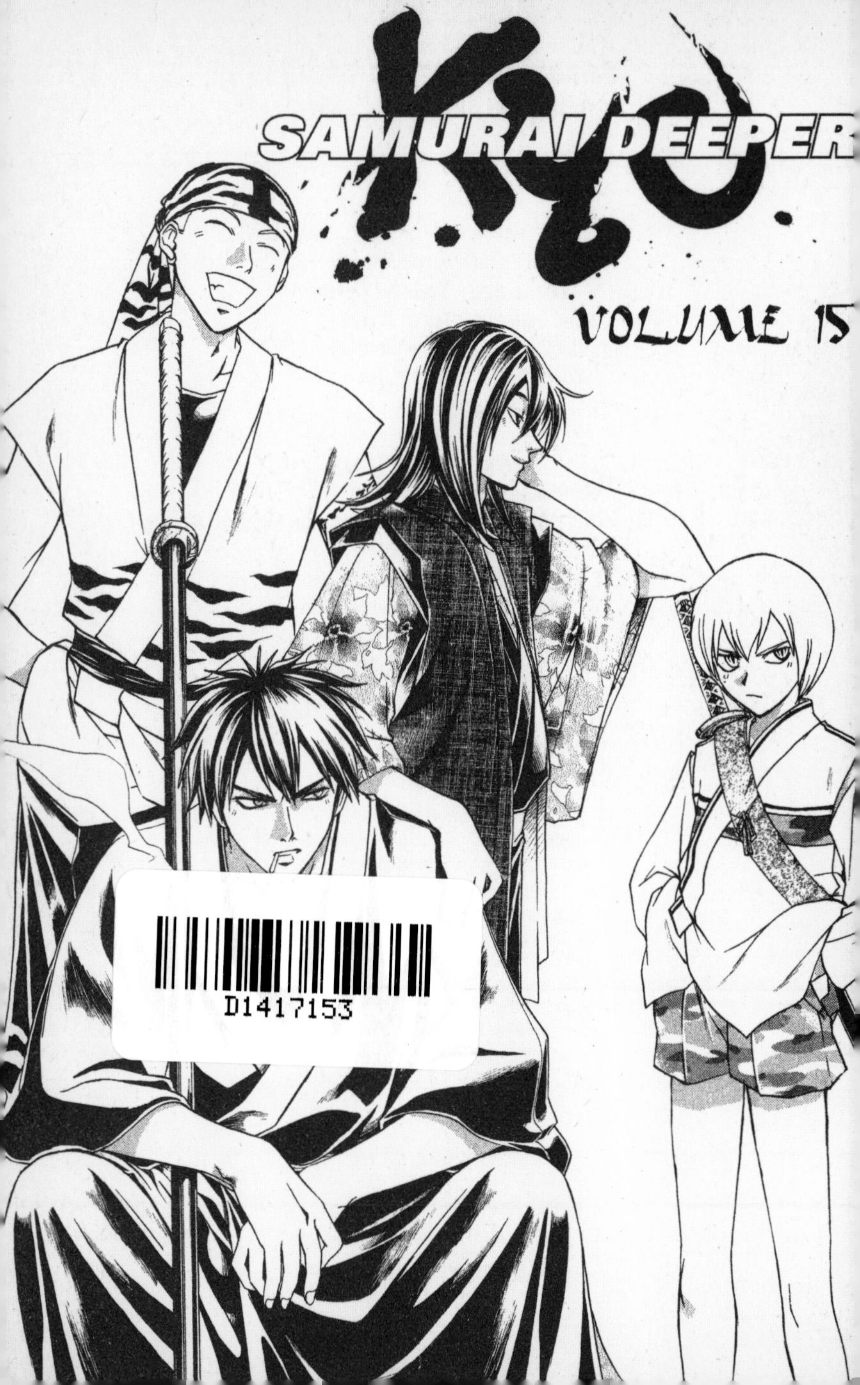

Samurai Deeper Kyo Vol. 15
Created by Akimine Kamijyo

Translation - Alexander O. Smith
Script Editor - Rich Amtower
Copy Editor - Suzanne Waldman
Retouch and Lettering - Lucas Rivera
Production Artist - Irene Woori Choi
Cover Design - Seth Cable

Editor - Aaron Suhr
Digital Imaging Manager - Chris Buford
Production Managers - Jennifer Miller and Mutsumi Miyazaki
Managing Editor - Jill Freshney
VP of Production - Ron Klamert
Editor-In-Chief - Mike Kiley
President and C.O.O. - John Parker
Publisher and C.E.O. - Stuart Levy

A  Manga

TOKYOPOP Inc.
5900 Wilshire Blvd. Suite 2000
Los Angeles, CA 90036

E-mail: info@TOKYOPOP.com
Come visit us online at www.TOKYOPOP.com

ISBN: 1-59532-455-0

First TOKYOPOP printing: Augusst 2005
10 9 8 7 6 5 4 3 2
Printed in the USA

SAMURAI DEEPER Kyo

Vol. 15
by Akimine Kamijyo

TOKYOPOP®

HAMBURG // LONDON // LOS ANGELES // TOKYO

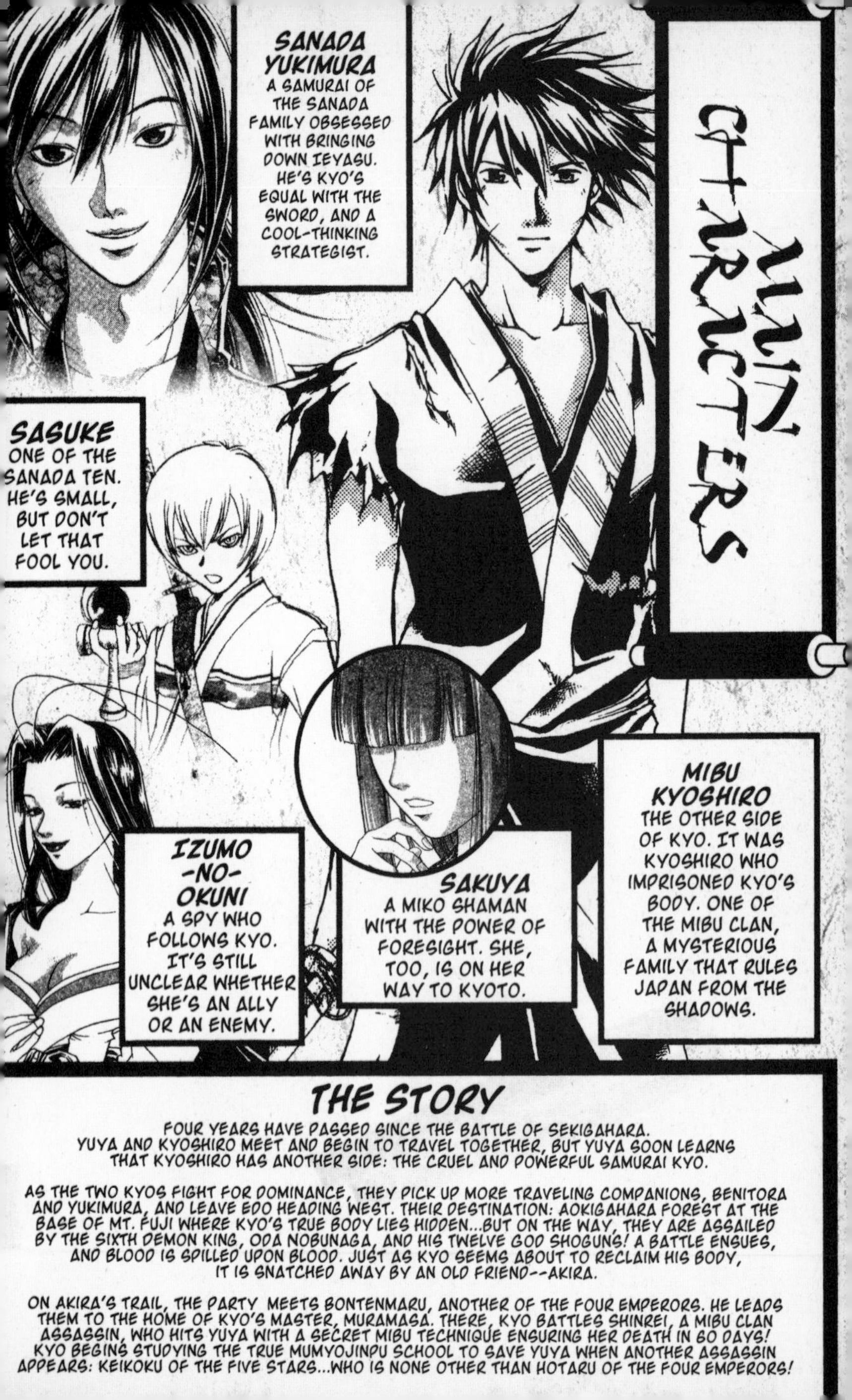
MAIN CHARACTERS
SANADA YUKIMURA
A SAMURAI OF THE SANADA FAMILY OBSESSED WITH BRINGING DOWN IEYASU. HE'S KYO'S EQUAL WITH THE SWORD, AND A COOL-THINKING STRATEGIST.
SASUKE
ONE OF THE SANADA TEN. HE'S SMALL, BUT DON'T LET THAT FOOL YOU.
MIBU KYOSHIRO
THE OTHER SIDE OF KYO. IT WAS KYOSHIRO WHO IMPRISONED KYO'S BODY. ONE OF THE MIBU CLAN, A MYSTERIOUS FAMILY THAT RULES JAPAN FROM THE SHADOWS.
SAKUYA
A MIKO SHAMAN WITH THE POWER OF FORESIGHT. SHE, TOO, IS ON HER WAY TO KYOTO.
IZUMO -NO- OKUNI
A SPY WHO FOLLOWS KYO. IT'S STILL UNCLEAR WHETHER SHE'S AN ALLY OR AN ENEMY.

THE STORY

FOUR YEARS HAVE PASSED SINCE THE BATTLE OF SEKIGAHARA. YUYA AND KYOSHIRO MEET AND BEGIN TO TRAVEL TOGETHER, BUT YUYA SOON LEARNS THAT KYOSHIRO HAS ANOTHER SIDE: THE CRUEL AND POWERFUL SAMURAI KYO.

AS THE TWO KYOS FIGHT FOR DOMINANCE, THEY PICK UP MORE TRAVELING COMPANIONS, BENITORA AND YUKIMURA, AND LEAVE EDO HEADING WEST. THEIR DESTINATION: AOKIGAHARA FOREST AT THE BASE OF MT. FUJI WHERE KYO'S TRUE BODY LIES HIDDEN...BUT ON THE WAY, THEY ARE ASSAILED BY THE SIXTH DEMON KING, ODA NOBUNAGA, AND HIS TWELVE GOD SHOGUNS! A BATTLE ENSUES, AND BLOOD IS SPILLED UPON BLOOD. JUST AS KYO SEEMS ABOUT TO RECLAIM HIS BODY, IT IS SNATCHED AWAY BY AN OLD FRIEND--AKIRA.

ON AKIRA'S TRAIL, THE PARTY MEETS BONTENMARU, ANOTHER OF THE FOUR EMPERORS. HE LEADS THEM TO THE HOME OF KYO'S MASTER, MURAMASA. THERE, KYO BATTLES SHINREI, A MIBU CLAN ASSASSIN, WHO HITS YUYA WITH A SECRET MIBU TECHNIQUE ENSURING HER DEATH IN 60 DAYS! KYO BEGINS STUDYING THE TRUE MUMYOJINPU SCHOOL TO SAVE YUYA WHEN ANOTHER ASSASSIN APPEARS: KEIKOKU OF THE FIVE STARS...WHO IS NONE OTHER THAN HOTARU OF THE FOUR EMPERORS!

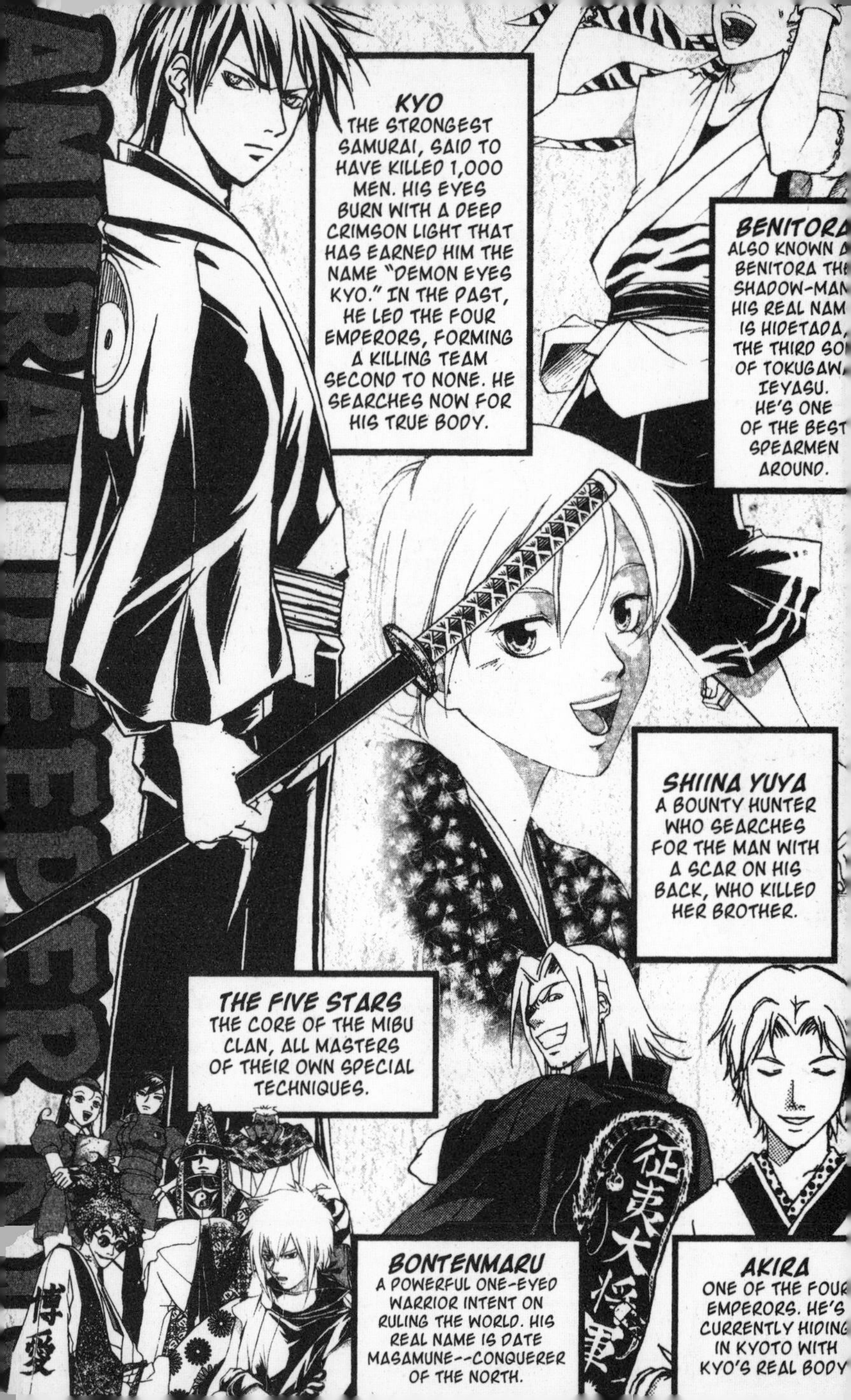

BENITORA
ALSO KNOWN A
BENITORA THE
SHADOW-MAN
HIS REAL NAM
IS HIDETADA,
THE THIRD SO
OF TOKUGAW
IEYASU.
HE'S ONE
OF THE BEST
SPEARMEN
AROUND.
KYO
THE STRONGEST SAMURAI, SAID TO HAVE KILLED 1,000 MEN. HIS EYES BURN WITH A DEEP CRIMSON LIGHT THAT HAS EARNED HIM THE NAME "DEMON EYES KYO." IN THE PAST, HE LED THE FOUR EMPERORS, FORMING A KILLING TEAM SECOND TO NONE. HE SEARCHES NOW FOR HIS TRUE BODY.
SHIINA YUYA
A BOUNTY HUNTER WHO SEARCHES FOR THE MAN WITH A SCAR ON HIS BACK, WHO KILLED HER BROTHER.
THE FIVE STARS
THE CORE OF THE MIBU CLAN, ALL MASTERS OF THEIR OWN SPECIAL TECHNIQUES.
AKIRA
ONE OF THE FOUR EMPERORS. HE'S CURRENTLY HIDING IN KYOTO WITH KYO'S REAL BODY
BONTENMARU
A POWERFUL ONE-EYED WARRIOR INTENT ON RULING THE WORLD. HIS REAL NAME IS DATE MASAMUNE--CONQUERER OF THE NORTH.
征東大将軍
博愛

F KYO!

WHERE DID KYO MEET ALL HIS FRIENDS? WHO DID THEY FIGHT? SWIFTER THAN KYO CAN SWING HIS SWORD, HERE'S A RECAP OF ALL THAT'S HAPPENED IN SDK SO FAR!

(1) THE JOURNEY OF KYOSHIRO AND YUYA BEGINS! (SDK VOL.1)

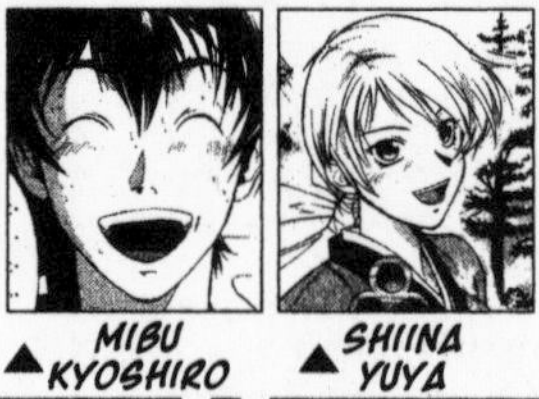

MIBU KYOSHIRO
SHIINA YUYA

THE BEAUTIFUL BOUNTY HUNTER YUYA MEETS MIBU KYOSHIRO BY CHANCE (OR WAS IT FATE?!). WHEN THEY FOUGHT THE BANTOUJI BROTHERS, KYOSHIRO'S OTHER SIDE WAS REVEALED: THAT OF DEMON EYES KYO!

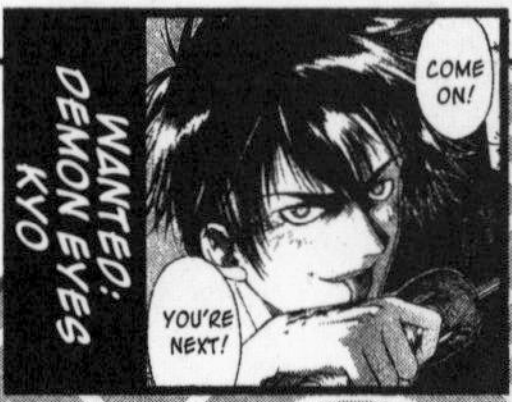

WANTED: DEMON EYES KYO
COME ON!
YOU'RE NEXT!

(2) THE WOMAN IZUMO-NO-OKUNI (SDK VOL.1-2)

THEY MEET THE WOMAN IZUMO-NO-OKUNI IN AN INN TOWN--AND SHE SEEMS TO KNOW A LOT ABOUT KYO AND KYOSHIRO'S PAST. THEN, IN THE VILLAGE OF DESERTERS, KYO AWAKENS AND SHOWS HIS FULL STRENGTH!

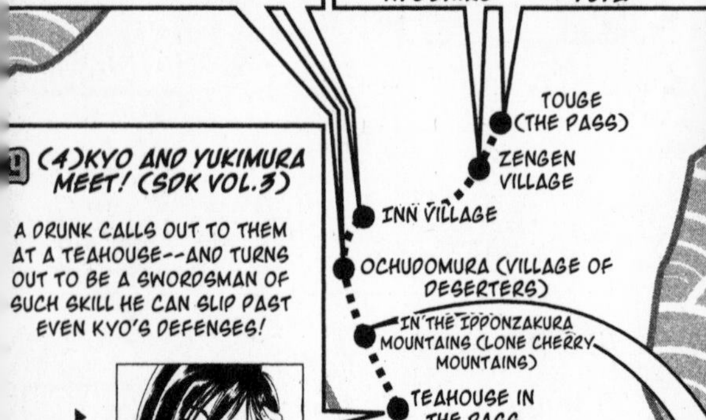

TOUGE (THE PASS)
ZENGEN VILLAGE
INN VILLAGE
OCHUDOMURA (VILLAGE OF DESERTERS)
IN THE IPPONZAKURA MOUNTAINS (LONE CHERRY MOUNTAINS)
TEAHOUSE IN THE PASS
EDO
THE FOREST OF AOKIGAHARA
HAKONE
MT. FUJI

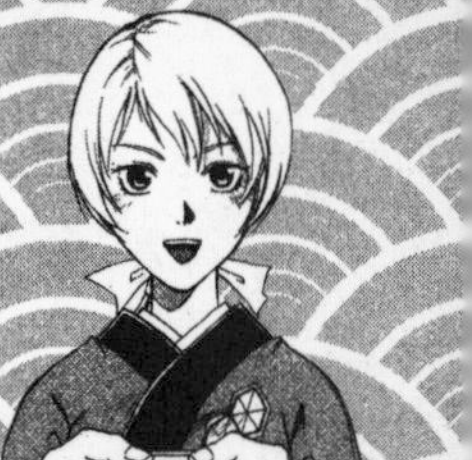

(4)KYO AND YUKIMURA MEET! (SDK VOL.3)

A DRUNK CALLS OUT TO THEM AT A TEAHOUSE--AND TURNS OUT TO BE A SWORDSMAN OF SUCH SKILL HE CAN SLIP PAST EVEN KYO'S DEFENSES!

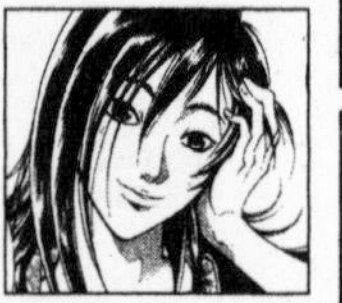

SANADA YUKIMURA

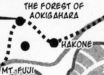

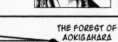

(3) BENITORA JOINS THE PARTY! (SDK VOL. 2-3)

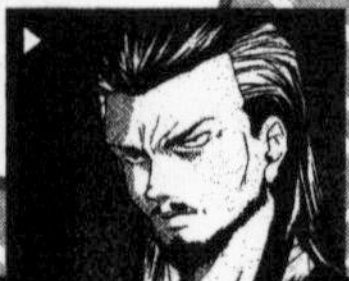

THE PARTY GETS INTO A FIGHT WITH A TREASURE-SEEKING GROUP OF ASSASSINS KNOWN AS THE KITOU FAMILY SANSAISHU. ONE OF THEIR NUMBER, BENITORA, ENDS UP JOINING SIDES WITH KYO. KYO FIGHTS THE SHIROKARASU (WHITE CROW) AND FULLY AWAKENS! KYOSHIRO, HOWEVER, IS NOWHERE TO BE SEEN.

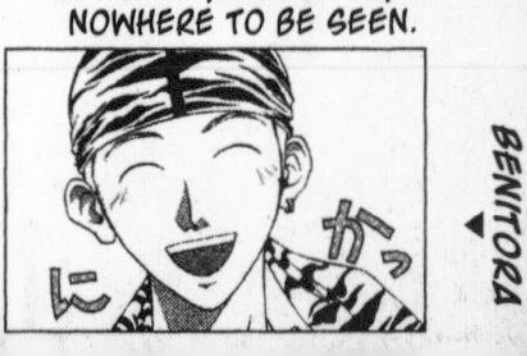

BENITORA

(5)FIGHT BEFORE THE SHOGUN! (SDK VOL.3-5)

KYO, YUKIMURA, AND BENITORA ENTER A TOURNEY HELD BY THE RULER OF THE LAND, TOKUGAWA IEYASU. BUT THE TOURNEY WAS A TRAP! SET UPON BY TOKUGAWA'S ELITES, THE THREE MANAGE TO DESTROY THEM ALL WITHOUT BREAKING A SWEAT! THEN YUKIMURA TELLS KYO A SECRET: THE LOCATION OF HIS BODY!

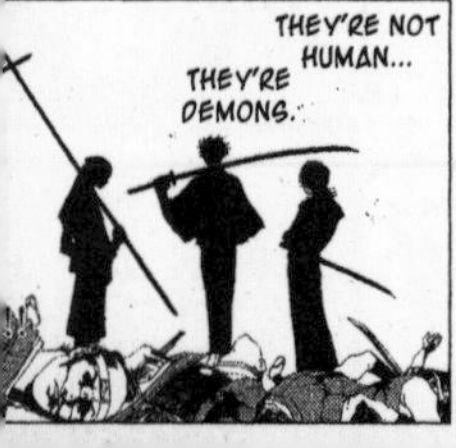

THEY'RE NOT HUMAN...
THEY'RE DEMONS.

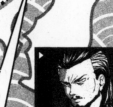

LEARN THE LEGEND

六 (6) MORTAL COMBAT VERSUS ODA NOBUNAGA AND THE TWELVE GOD SHOGUNS! (SDK VOL. 5-10)

KYO'S BODY LIES HIDDEN IN THE DEEPEST REACHES OF THE AOKIGAHARA FOREST AT THE FOOT OF MT. FUJI. BUT BETWEEN KYO AND HIS BODY STAND THE TWELVE GUARDIANS OF THE MASTER, ODA NOBUNAGA. AFTER A STRING OF BLOODY BATTLES, KYO'S DEMONBLADE, MURAMASA, RELIEVES NOBUNAGA'S BODY OF ITS HEAD, BUT AKIRA MAKES HIS ESCAPE WITH KYO'S BODY!

AKIRA	ANTERA
SHINDARA	MAKORA
SANTERA	INDARA = IZUMO-NO-OKUNI
SHATORA	

--R.I.P.--
BIKARA
BASARA
MEKIRA
KUBIRA
HAIRA

NOBUNAGA AWAITS THE TIME OF HIS RESURRECTION IN THE VILLAGE OF THE MIBU, DEEP WITHIN THE LAND OF THE FIRE LOTUS.

▲ ODA NOBUNAGA

▲ SASUKE

ONE OF THE SANADA TEN. HE RETURNED TO THE FOREST WHERE HE WAS BORN ON YUKIMURA'S ORDERS.

八 (8) FIERCE FIGHTING AGAINST THE PRIDE OF THE MIBU CLAN! (SDK VOL. 11-)

THE ENIGMATIC MIBU FAMILY HOLDS THE KEY TO THE MYSTERY BEHIND KYO'S BIRTH. AFTER HOLDING THE POWER TO CONTROL JAPAN'S HISTORY FROM THE DARK SIDE, SUDDENLY THE FACE-TO-FACE SHOWDOWN HAS BEGUN! AT THE SAME TIME, THE POWER TO SAVE YUYA'S LIFE LIES WITH THE ENEMY. KYO HAS CONFRONTED THE FIVE STARS, THE FOUR EMPERORS AND MOST RECENTLY, THE RED KING (AKA NO OU), HIS LATEST ULTIMATELY STRONG FOE. ON THE OTHER HAND, KYO IS MARCHING INTO ENEMY TERRITORY ARMED WITH THE MUMYO JINPU TECHNIQUE THAT MURAMASA TRADED HIS LIFE TO OBTAIN.

SHINREI

KYOTO: WHERE KYO'S BODY LIES!

● KYOTO

TOKAIDO ROAD

OWARI

七 (7) ENTER BONTENMARU! (SDK VOL. 10)

THE ONE-EYED DATE MASAMUNE APPEARS BEFORE KYO AND LEADS THE PARTY TO KYO'S MASTER, MURAMASA.

The rejected cover for Vol. 14.
Sorry, Akira-- Maybe next time.

SAMURAI DEEPER KYO

CHAPTER 115   CASTLE TOWN

CHAPTER 116   THE COLOR OF THE HEART

CHAPTER 117   ROAD TO HOPE

CHAPTER 118   THE CHAMBER OF TIME

CHAPTER 119   THREADS OF FATE

CHAPTER 120   LABORATORY OF LIFE

CHAPTER 121   TEARS

CHAPTER 122   BLOOD OATH

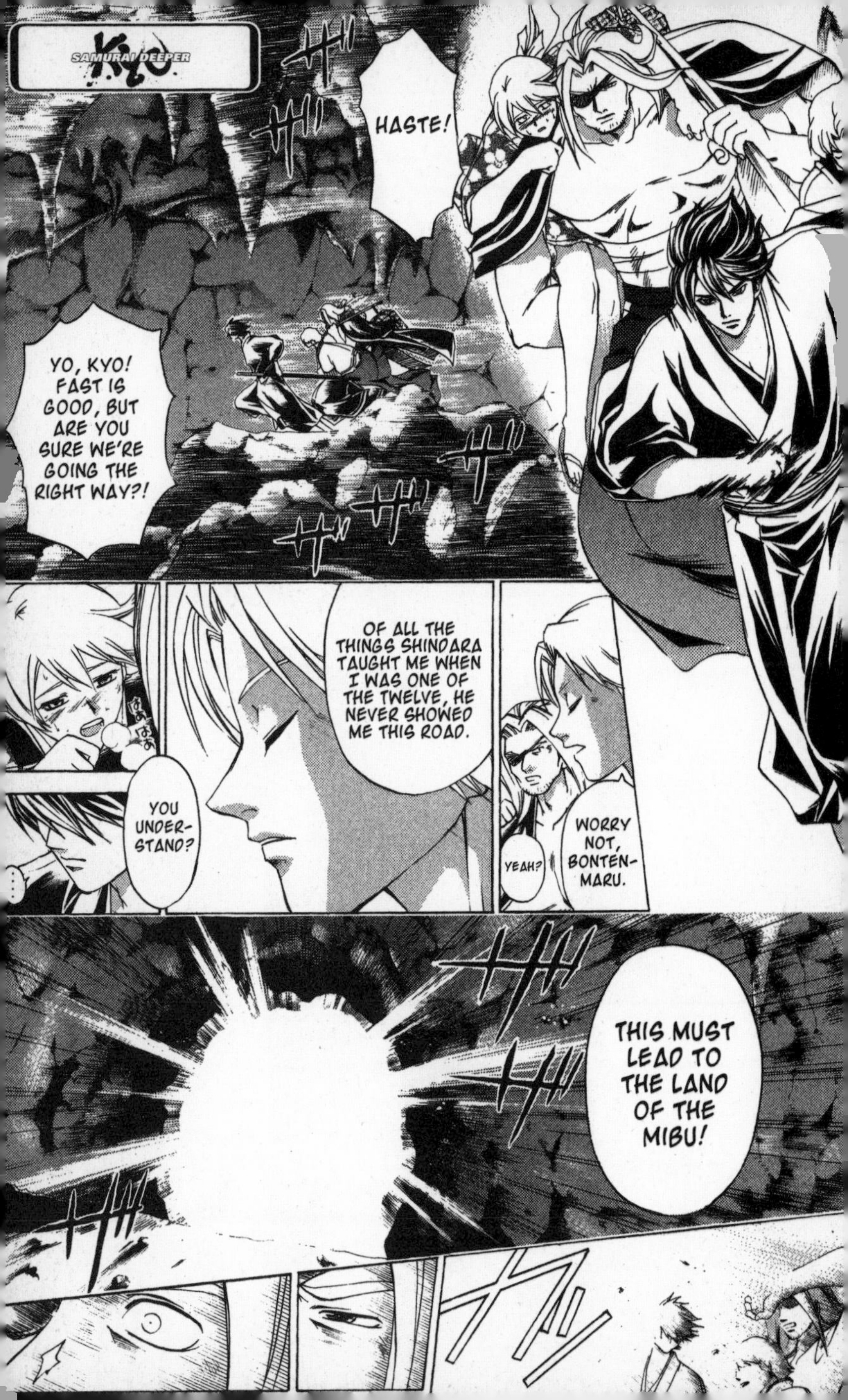
HASTE!
YO, KYO! FAST IS GOOD, BUT ARE YOU SURE WE'RE GOING THE RIGHT WAY?!
WORRY NOT, BONTEN-MARU.
YEAH?
OF ALL THE THINGS SHINDARA TAUGHT ME WHEN I WAS ONE OF THE TWELVE, HE NEVER SHOWED ME THIS ROAD.
YOU UNDER-STAND?
...
THIS MUST LEAD TO THE LAND OF THE MIBU!

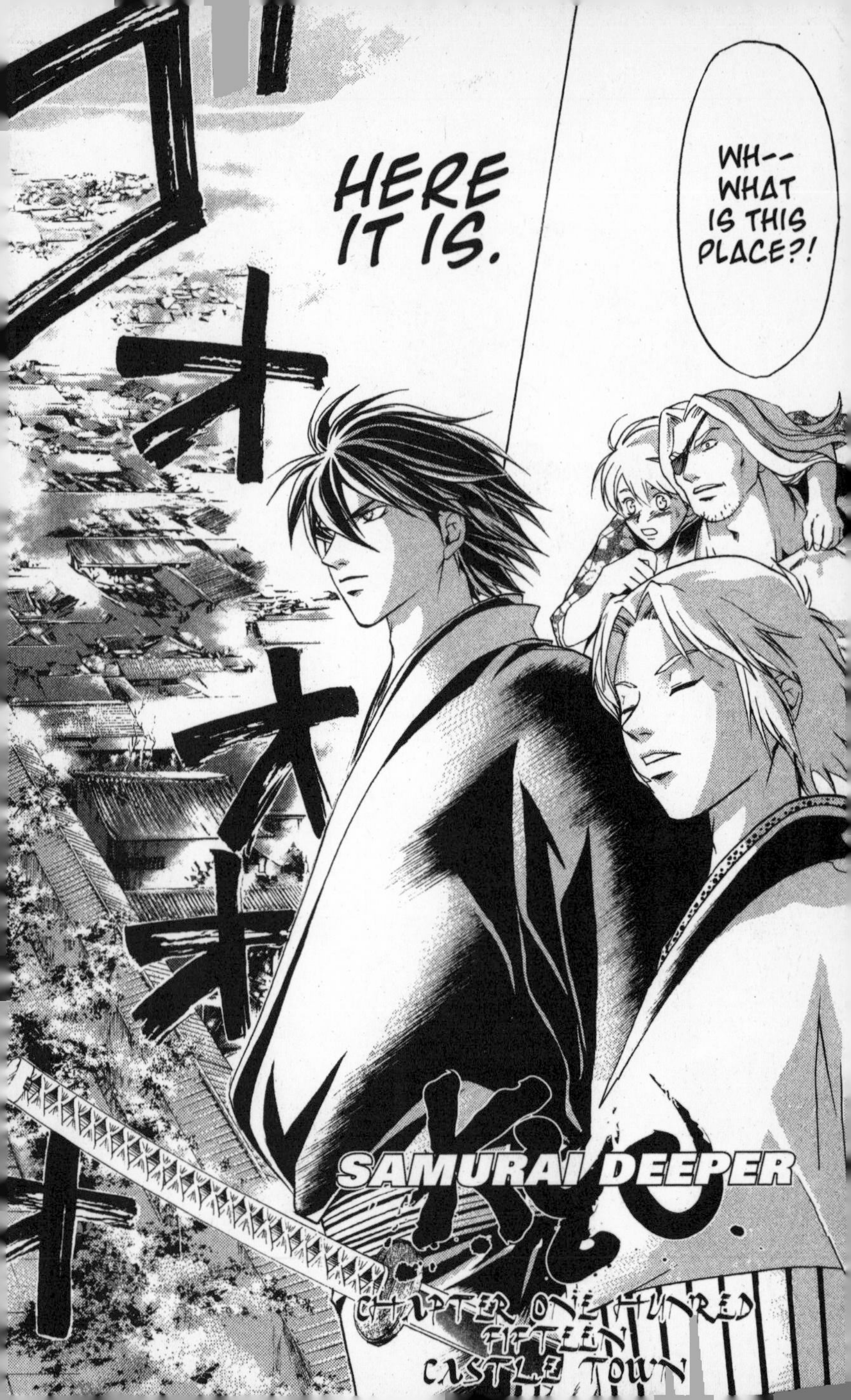
WH-- WHAT IS THIS PLACE?!
HERE IT IS.
ゴオオオ
SAMURAI DEEPER
CHAPTER ONE HUNRED FIFTEEN
CASTLE TOWN

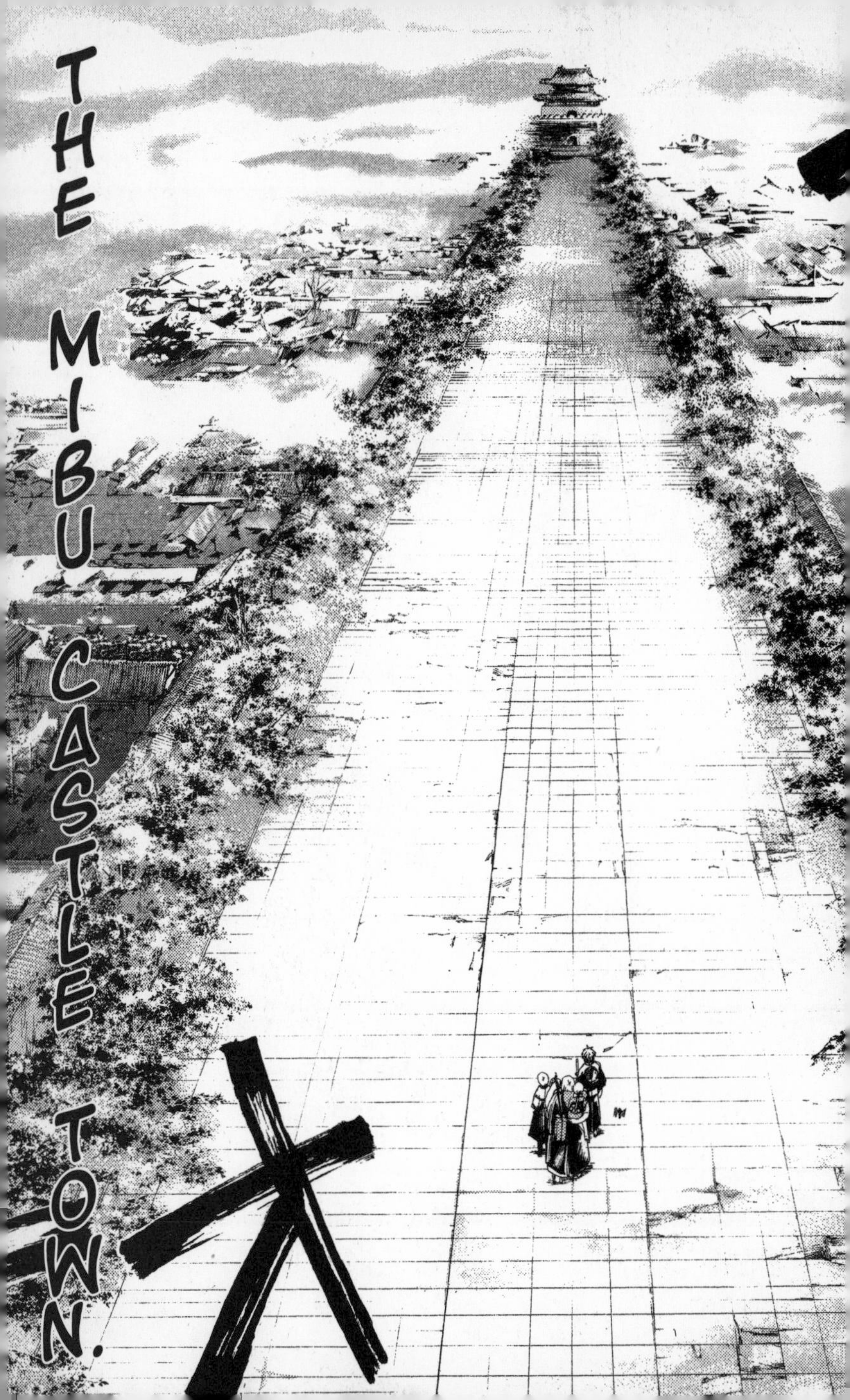
THE MIBU CASTLE TOWN.

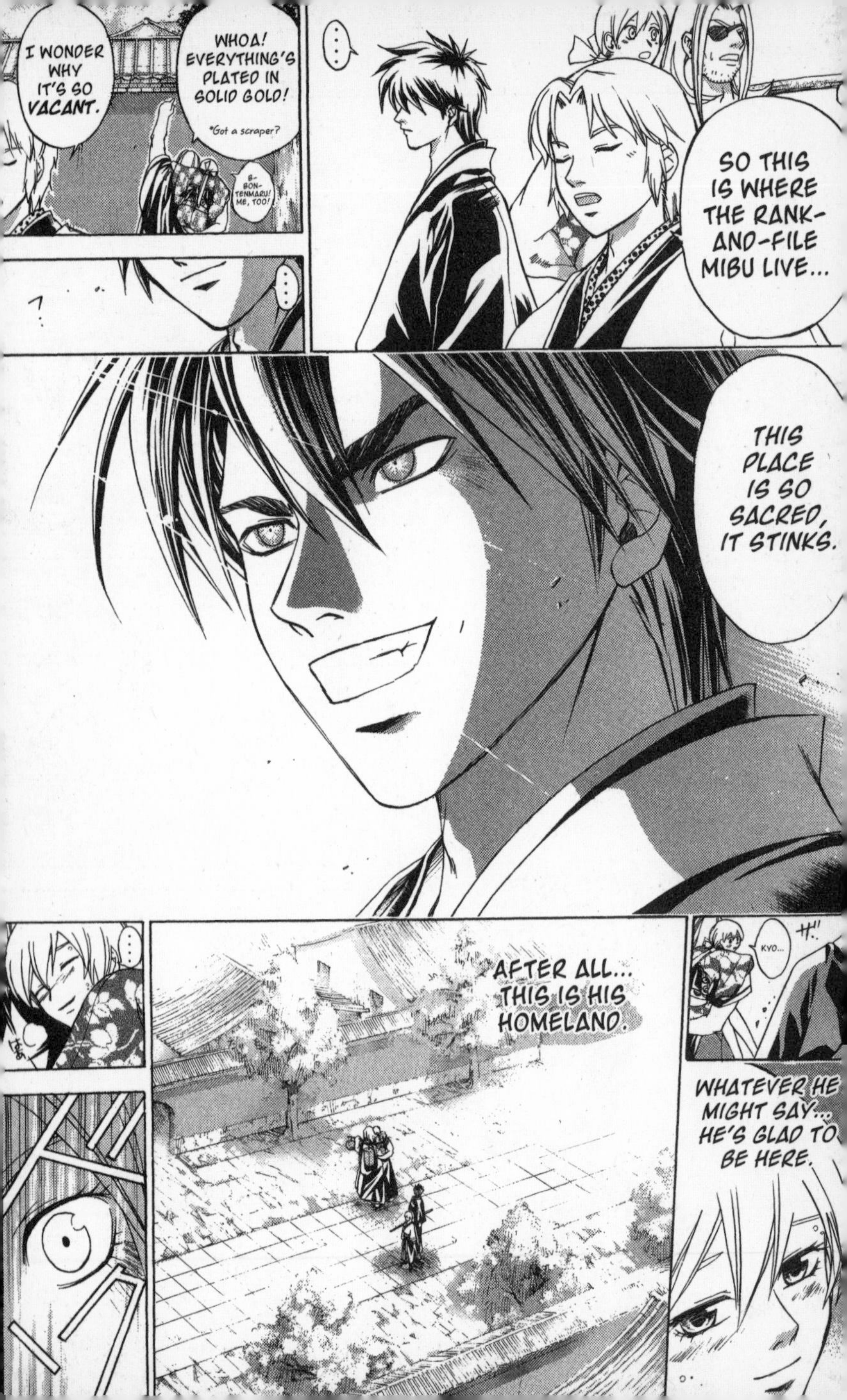
SO THIS IS WHERE THE RANK-AND-FILE MIBU LIVE...
...
WHOA! EVERYTHING'S PLATED IN SOLID GOLD!
*Got a scraper?
B-BONTENMARU! ME, TOO!
I WONDER WHY IT'S SO VACANT.
...
?
THIS PLACE IS SO SACRED, IT STINKS.
KYO...
WHATEVER HE MIGHT SAY... HE'S GLAD TO BE HERE.
AFTER ALL... THIS IS HIS HOMELAND.
...

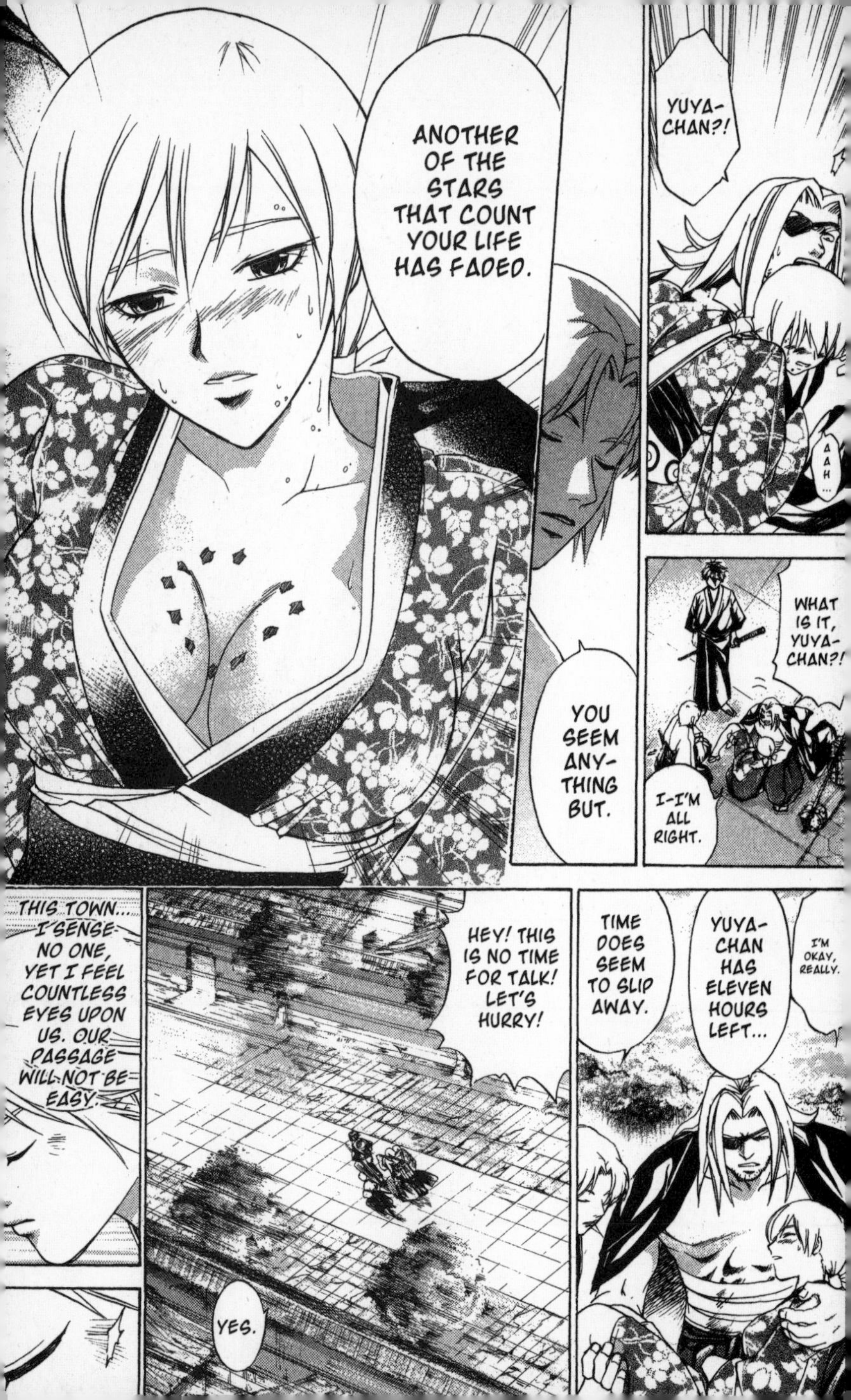
YUYA-CHAN?!
AAH...
WHAT IS IT, YUYA-CHAN?!
I-I'M ALL RIGHT.
YOU SEEM ANYTHING BUT.
ANOTHER OF THE STARS THAT COUNT YOUR LIFE HAS FADED.
I'M OKAY, REALLY.
YUYA-CHAN HAS ELEVEN HOURS LEFT...
TIME DOES SEEM TO SLIP AWAY.
HEY! THIS IS NO TIME FOR TALK! LET'S HURRY!
YES.
THIS TOWN... I SENSE NO ONE, YET I FEEL COUNTLESS EYES UPON US. OUR PASSAGE WILL NOT BE EASY.

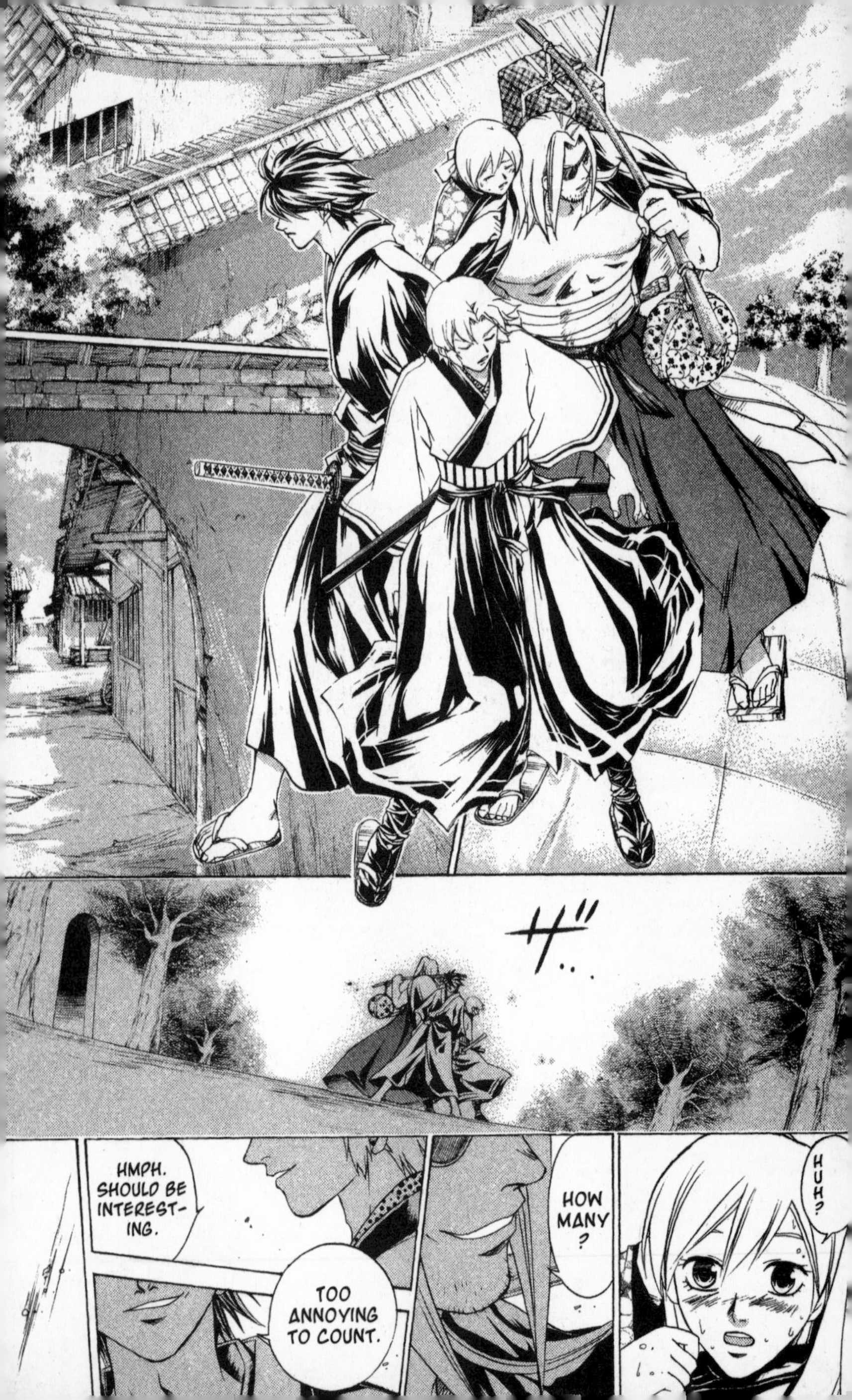
ザ...
HUH?
HOW MANY?
TOO ANNOYING TO COUNT.
HMPH. SHOULD BE INTEREST-ING.

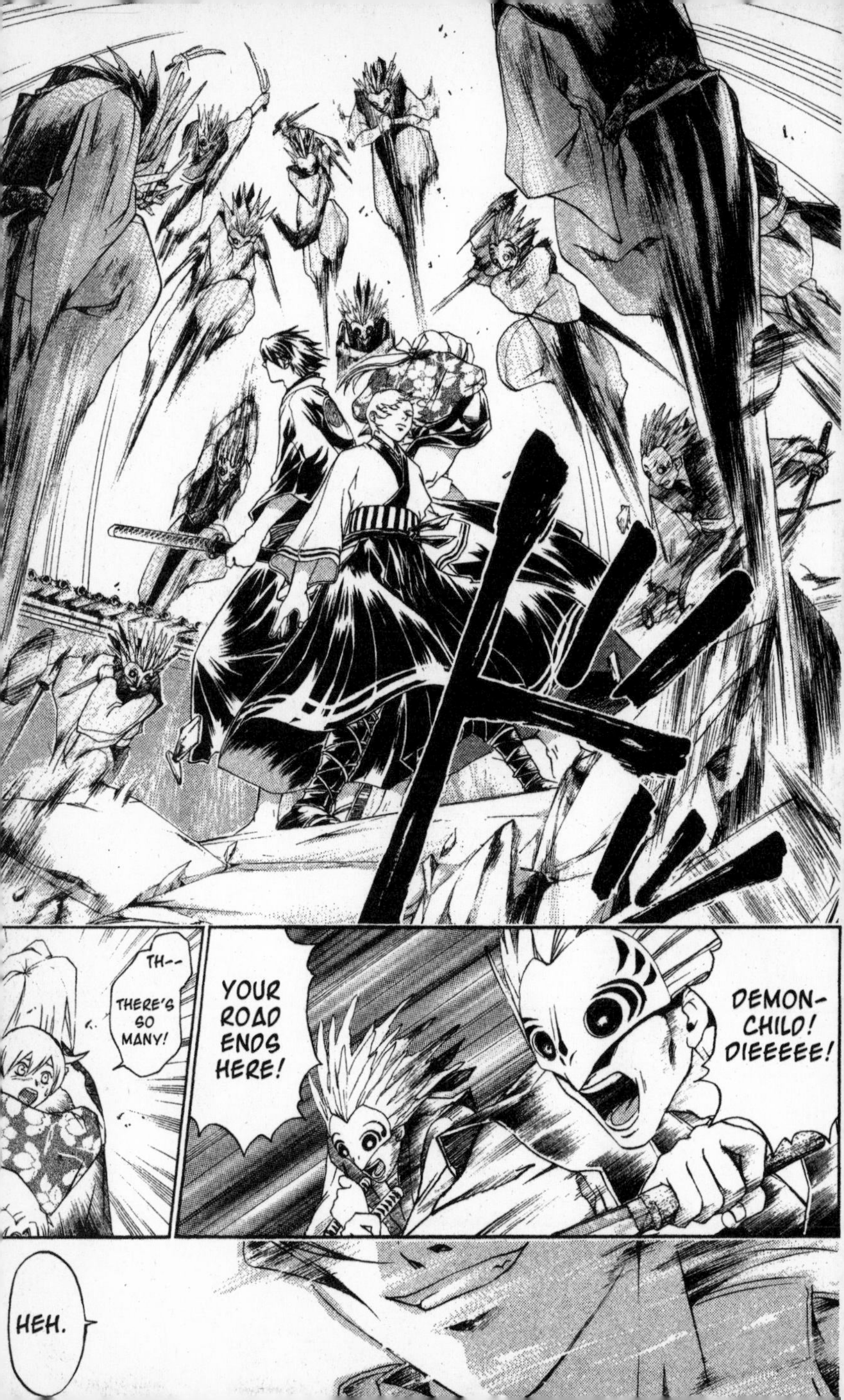
DEMON-CHILD! DIEEEEE!
YOUR ROAD ENDS HERE!
TH--
THERE'S SO MANY!
HEH.

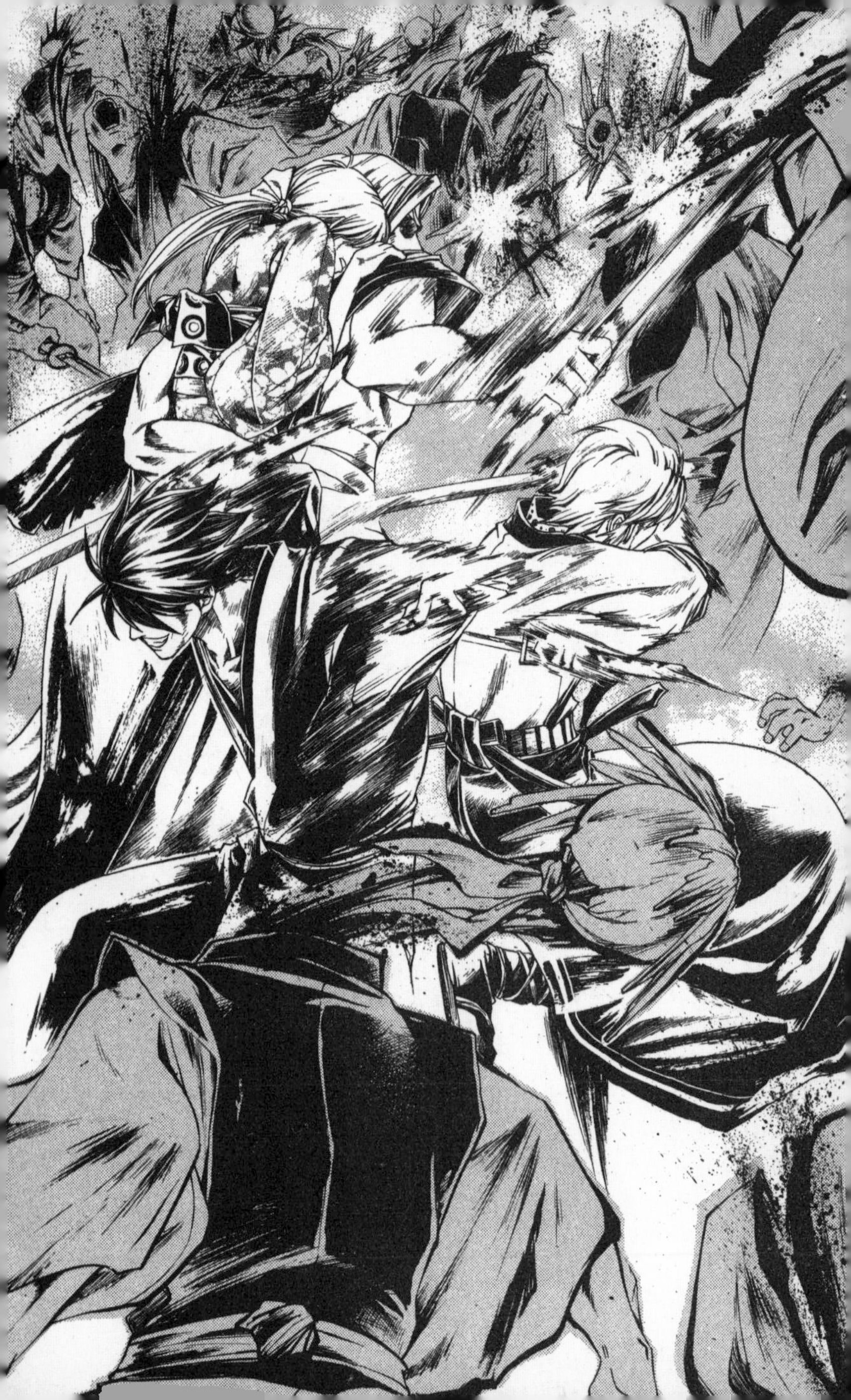

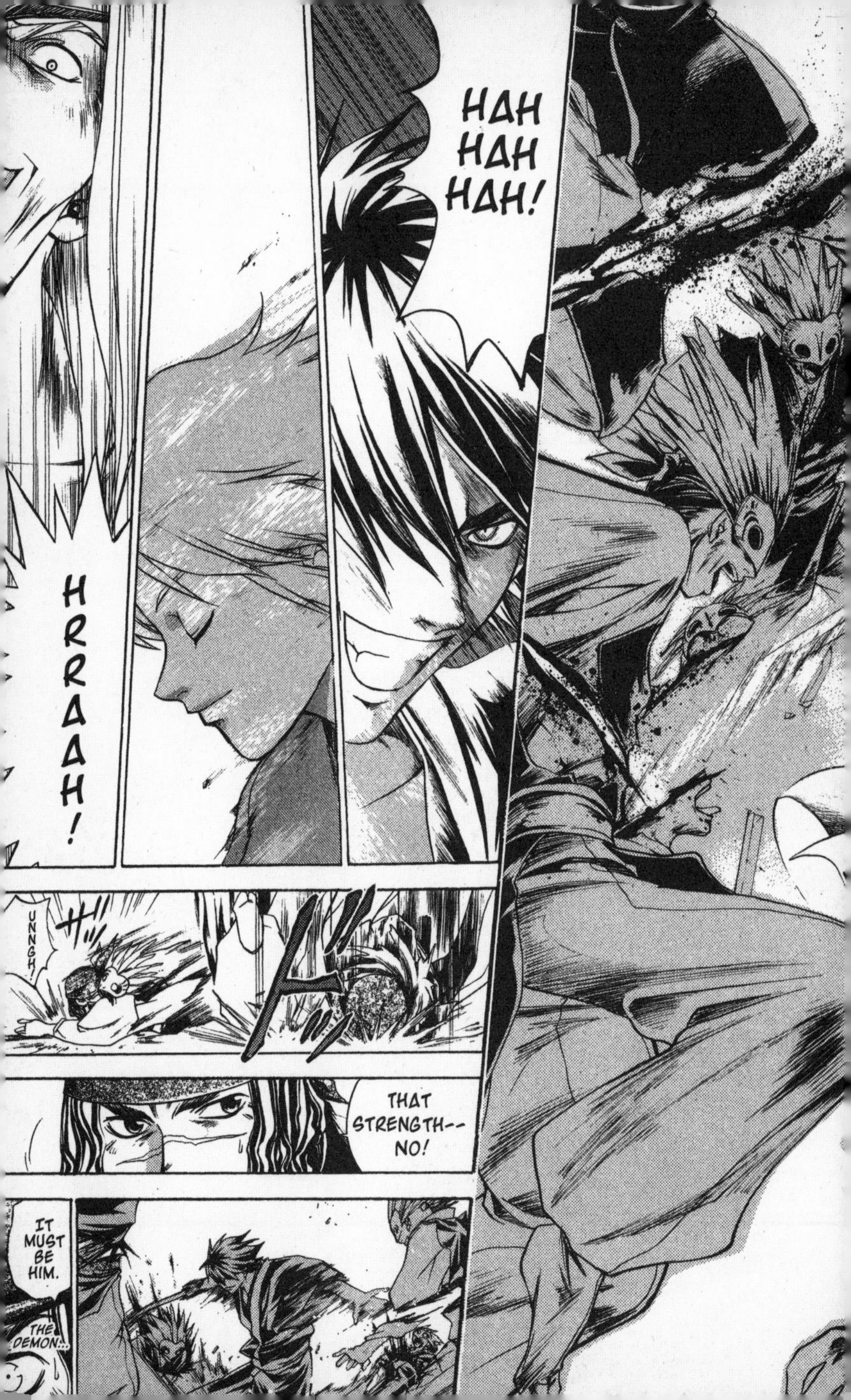
HAH HAH HAH!
HRRAAAH!
UNNGH!
THAT STRENGTH-- NO!
IT MUST BE HIM.
THE DEMON...

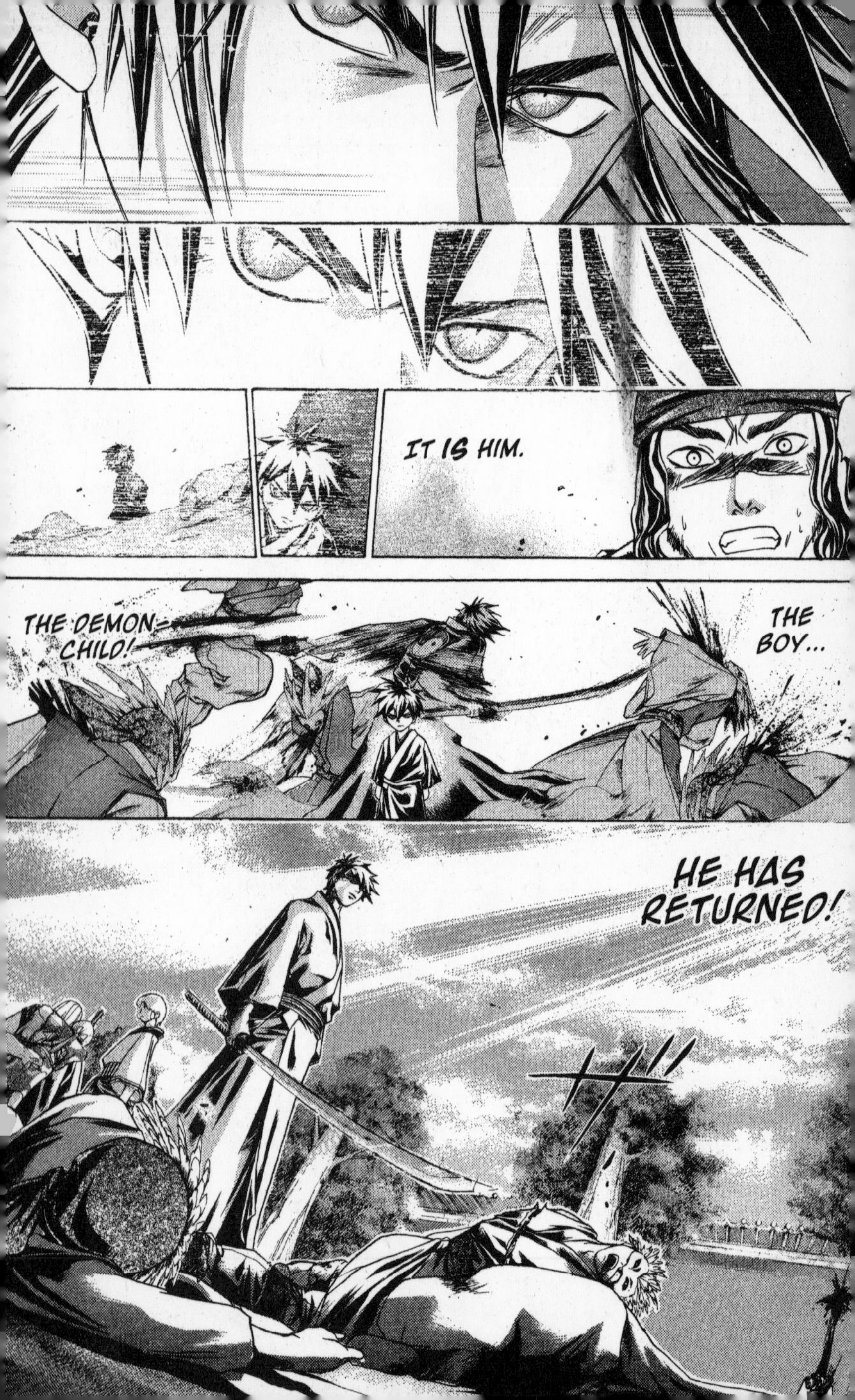
IT IS HIM.
THE BOY...
THE DEMON-CHILD!
HE HAS RETURNED!

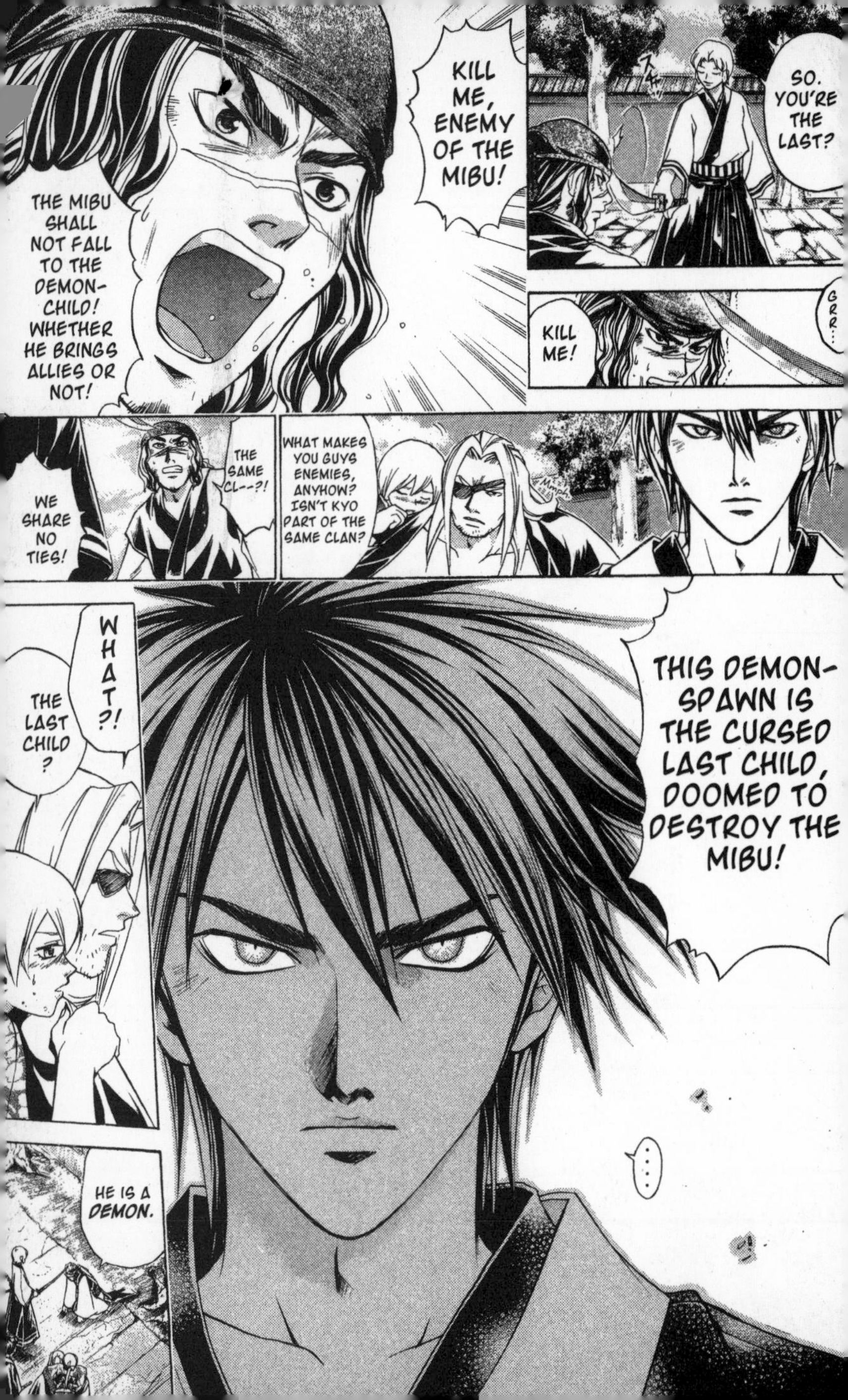
SO. YOU'RE THE LAST?
GRR...
KILL ME!
KILL ME, ENEMY OF THE MIBU!
THE MIBU SHALL NOT FALL TO THE DEMON-CHILD! WHETHER HE BRINGS ALLIES OR NOT!
Mmph.
WHAT MAKES YOU GUYS ENEMIES, ANYHOW? ISN'T KYO PART OF THE SAME CLAN?
THE SAME CL--?!
WE SHARE NO TIES!
THIS DEMON-SPAWN IS THE CURSED LAST CHILD, DOOMED TO DESTROY THE MIBU!
....
WHAT?!
THE LAST CHILD?
HE IS A DEMON.

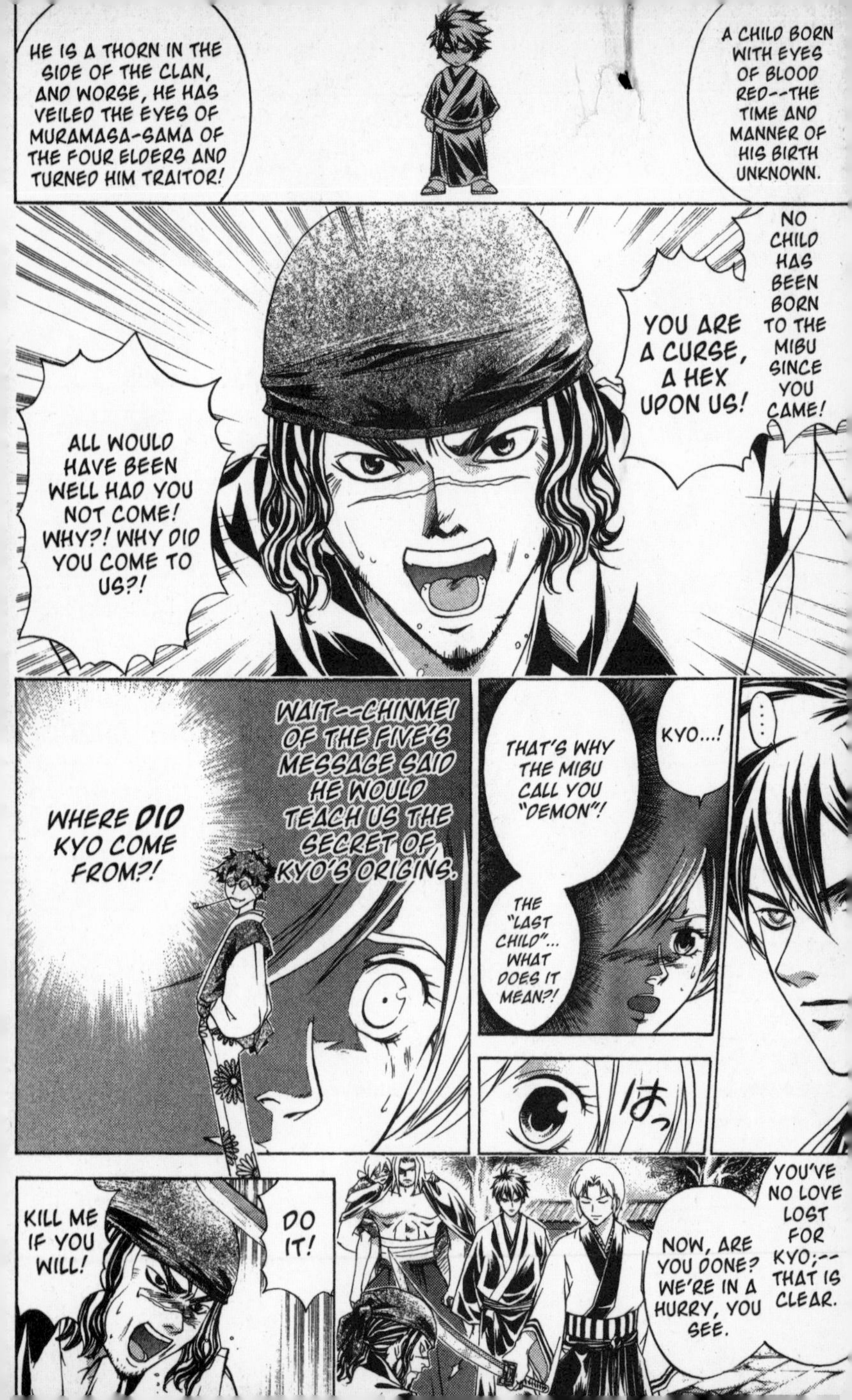
A CHILD BORN WITH EYES OF BLOOD RED--THE TIME AND MANNER OF HIS BIRTH UNKNOWN.
HE IS A THORN IN THE SIDE OF THE CLAN, AND WORSE, HE HAS VEILED THE EYES OF MURAMASA-SAMA OF THE FOUR ELDERS AND TURNED HIM TRAITOR!
NO CHILD HAS BEEN BORN TO THE MIBU SINCE YOU CAME!
YOU ARE A CURSE, A HEX UPON US!
ALL WOULD HAVE BEEN WELL HAD YOU NOT COME! WHY?! WHY DID YOU COME TO US?!
...
KYO...!
THAT'S WHY THE MIBU CALL YOU "DEMON"!
THE "LAST CHILD"... WHAT DOES IT MEAN?!
はっ
WAIT--CHINMEI OF THE FIVE'S MESSAGE SAID HE WOULD TEACH US THE SECRET OF KYO'S ORIGINS.
WHERE DID KYO COME FROM?!
YOU'VE NO LOVE LOST FOR KYO;--THAT IS CLEAR.
NOW, ARE YOU DONE? WE'RE IN A HURRY, YOU SEE.
DO IT!
KILL ME IF YOU WILL!

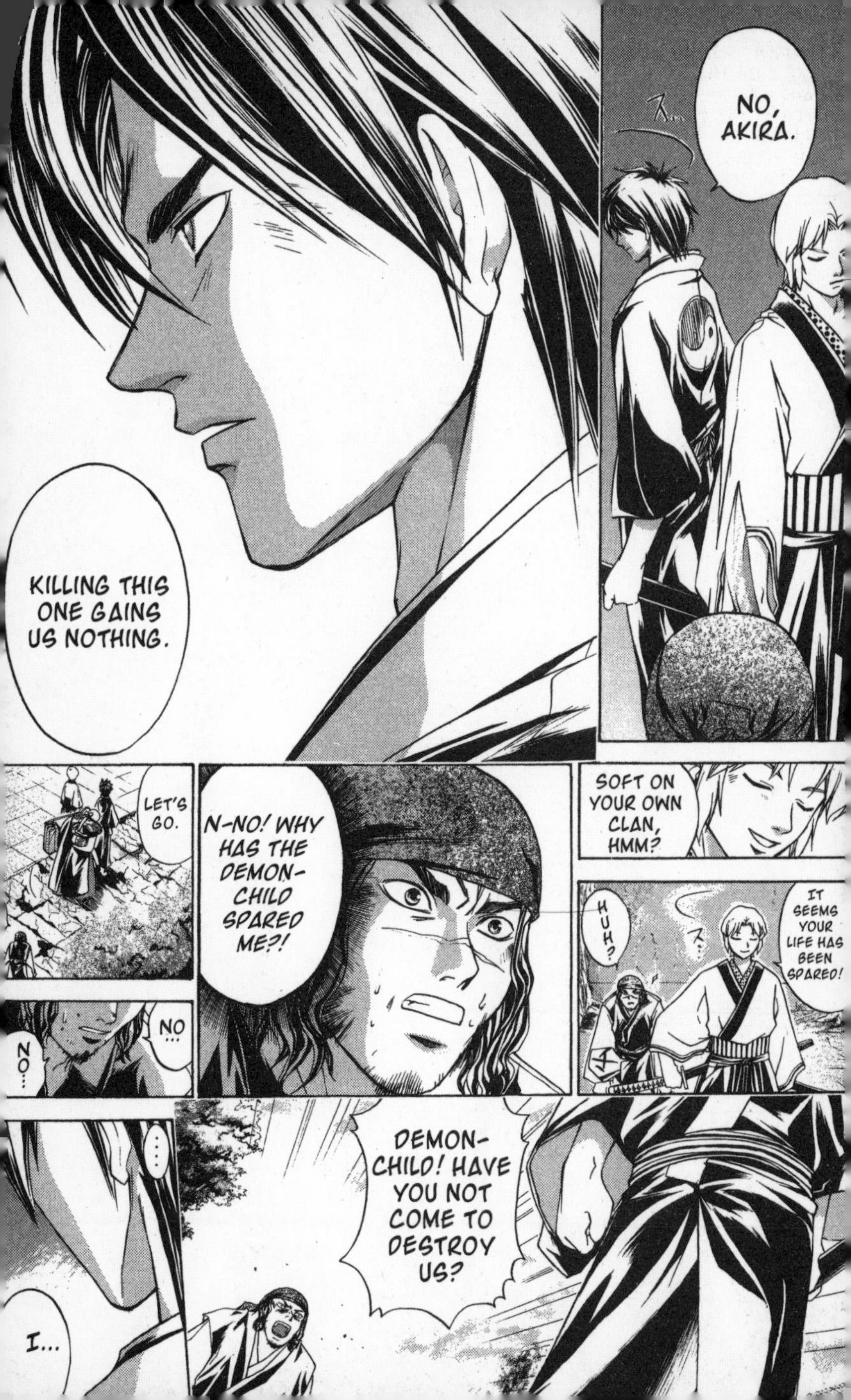
NO, AKIRA.
KILLING THIS ONE GAINS US NOTHING.
SOFT ON YOUR OWN CLAN, HMM?
IT SEEMS YOUR LIFE HAS BEEN SPARED!
HUH?
N-NO! WHY HAS THE DEMON-CHILD SPARED ME?!
LET'S GO.
NO...
NO...
DEMON-CHILD! HAVE YOU NOT COME TO DESTROY US?
...
I...

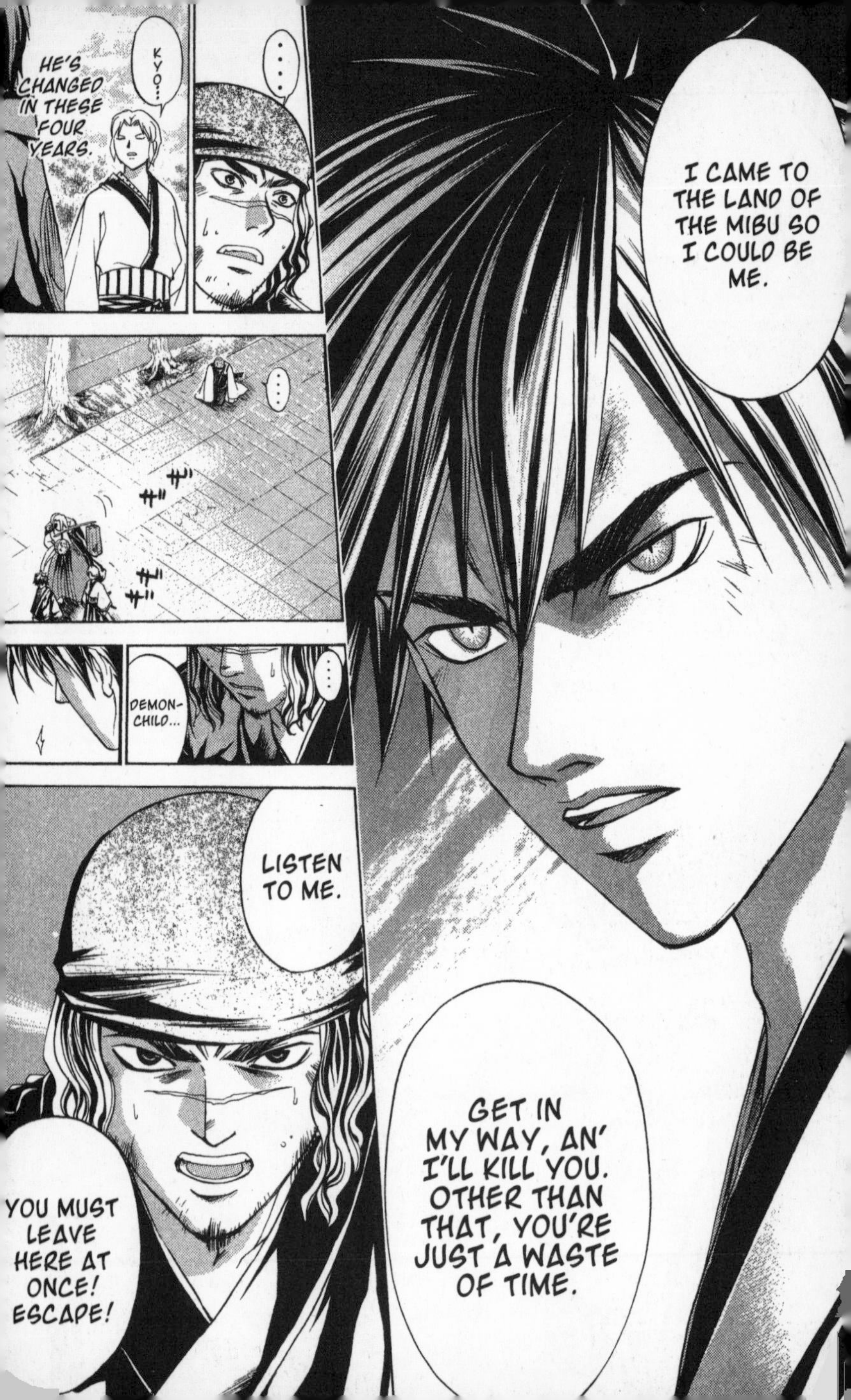
I CAME TO THE LAND OF THE MIBU SO I COULD BE ME.
GET IN MY WAY, AN' I'LL KILL YOU. OTHER THAN THAT, YOU'RE JUST A WASTE OF TIME.
. . . .
KYO...
HE'S CHANGED IN THESE FOUR YEARS.
. . .
. . .
DEMON-CHILD...
LISTEN TO ME.
YOU MUST LEAVE HERE AT ONCE! ESCAPE!

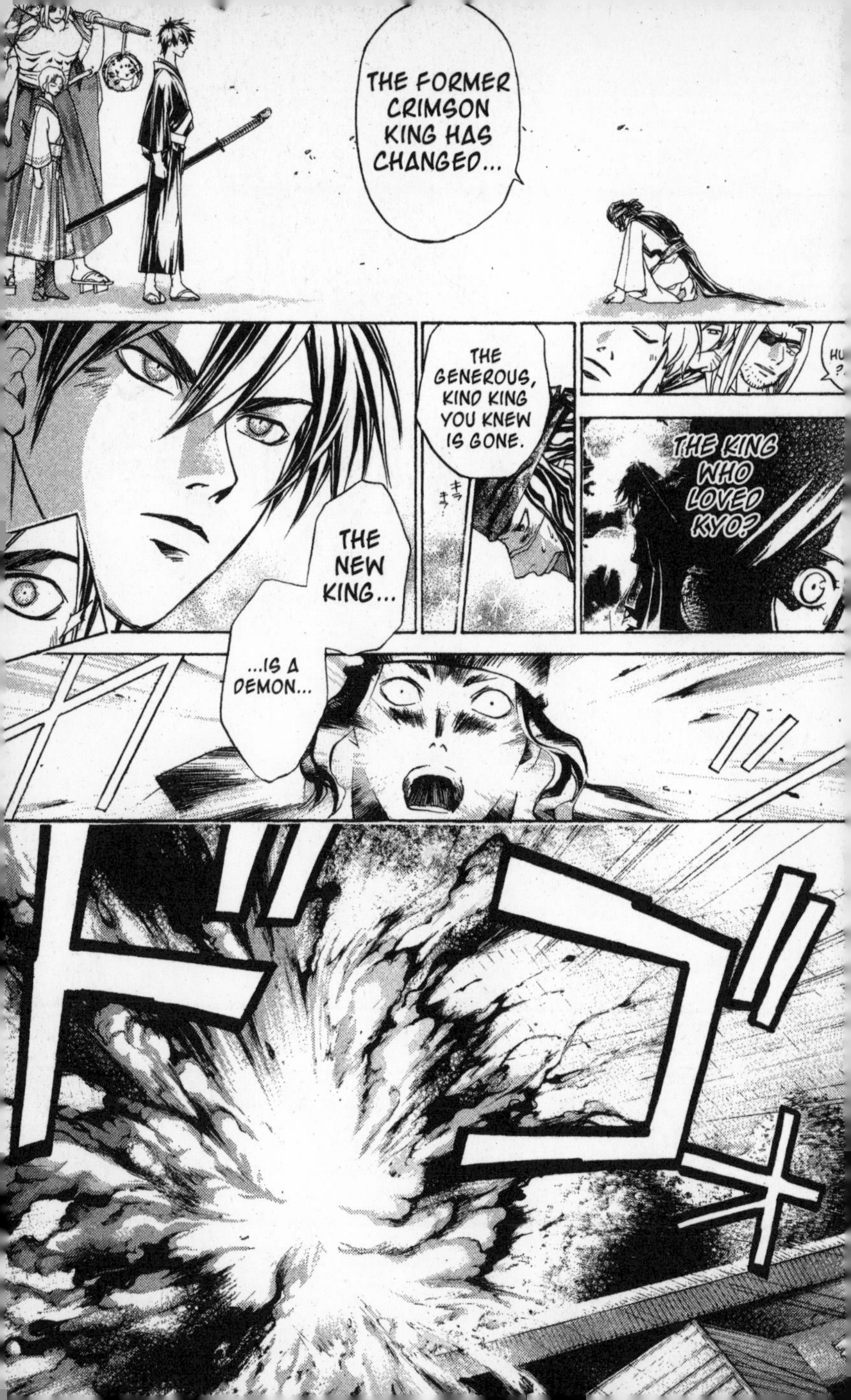
THE FORMER CRIMSON KING HAS CHANGED...
HU ?
THE KING WHO LOVED KYO?
THE GENEROUS, KIND KING YOU KNEW IS GONE.
キラ キラ
THE NEW KING...
...IS A DEMON...

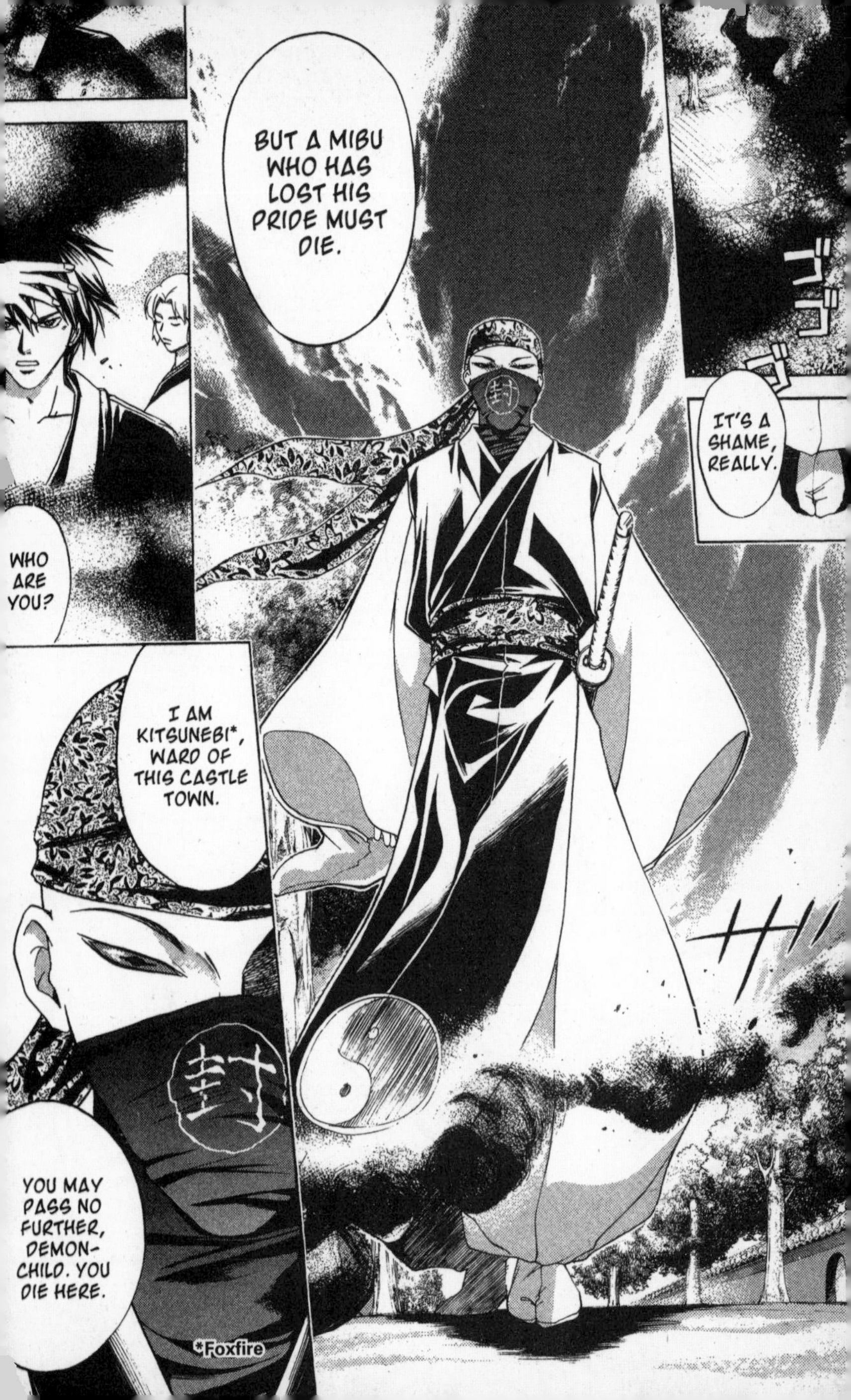
ゴゴゴ
IT'S A SHAME, REALLY.
BUT A MIBU WHO HAS LOST HIS PRIDE MUST DIE.
WHO ARE YOU?
I AM KITSUNEBI*, WARD OF THIS CASTLE TOWN.
YOU MAY PASS NO FURTHER, DEMON-CHILD. YOU DIE HERE.
*Foxfire

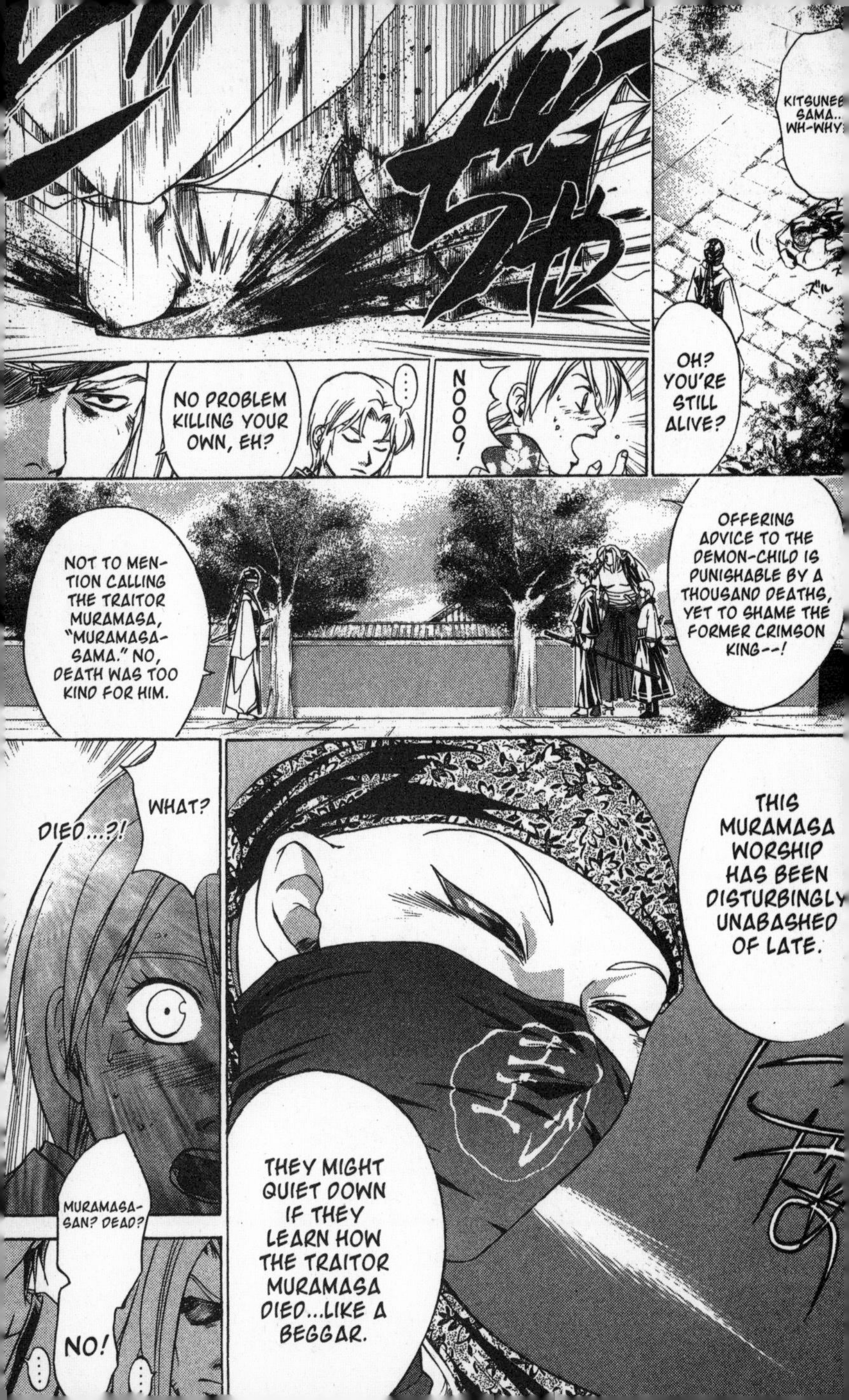
KITSUNEE SAMA.. WH-WHY?
ズル
OH? YOU'RE STILL ALIVE?
NOOO!
...
NO PROBLEM KILLING YOUR OWN, EH?
OFFERING ADVICE TO THE DEMON-CHILD IS PUNISHABLE BY A THOUSAND DEATHS, YET TO SHAME THE FORMER CRIMSON KING--!
NOT TO MENTION CALLING THE TRAITOR MURAMASA, "MURAMASA-SAMA." NO, DEATH WAS TOO KIND FOR HIM.
THIS MURAMASA WORSHIP HAS BEEN DISTURBINGLY UNABASHED OF LATE.
THEY MIGHT QUIET DOWN IF THEY LEARN HOW THE TRAITOR MURAMASA DIED...LIKE A BEGGAR.
WHAT?
DIED...?!
MURAMASA-SAN? DEAD?
NO!
...
...

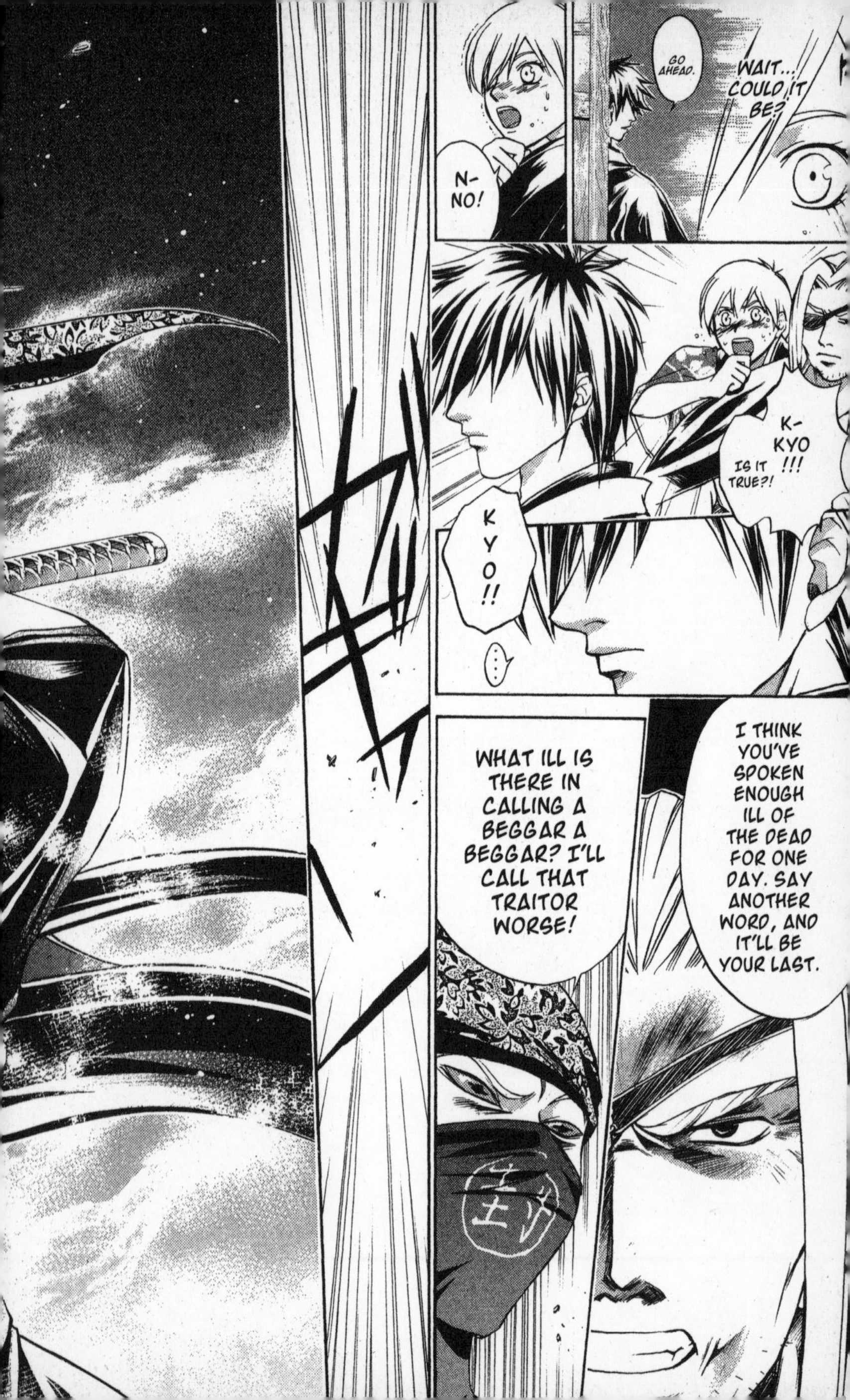
WAIT... COULD IT BE?
GO AHEAD.
N-NO!
K-KYO!!!
IS IT TRUE?!
KYO!!
...
I THINK YOU'VE SPOKEN ENOUGH ILL OF THE DEAD FOR ONE DAY. SAY ANOTHER WORD, AND IT'LL BE YOUR LAST.
WHAT ILL IS THERE IN CALLING A BEGGAR A BEGGAR? I'LL CALL THAT TRAITOR WORSE!

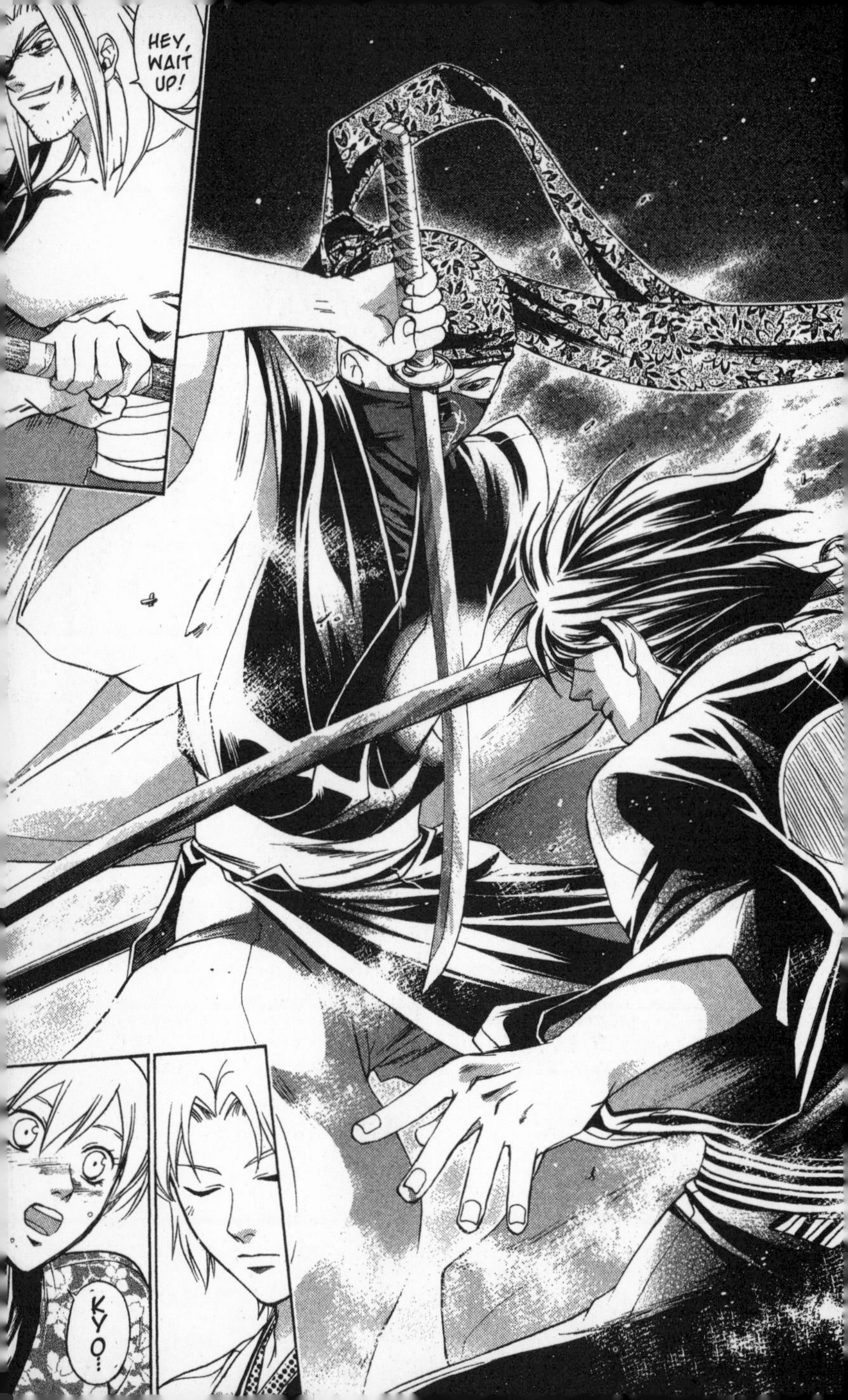
HEY, WAIT UP!
KYO...

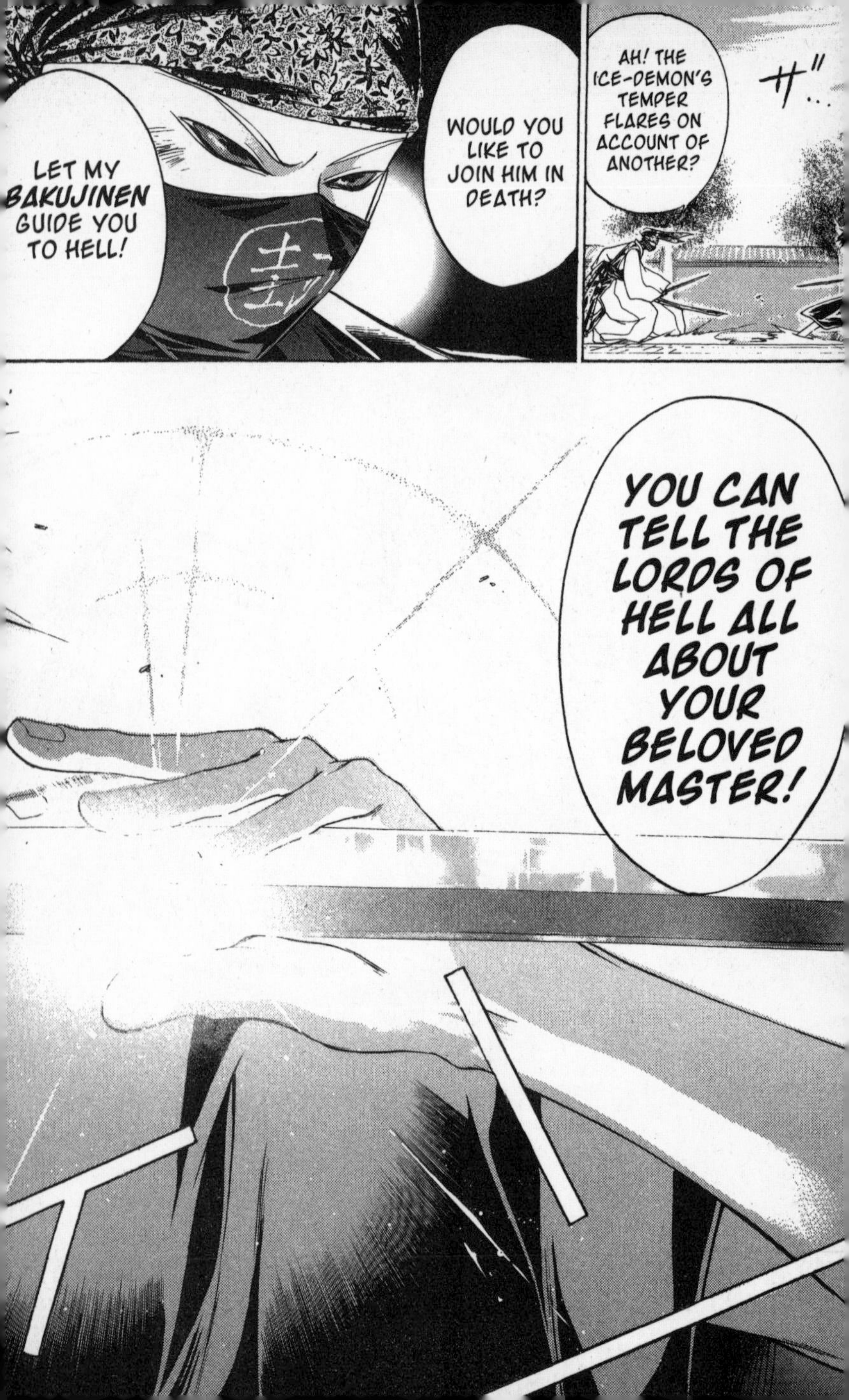
AH! THE ICE-DEMON'S TEMPER FLARES ON ACCOUNT OF ANOTHER?
WOULD YOU LIKE TO JOIN HIM IN DEATH?
LET MY BAKUJINEN GUIDE YOU TO HELL!
YOU CAN TELL THE LORDS OF HELL ALL ABOUT YOUR BELOVED MASTER!

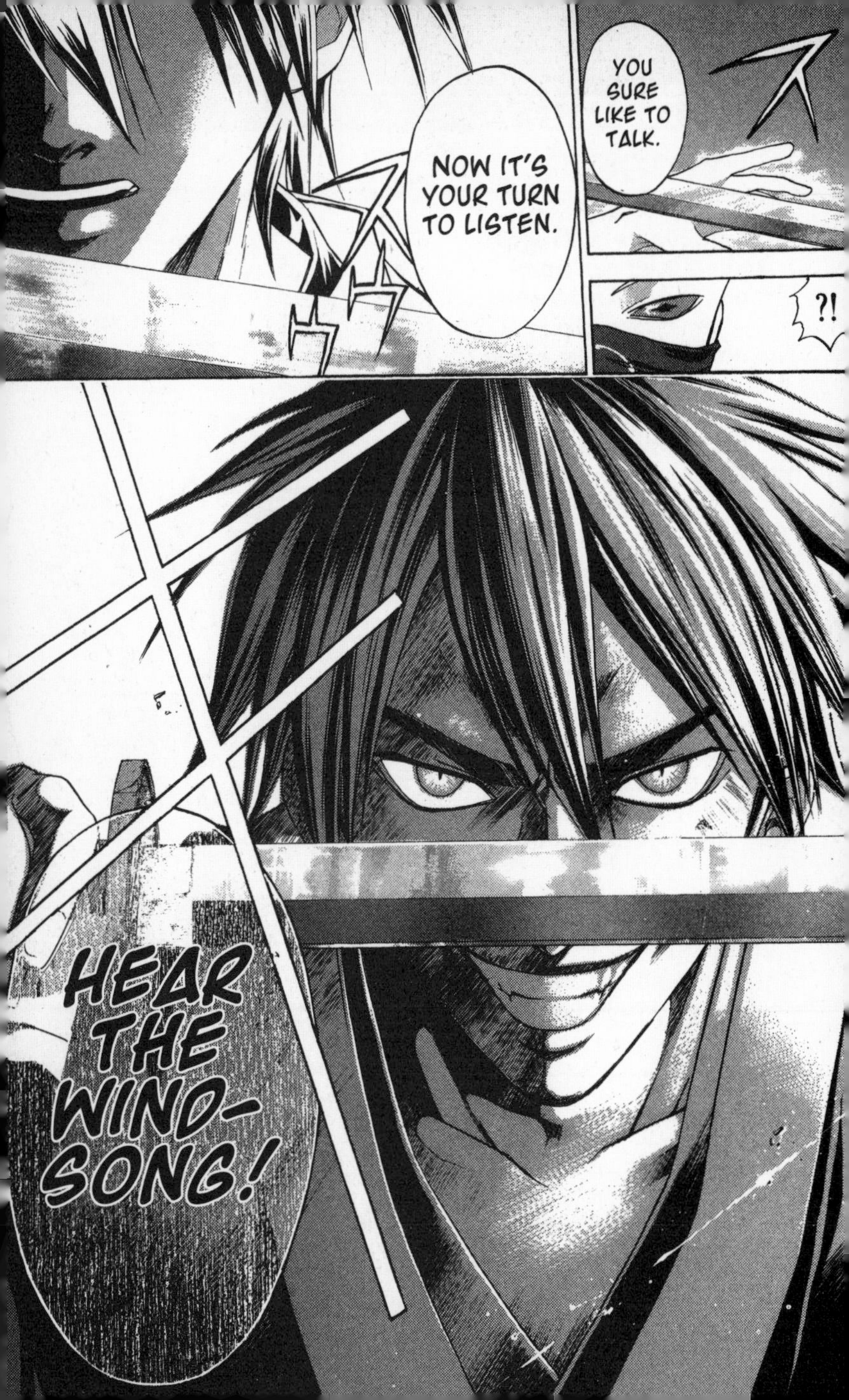
YOU SURE LIKE TO TALK.
?!
NOW IT'S YOUR TURN TO LISTEN.
HEAR THE WIND-SONG!

Report

Yo! Kamijyo here. Thanks to you, Kyo can now count to 15! Amazing! (I'm so humble!) The only reason I've made it drawing this long is all thanks to you, the readers, and the people around me who make SDK possible. Thank you all!

Oh, and one more thing:

Samurai Deeper Kyo is going ANIME!

Good news for all of you who were waiting--and the rest of you, too! More details soon.

Stay tuned: in the next part, Kyo gets WHUPPIN' MAD for the first time in a while! See you in vol. 16!

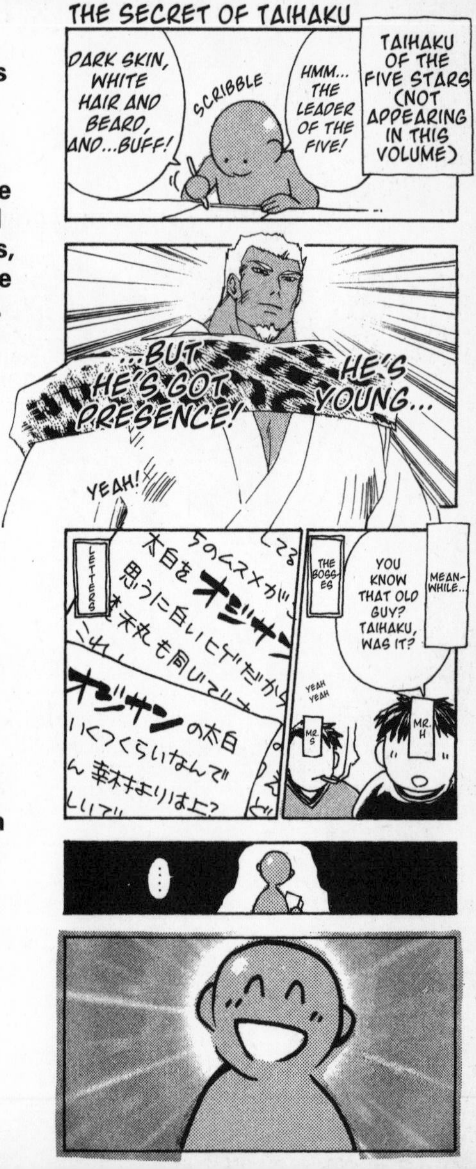
THE SECRET OF TAIHAKU
TAIHAKU OF THE FIVE STARS (NOT APPEARING IN THIS VOLUME)
HMM... THE LEADER OF THE FIVE!
SCRIBBLE
DARK SKIN, WHITE HAIR AND BEARD, AND...BUFF!
HE'S YOUNG...
...BUT HE'S GOT PRESENCE!
YEAH!
MEANWHILE...
YOU KNOW THAT OLD GUY? TAIHAKU, WAS IT?
MR. H
YEAH YEAH
MR. S
THE BOSSES
LETTERS
...

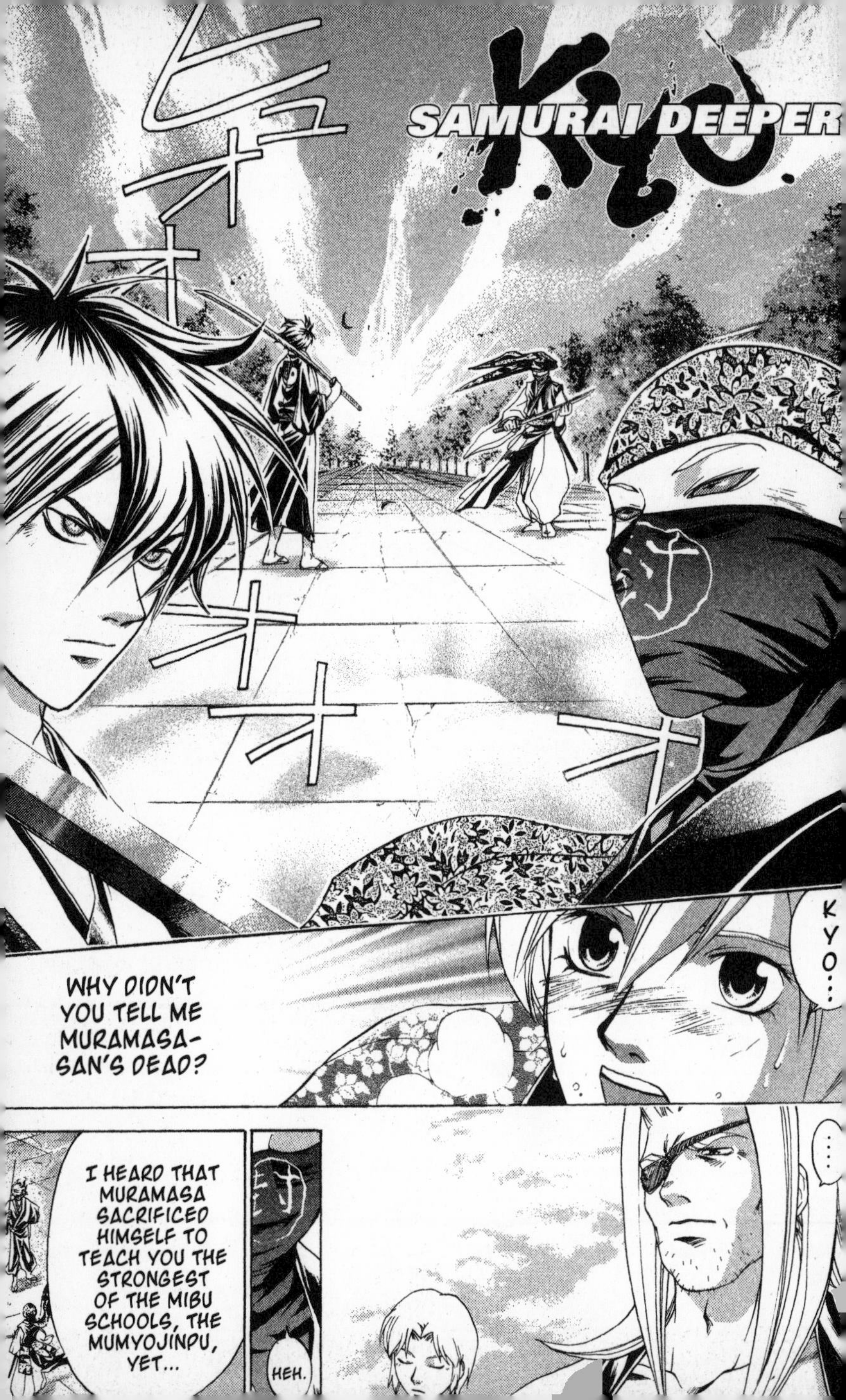
SAMURAI DEEPER KYO
ヒュオオオオオ
KYO...
WHY DIDN'T YOU TELL ME MURAMASA-SAN'S DEAD?
...
I HEARD THAT MURAMASA SACRIFICED HIMSELF TO TEACH YOU THE STRONGEST OF THE MIBU SCHOOLS, THE MUMYOJINPU, YET...
HEH.

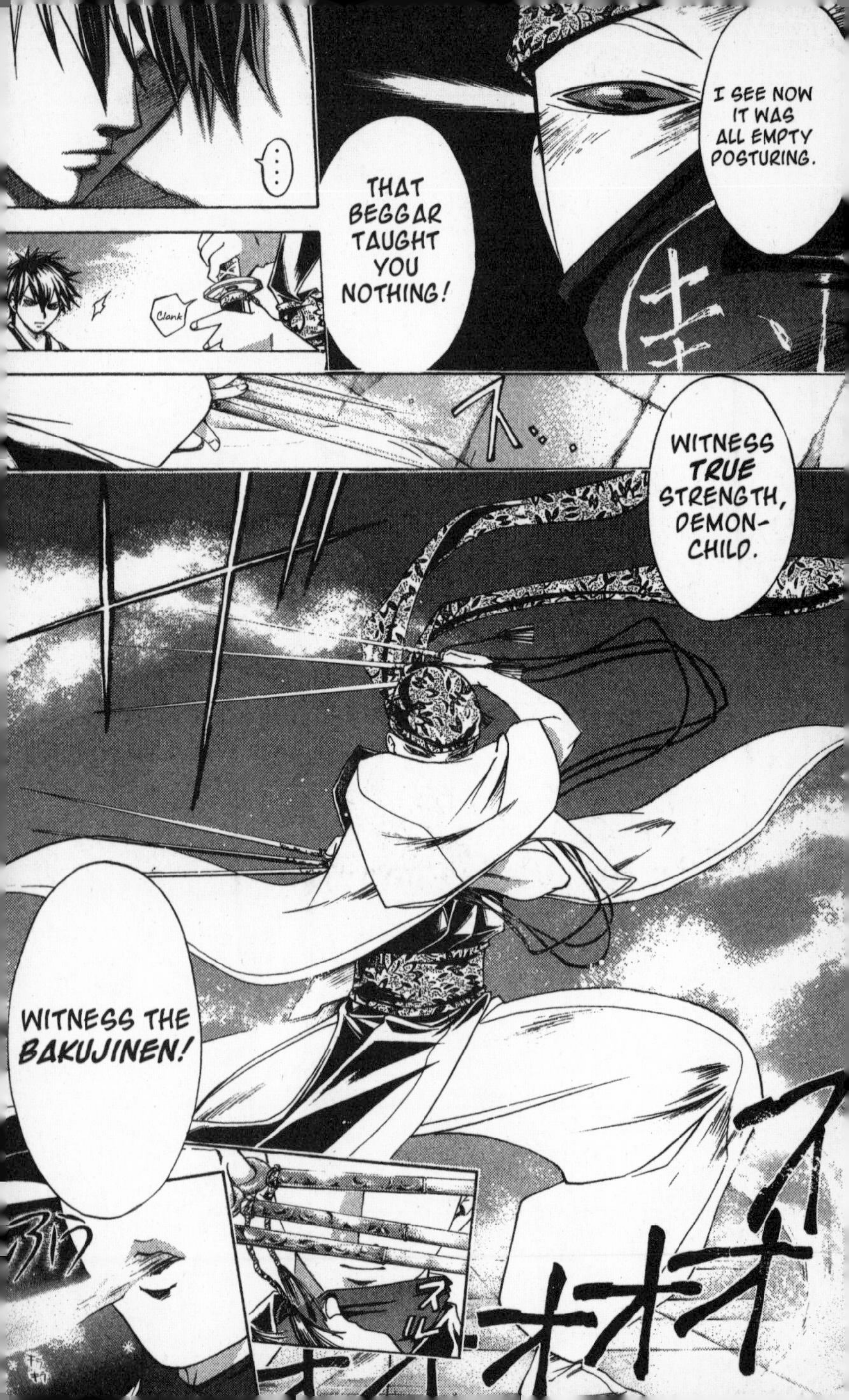
I SEE NOW IT WAS ALL EMPTY POSTURING.
THAT BEGGAR TAUGHT YOU NOTHING!
...
Clank
WITNESS TRUE STRENGTH, DEMON-CHILD.
WITNESS THE BAKUJINEN!

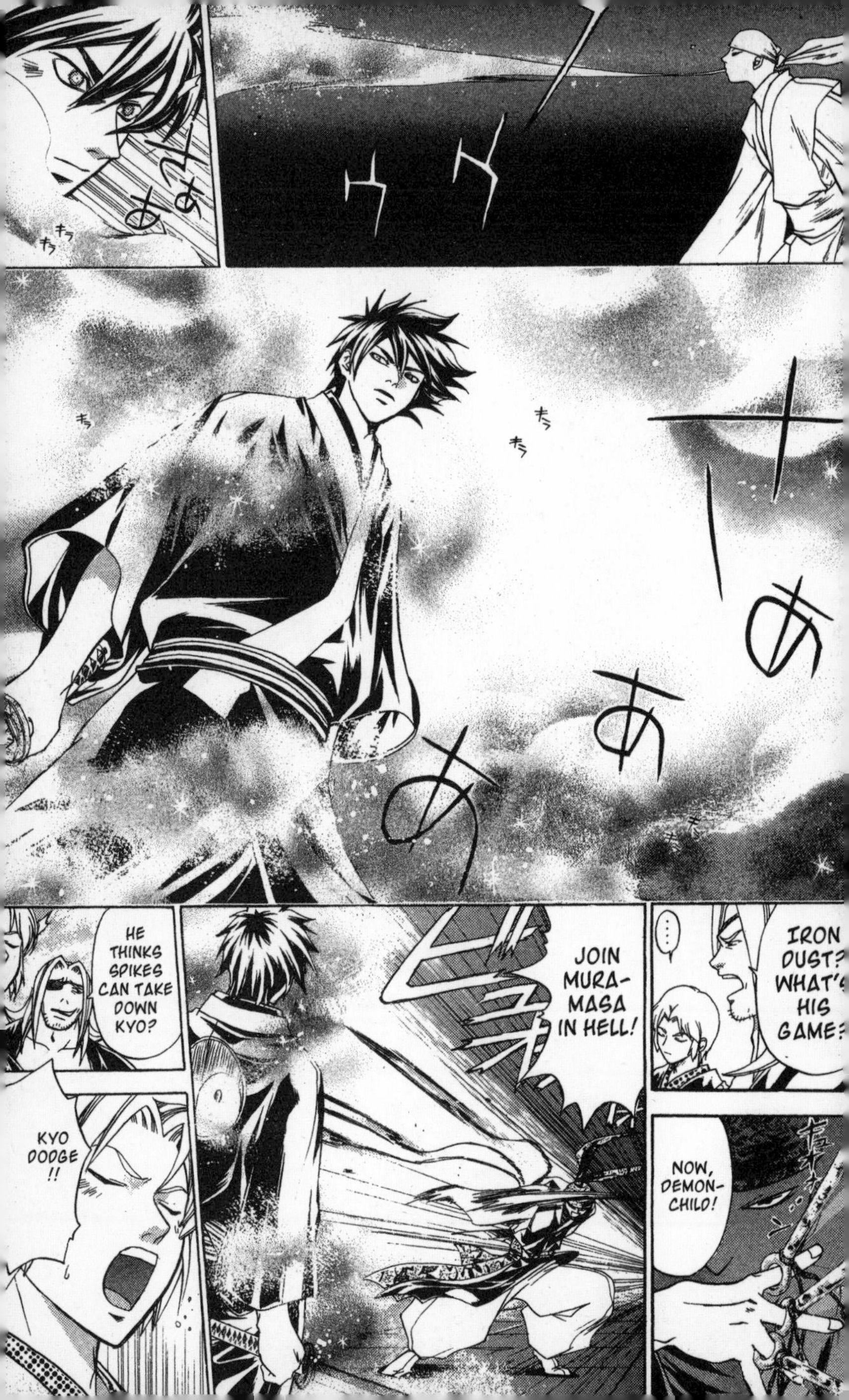
...
IRON DUST? WHAT'
HIS GAME?
NOW, DEMON-CHILD!
JOIN MURA-MASA IN HELL!
HE THINKS SPIKES CAN TAKE DOWN KYO?
KYO DODGE!!

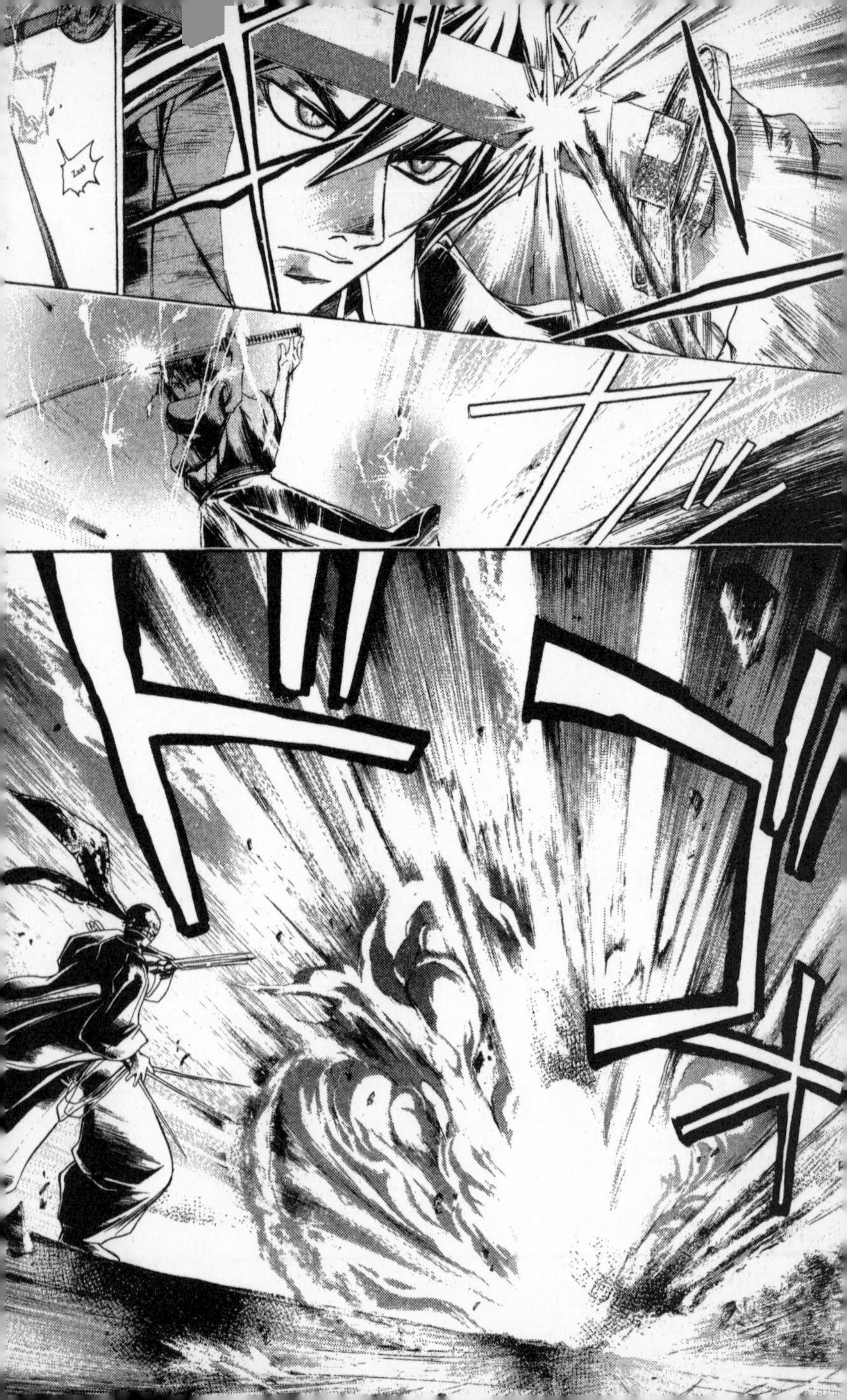
Zzat

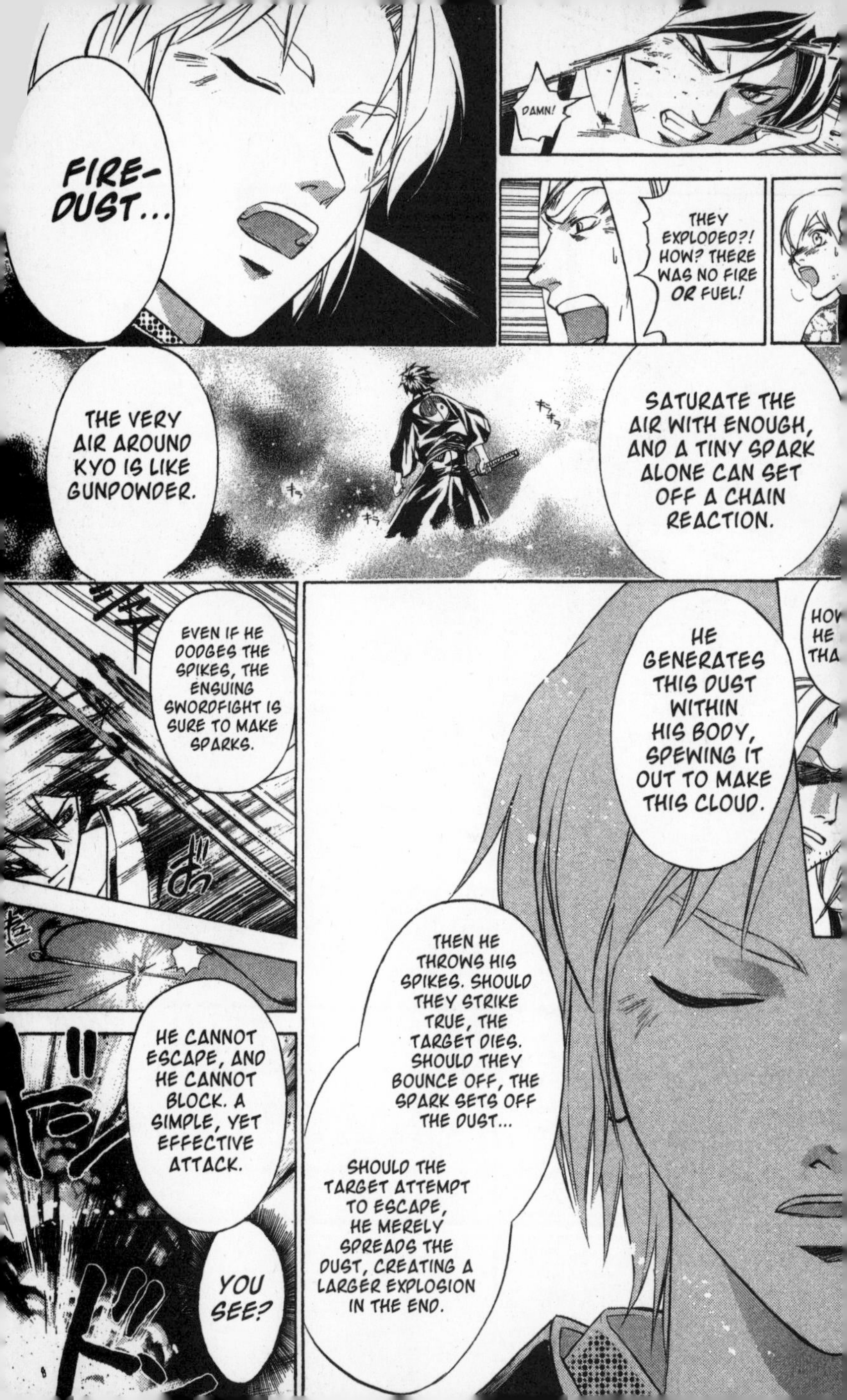
DAMN!
THEY EXPLODED?! HOW? THERE WAS NO FIRE OR FUEL!
FIRE-DUST...
SATURATE THE AIR WITH ENOUGH, AND A TINY SPARK ALONE CAN SET OFF A CHAIN REACTION.
THE VERY AIR AROUND KYO IS LIKE GUNPOWDER.
HOW HE THA
HE GENERATES THIS DUST WITHIN HIS BODY, SPEWING IT OUT TO MAKE THIS CLOUD.
THEN HE THROWS HIS SPIKES. SHOULD THEY STRIKE TRUE, THE TARGET DIES. SHOULD THEY BOUNCE OFF, THE SPARK SETS OFF THE DUST...
SHOULD THE TARGET ATTEMPT TO ESCAPE, HE MERELY SPREADS THE DUST, CREATING A LARGER EXPLOSION IN THE END.
EVEN IF HE DODGES THE SPIKES, THE ENSUING SWORDFIGHT IS SURE TO MAKE SPARKS.
HE CANNOT ESCAPE, AND HE CANNOT BLOCK. A SIMPLE, YET EFFECTIVE ATTACK.
YOU SEE?

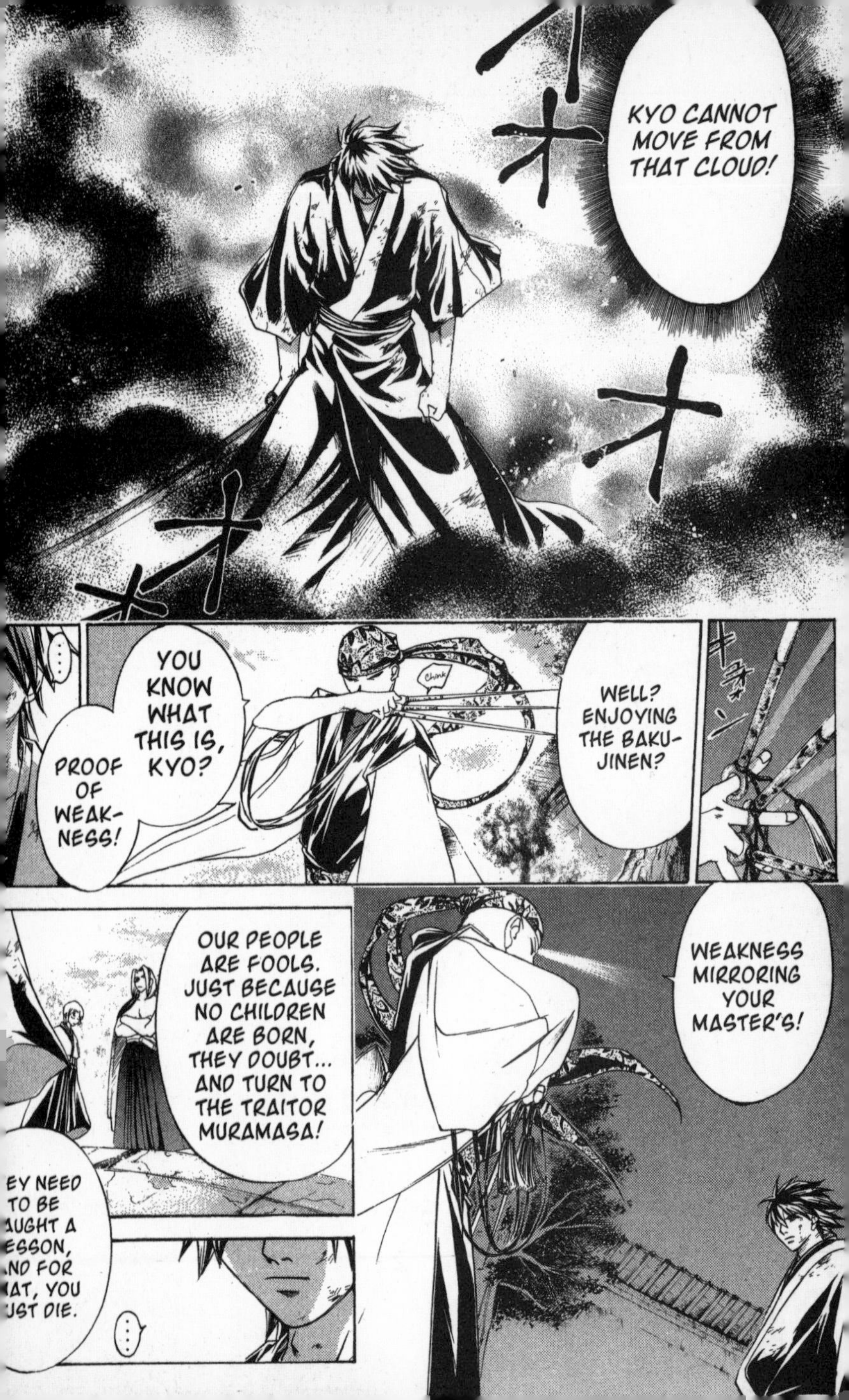
KYO CANNOT MOVE FROM THAT CLOUD!
WELL? ENJOYING THE BAKU-JINEN?
Chink
YOU KNOW WHAT THIS IS, KYO?
PROOF OF WEAK-NESS!
...
WEAKNESS MIRRORING YOUR MASTER'S!
OUR PEOPLE ARE FOOLS. JUST BECAUSE NO CHILDREN ARE BORN, THEY DOUBT... AND TURN TO THE TRAITOR MURAMASA!
EY NEED TO BE AUGHT A ESSON, ND FOR AT, YOU UST DIE.
...

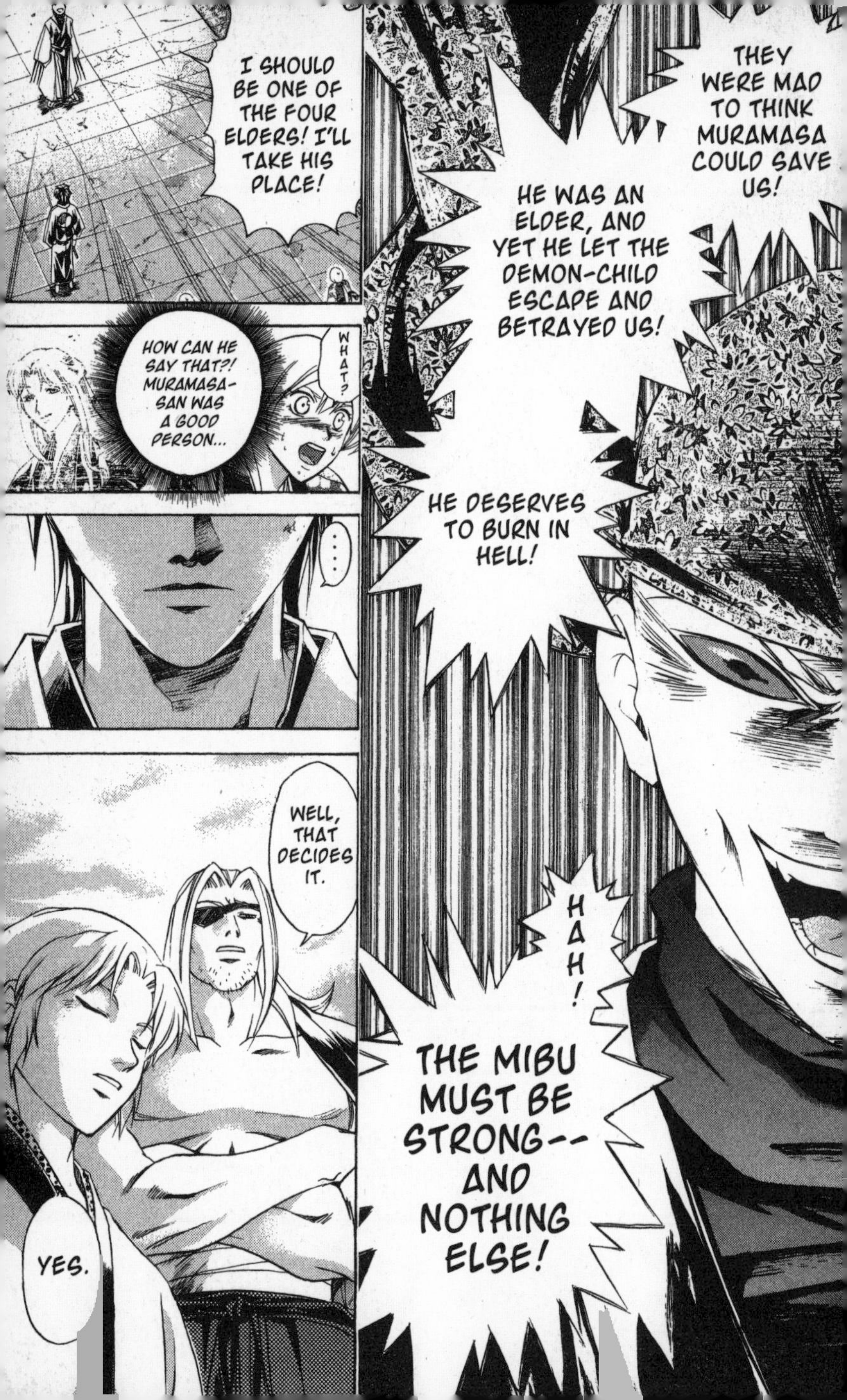
THEY WERE MAD TO THINK MURAMASA COULD SAVE US!
HE WAS AN ELDER, AND YET HE LET THE DEMON-CHILD ESCAPE AND BETRAYED US!
HE DESERVES TO BURN IN HELL!
HAH!
THE MIBU MUST BE STRONG-- AND NOTHING ELSE!
I SHOULD BE ONE OF THE FOUR ELDERS! I'LL TAKE HIS PLACE!
WHAT?
HOW CAN HE SAY THAT?! MURAMASA-SAN WAS A GOOD PERSON...
...
WELL, THAT DECIDES IT.
YES.

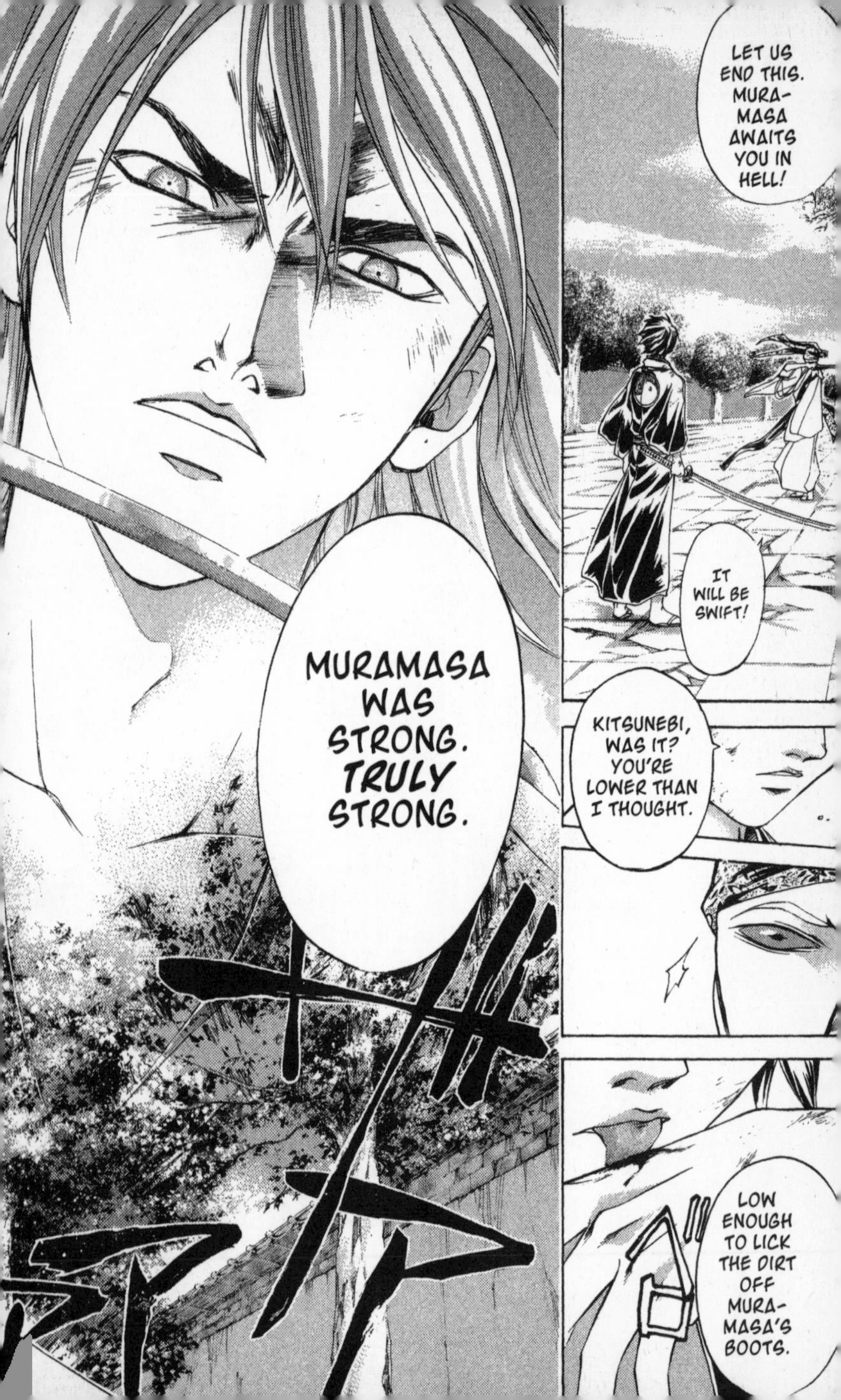
LET US END THIS. MURA-MASA AWAITS YOU IN HELL!
IT WILL BE SWIFT!
KITSUNEBI, WAS IT? YOU'RE LOWER THAN I THOUGHT.
LOW ENOUGH TO LICK THE DIRT OFF MURA-MASA'S BOOTS.
MURAMASA WAS STRONG. *TRULY* STRONG.

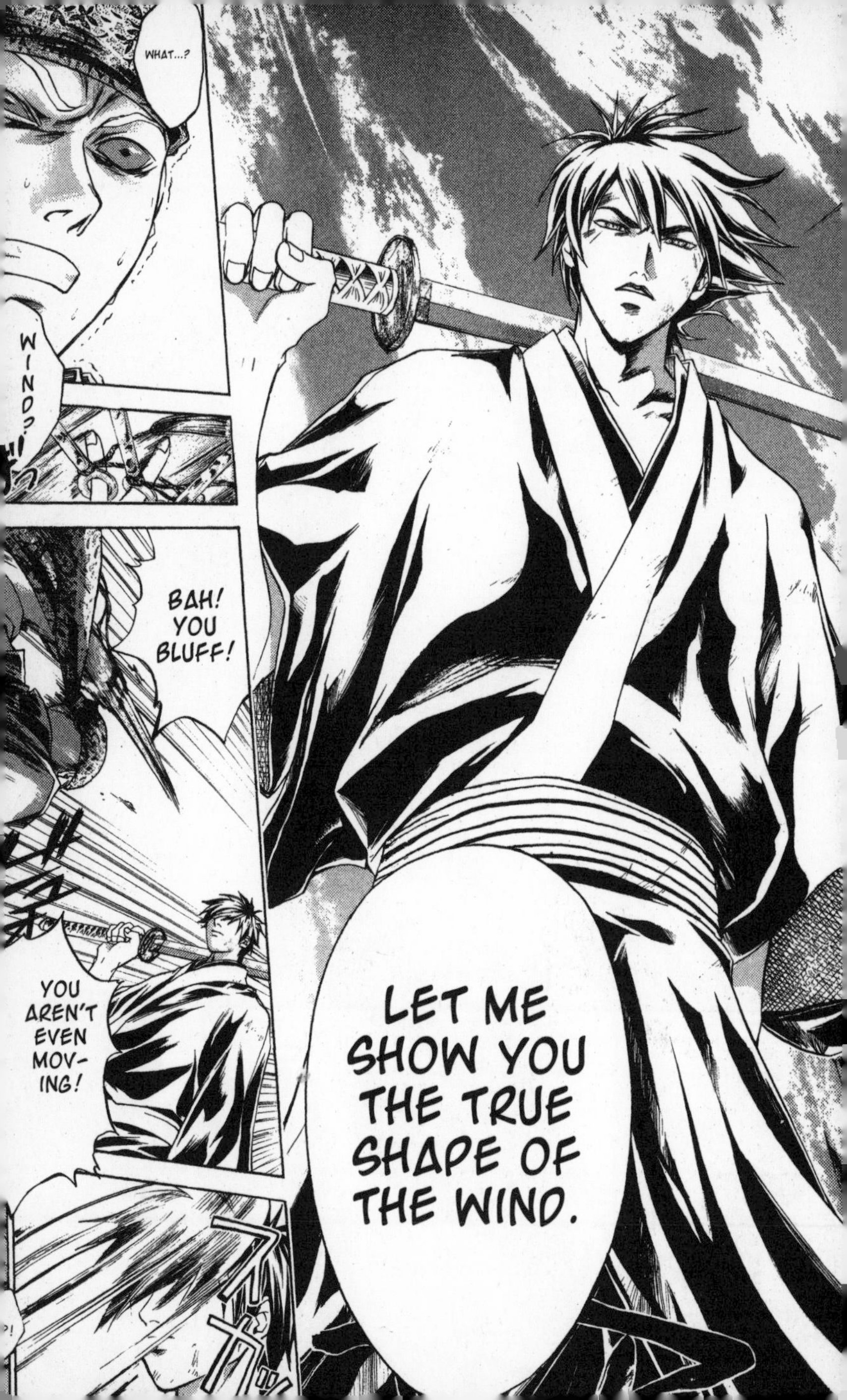
LET ME SHOW YOU THE TRUE SHAPE OF THE WIND.
WHAT...?
WIND?!
BAH! YOU BLUFF!
YOU AREN'T EVEN MOV-ING!

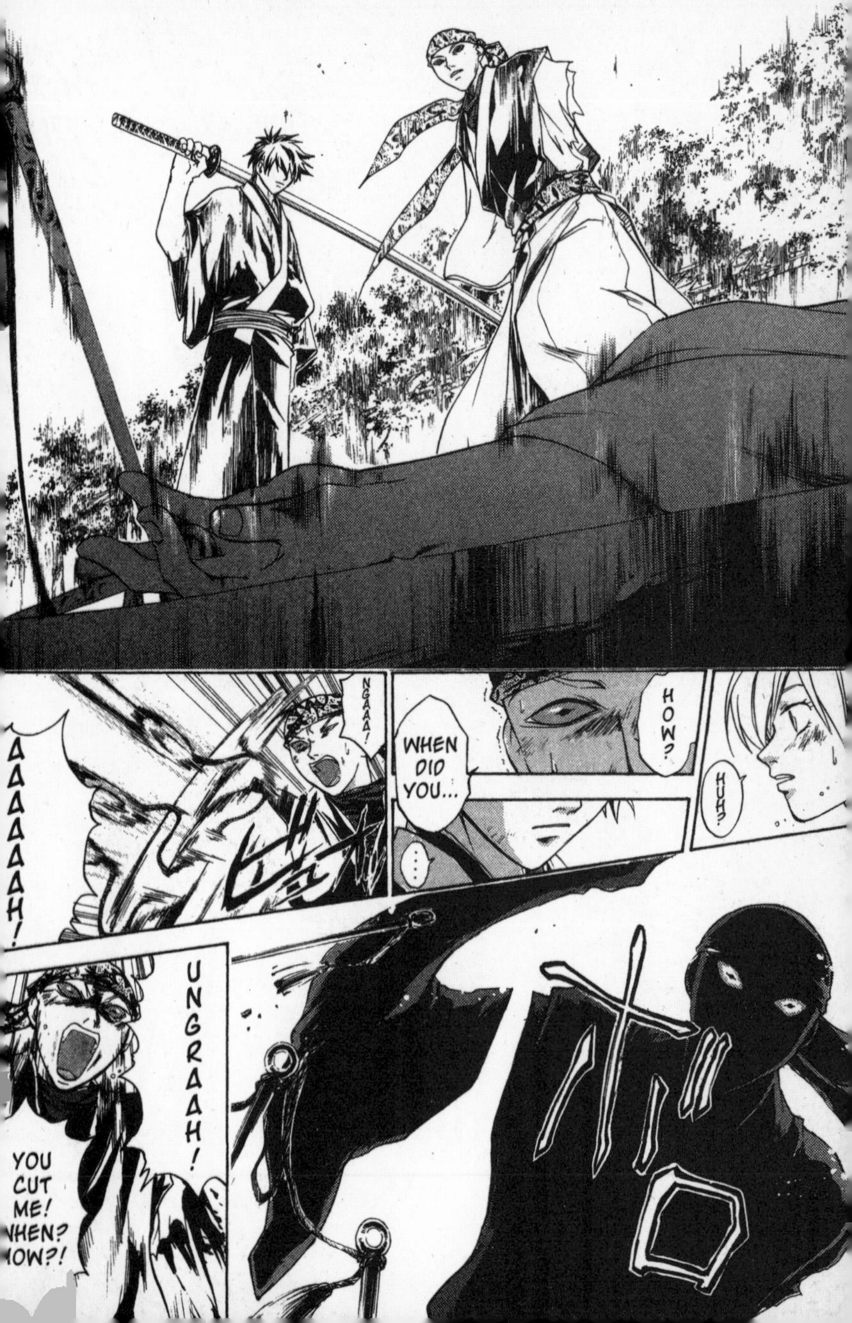
HUH?
HOW?
WHEN DID YOU...
...
NGAAA!
AAAAAAAAAAH!
UNGRAAH!
YOU CUT ME! WHEN? HOW?!

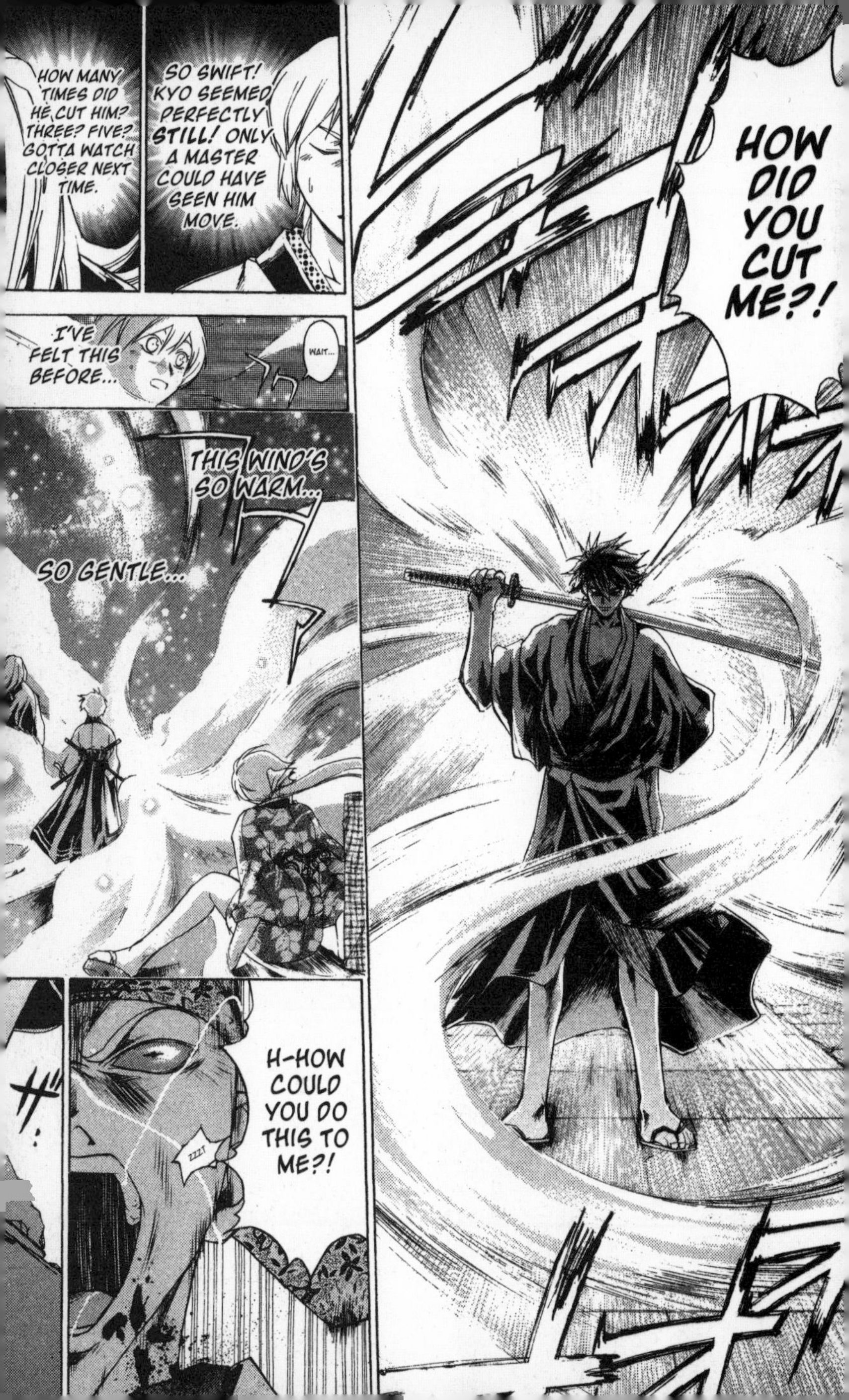
HOW DID YOU CUT ME?!
SO SWIFT! KYO SEEMED PERFECTLY STILL! ONLY A MASTER COULD HAVE SEEN HIM MOVE.
HOW MANY TIMES DID HE CUT HIM? THREE? FIVE? GOTTA WATCH CLOSER NEXT TIME.
WAIT...
I'VE FELT THIS BEFORE...
THIS WIND'S SO WARM...
SO GENTLE...
H-HOW COULD YOU DO THIS TO ME?!
ZZZT

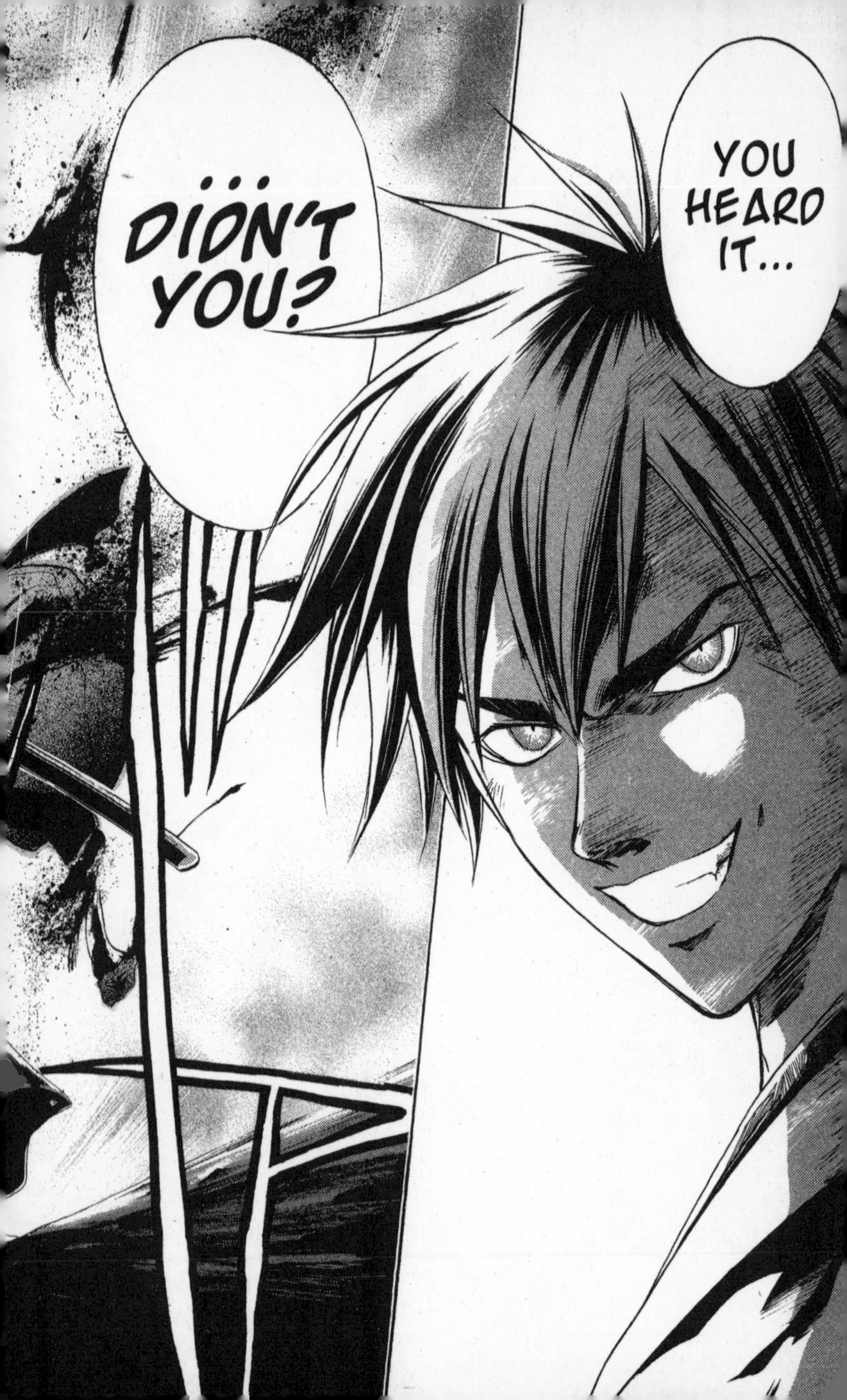
YOU HEARD IT...
...DIDN'T YOU?

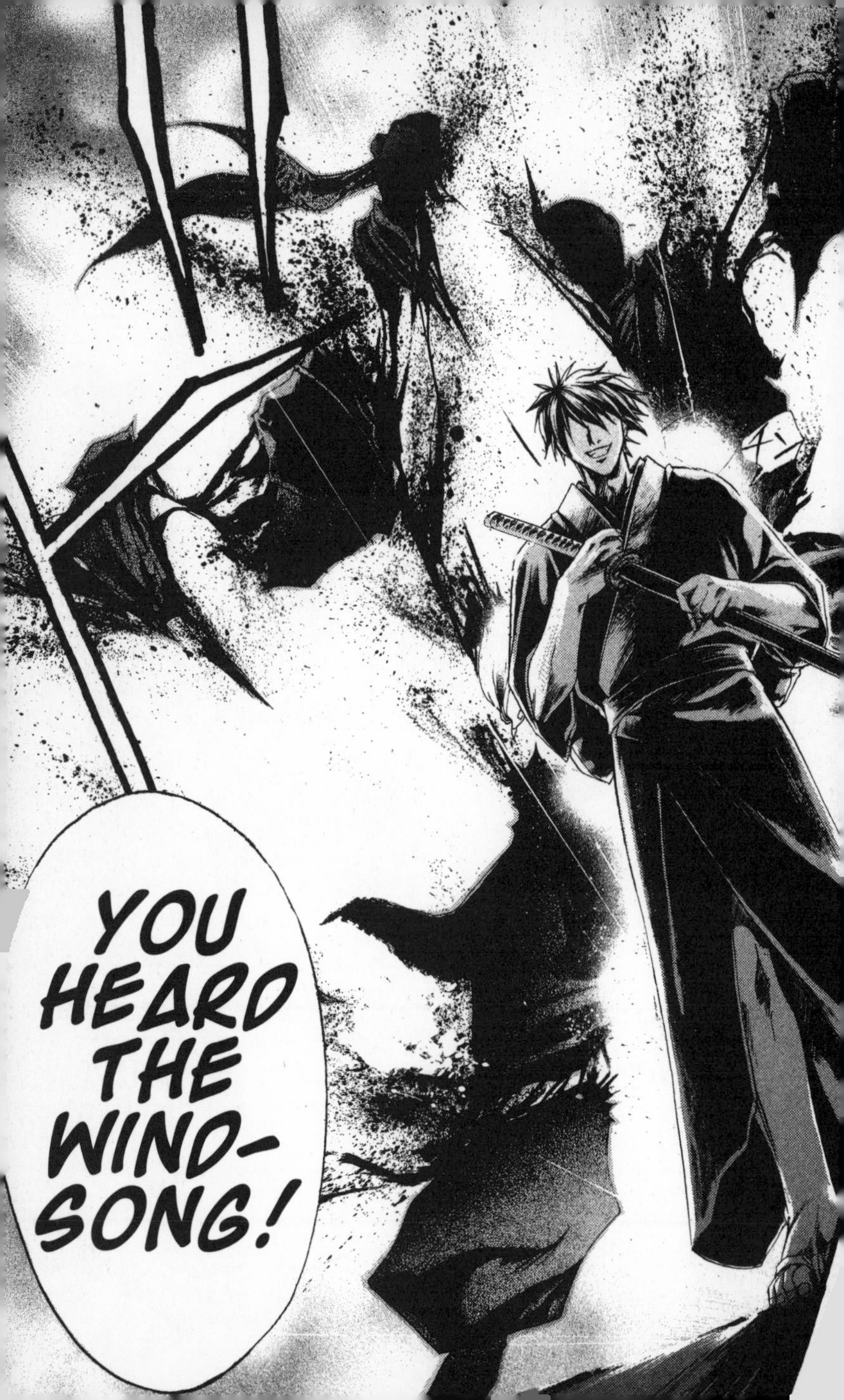
YOU HEARD THE WIND-SONG!

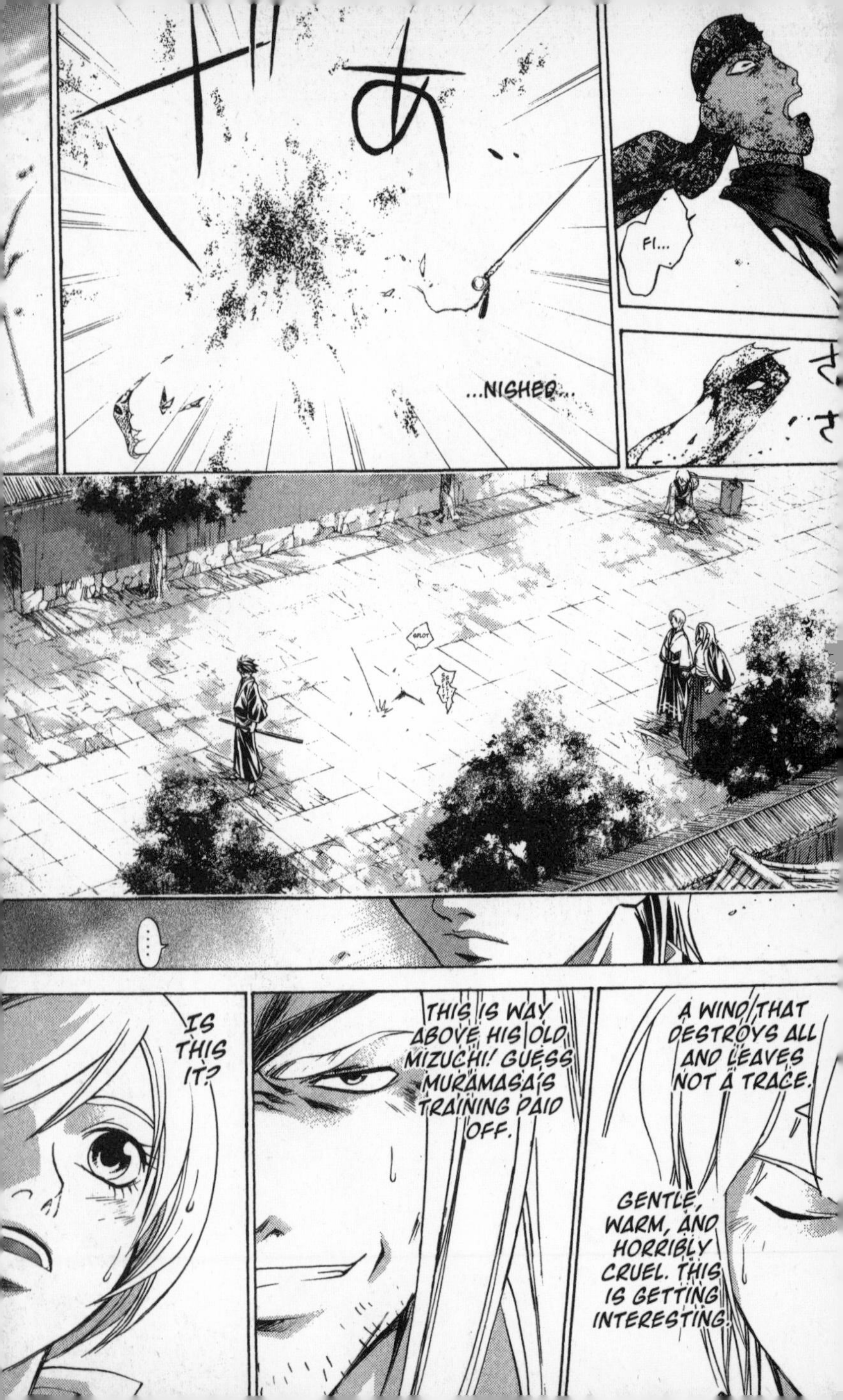

FI...
さ
さ
ザあ
...NISHED...
SPLOT
....
A WIND THAT DESTROYS ALL AND LEAVES NOT A TRACE.
GENTLE, WARM, AND HORRIBLY CRUEL. THIS IS GETTING INTERESTING.
THIS IS WAY ABOVE HIS OLD MIZUCHI! GUESS MURAMASA'S TRAINING PAID OFF.
IS THIS IT?

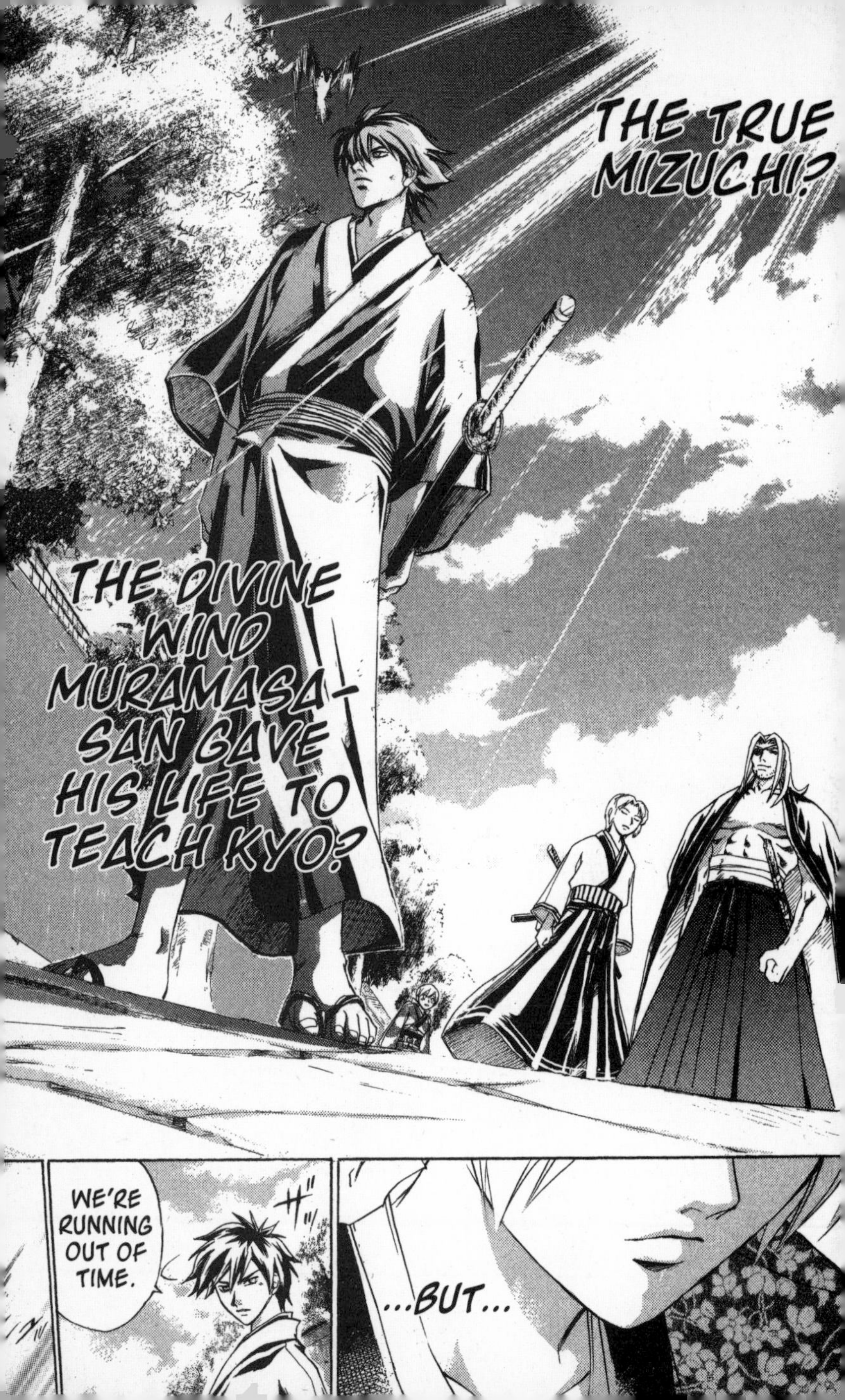
THE TRUE MIZUCHI?
THE DIVINE WIND MURAMASA-SAN GAVE HIS LIFE TO TEACH KYO?
...BUT...
WE'RE RUNNING OUT OF TIME.

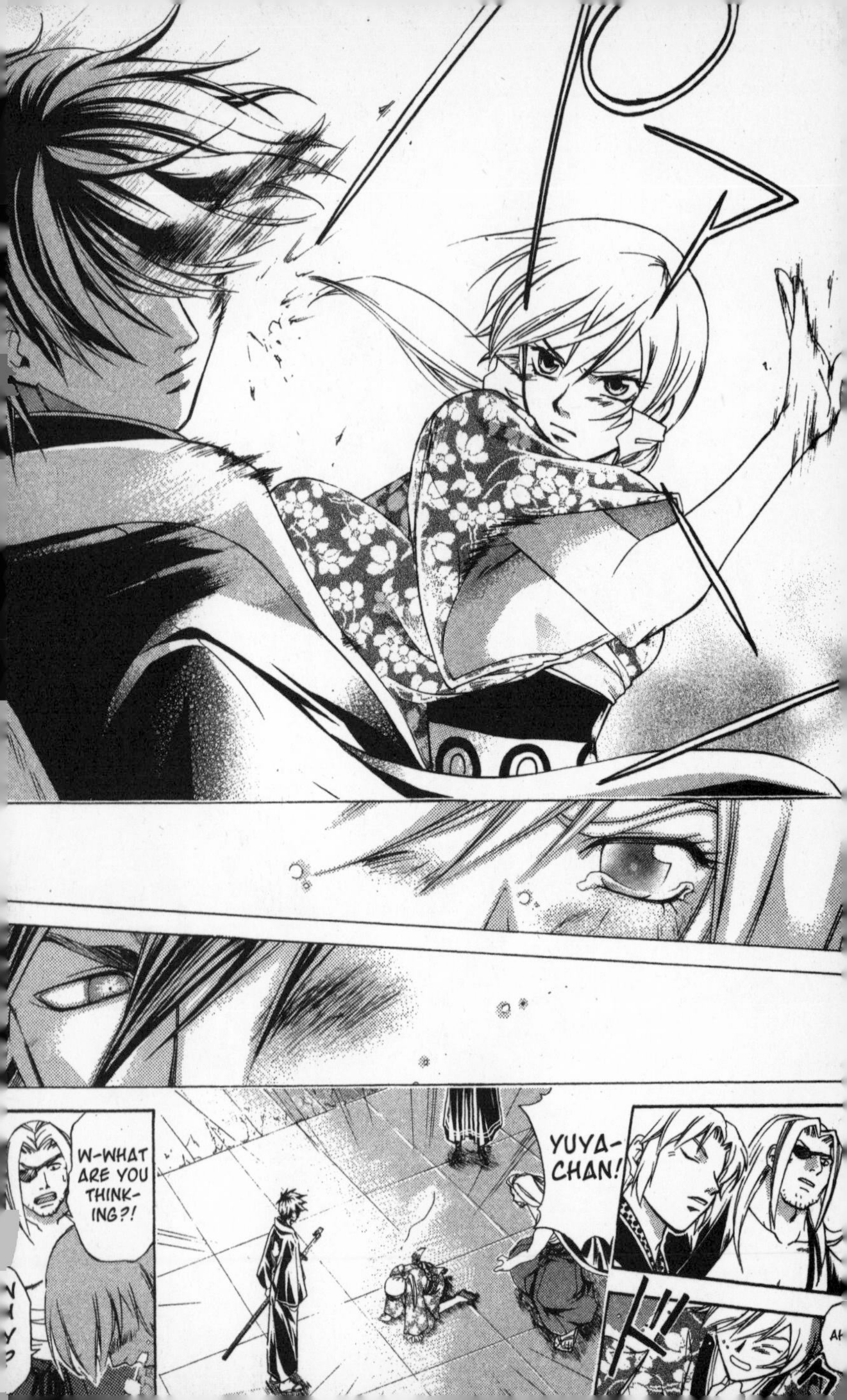
AH
YUYA-CHAN!
W-WHAT ARE YOU THINKING?!

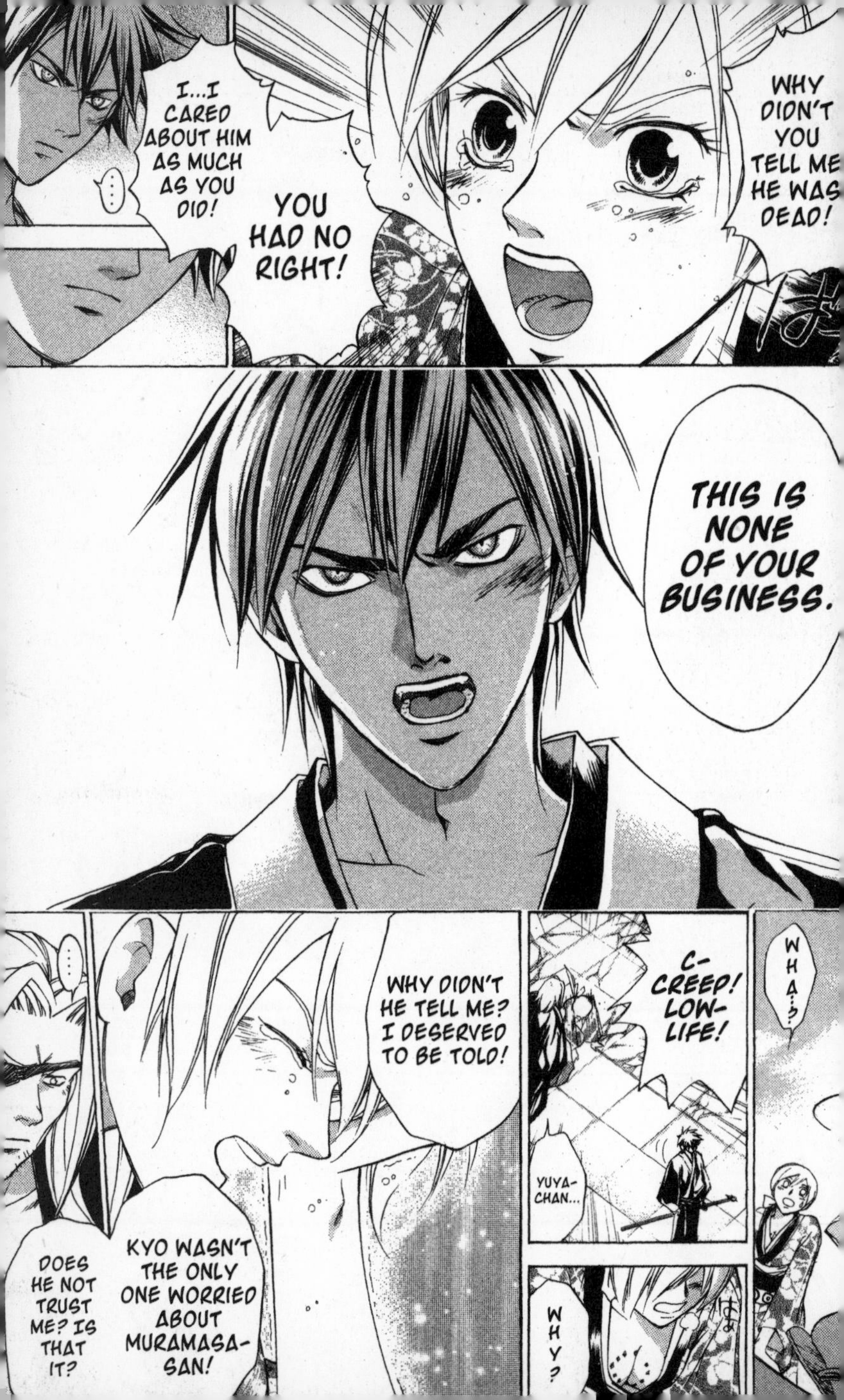
WHY DIDN'T YOU TELL ME HE WAS DEAD!
YOU HAD NO RIGHT!
I...I CARED ABOUT HIM AS MUCH AS YOU DID!
...
THIS IS NONE OF YOUR BUSINESS.
WHA...?
C-CREEP! LOW-LIFE!
YUYA-CHAN...
WHY?
WHY DIDN'T HE TELL ME? I DESERVED TO BE TOLD!
KYO WASN'T THE ONLY ONE WORRIED ABOUT MURAMASA-SAN!
DOES HE NOT TRUST ME? IS THAT IT?
...

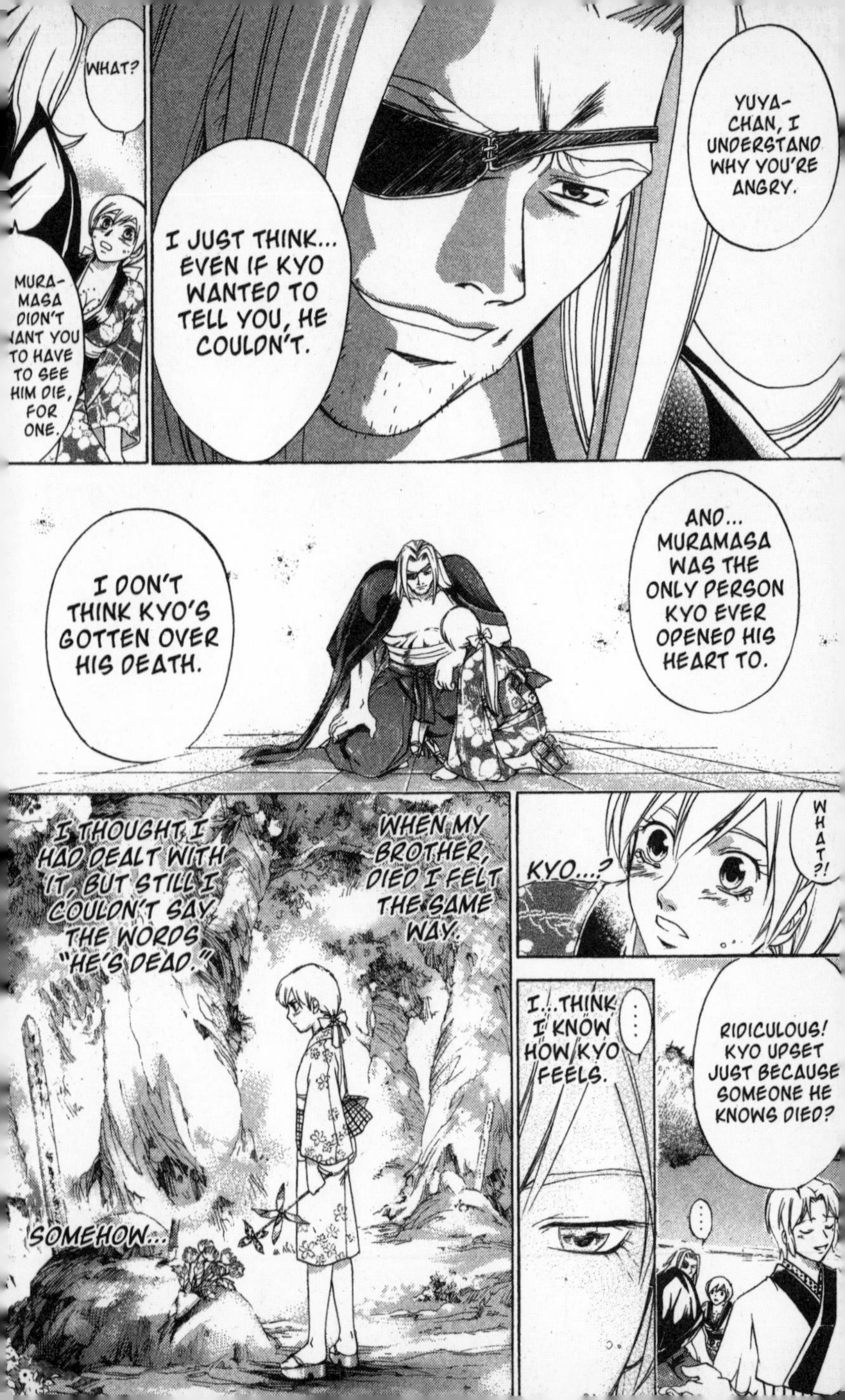
YUYA-CHAN, I UNDERSTAND WHY YOU'RE ANGRY.
I JUST THINK... EVEN IF KYO WANTED TO TELL YOU, HE COULDN'T.
WHAT?
MURA-MASA DIDN'T WANT YOU TO HAVE TO SEE HIM DIE, FOR ONE.
AND... MURAMASA WAS THE ONLY PERSON KYO EVER OPENED HIS HEART TO.
I DON'T THINK KYO'S GOTTEN OVER HIS DEATH.
WHAT?!
KYO...?
RIDICULOUS! KYO UPSET JUST BECAUSE SOMEONE HE KNOWS DIED?
....
I...THINK I KNOW HOW KYO FEELS.
....
WHEN MY BROTHER DIED I FELT THE SAME WAY.
I THOUGHT I HAD DEALT WITH IT, BUT STILL I COULDN'T SAY THE WORDS "HE'S DEAD."
SOMEHOW...

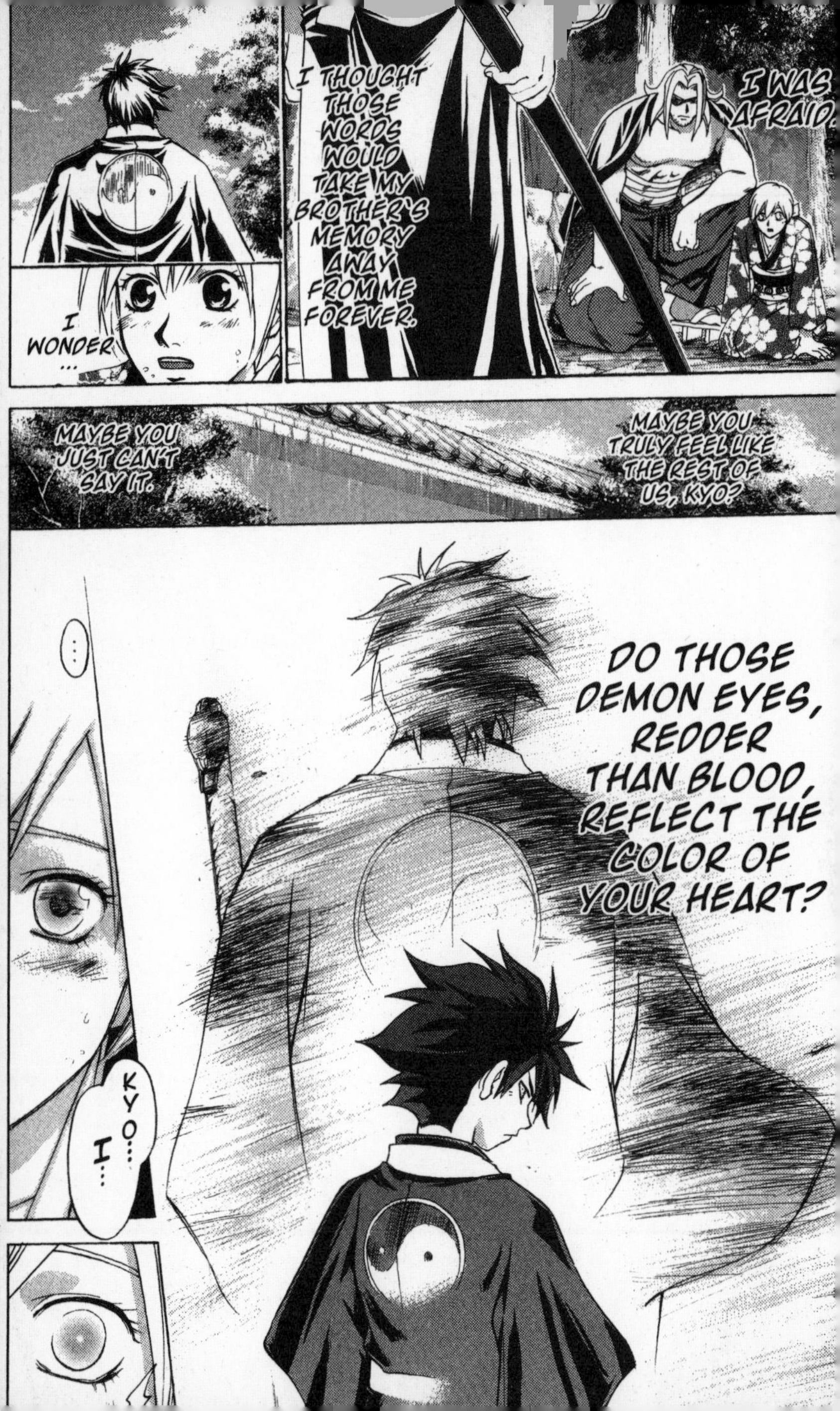
I WAS AFRAID.
I THOUGHT THOSE WORDS WOULD TAKE MY BROTHER'S MEMORY AWAY FROM ME FOREVER.
I WONDER...
MAYBE YOU TRULY FEEL LIKE THE REST OF US, KYO?
MAYBE YOU JUST CAN'T SAY IT.
DO THOSE DEMON EYES, REDDER THAN BLOOD, REFLECT THE COLOR OF YOUR HEART?
...
KYO... I...

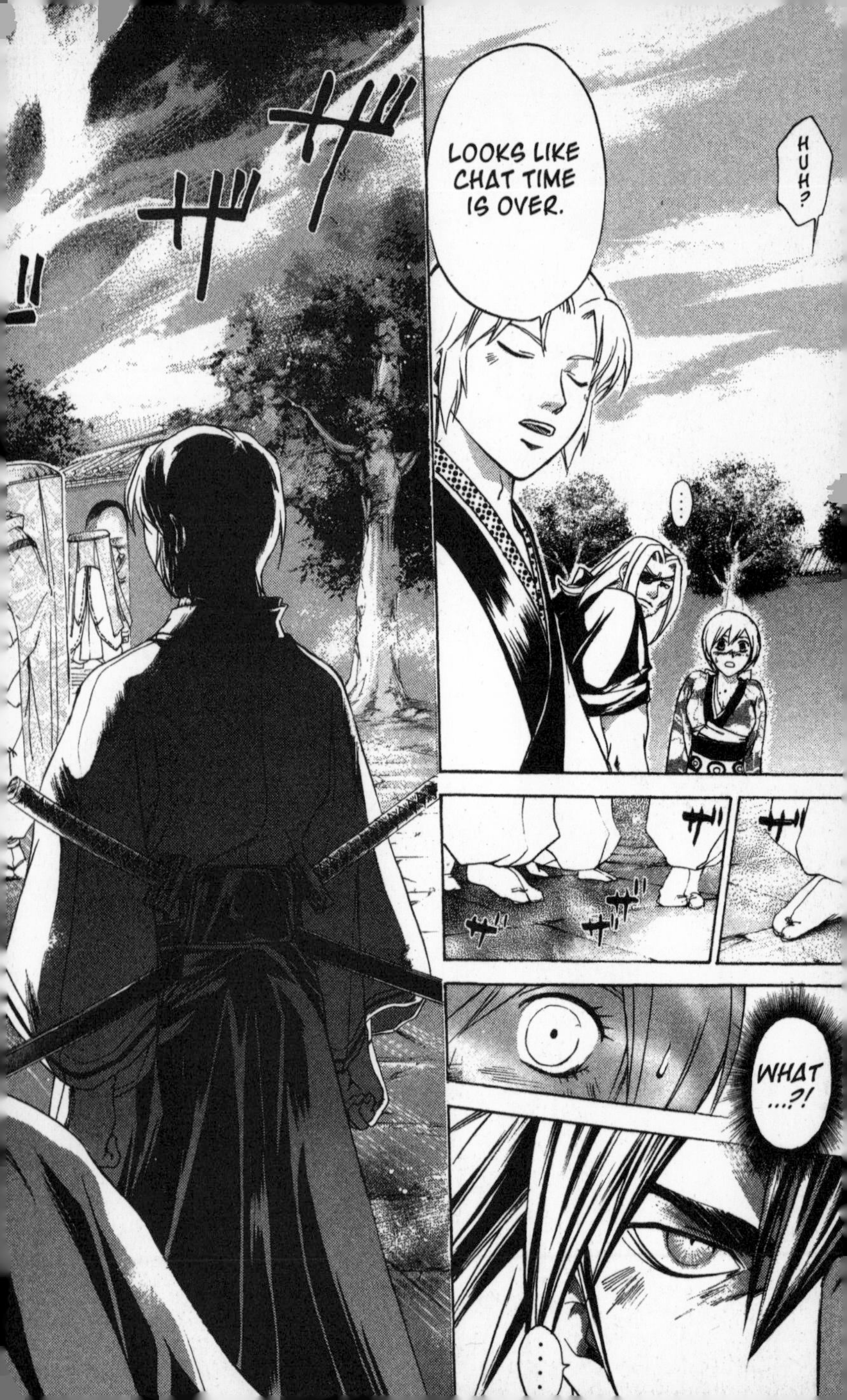
HUH?
LOOKS LIKE CHAT TIME IS OVER.
...
WHAT ...?!
...
!!

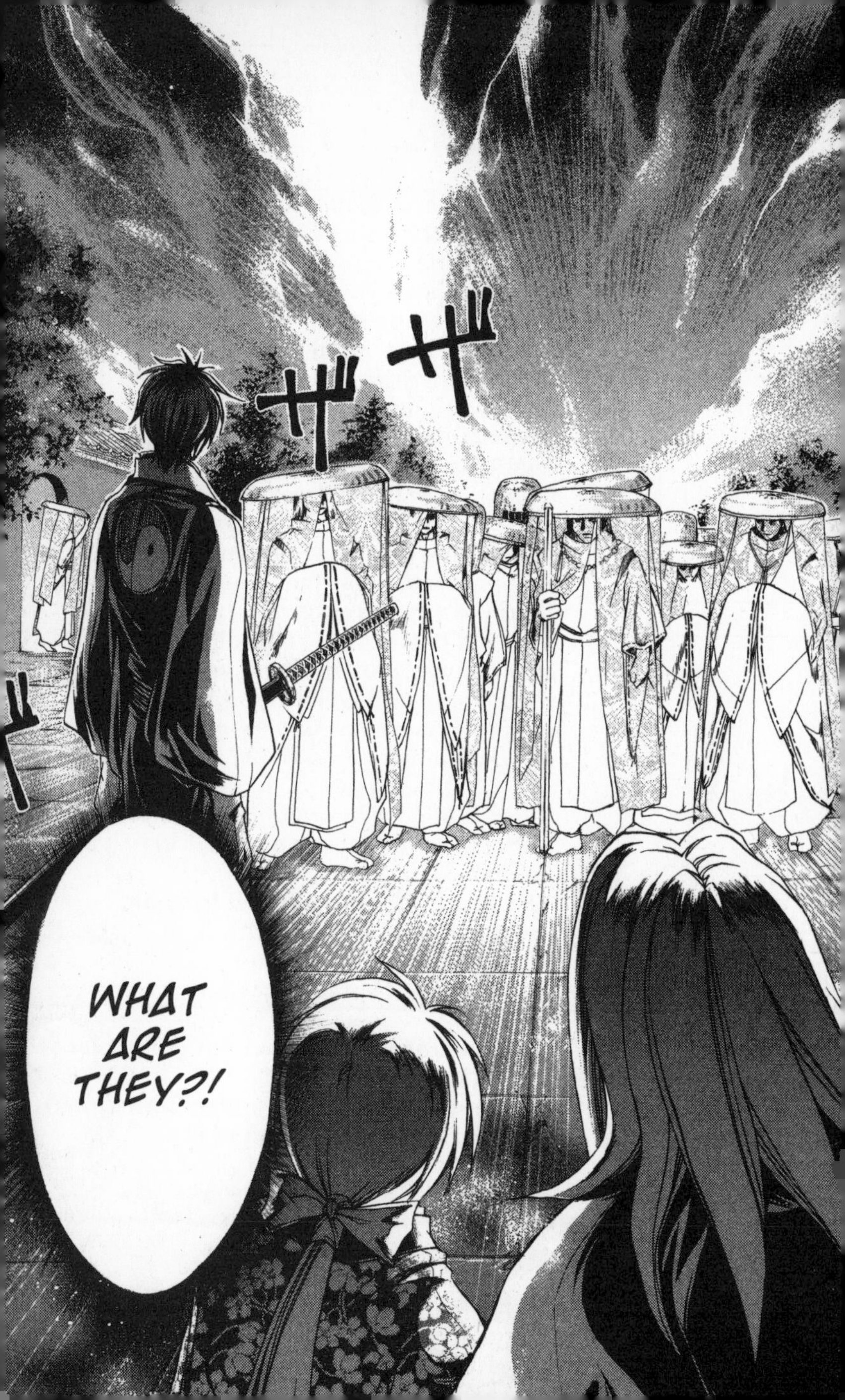
ザ ザ
WHAT ARE THEY?!

Character Profile

Bontenmaru (B, below):　　　　To my millions of fans: the long wait is over!!! At last, the day has come to tell...the legend of Bontenmaru!

Kamijyo (K, below):　　Well, "millions" might be overdoing it...

B:　(not listening) Bontenmaru was my childhood nickname. My real name is Date Masamune. Height: 198 cm. Weight: 85 kg. Hobbies: Smoking. Likes: the world, as in *ruling* it. Dislikes: defeat! Favorite food? If it's edible, I'll eat it! It's been a quick 37 years. The legend of the one-eyed dragon began when I was five. I got the measles, and the pus took out my right eye.

K:　(I'd better step in here!) S-so, I read in the history book that you were strikingly handsome and well attired. I guess you can't believe everything you read!

B:　You lookin' for a fight?

K:　Uh, no! No no no! Of course, you're quite stylish. Why, you've had three different eye patches already! Very, very stylish.

B:　Yes, it's true, it's true. I truly am destined to rule the world! Best ask quick if you want my signature!

K:　R-right. (No thanks...) Any parting words?

B:　Everyone, follow me! I'm going places! Bwah hah hah hah!

K:　(note to self: never praise Bontenmaru. You'll never hear the end of it.)

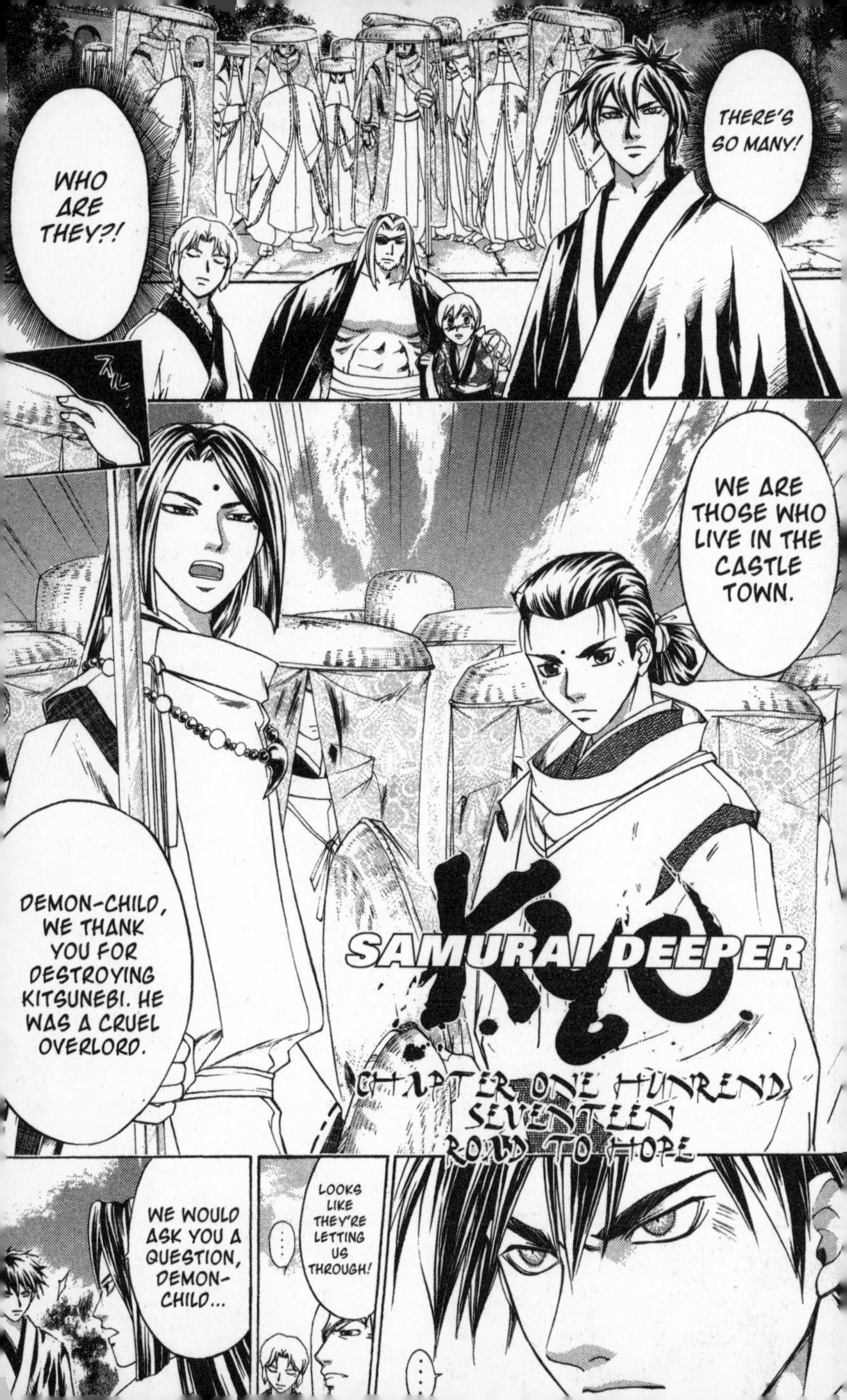
THERE'S SO MANY!
WHO ARE THEY?!
WE ARE THOSE WHO LIVE IN THE CASTLE TOWN.
DEMON-CHILD, WE THANK YOU FOR DESTROYING KITSUNEBI. HE WAS A CRUEL OVERLORD.
SAMURAI DEEPER KYO
CHAPTER ONE HUNREND SEVENTEEN
ROAD TO HOPE
LOOKS LIKE THEY'RE LETTING US THROUGH!
...
...
WE WOULD ASK YOU A QUESTION, DEMON-CHILD...

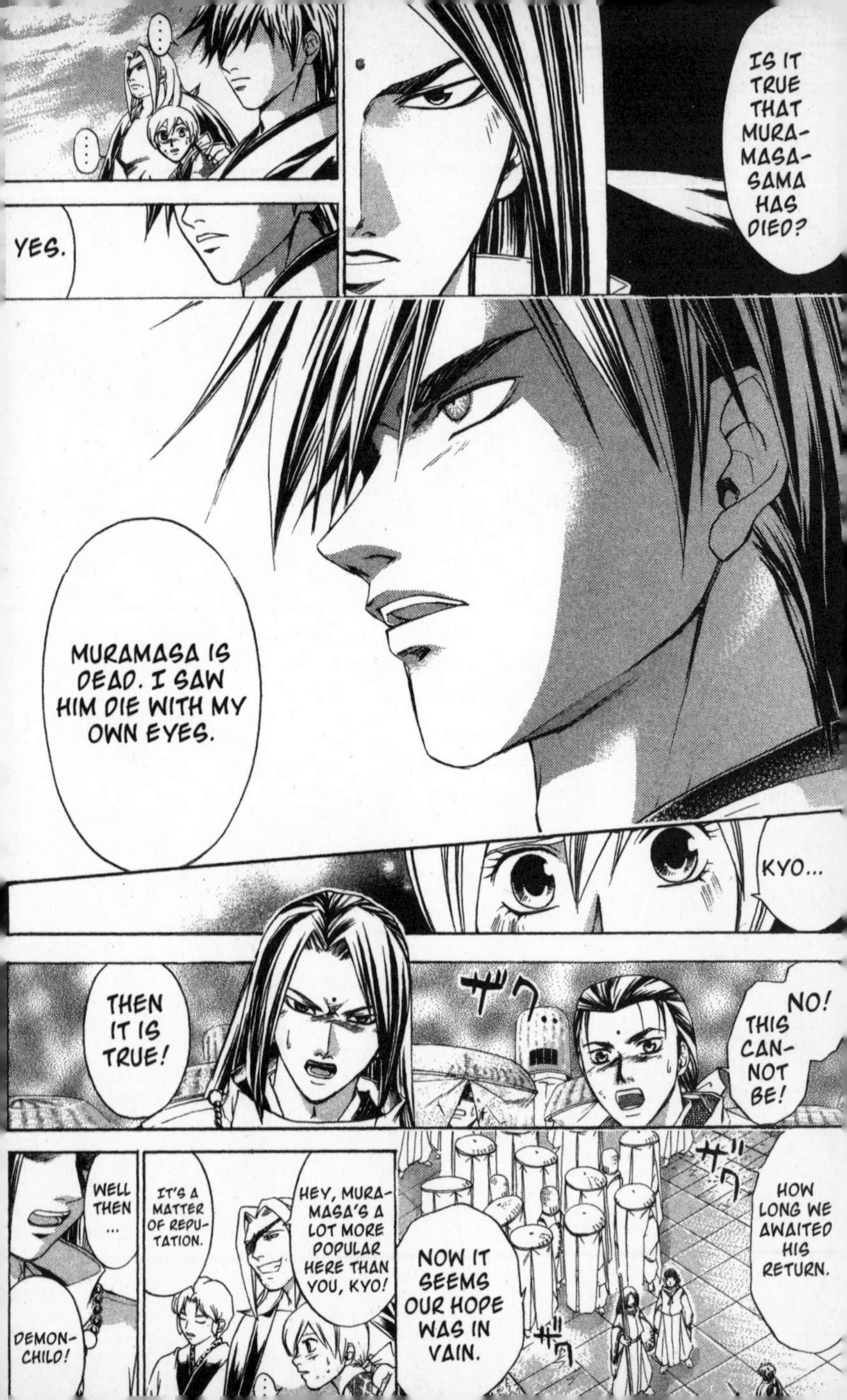
IS IT TRUE THAT MURA-MASA-SAMA HAS DIED?
...
...
YES.
MURAMASA IS DEAD. I SAW HIM DIE WITH MY OWN EYES.
KYO...
NO! THIS CAN-NOT BE!
ザワ
THEN IT IS TRUE!
HOW LONG WE AWAITED HIS RETURN.
ザワ
NOW IT SEEMS OUR HOPE WAS IN VAIN.
HEY, MURA-MASA'S A LOT MORE POPULAR HERE THAN YOU, KYO!
IT'S A MATTER OF REPU-TATION.
WELL THEN ...
DEMON-CHILD!

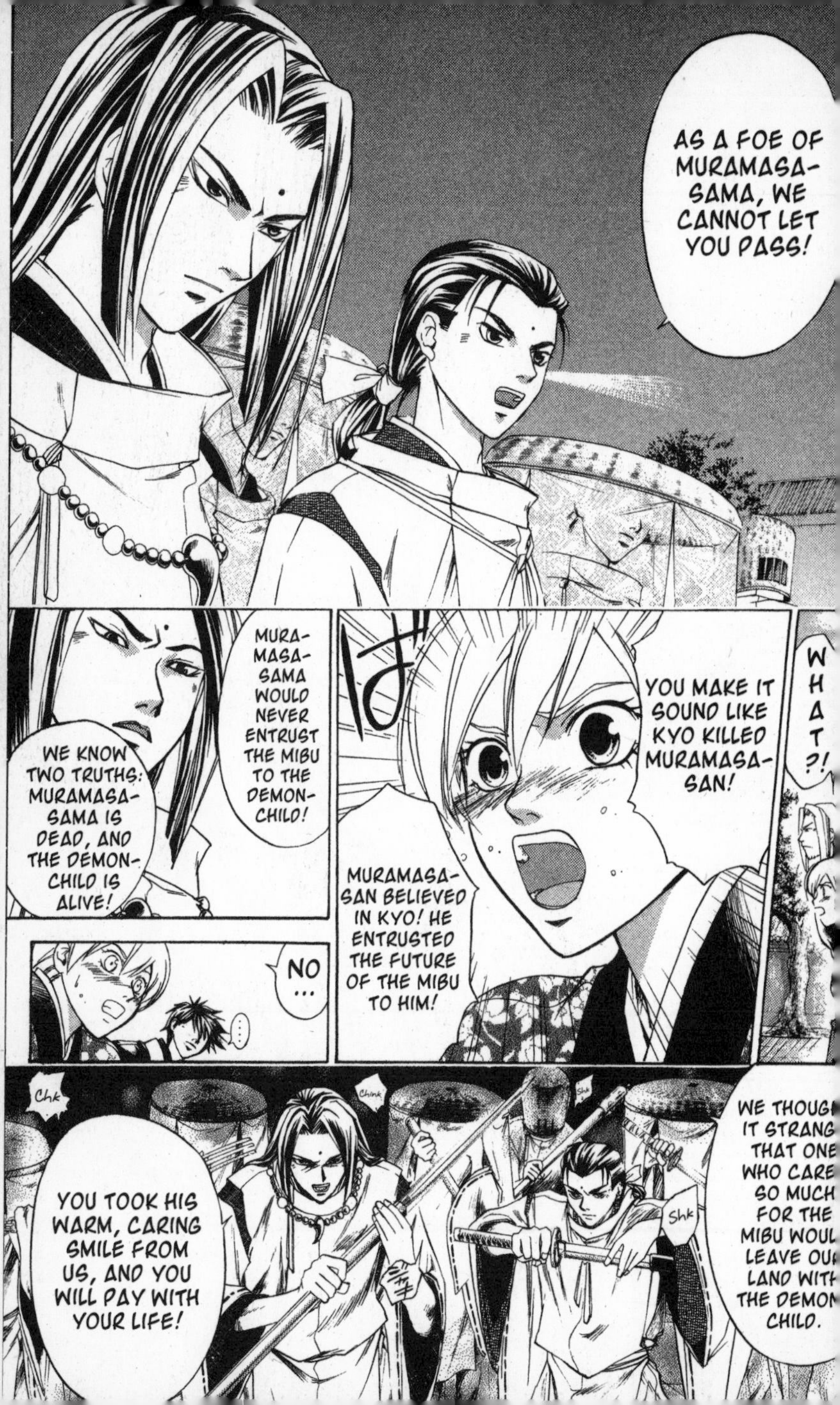
AS A FOE OF MURAMASA-SAMA, WE CANNOT LET YOU PASS!
WHAT?!
ば
YOU MAKE IT SOUND LIKE KYO KILLED MURAMASA-SAN!
MURAMASA-SAN BELIEVED IN KYO! HE ENTRUSTED THE FUTURE OF THE MIBU TO HIM!
MURA-MASA-SAMA WOULD NEVER ENTRUST THE MIBU TO THE DEMON-CHILD!
WE KNOW TWO TRUTHS: MURAMASA-SAMA IS DEAD, AND THE DEMON-CHILD IS ALIVE!
NO ...
...
WE THOUG IT STRANG THAT ONE WHO CARE SO MUCH FOR THE MIBU WOUL LEAVE OU LAND WITH THE DEMON CHILD.
Shk
Shk
Chink
Chk
YOU TOOK HIS WARM, CARING SMILE FROM US, AND YOU WILL PAY WITH YOUR LIFE!

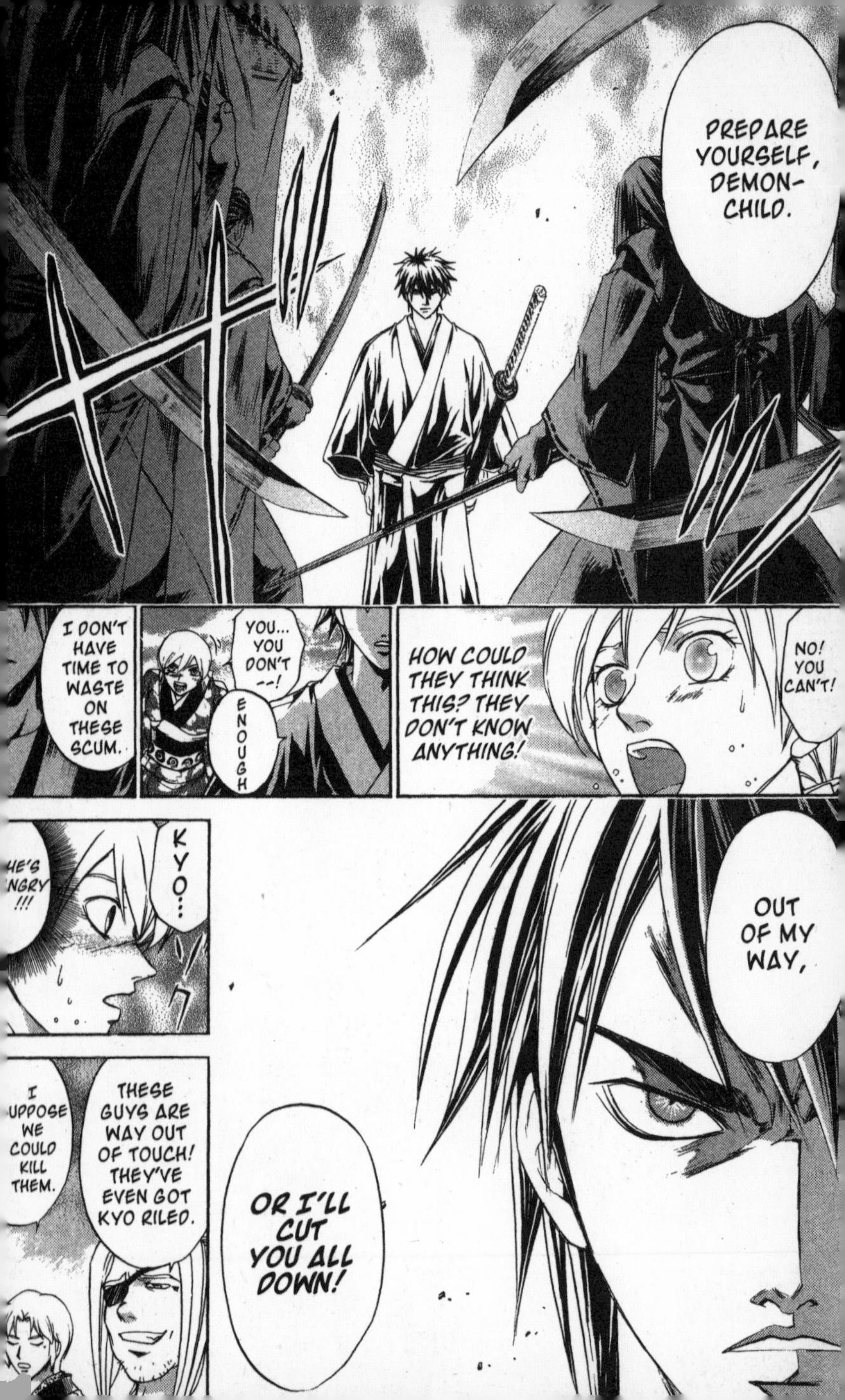
PREPARE YOURSELF, DEMON-CHILD.
NO! YOU CAN'T!
HOW COULD THEY THINK THIS? THEY DON'T KNOW ANYTHING!
YOU... YOU DON'T --!
ENOUGH
I DON'T HAVE TIME TO WASTE ON THESE SCUM.
OUT OF MY WAY,
OR I'LL CUT YOU ALL DOWN!
KYO...
HE'S NGRY !!!
THESE GUYS ARE WAY OUT OF TOUCH! THEY'VE EVEN GOT KYO RILED.
I UPPOSE WE COULD KILL THEM.

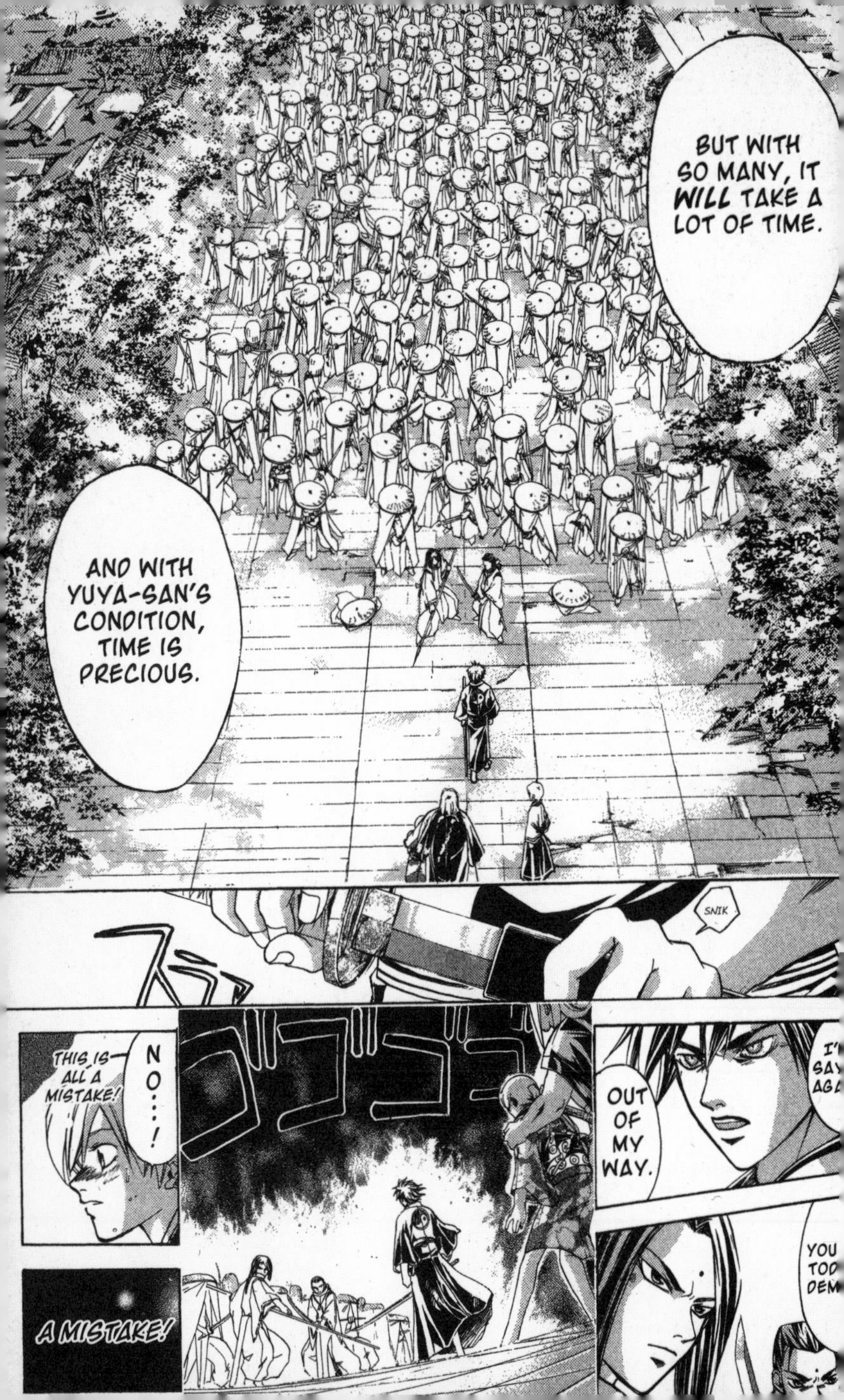
BUT WITH SO MANY, IT WILL TAKE A LOT OF TIME.
AND WITH YUYA-SAN'S CONDITION, TIME IS PRECIOUS.
SNIK
OUT OF MY WAY.
NO...!
THIS IS ALL A MISTAKE!
A MISTAKE!

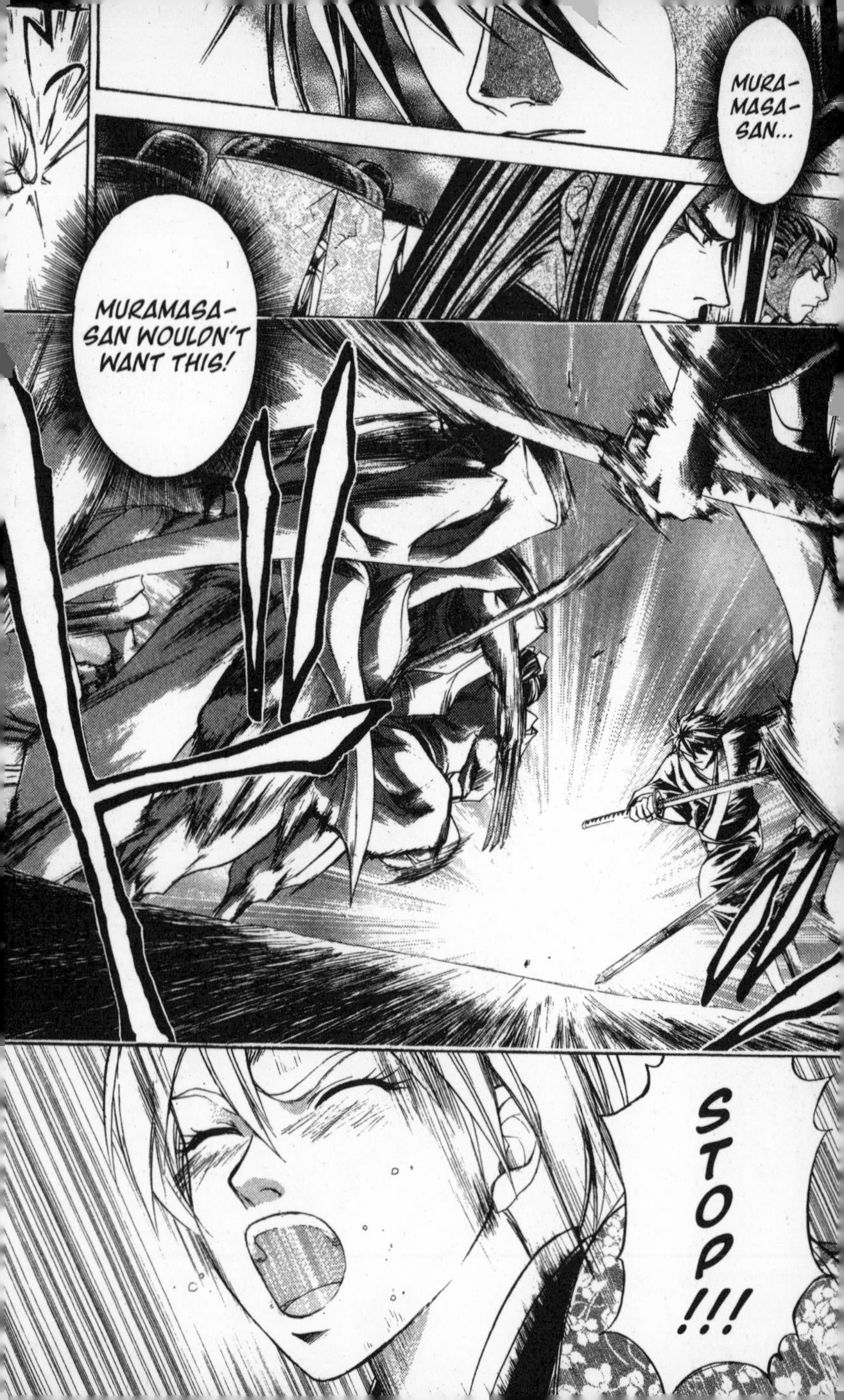
MURA-MASA-SAN...
MURAMASA-SAN WOULDN'T WANT THIS!
STOP!!!

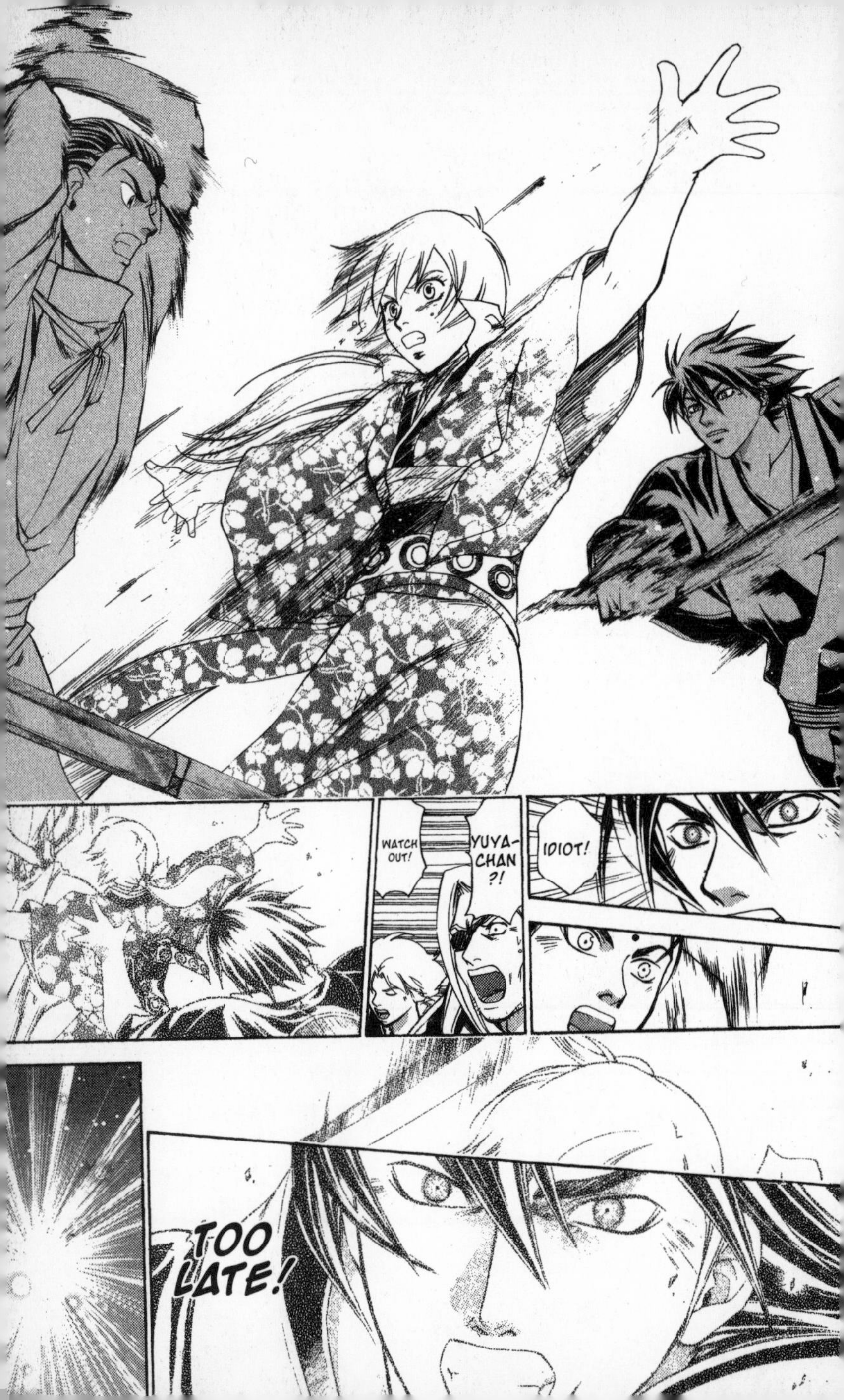
IDIOT!
YUYA-CHAN ?!
WATCH OUT!
TOO LATE!

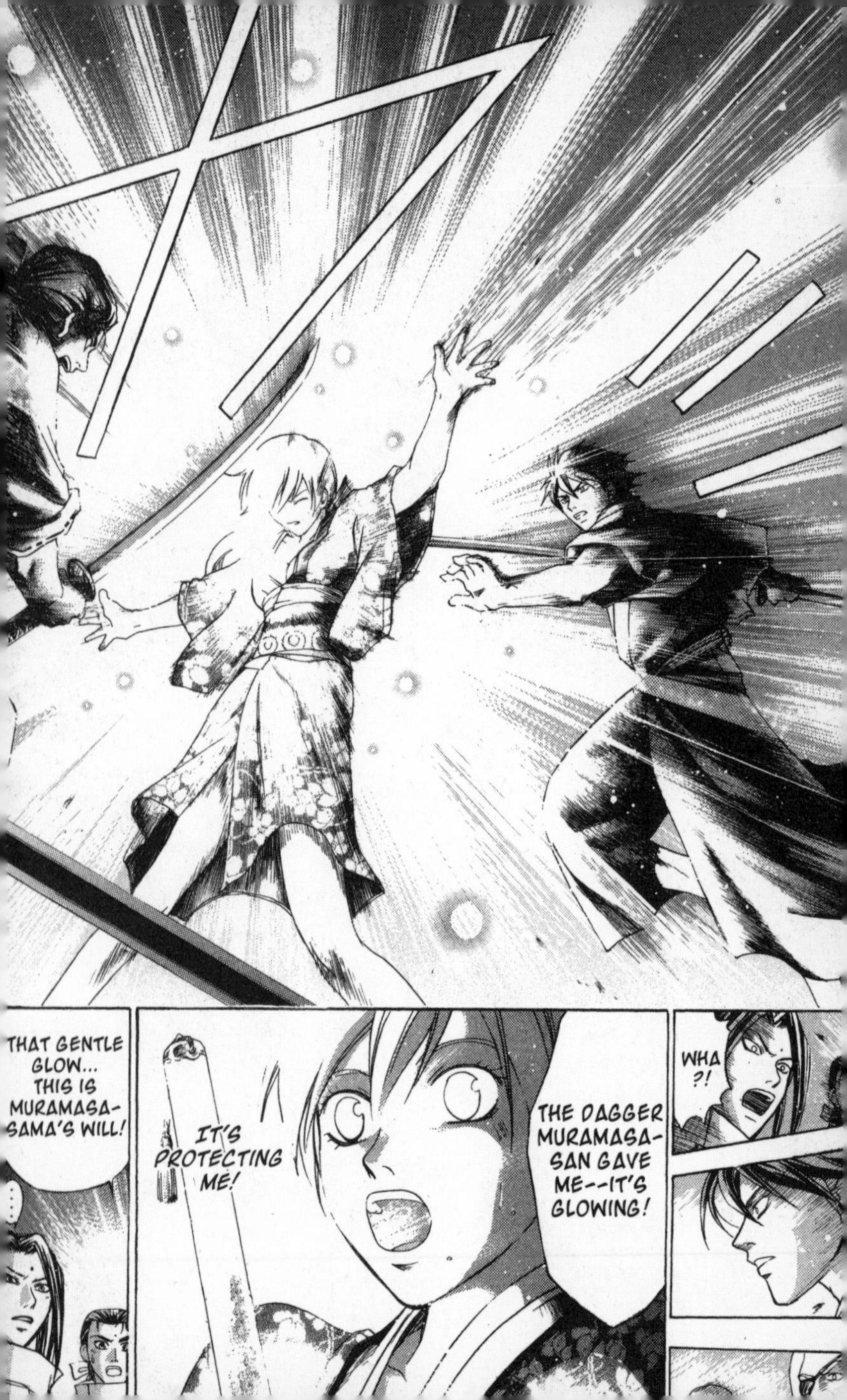
WHA?!
THE DAGGER MURAMASA-SAN GAVE ME--IT'S GLOWING!
IT'S PROTECTING ME!
THAT GENTLE GLOW... THIS IS MURAMASA-SAMA'S WILL!
......

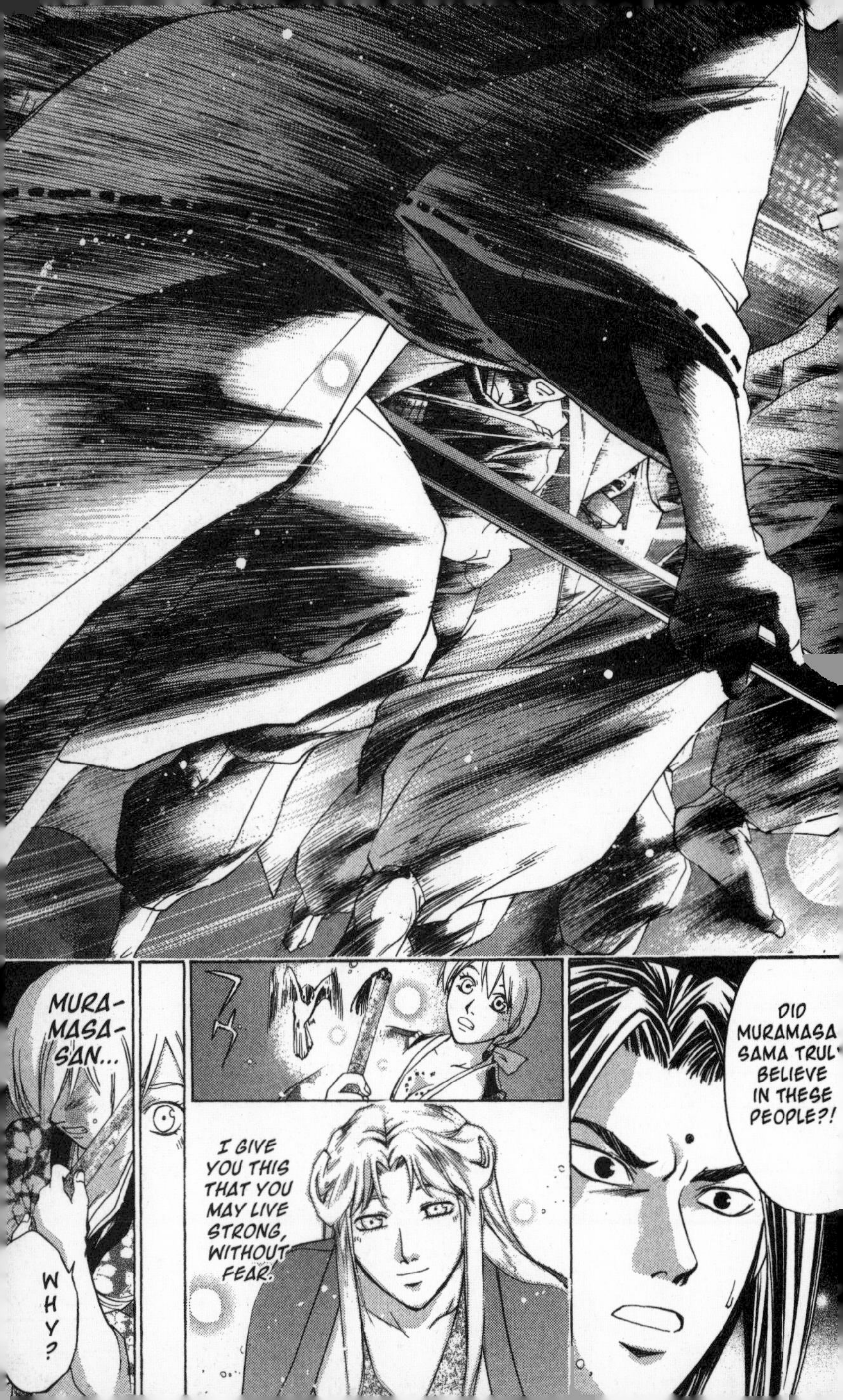
DID MURAMASA SAMA TRUL BELIEVE IN THESE PEOPLE?!
I GIVE YOU THIS THAT YOU MAY LIVE STRONG, WITHOUT FEAR.
MURA-MASA-SAN...
WHY?

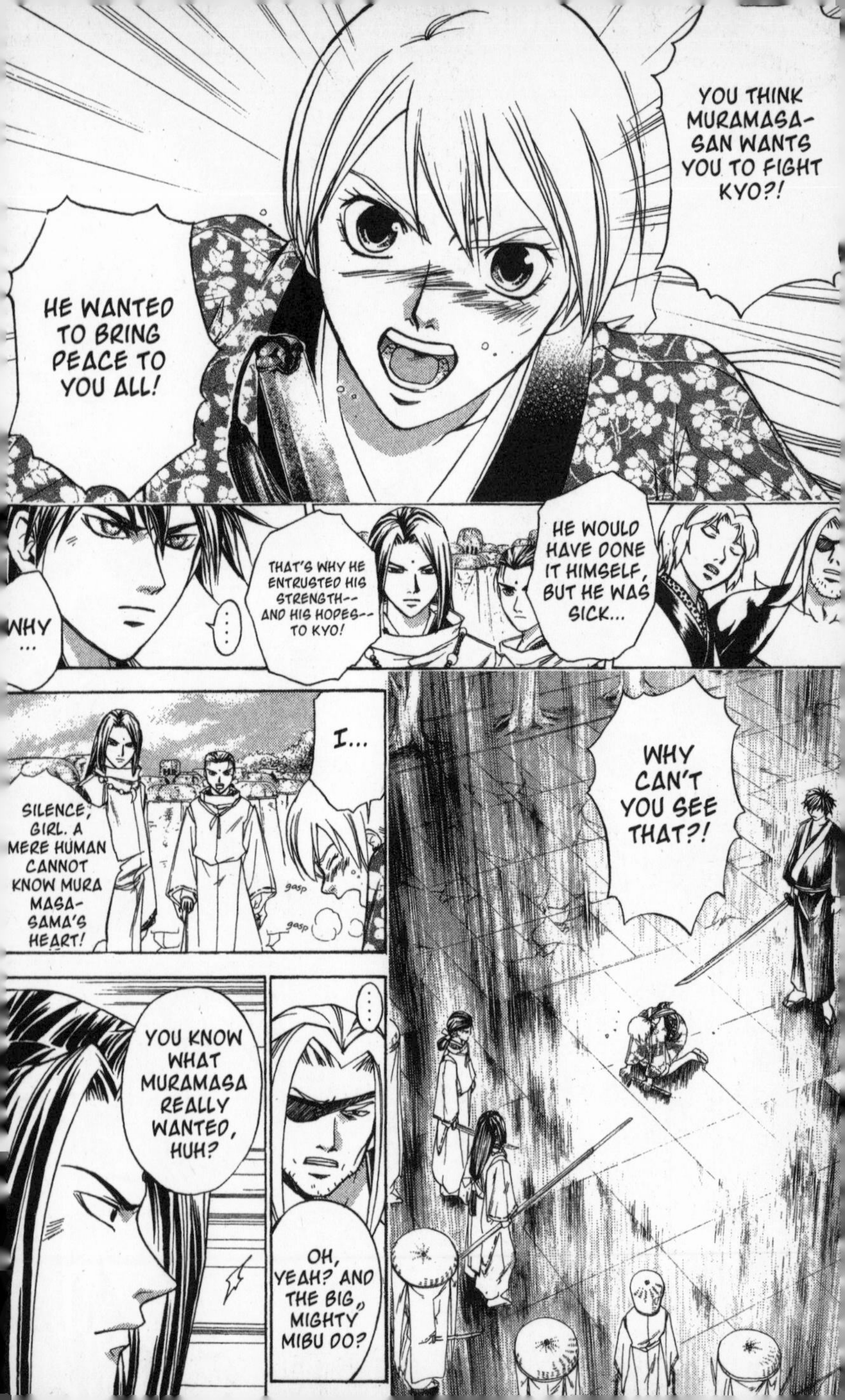
YOU THINK MURAMASA-SAN WANTS YOU TO FIGHT KYO?!
HE WANTED TO BRING PEACE TO YOU ALL!
HE WOULD HAVE DONE IT HIMSELF, BUT HE WAS SICK...
THAT'S WHY HE ENTRUSTED HIS STRENGTH-- AND HIS HOPES-- TO KYO!
...
WHY ...
WHY CAN'T YOU SEE THAT?!
I...
SILENCE, GIRL. A MERE HUMAN CANNOT KNOW MURA MASA-SAMA'S HEART!
gasp
gasp
...
YOU KNOW WHAT MURAMASA REALLY WANTED, HUH?
OH, YEAH? AND THE BIG, MIGHTY MIBU DO?

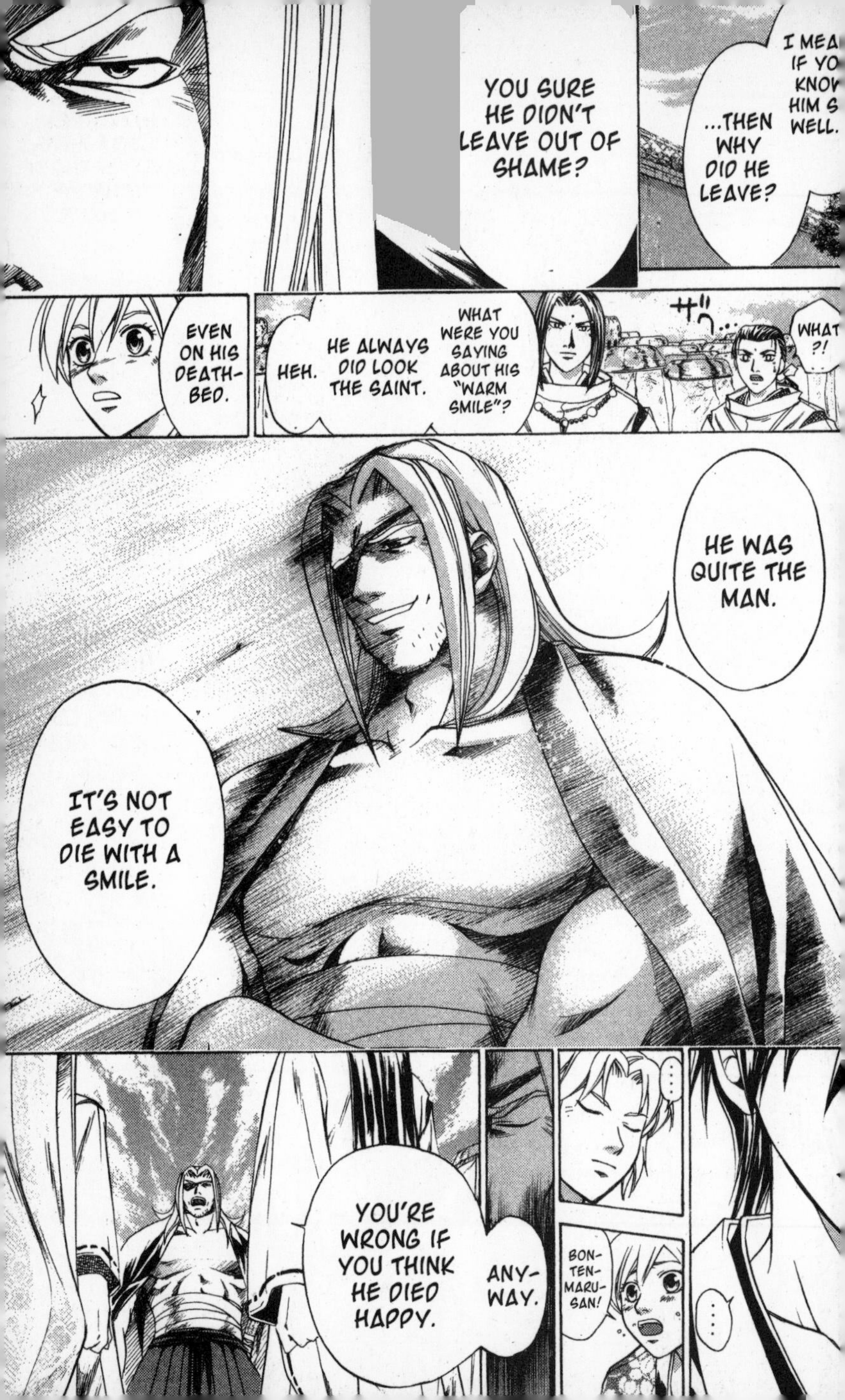

I MEA IF YO KNOW HIM S WELL.
...THEN WHY DID HE LEAVE?
YOU SURE HE DIDN'T LEAVE OUT OF SHAME?
WHAT ?!
ザッ...
WHAT WERE YOU SAYING ABOUT HIS "WARM SMILE"?
HE ALWAYS DID LOOK THE SAINT.
HEH.
EVEN ON HIS DEATH-BED.
HE WAS QUITE THE MAN.
IT'S NOT EASY TO DIE WITH A SMILE.
....
BON-TEN-MARU-SAN!
....
ANY-WAY.
YOU'RE WRONG IF YOU THINK HE DIED HAPPY.

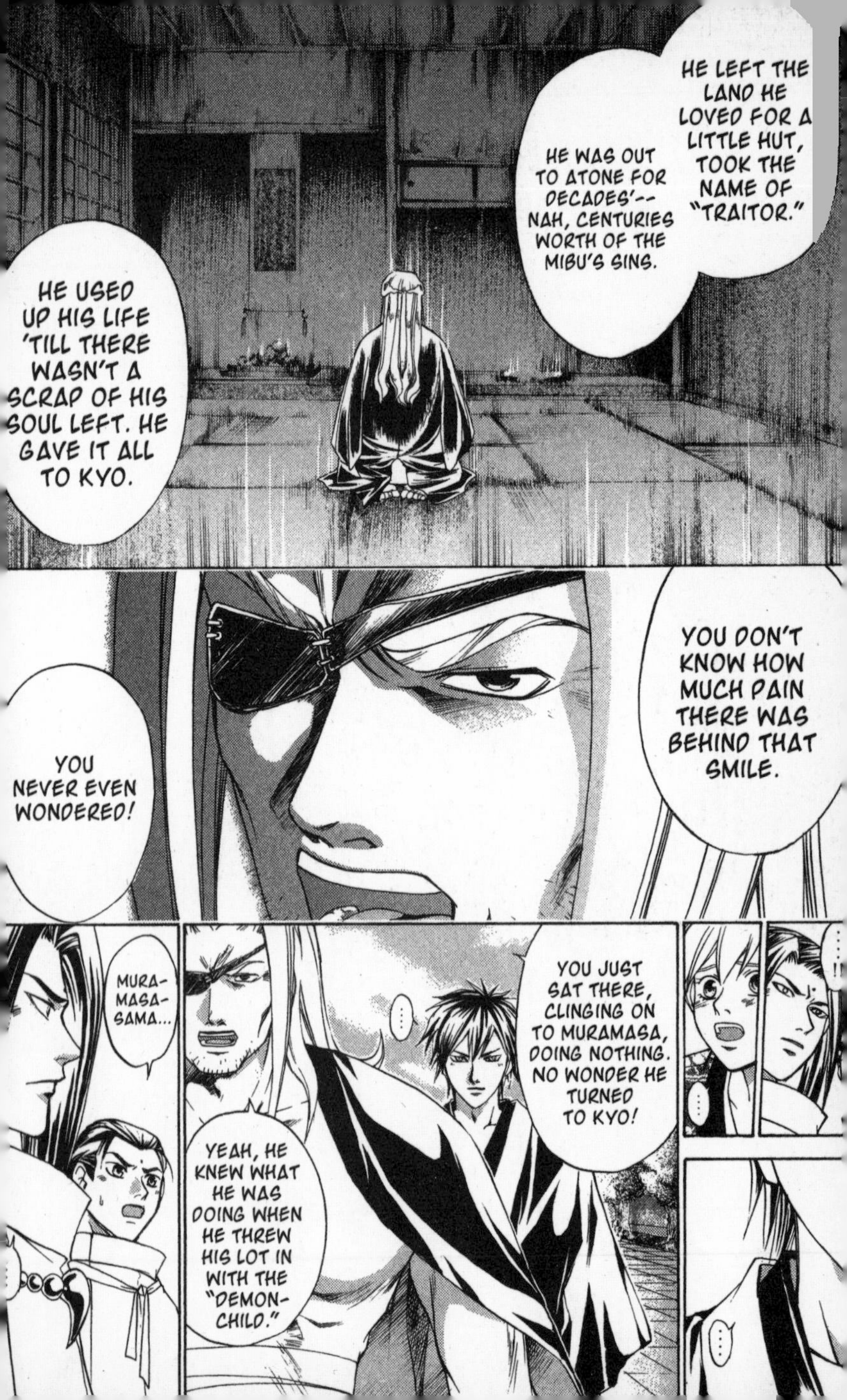
HE LEFT THE LAND HE LOVED FOR A LITTLE HUT, TOOK THE NAME OF "TRAITOR."
HE WAS OUT TO ATONE FOR DECADES'-- NAH, CENTURIES WORTH OF THE MIBU'S SINS.
HE USED UP HIS LIFE 'TILL THERE WASN'T A SCRAP OF HIS SOUL LEFT. HE GAVE IT ALL TO KYO.
YOU DON'T KNOW HOW MUCH PAIN THERE WAS BEHIND THAT SMILE.
YOU NEVER EVEN WONDERED!
...!!
...
...
YOU JUST SAT THERE, CLINGING ON TO MURAMASA, DOING NOTHING. NO WONDER HE TURNED TO KYO!
...
YEAH, HE KNEW WHAT HE WAS DOING WHEN HE THREW HIS LOT IN WITH THE "DEMON-CHILD."
MURA-MASA-SAMA...

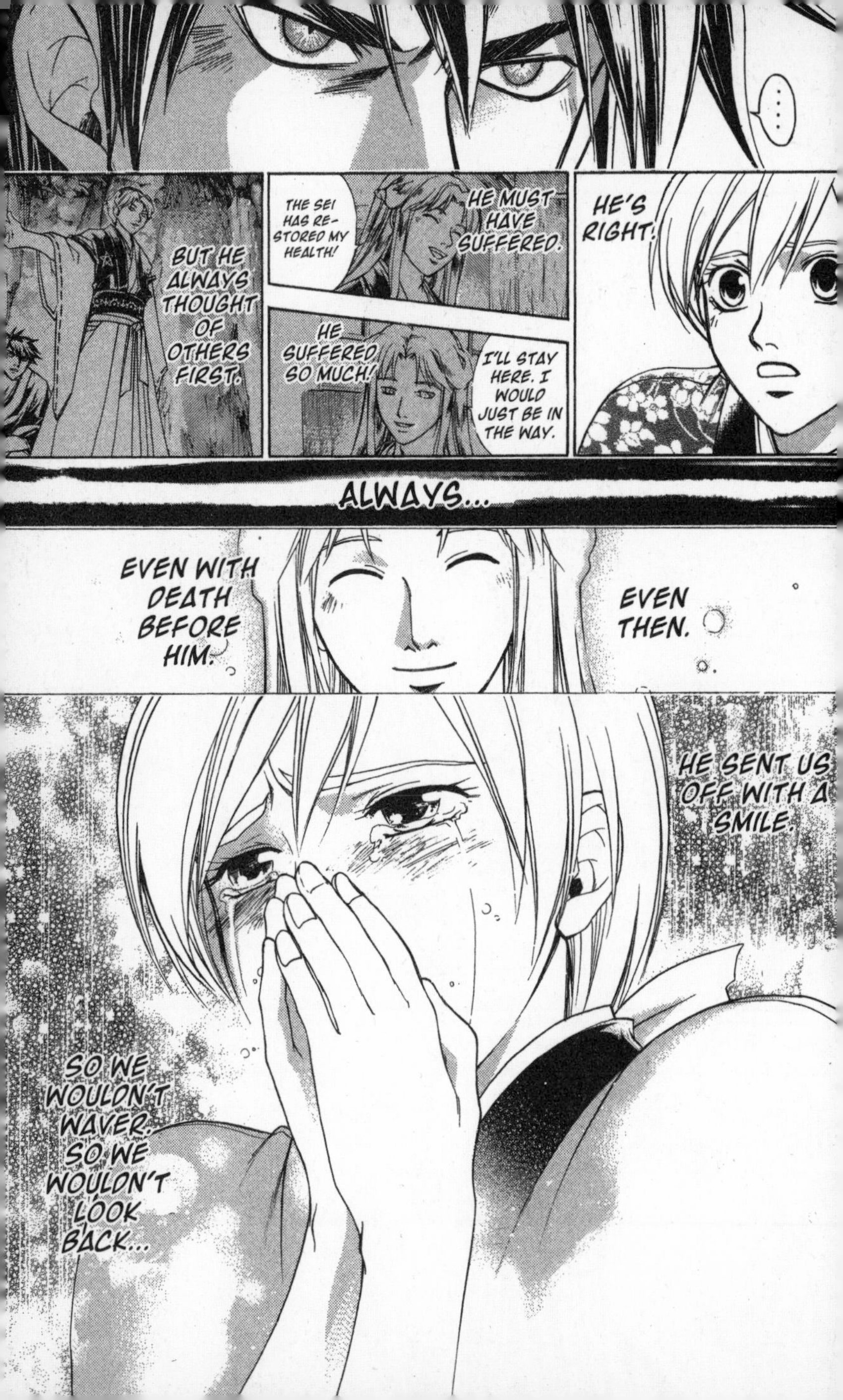
……
HE'S RIGHT!
HE MUST HAVE SUFFERED.
THE SEI HAS RE-STORED MY HEALTH!
I'LL STAY HERE. I WOULD JUST BE IN THE WAY.
HE SUFFERED SO MUCH!
BUT HE ALWAYS THOUGHT OF OTHERS FIRST.
ALWAYS...
EVEN THEN.
EVEN WITH DEATH BEFORE HIM.
HE SENT US OFF WITH A SMILE.
SO WE WOULDN'T WAVER. SO WE WOULDN'T LOOK BACK...

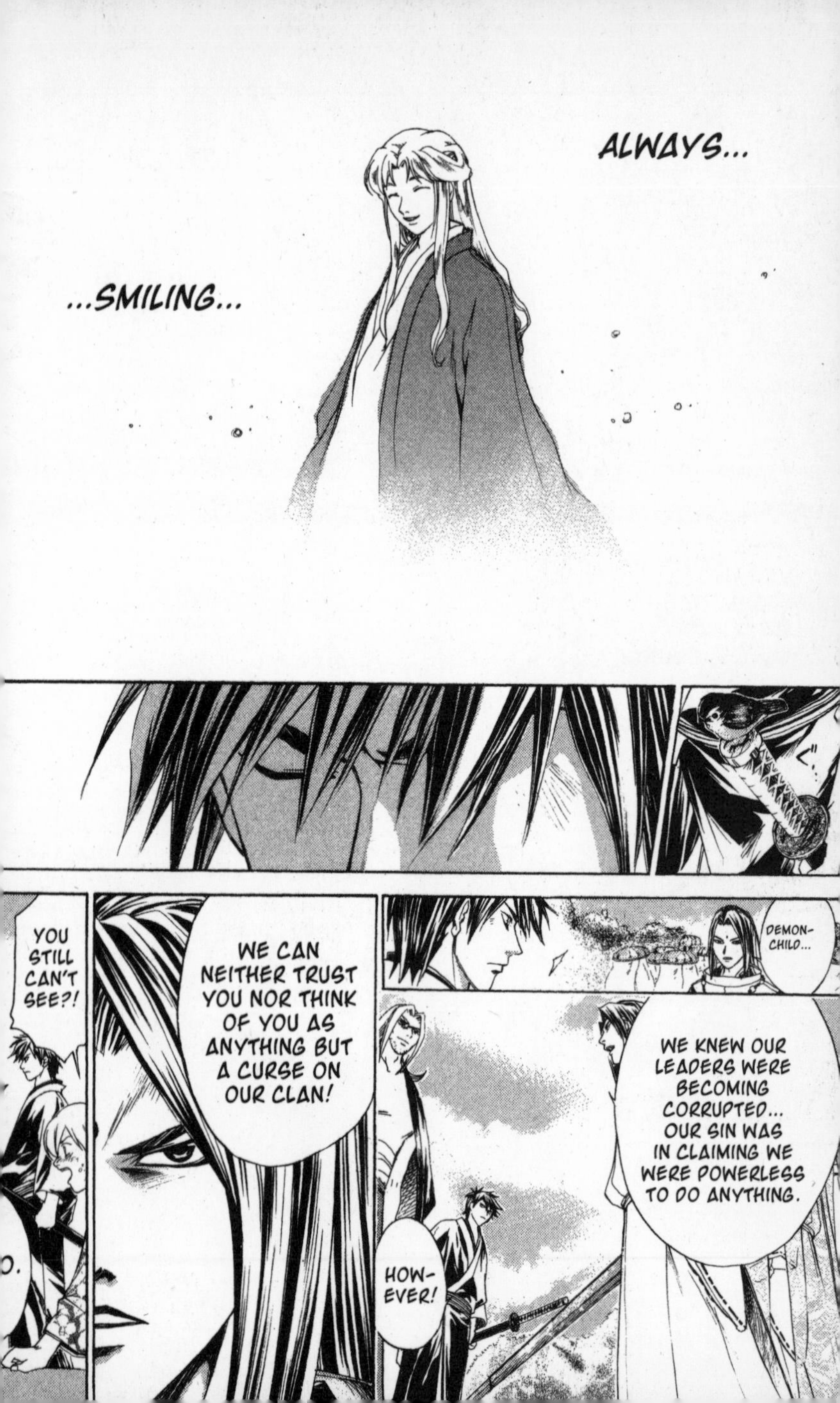
ALWAYS...
...SMILING...
DEMON-CHILD...
WE KNEW OUR LEADERS WERE BECOMING CORRUPTED... OUR SIN WAS IN CLAIMING WE WERE POWERLESS TO DO ANYTHING.
HOW-EVER!
WE CAN NEITHER TRUST YOU NOR THINK OF YOU AS ANYTHING BUT A CURSE ON OUR CLAN!
YOU STILL CAN'T SEE?!

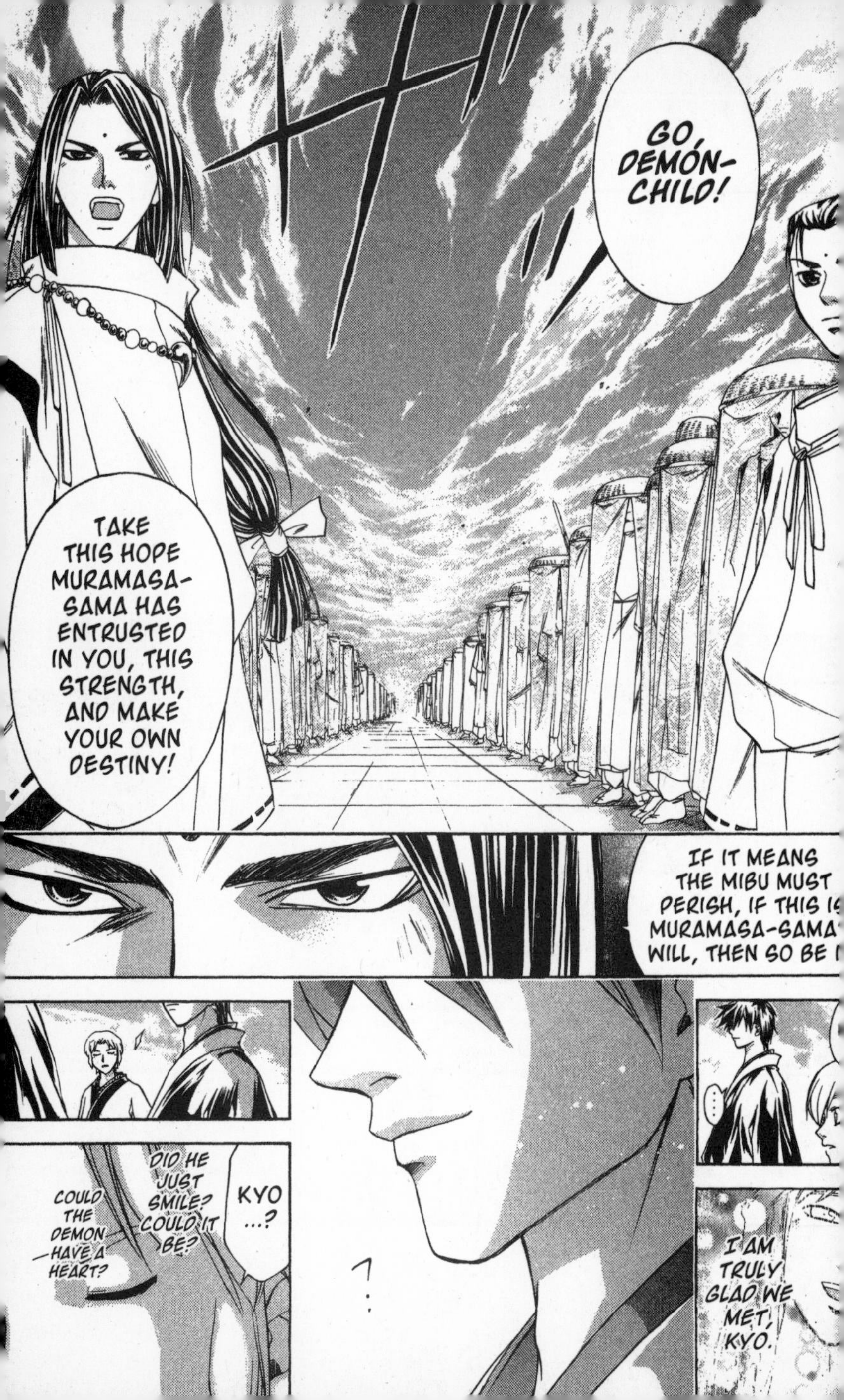
GO, DEMON-CHILD!
TAKE THIS HOPE MURAMASA-SAMA HAS ENTRUSTED IN YOU, THIS STRENGTH, AND MAKE YOUR OWN DESTINY!
IF IT MEANS THE MIBU MUST PERISH, IF THIS IS MURAMASA-SAMA' WILL, THEN SO BE I
...
I AM TRULY GLAD WE MET, KYO.
?
KYO ...?
DID HE JUST SMILE? COULD IT BE?
COULD THE DEMON HAVE A HEART?

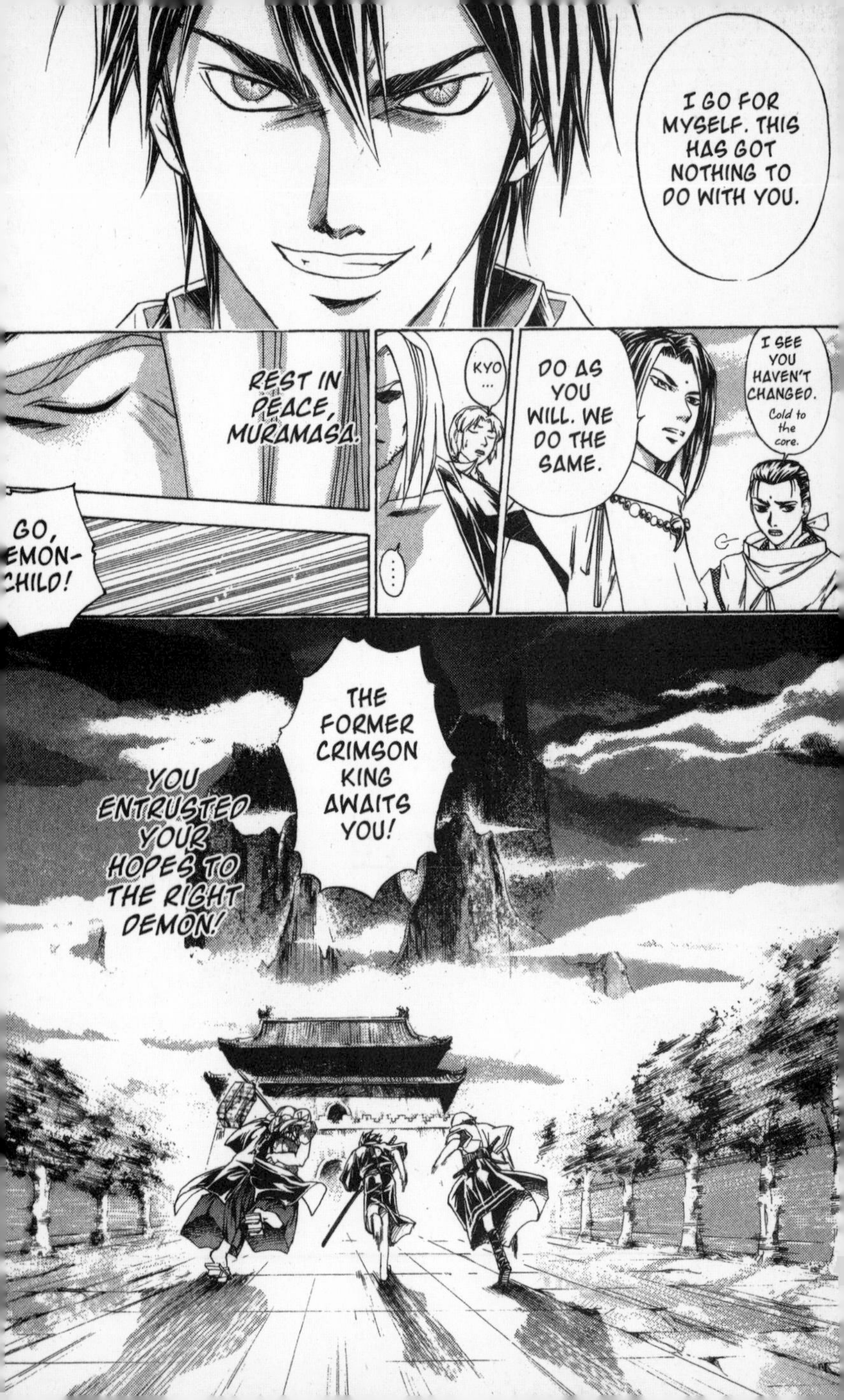
I GO FOR MYSELF. THIS HAS GOT NOTHING TO DO WITH YOU.
I SEE YOU HAVEN'T CHANGED.
Cold to the core.
DO AS YOU WILL. WE DO THE SAME.
KYO ...
...
REST IN PEACE, MURAMASA.
GO, EMON-CHILD!
THE FORMER CRIMSON KING AWAITS YOU!
YOU ENTRUSTED YOUR HOPES TO THE RIGHT DEMON!

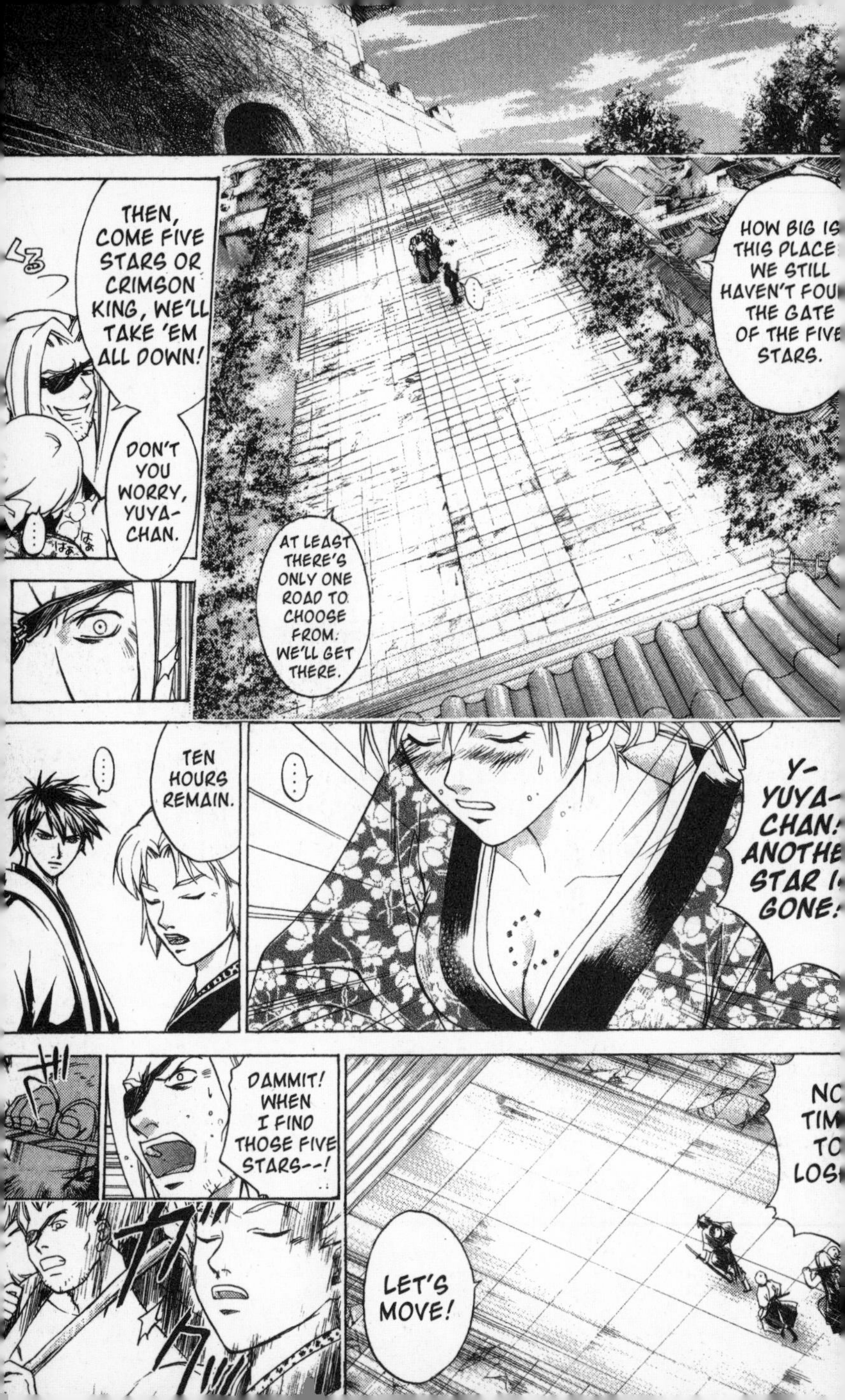
HOW BIG IS THIS PLACE WE STILL HAVEN'T FOU THE GATE OF THE FIVE STARS.
...
AT LEAST THERE'S ONLY ONE ROAD TO CHOOSE FROM. WE'LL GET THERE.
THEN, COME FIVE STARS OR CRIMSON KING, WE'LL TAKE 'EM ALL DOWN!
くる
DON'T YOU WORRY, YUYA-CHAN.
...
はぁ はぁ
Y- YUYA-CHAN! ANOTHE STAR I GONE!
...
TEN HOURS REMAIN.
...
NO TIM TO LOS
LET'S MOVE!
DAMMIT! WHEN I FIND THOSE FIVE STARS--!

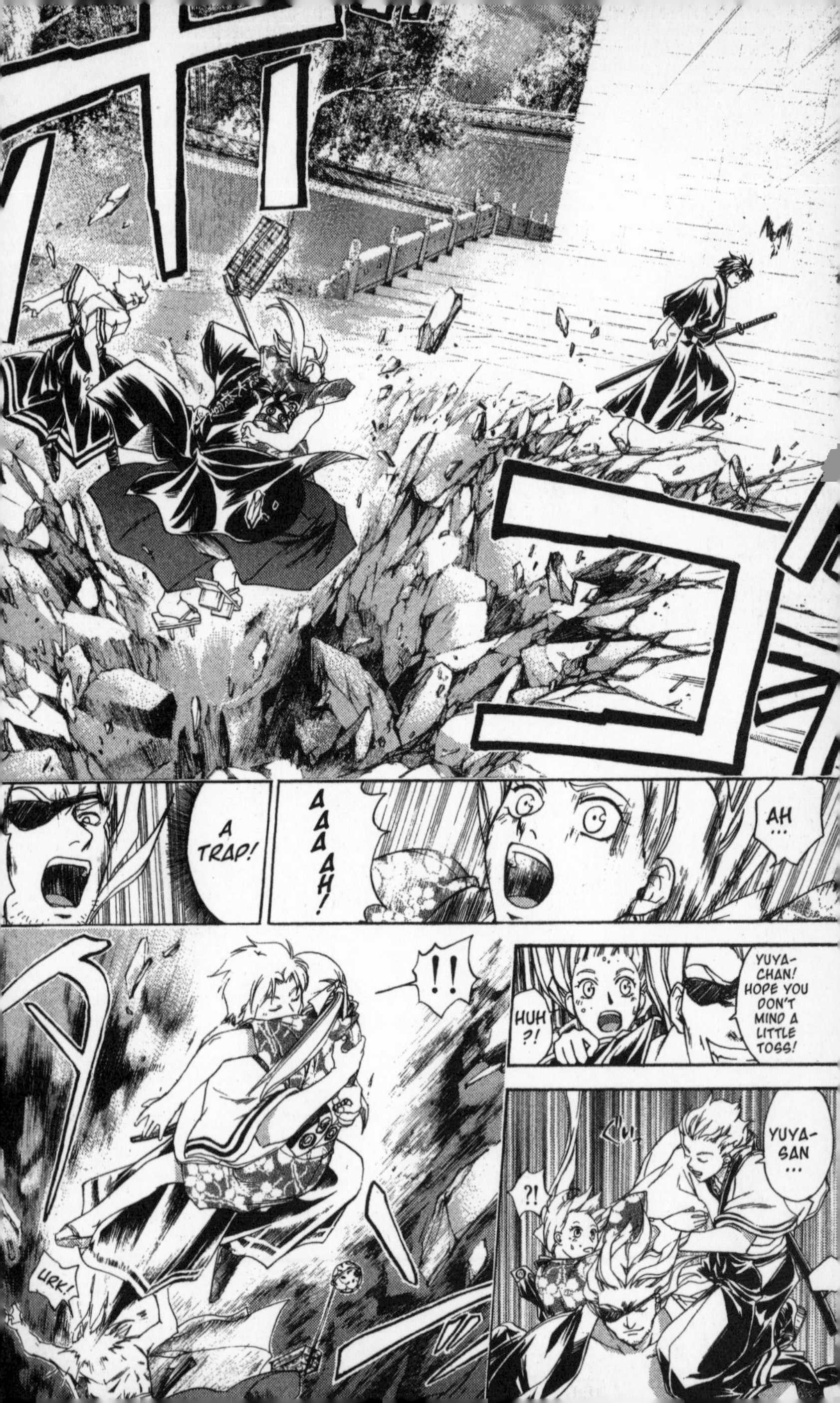

AH ...
AAAAAH!
A TRAP!
YUYA-CHAN! HOPE YOU DON'T MIND A LITTLE TOSS!
HUH ?!
YUYA-SAN ...
?!
!!
URK!

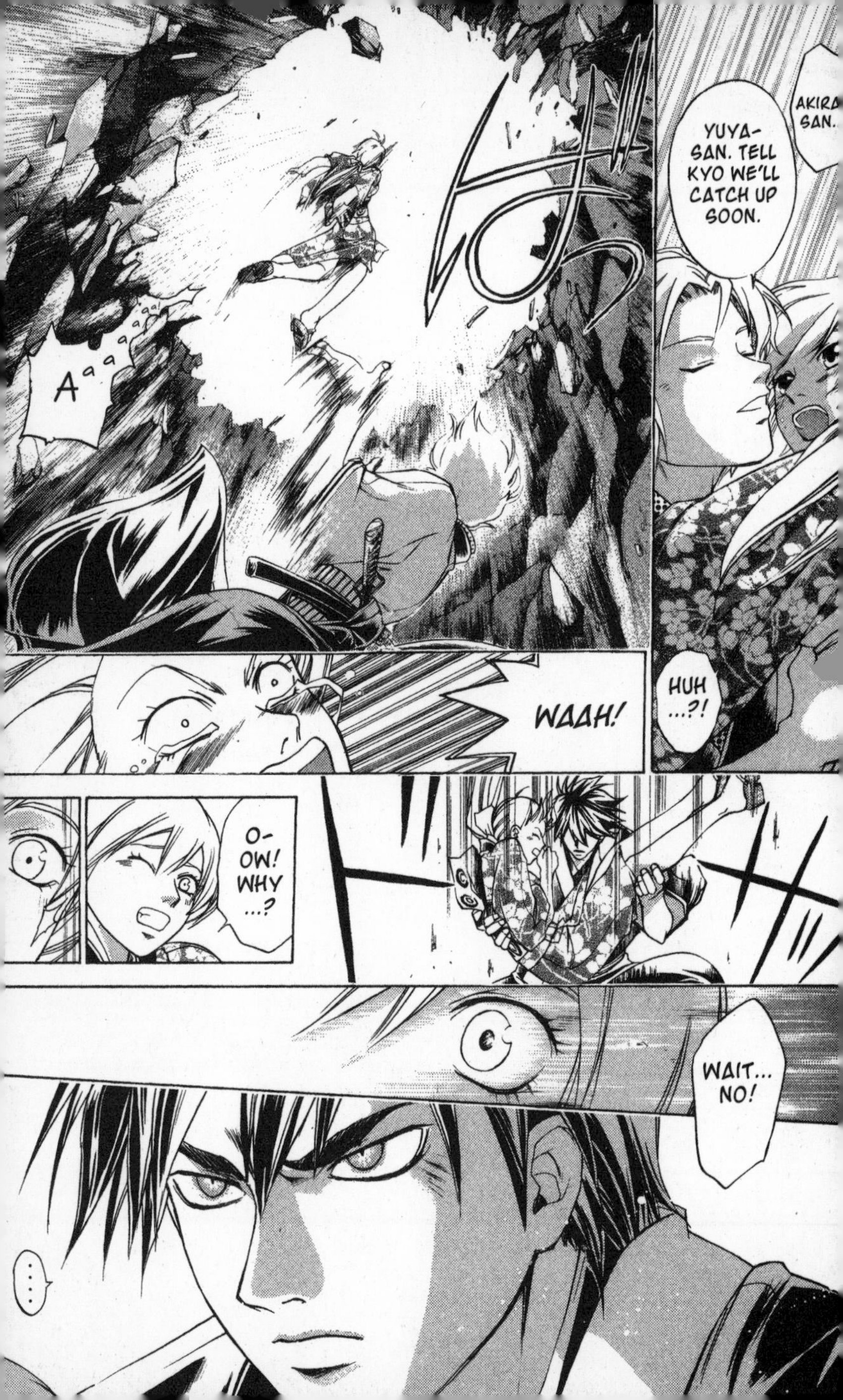
AKIRA SAN...
YUYA-SAN. TELL KYO WE'LL CATCH UP SOON.
Aaaaaaa!
HUH ...?!
WAAH!
O-OW! WHY ...?
WAIT... NO!
...

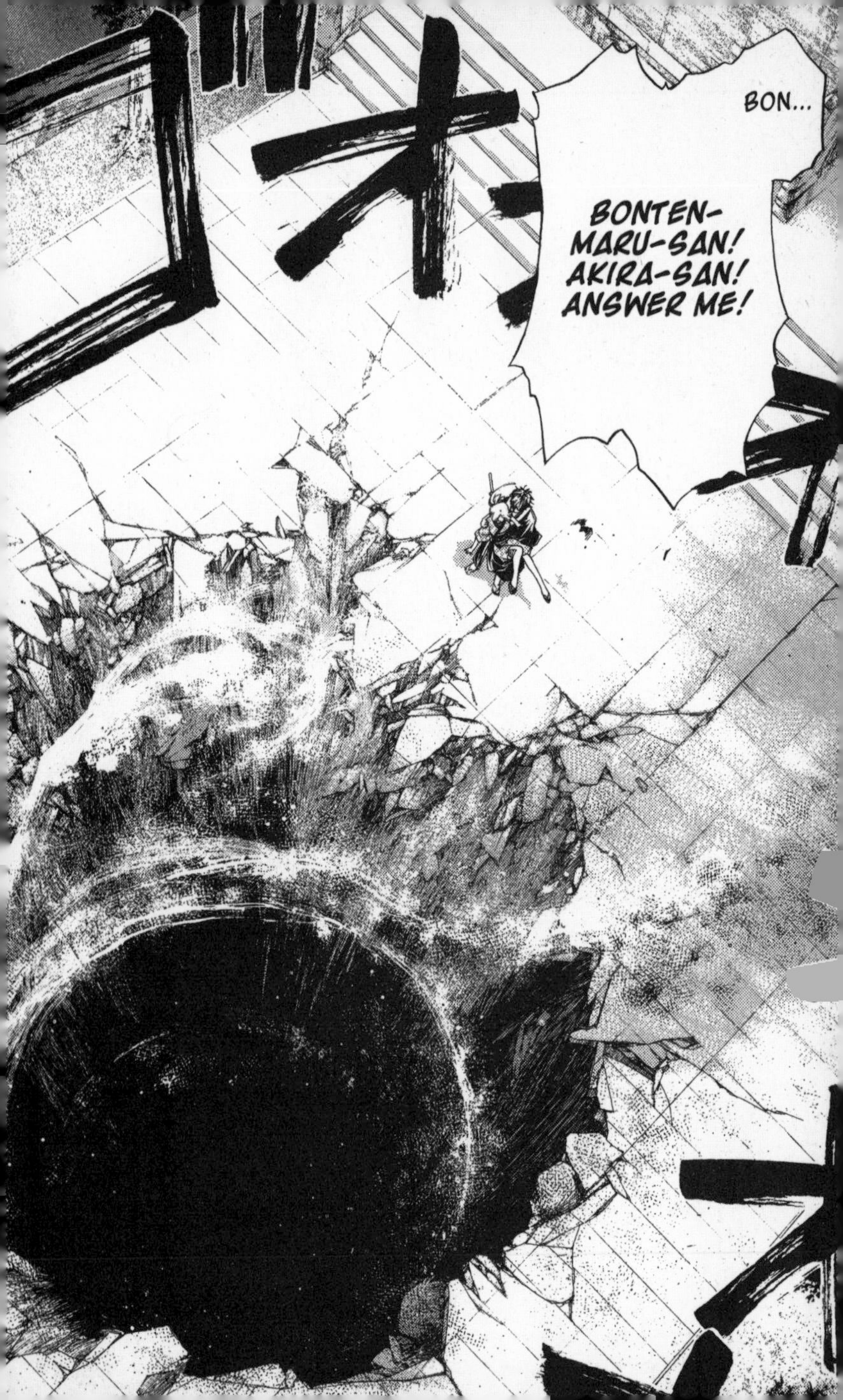
BON...
BONTEN-MARU-SAN! AKIRA-SAN! ANSWER ME!

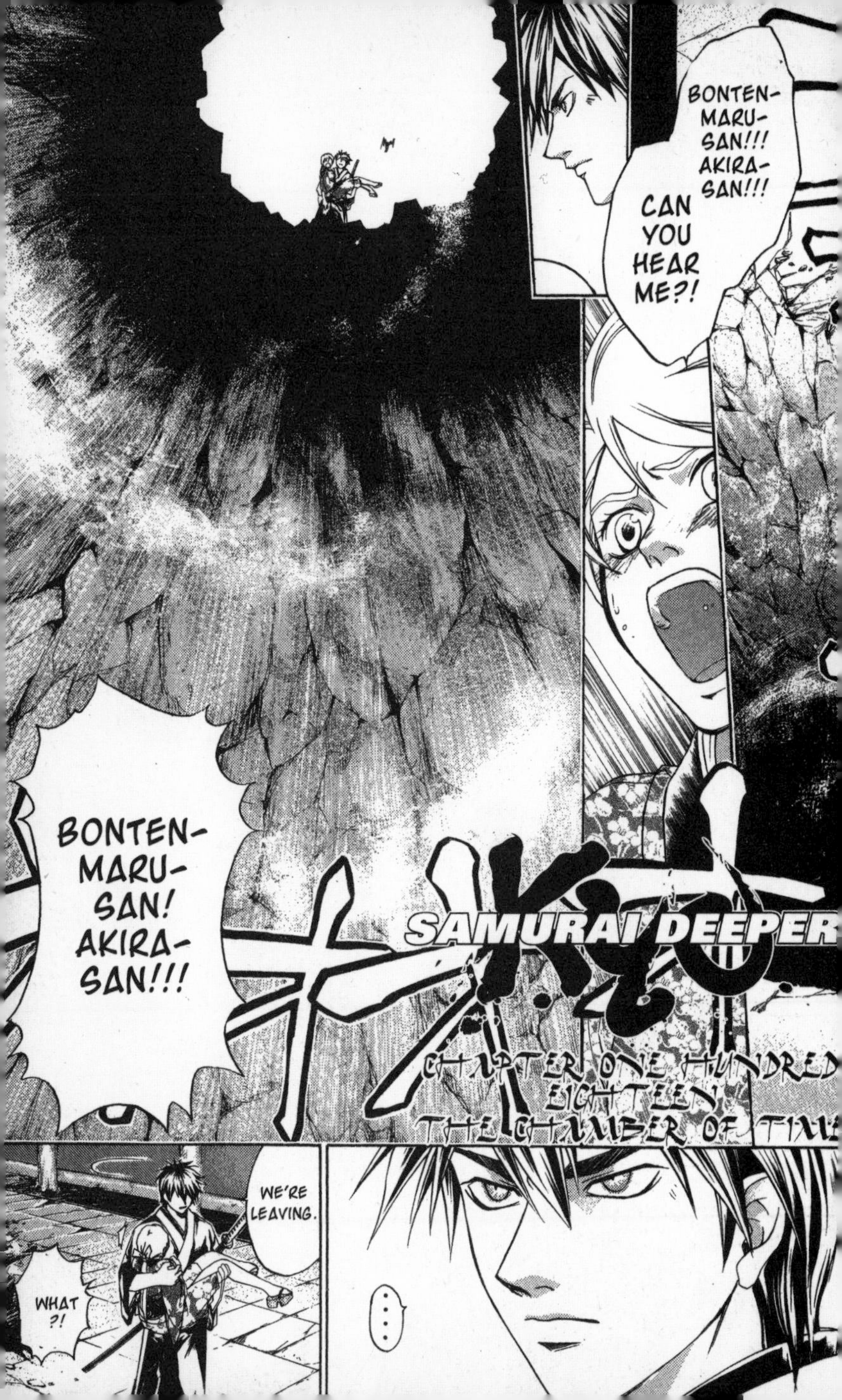
BONTEN-MARU-SAN!!! AKIRA-SAN!!!
CAN YOU HEAR ME?!
BONTEN-MARU-SAN! AKIRA-SAN!!!
SAMURAI DEEPER
CHAPTER ONE HUNDRED EIGHTEEN
THE CHAMBER OF TIM
...
WE'RE LEAVING.
WHAT?!

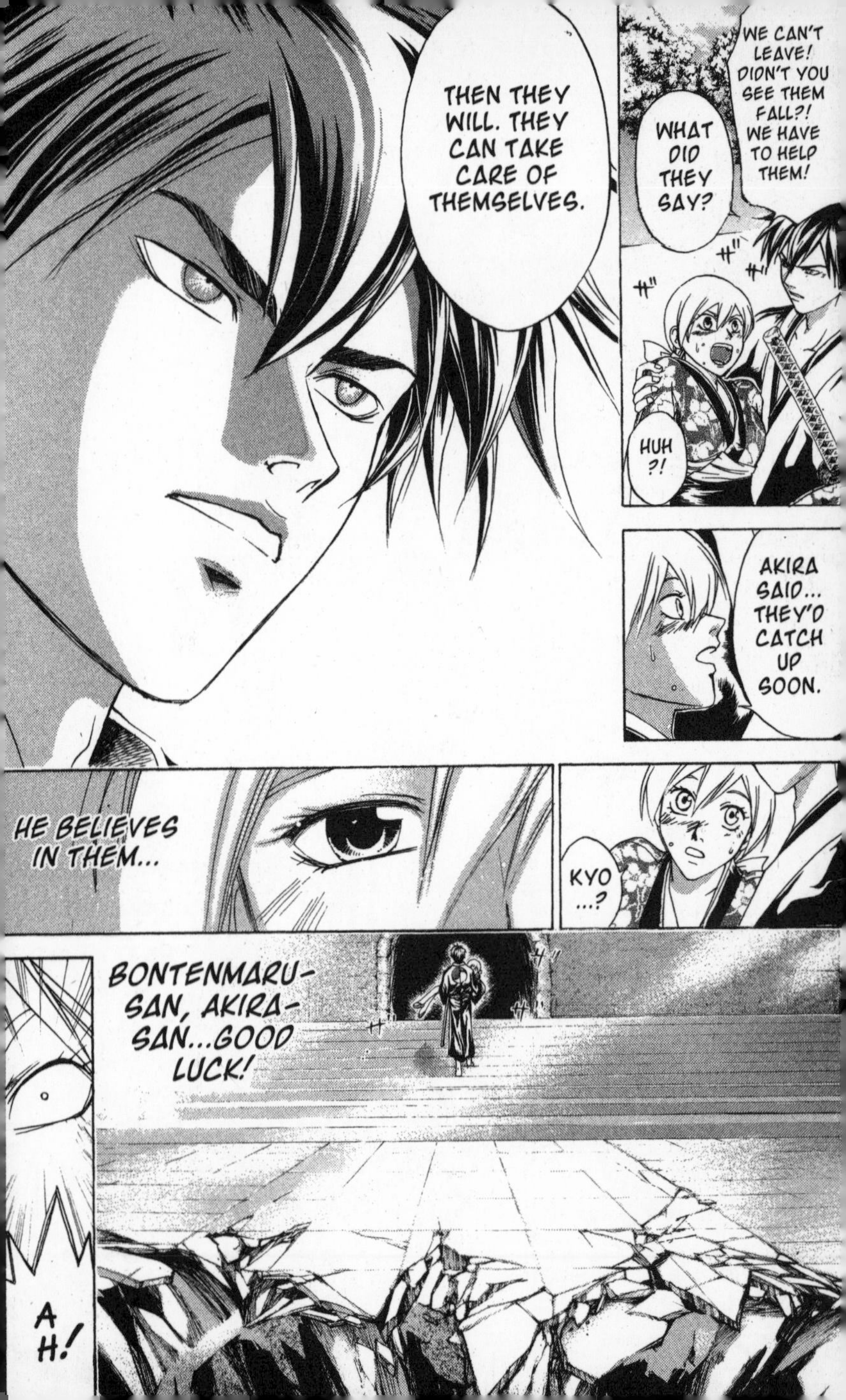
WE CAN'T LEAVE! DIDN'T YOU SEE THEM FALL?! WE HAVE TO HELP THEM!
WHAT DID THEY SAY?
HUH?!
AKIRA SAID... THEY'D CATCH UP SOON.
THEN THEY WILL. THEY CAN TAKE CARE OF THEMSELVES.
KYO ...?
HE BELIEVES IN THEM...
BONTENMARU-SAN, AKIRA-SAN...GOOD LUCK!
AH!

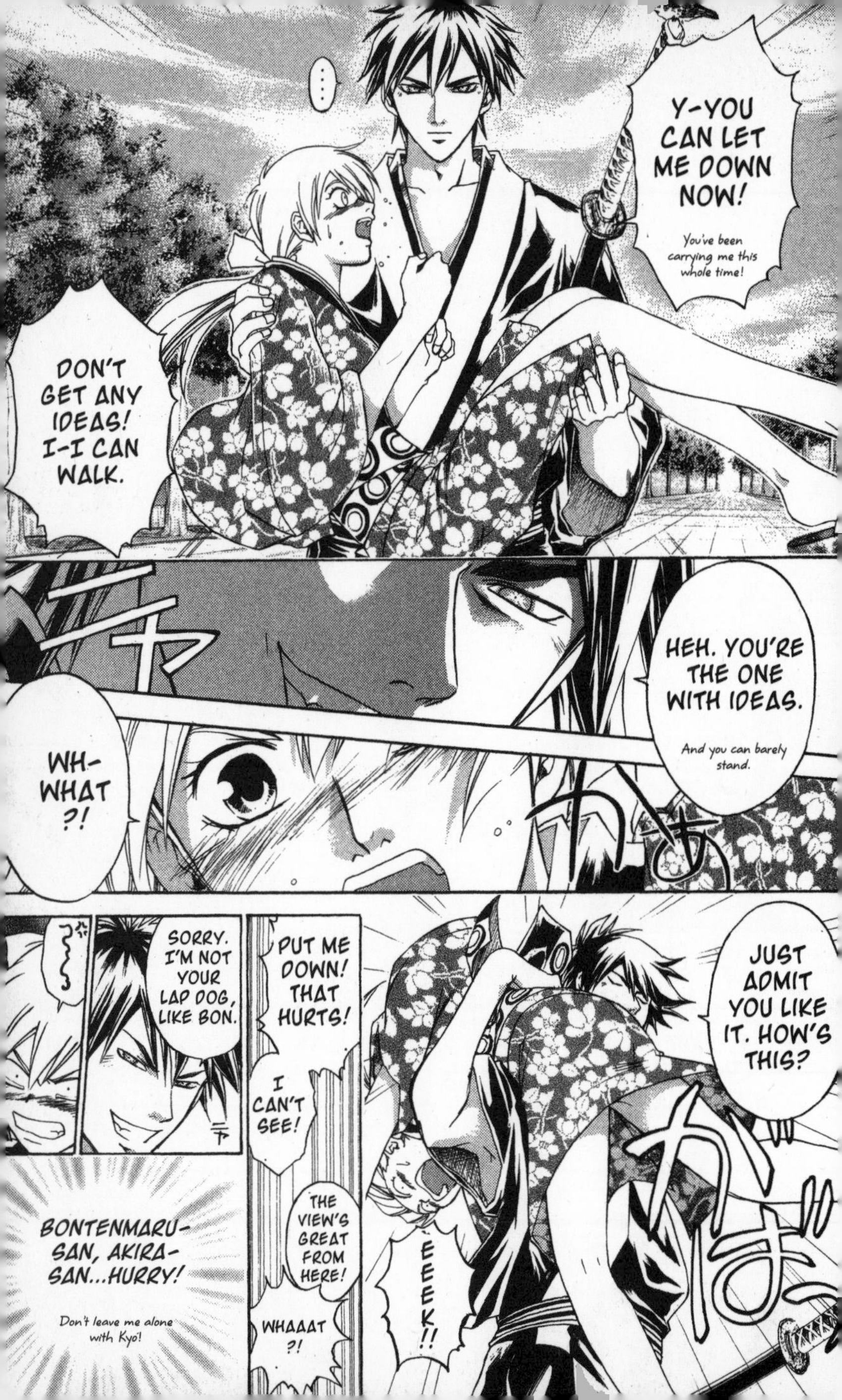
Y-YOU CAN LET ME DOWN NOW!
You've been carrying me this whole time!
...
DON'T GET ANY IDEAS! I-I CAN WALK.
HEH. YOU'RE THE ONE WITH IDEAS.
And you can barely stand.
WH-WHAT?!
JUST ADMIT YOU LIKE IT. HOW'S THIS?
EEEEK!!
PUT ME DOWN! THAT HURTS!
I CAN'T SEE!
THE VIEW'S GREAT FROM HERE!
WHAAAT?!
SORRY. I'M NOT YOUR LAP DOG, LIKE BON.
BONTENMARU-SAN, AKIRA-SAN...HURRY!
Don't leave me alone with Kyo!

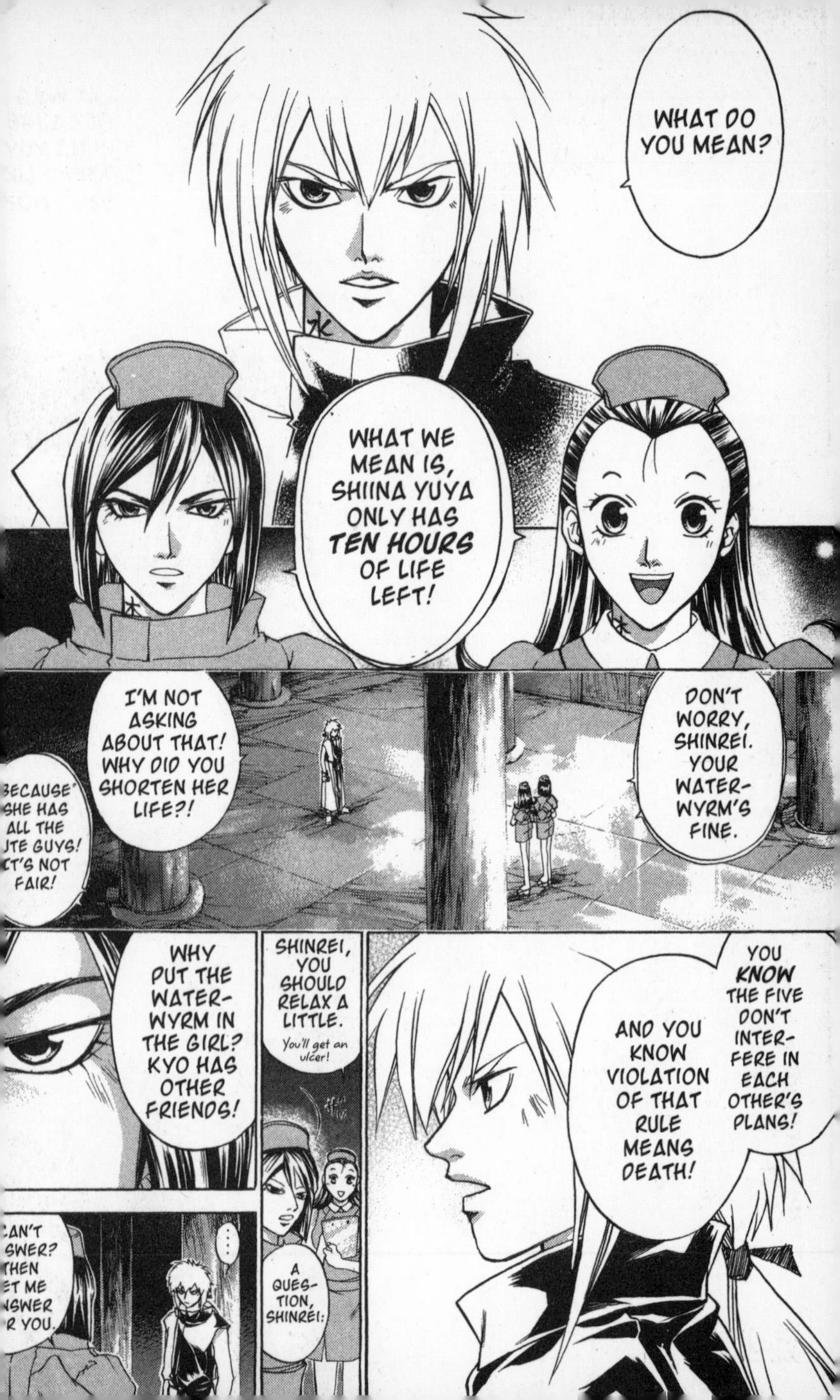
WHAT DO YOU MEAN?
WHAT WE MEAN IS, SHIINA YUYA ONLY HAS **TEN HOURS** OF LIFE LEFT!
DON'T WORRY, SHINREI. YOUR WATER-WYRM'S FINE.
I'M NOT ASKING ABOUT THAT! WHY DID YOU SHORTEN HER LIFE?!
BECAUSE SHE HAS ALL THE UTE GUYS! T'S NOT FAIR!
YOU **KNOW** THE FIVE DON'T INTER-FERE IN EACH OTHER'S PLANS!
AND YOU KNOW VIOLATION OF THAT RULE MEANS DEATH!
SHINREI, YOU SHOULD RELAX A LITTLE.
You'll get an ulcer!
A QUES-TION, SHINREI:
WHY PUT THE WATER-WYRM IN THE GIRL? KYO HAS OTHER FRIENDS!
...
AN'T SWER? THEN T ME NSWER R YOU.

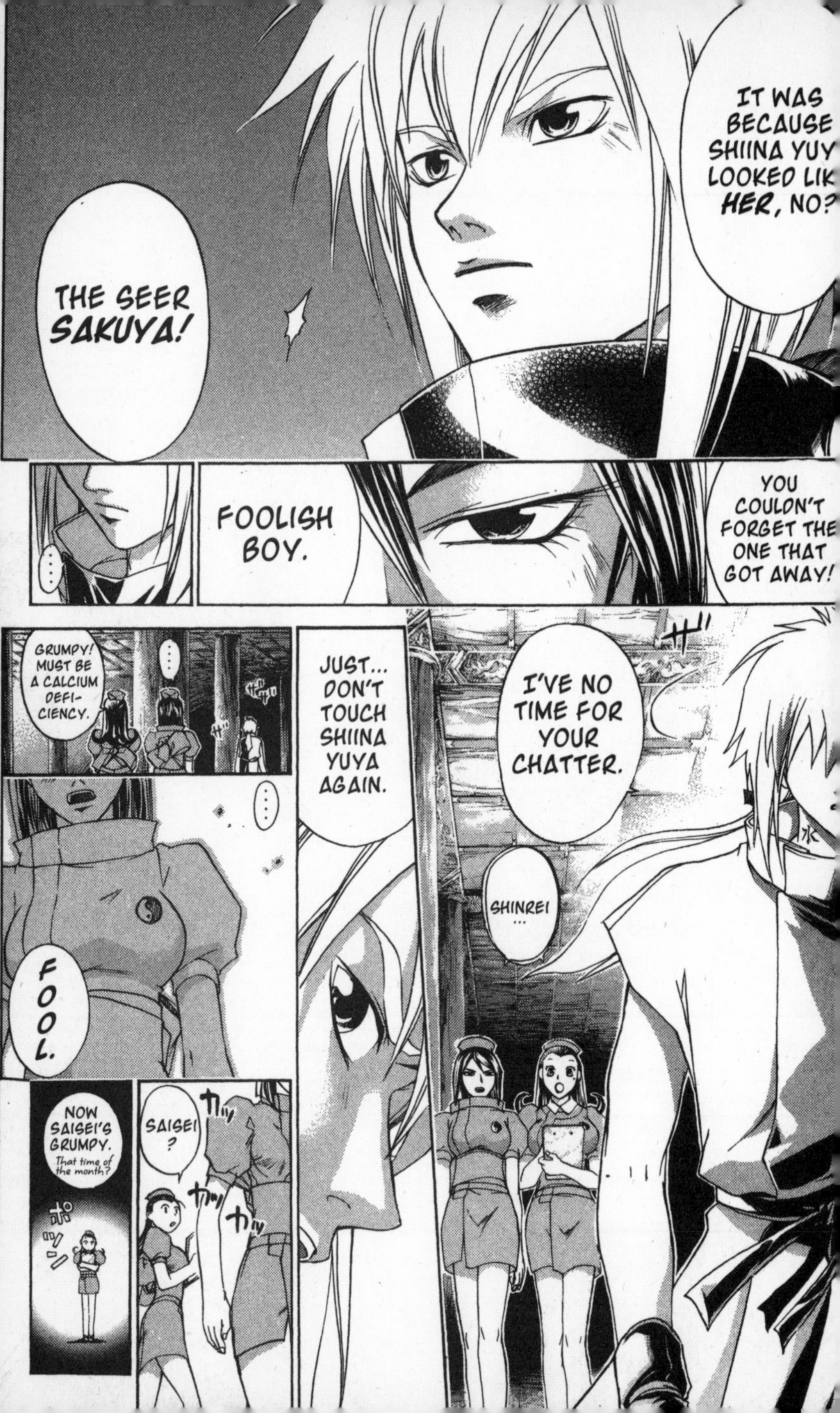
IT WAS BECAUSE SHIINA YUY LOOKED LIK HER, NO?
THE SEER SAKUYA!
YOU COULDN'T FORGET THE ONE THAT GOT AWAY!
FOOLISH BOY.
...
I'VE NO TIME FOR YOUR CHATTER.
JUST... DON'T TOUCH SHIINA YUYA AGAIN.
SHINREI ...
GRUMPY! MUST BE A CALCIUM DEFI-CIENCY.
...
...
FOOL.
SAISEI ?
NOW SAISEI'S GRUMPY.
That time of the month?

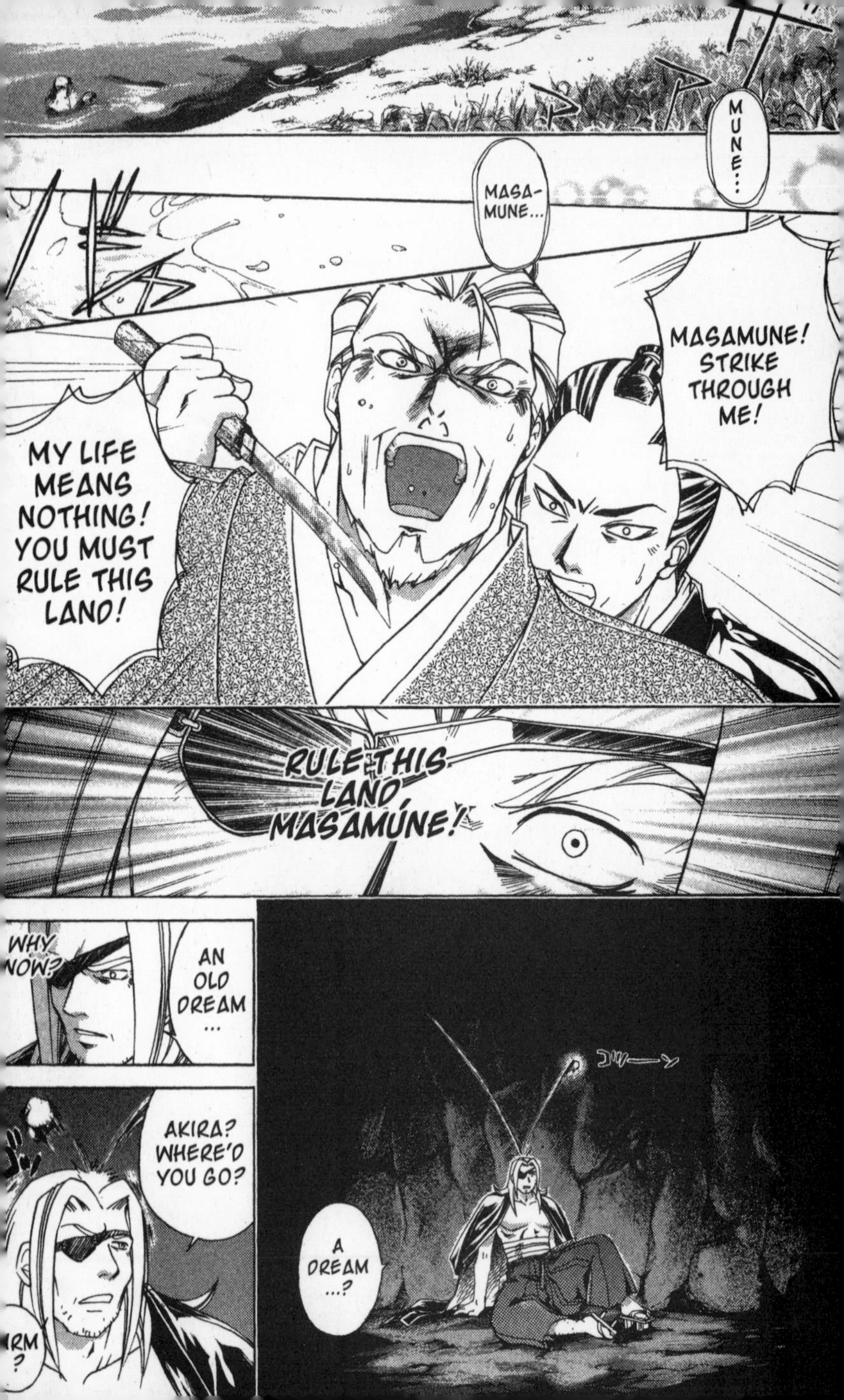
MUNE...
MASA-MUNE...
MASAMUNE! STRIKE THROUGH ME!
MY LIFE MEANS NOTHING! YOU MUST RULE THIS LAND!
RULE THIS LAND, MASAMUNE!
A DREAM ...?
AN OLD DREAM ...
WHY NOW?
AKIRA? WHERE'D YOU GO?
RM?

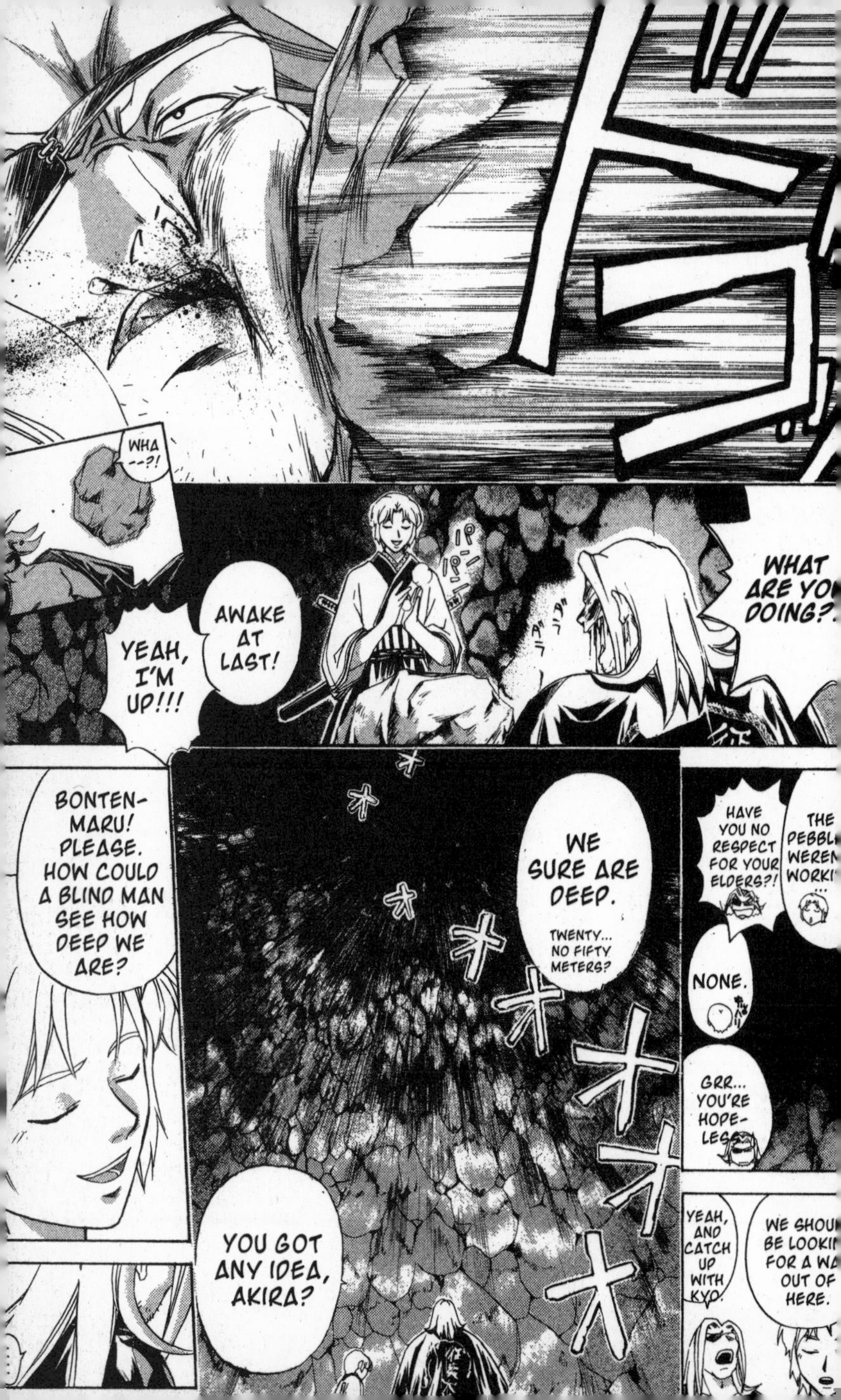

WHA --?!
WHAT ARE YO DOING?..
AWAKE AT LAST!
YEAH, I'M UP!!!
THE PEBBL WEREN WORKI...
HAVE YOU NO RESPECT FOR YOUR ELDERS?!
NONE.
GRR... YOU'RE HOPE-LESS
WE SHOU BE LOOKI FOR A WA OUT OF HERE.
YEAH, AND CATCH UP WITH KYO.
WE SURE ARE DEEP.
TWENTY... NO FIFTY METERS?
YOU GOT ANY IDEA, AKIRA?
BONTEN-MARU! PLEASE. HOW COULD A BLIND MAN SEE HOW DEEP WE ARE?

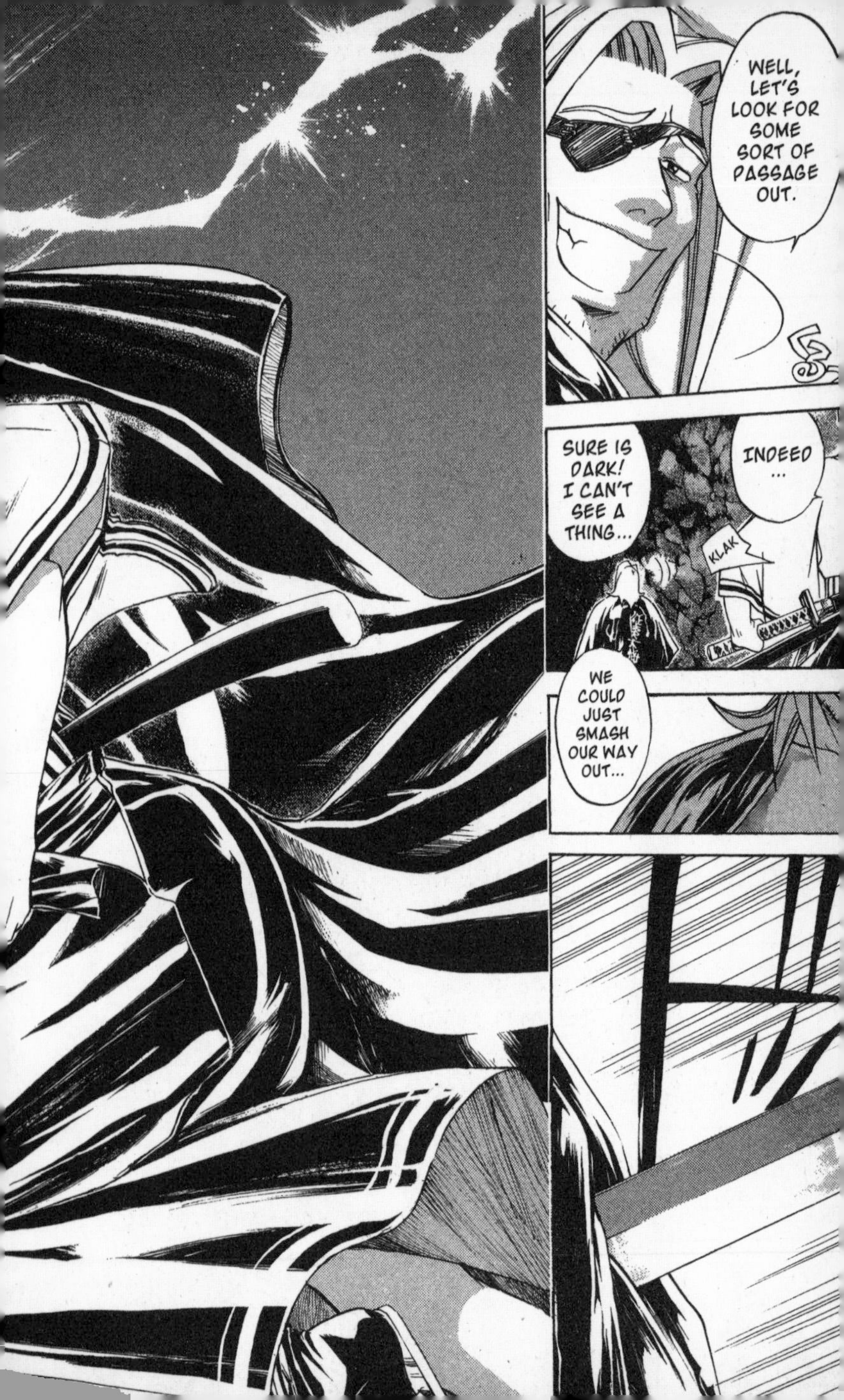
WELL, LET'S LOOK FOR SOME SORT OF PASSAGE OUT.
INDEED...
SURE IS DARK! I CAN'T SEE A THING...
KLAK
WE COULD JUST SMASH OUR WAY OUT...

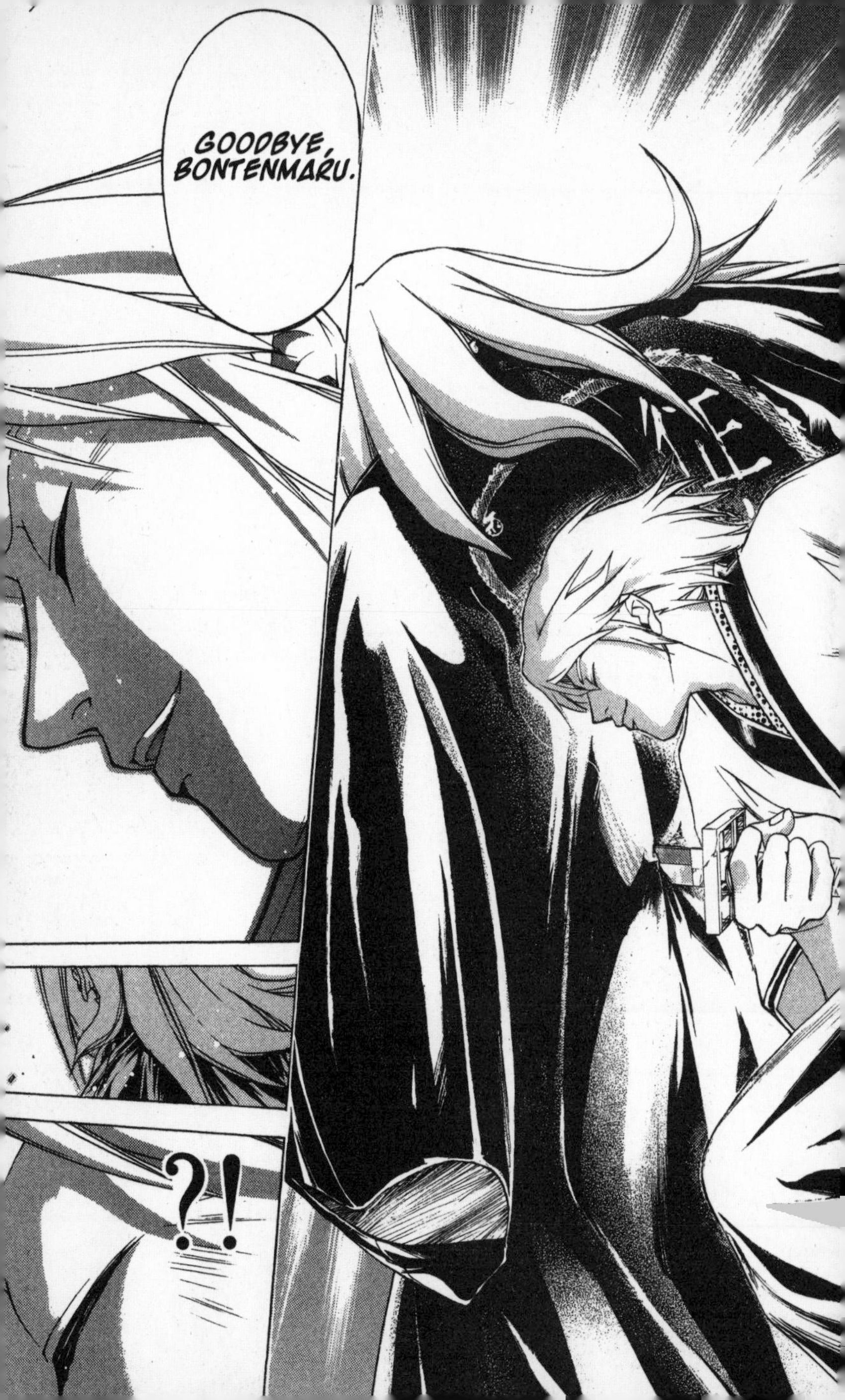
GOODBYE, BONTENMARU.
?!

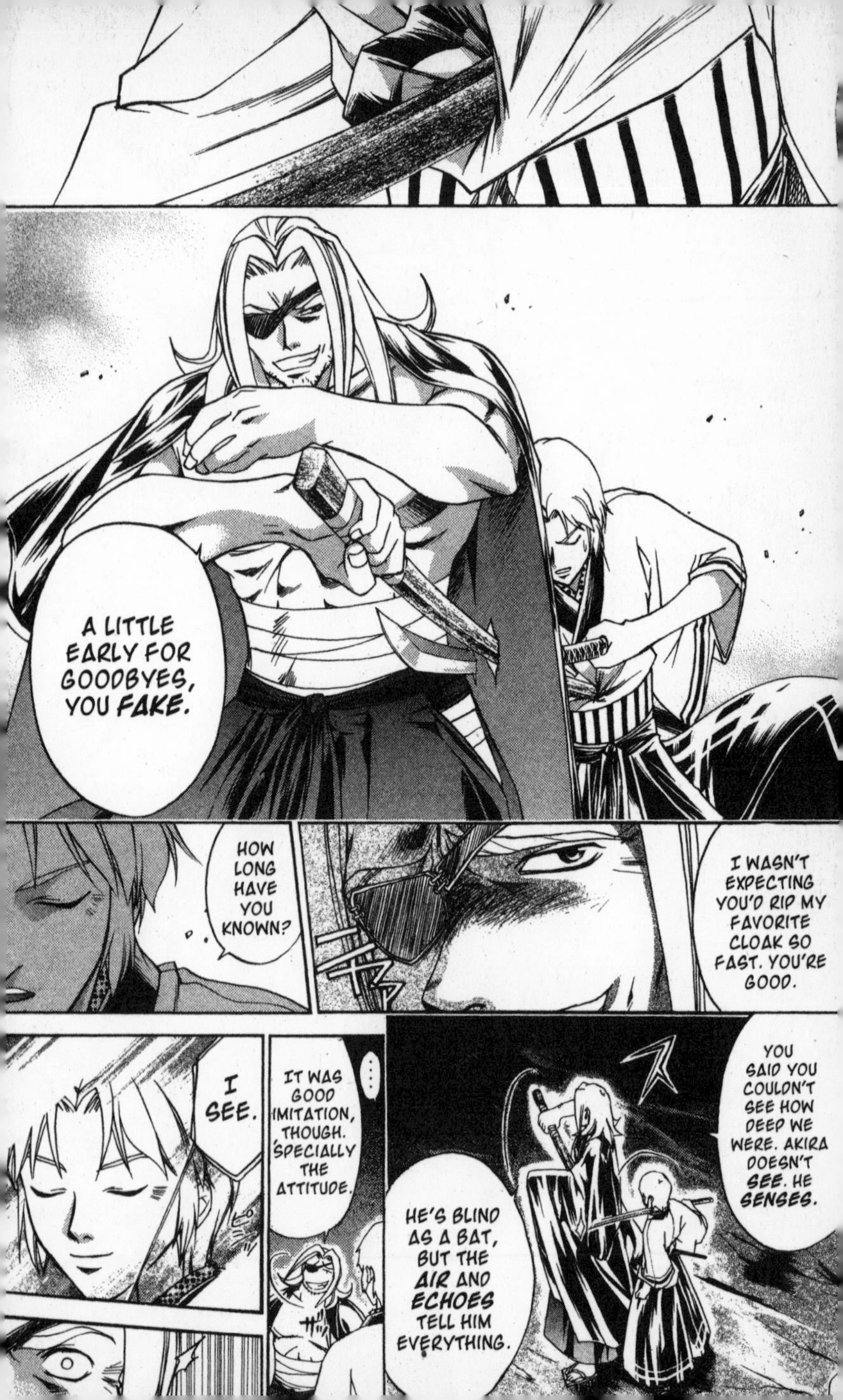
A LITTLE EARLY FOR GOODBYES, YOU FAKE.
I WASN'T EXPECTING YOU'D RIP MY FAVORITE CLOAK SO FAST. YOU'RE GOOD.
HOW LONG HAVE YOU KNOWN?
YOU SAID YOU COULDN'T SEE HOW DEEP WE WERE. AKIRA DOESN'T SEE. HE SENSES.
HE'S BLIND AS A BAT, BUT THE AIR AND ECHOES TELL HIM EVERYTHING.
...
IT WAS GOOD IMITATION, THOUGH. 'SPECIALLY THE ATTITUDE.
I SEE.

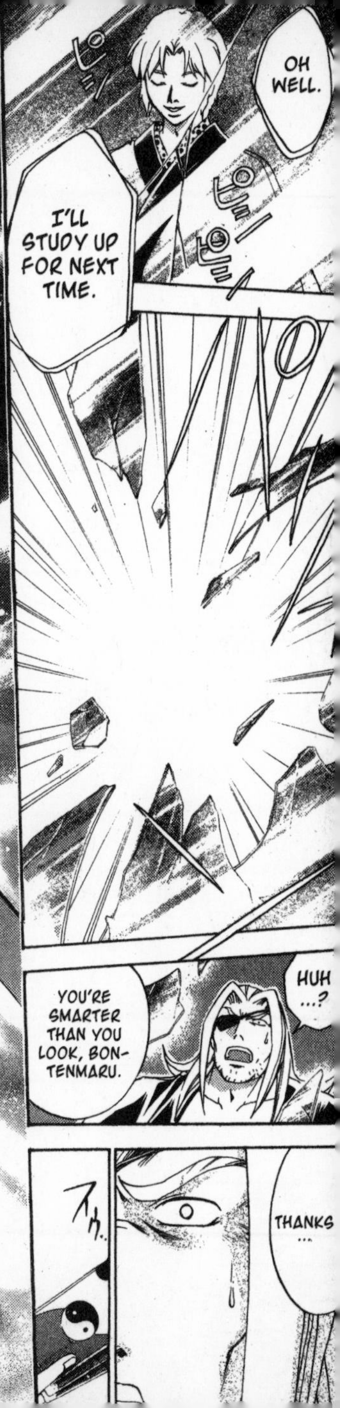
OH WELL.
I'LL STUDY UP FOR NEXT TIME.
HUH ...?
YOU'RE SMARTER THAN YOU LOOK, BON-TENMARU.
THANKS ...
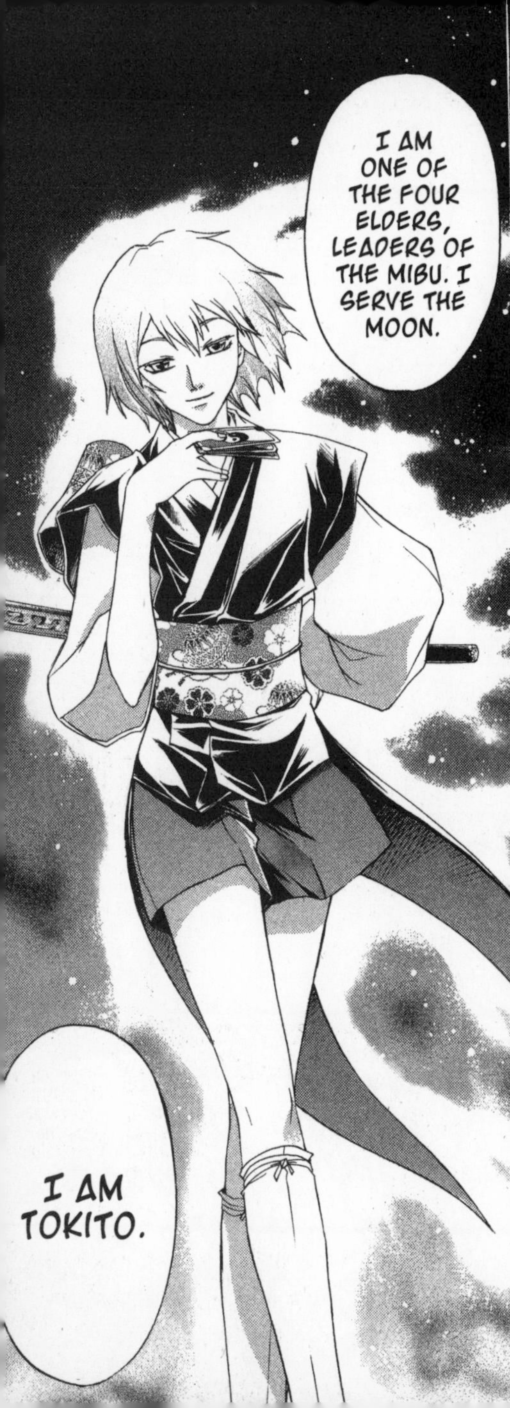
I AM ONE OF THE FOUR ELDERS, LEADERS OF THE MIBU. I SERVE THE MOON.
I AM TOKITO.

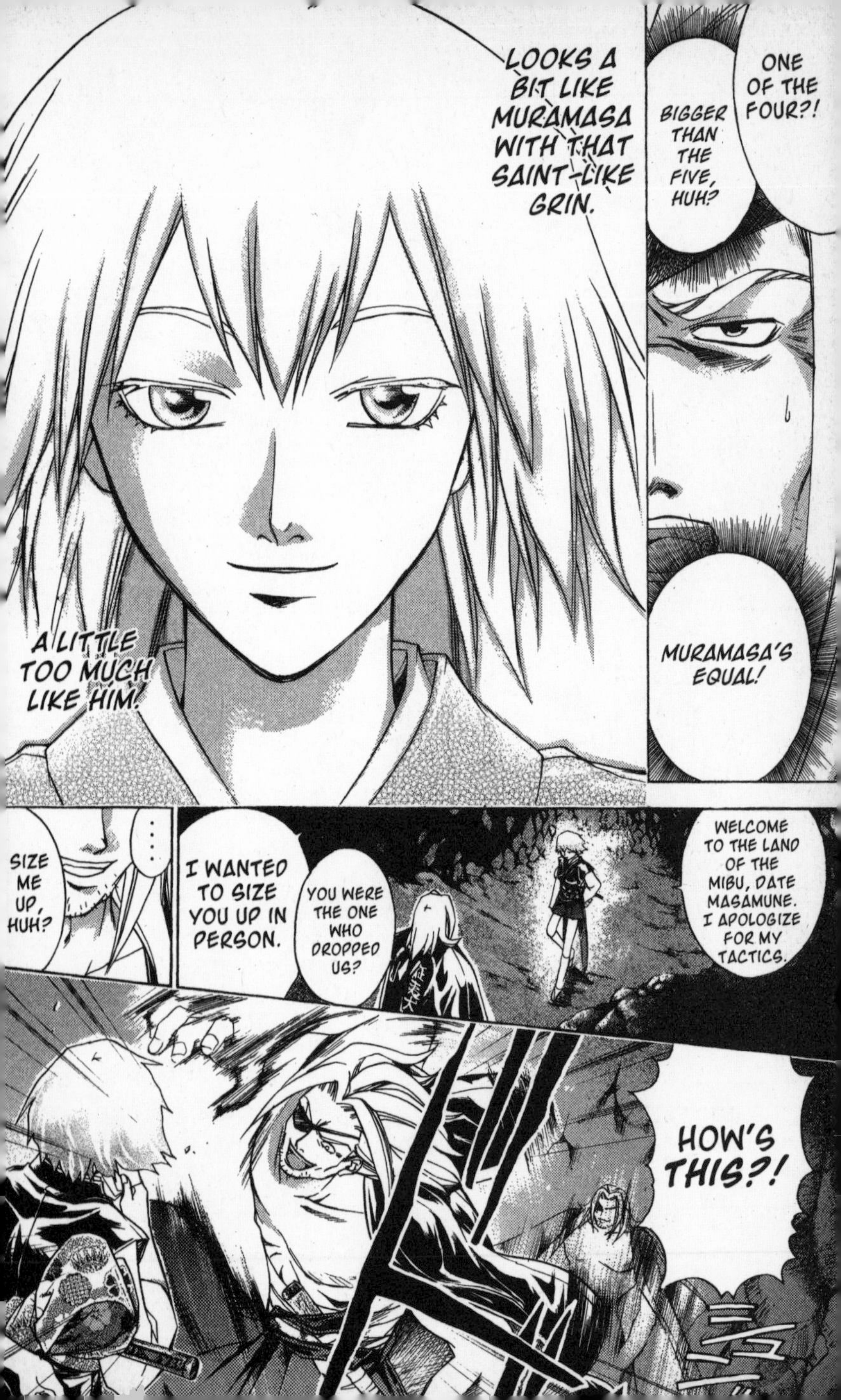
ONE OF THE FOUR?!
BIGGER THAN THE FIVE, HUH?
MURAMASA'S EQUAL!
LOOKS A BIT LIKE MURAMASA WITH THAT SAINT-LIKE GRIN.
A LITTLE TOO MUCH LIKE HIM.
WELCOME TO THE LAND OF THE MIBU, DATE MASAMUNE. I APOLOGIZE FOR MY TACTICS.
YOU WERE THE ONE WHO DROPPED US?
I WANTED TO SIZE YOU UP IN PERSON.
....
SIZE ME UP, HUH?
HOW'S THIS?!

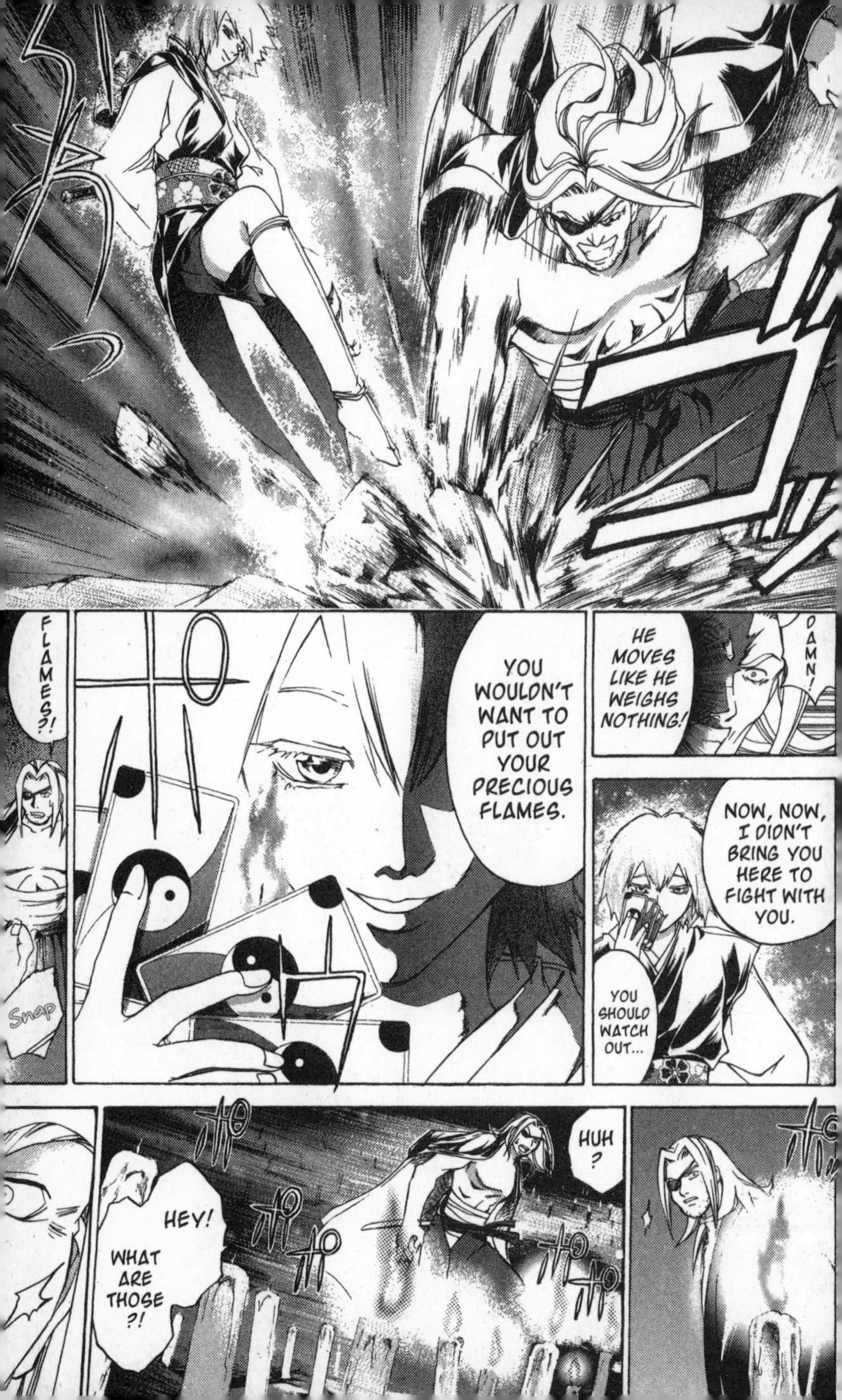
DAMN!
HE MOVES LIKE HE WEIGHS NOTHING!
NOW, NOW, I DIDN'T BRING YOU HERE TO FIGHT WITH YOU.
YOU SHOULD WATCH OUT...
YOU WOULDN'T WANT TO PUT OUT YOUR PRECIOUS FLAMES.
FLAMES?!
Snap
HUH?
HEY!
WHAT ARE THOSE?!

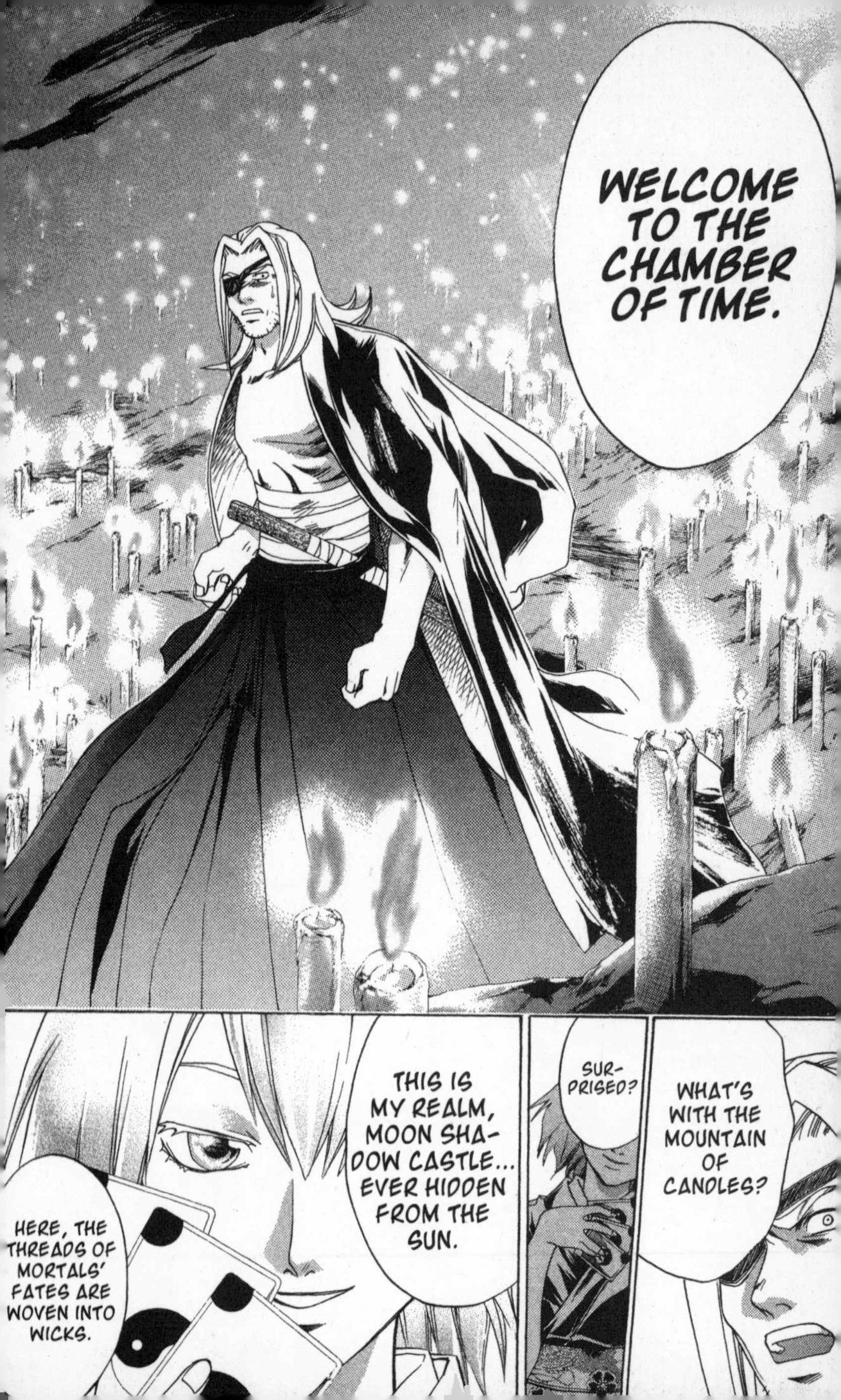
WELCOME TO THE CHAMBER OF TIME.
WHAT'S WITH THE MOUNTAIN OF CANDLES?
SUR-PRISED?
THIS IS MY REALM, MOON SHA-DOW CASTLE... EVER HIDDEN FROM THE SUN.
HERE, THE THREADS OF MORTALS' FATES ARE WOVEN INTO WICKS.

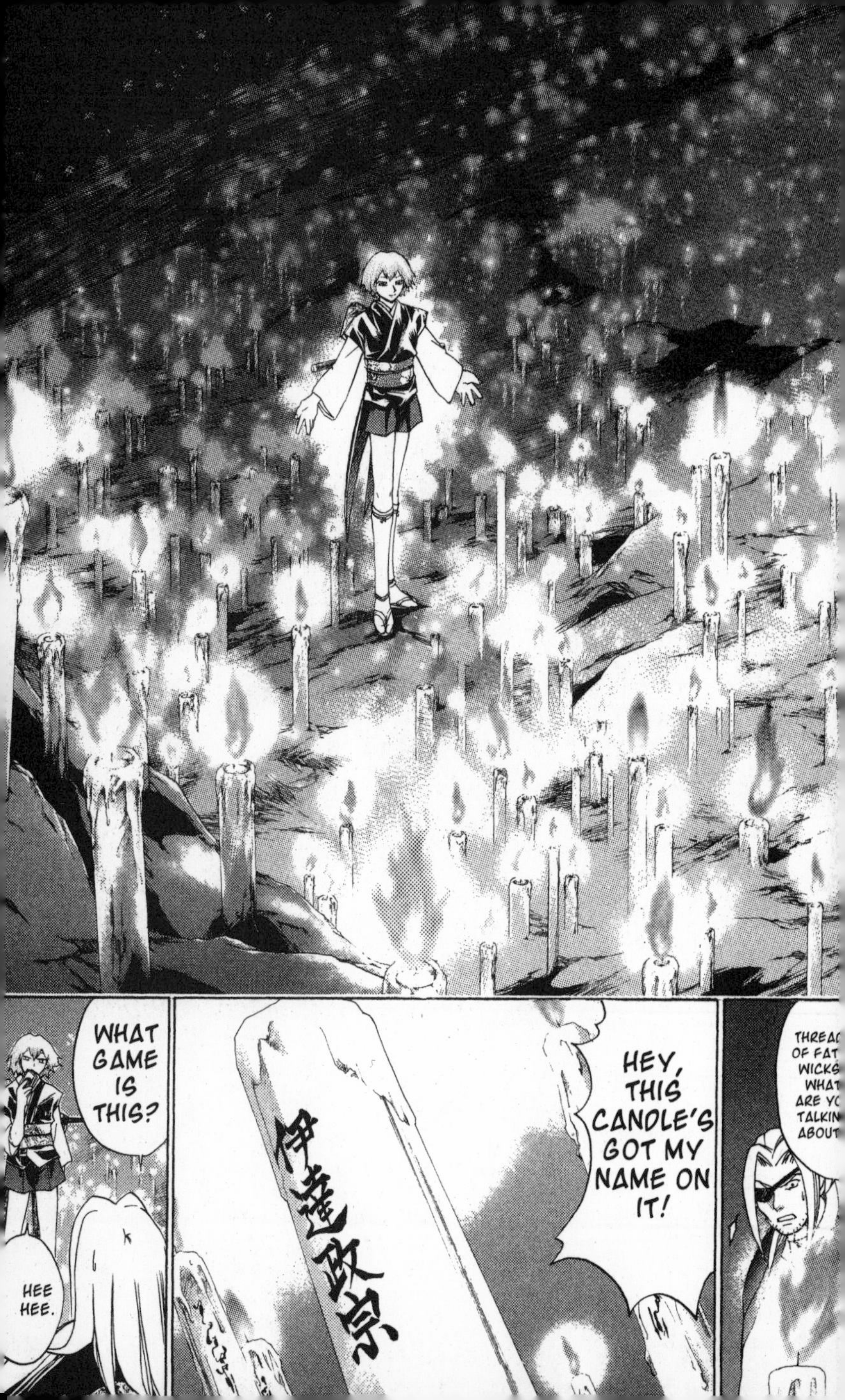
THREA OF FAT WICKS WHAT ARE YO TALKING ABOUT
HEY, THIS CANDLE'S GOT MY NAME ON IT!
伊達政宗
WHAT GAME IS THIS?
HEE HEE.

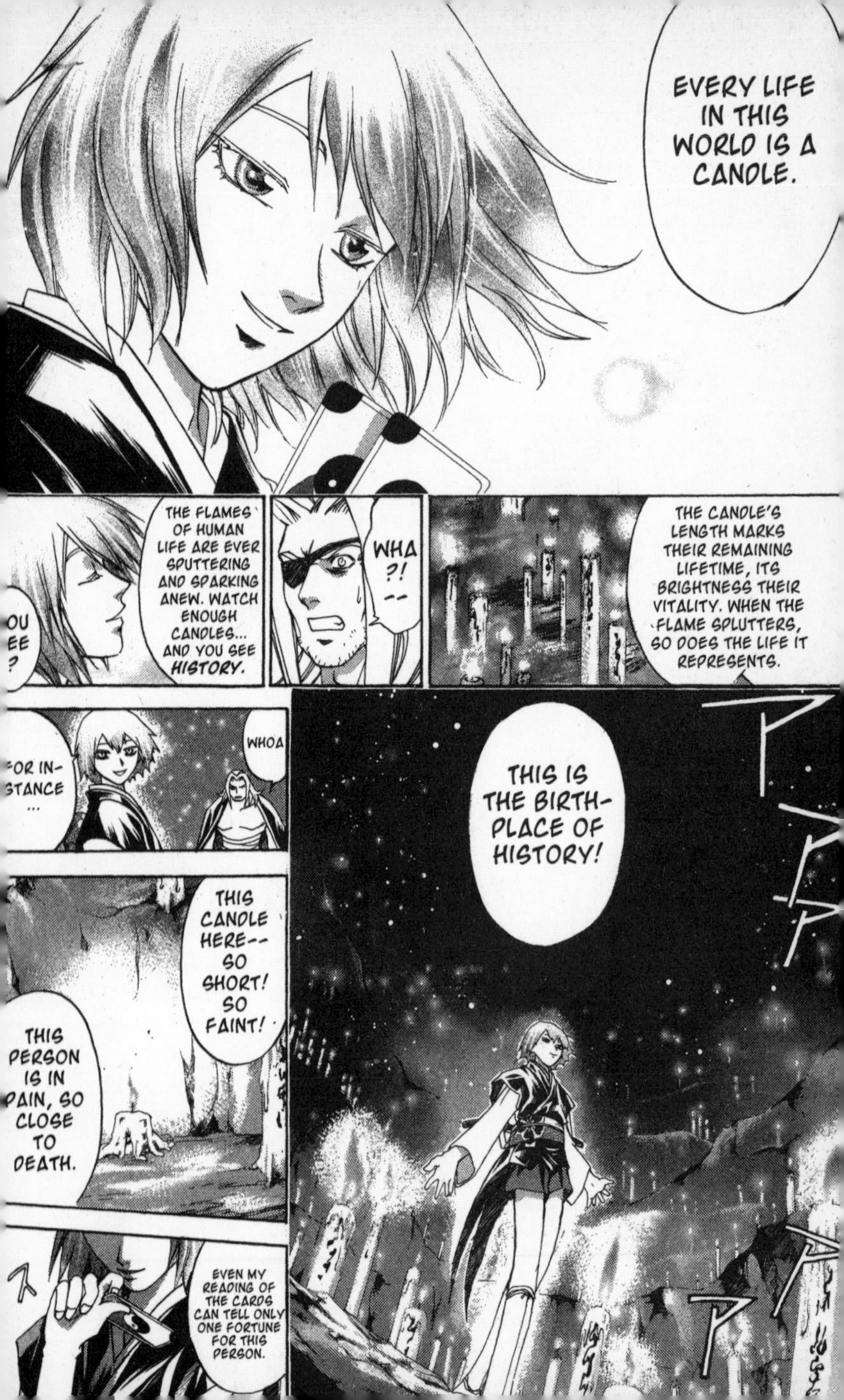

EVERY LIFE IN THIS WORLD IS A CANDLE.
THE CANDLE'S LENGTH MARKS THEIR REMAINING LIFETIME, ITS BRIGHTNESS THEIR VITALITY. WHEN THE FLAME SPLUTTERS, SO DOES THE LIFE IT REPRESENTS.
WHA ?! --
THE FLAMES OF HUMAN LIFE ARE EVER SPUTTERING AND SPARKING ANEW. WATCH ENOUGH CANDLES... AND YOU SEE HISTORY.
OU EE ?
THIS IS THE BIRTH-PLACE OF HISTORY!
WHOA
FOR IN-STANCE ...
THIS CANDLE HERE-- SO SHORT! SO FAINT!
THIS PERSON IS IN PAIN, SO CLOSE TO DEATH.
EVEN MY READING OF THE CARDS CAN TELL ONLY ONE FORTUNE FOR THIS PERSON.

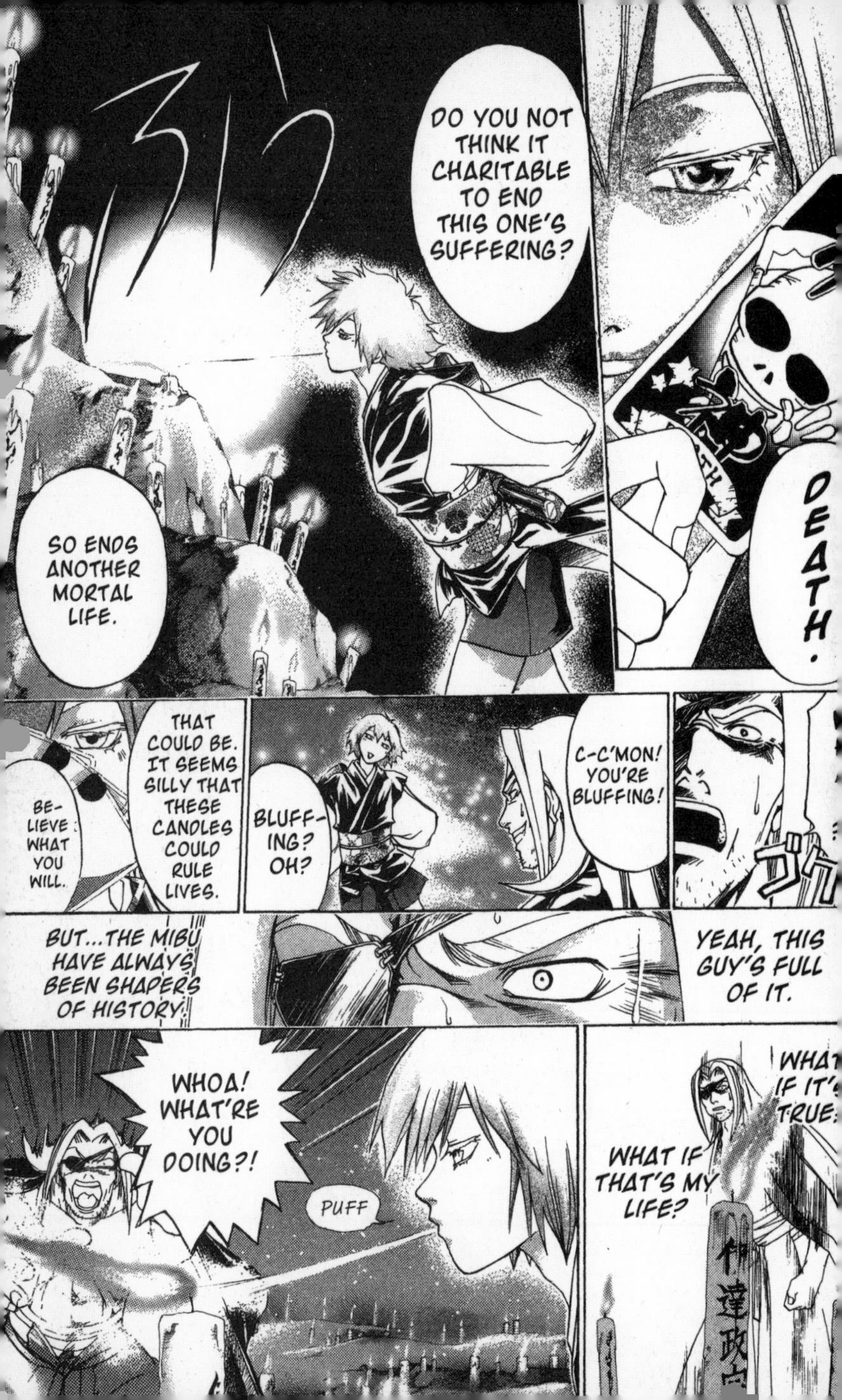
DEATH.
DO YOU NOT THINK IT CHARITABLE TO END THIS ONE'S SUFFERING?
SO ENDS ANOTHER MORTAL LIFE.
C-C'MON! YOU'RE BLUFFING!
BLUFF-ING? OH?
THAT COULD BE. IT SEEMS SILLY THAT THESE CANDLES COULD RULE LIVES.
BE-LIEVE WHAT YOU WILL.
YEAH, THIS GUY'S FULL OF IT.
BUT...THE MIBU HAVE ALWAYS BEEN SHAPERS OF HISTORY.
WHAT IF IT'S TRUE?
WHAT IF THAT'S MY LIFE?
WHOA! WHAT'RE YOU DOING?!
PUFF

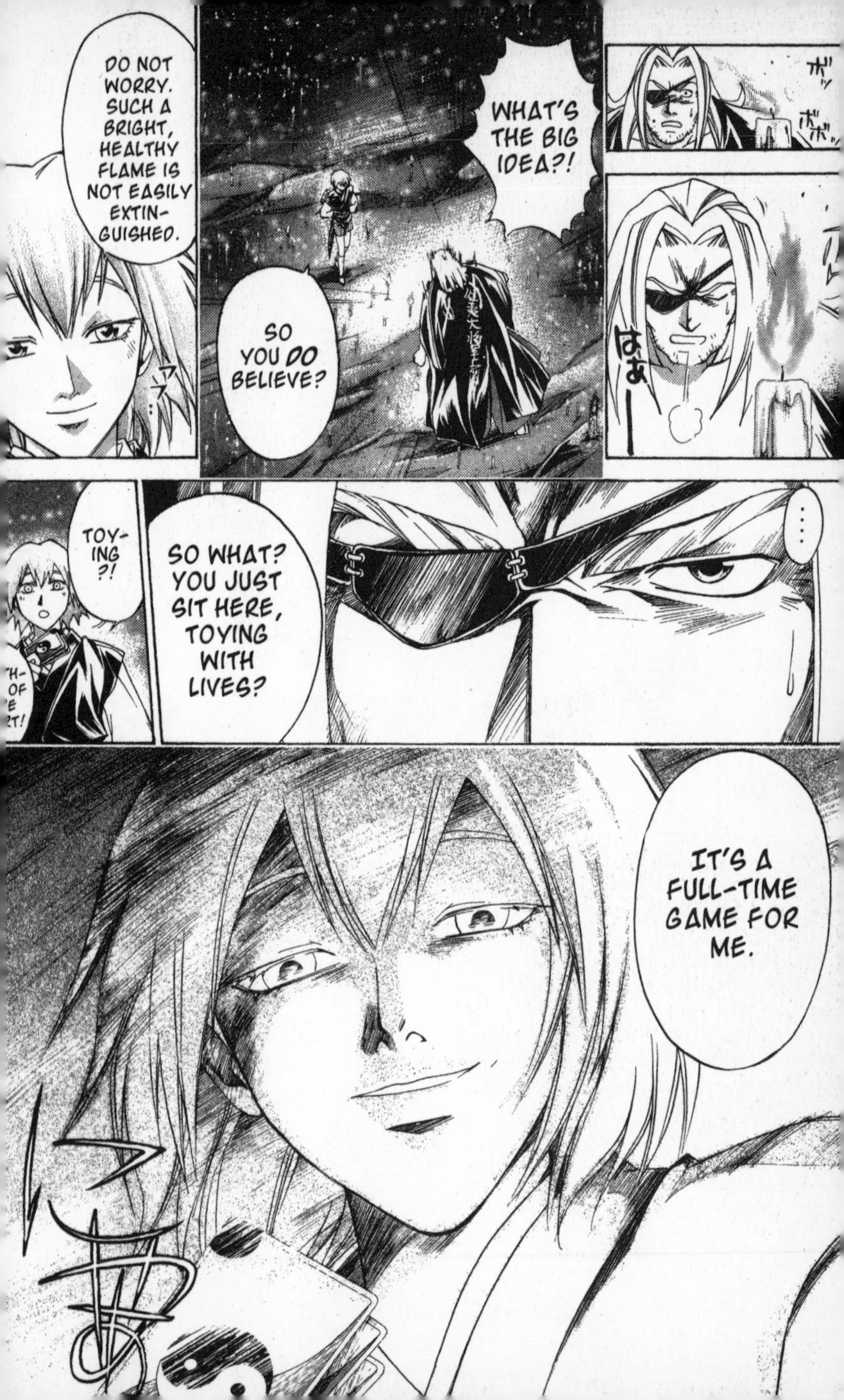

ボッ
ボボッ
はぁー
WHAT'S THE BIG IDEA?!
SO YOU *DO* BELIEVE?
DO NOT WORRY. SUCH A BRIGHT, HEALTHY FLAME IS NOT EASILY EXTIN-GUISHED.
....
SO WHAT? YOU JUST SIT HERE, TOYING WITH LIVES?
TOY-ING?!
IT'S A FULL-TIME GAME FOR ME.

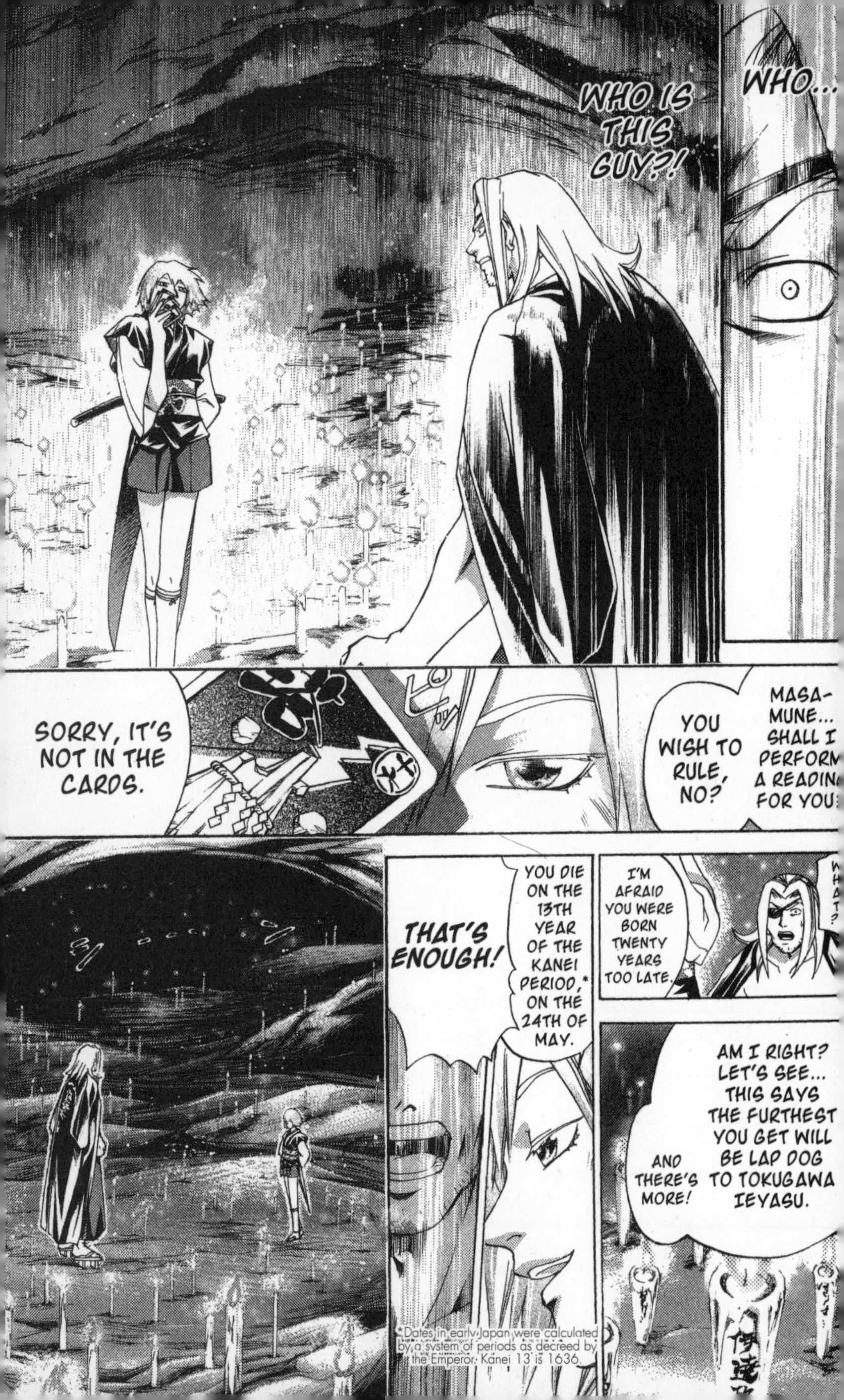
WHO...
WHO IS THIS GUY?!
MASA-MUNE... SHALL I PERFORM A READING FOR YOU?
YOU WISH TO RULE, NO?
SORRY, IT'S NOT IN THE CARDS.
WHAT?
I'M AFRAID YOU WERE BORN TWENTY YEARS TOO LATE.
AM I RIGHT? LET'S SEE... THIS SAYS THE FURTHEST YOU GET WILL BE LAP DOG TO TOKUGAWA IEYASU.
AND THERE'S MORE!
YOU DIE ON THE 13TH YEAR OF THE KANEI PERIOD,* ON THE 24TH OF MAY.
THAT'S ENOUGH!

*Dates in early Japan were calculated by a system of periods as decreed by the Emperor. Kanei 13 is 1636.

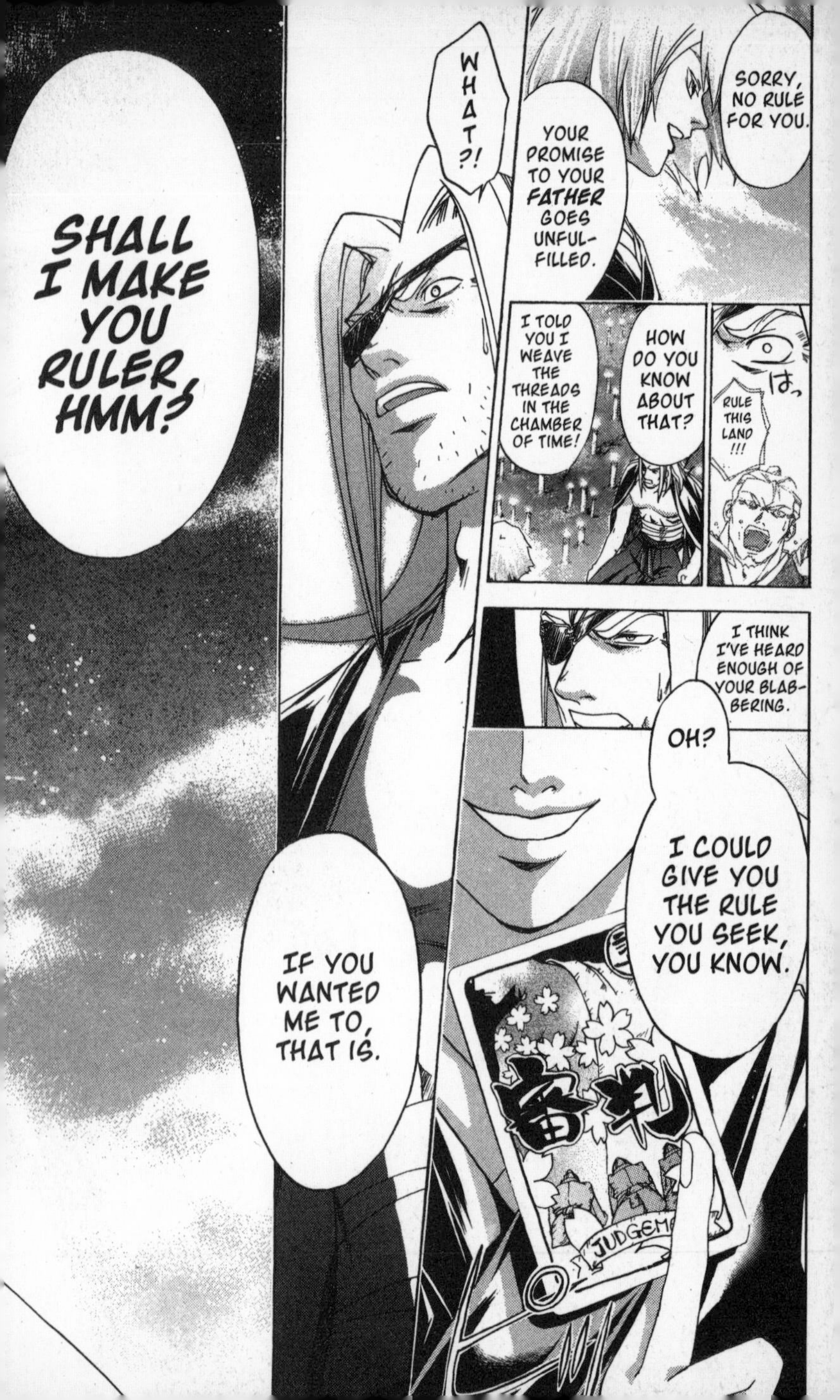
SORRY, NO RULE FOR YOU.
YOUR PROMISE TO YOUR **FATHER** GOES UNFUL-FILLED.
WHAT?!
はっ
RULE THIS LAND!!!
HOW DO YOU KNOW ABOUT THAT?
I TOLD YOU I WEAVE THE THREADS IN THE CHAMBER OF TIME!
I THINK I'VE HEARD ENOUGH OF YOUR BLAB-BERING.
OH?
I COULD GIVE YOU THE RULE YOU SEEK, YOU KNOW.
IF YOU WANTED ME TO, THAT IS.
審判
SHALL I MAKE YOU RULER HMM?

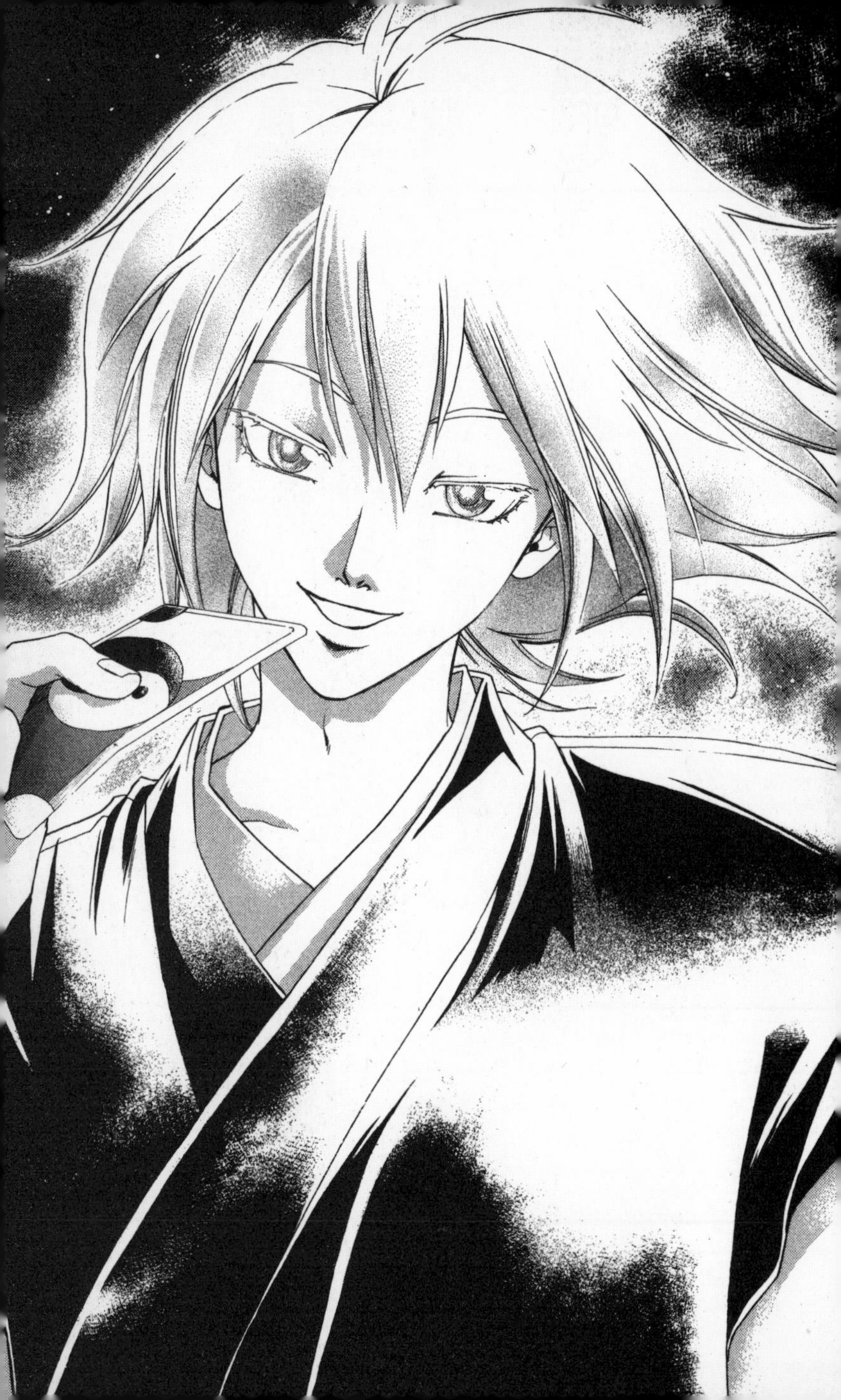

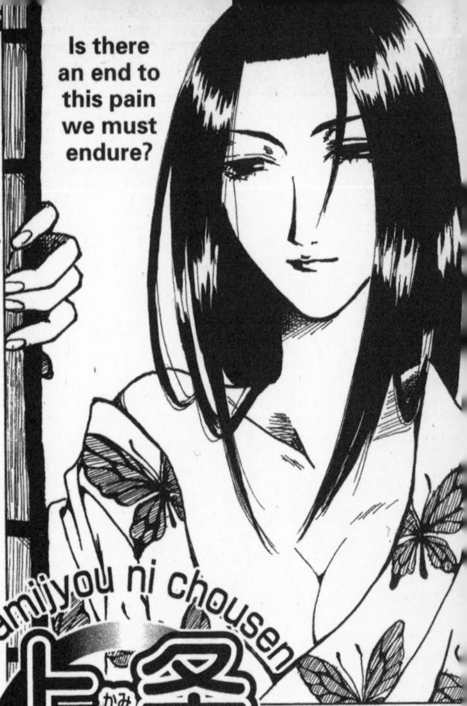

Is there an end to this pain we must endure?

Hmm... very mature. [Nenashi Niigata

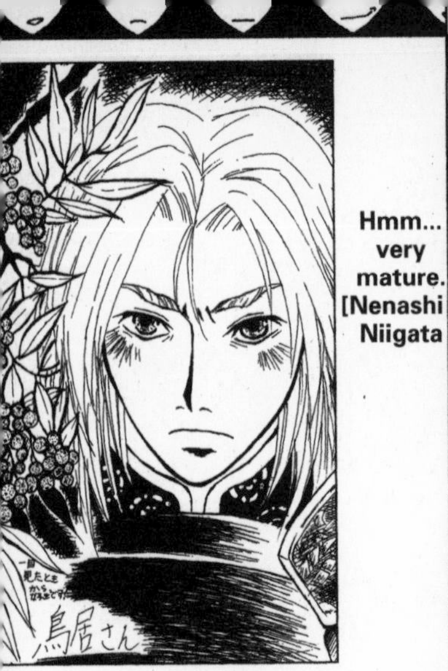
鳥居さん

like the strength in the eyes.

[Yukusa Akiiro / Kanagawa]

kamijyou ni chousen
上条(かみじょう)に挑戦(ちょうせん)!

Try to Draw Like Kamijyo Akimine

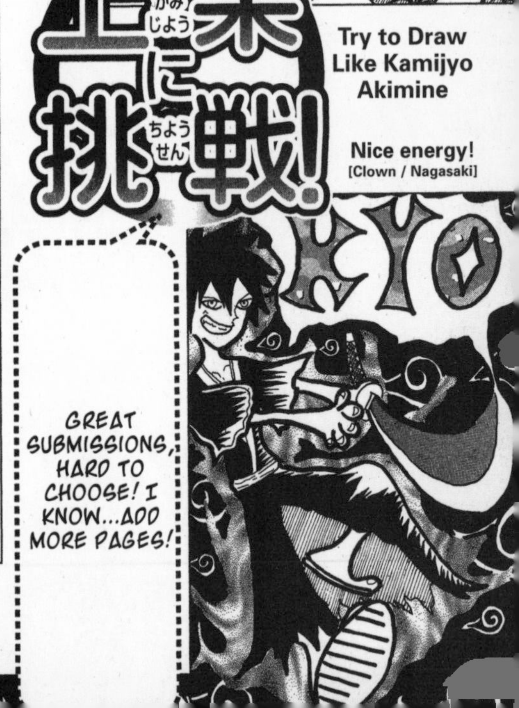
KYO

Nice energy!

[Clown / Nagasaki]

GREAT SUBMISSIONS, HARD TO CHOOSE! I KNOW...ADD MORE PAGES!

Why's his mouth always open? Stuffy nose! I think.

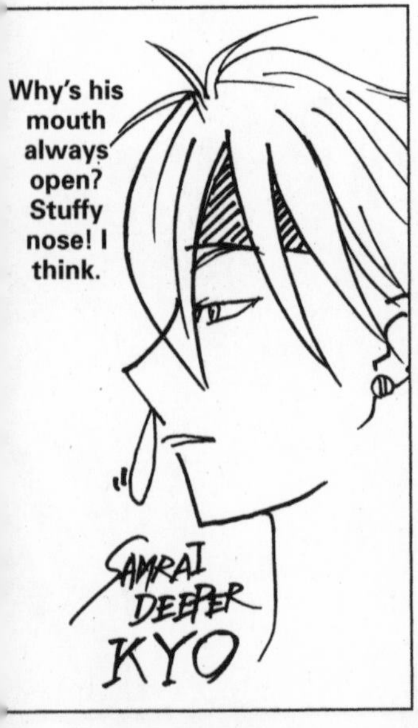
SAMRAI DEEPER KYO

It's all true! :-)

[Shion Kisaragi / Hokkaido]

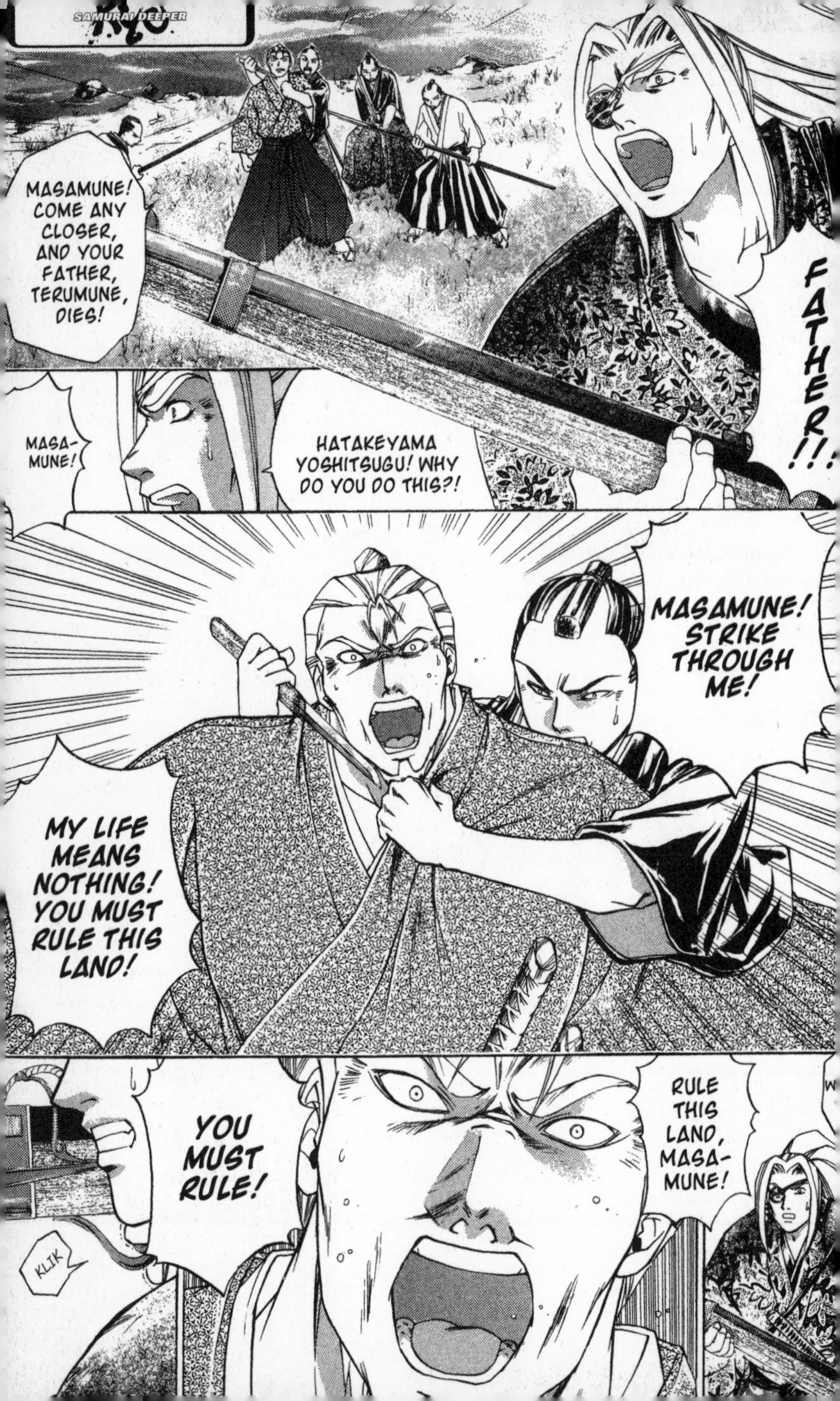
SAMURAI DEEPER
MASAMUNE! COME ANY CLOSER, AND YOUR FATHER, TERUMUNE, DIES!
FATHER!!
HATAKEYAMA YOSHITSUGU! WHY DO YOU DO THIS?!
MASA-MUNE!
MASAMUNE! STRIKE THROUGH ME!
MY LIFE MEANS NOTHING! YOU MUST RULE THIS LAND!
RULE THIS LAND, MASA-MUNE!
YOU MUST RULE!
KLIK

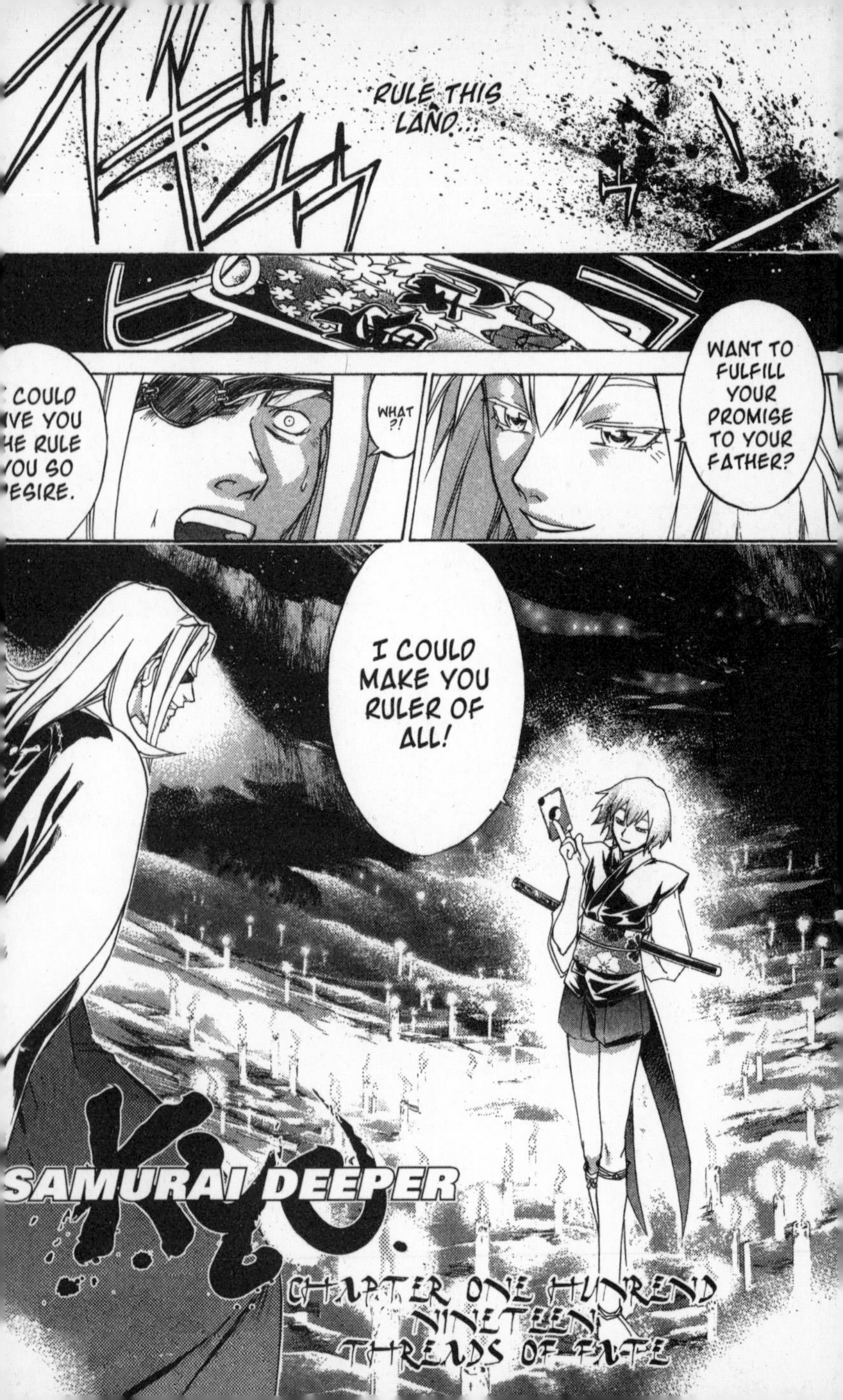

RULE THIS LAND...
WANT TO FULFILL YOUR PROMISE TO YOUR FATHER?
WHAT?!
COULD IVE YOU HE RULE YOU SO ESIRE.
I COULD MAKE YOU RULER OF ALL!
SAMURAI DEEPER KYO
CHAPTER ONE HUNDRED NINETEEN THREADS OF FATE

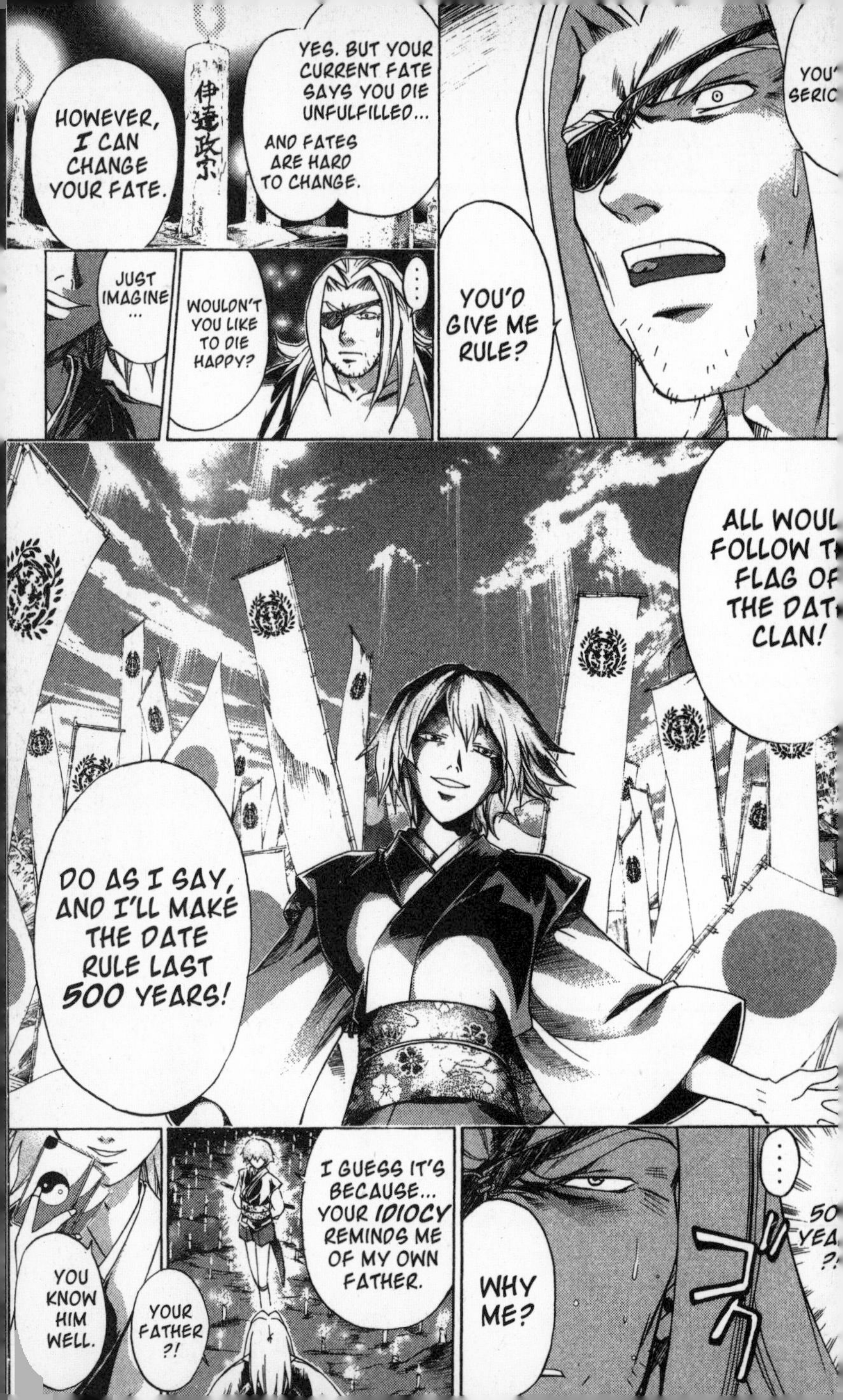
YOU'
SERIO
YOU'D GIVE ME RULE?
YES. BUT YOUR CURRENT FATE SAYS YOU DIE UNFULFILLED...
AND FATES ARE HARD TO CHANGE.
伊達政宗
HOWEVER, I CAN CHANGE YOUR FATE.
...
WOULDN'T YOU LIKE TO DIE HAPPY?
JUST IMAGINE ...
ALL WOUL FOLLOW T FLAG OF THE DAT CLAN!
DO AS I SAY, AND I'LL MAKE THE DATE RULE LAST 500 YEARS!
...
50 YEA ?!
ゴク
WHY ME?
I GUESS IT'S BECAUSE... YOUR IDIOCY REMINDS ME OF MY OWN FATHER.
YOUR FATHER ?!
YOU KNOW HIM WELL.

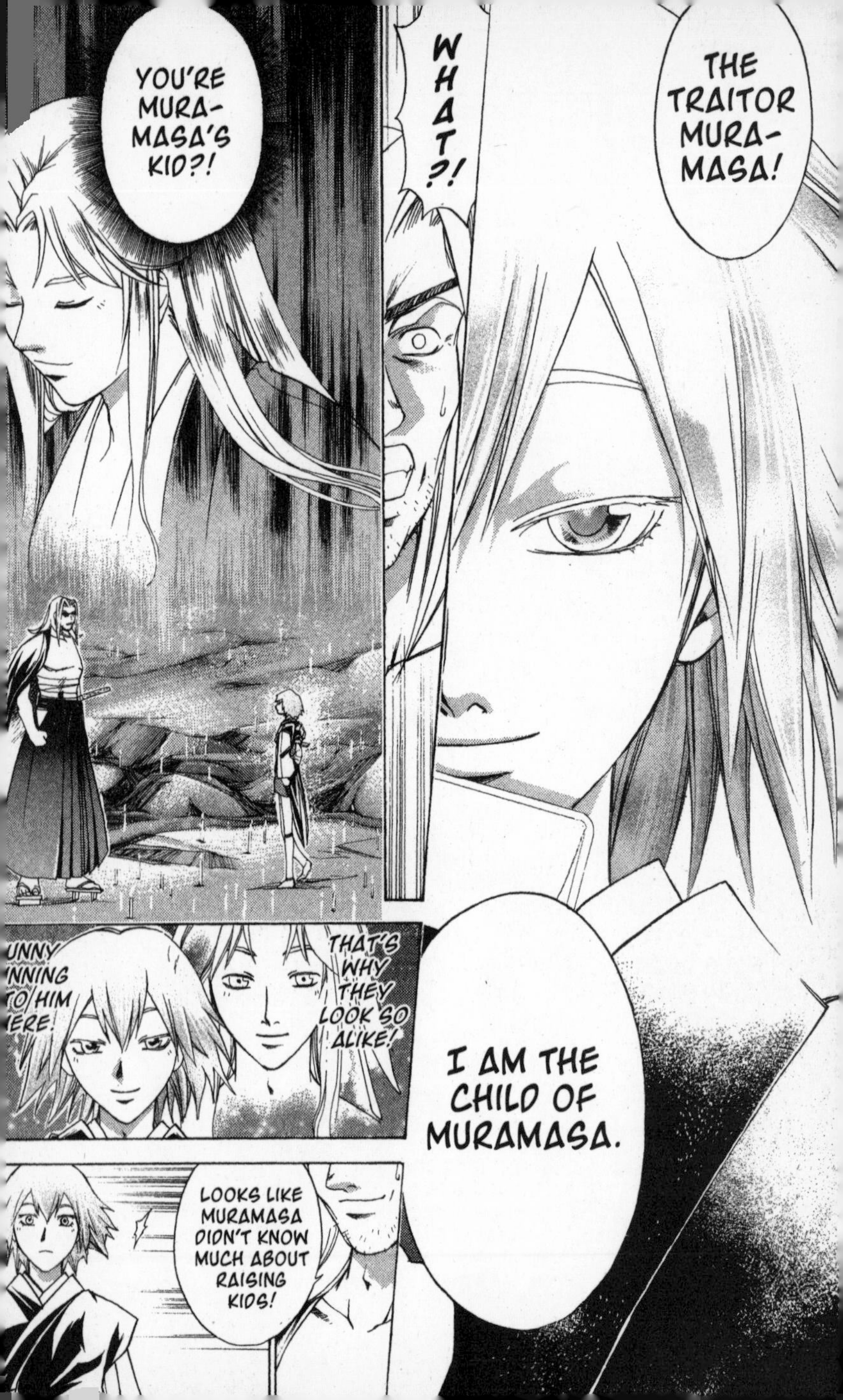
THE TRAITOR MURA-MASA!
WHAT?!
I AM THE CHILD OF MURAMASA.
YOU'RE MURA-MASA'S KID?!
THAT'S WHY THEY LOOK SO ALIKE!
UNNY NNING TO HIM ERE!
LOOKS LIKE MURAMASA DIDN'T KNOW MUCH ABOUT RAISING KIDS!

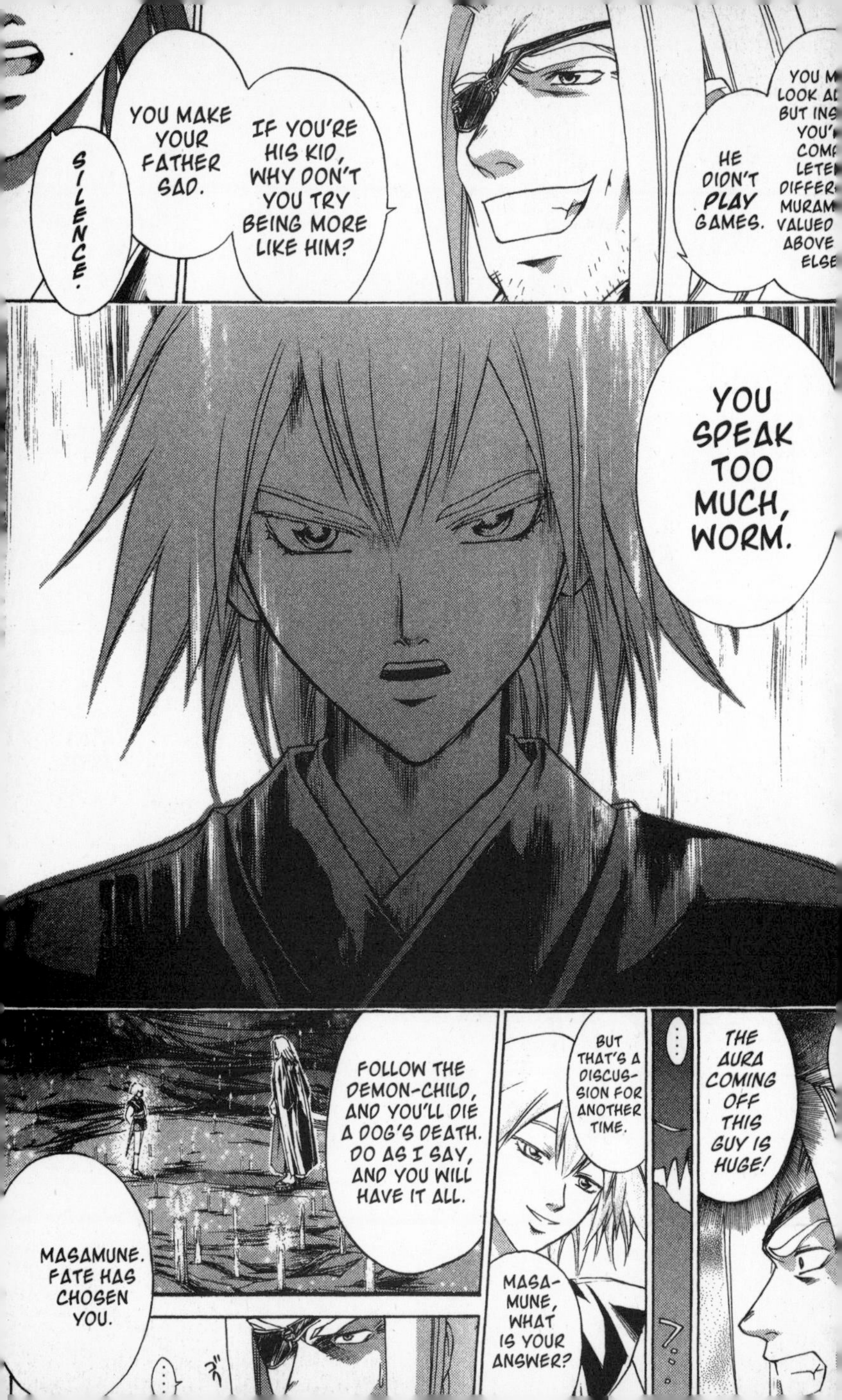
YOU M
LOOK AL
BUT INS
YOU'
COMP
LETEL
DIFFER
MURAM
VALUED
ABOVE
ELSE
HE DIDN'T PLAY GAMES.
IF YOU'RE HIS KID, WHY DON'T YOU TRY BEING MORE LIKE HIM?
YOU MAKE YOUR FATHER SAD.
SILENCE.
YOU SPEAK TOO MUCH, WORM.
THE AURA COMING OFF THIS GUY IS HUGE!
...
BUT THAT'S A DISCUSSION FOR ANOTHER TIME.
MASAMUNE, WHAT IS YOUR ANSWER?
FOLLOW THE DEMON-CHILD, AND YOU'LL DIE A DOG'S DEATH. DO AS I SAY, AND YOU WILL HAVE IT ALL.
MASAMUNE. FATE HAS CHOSEN YOU.
...

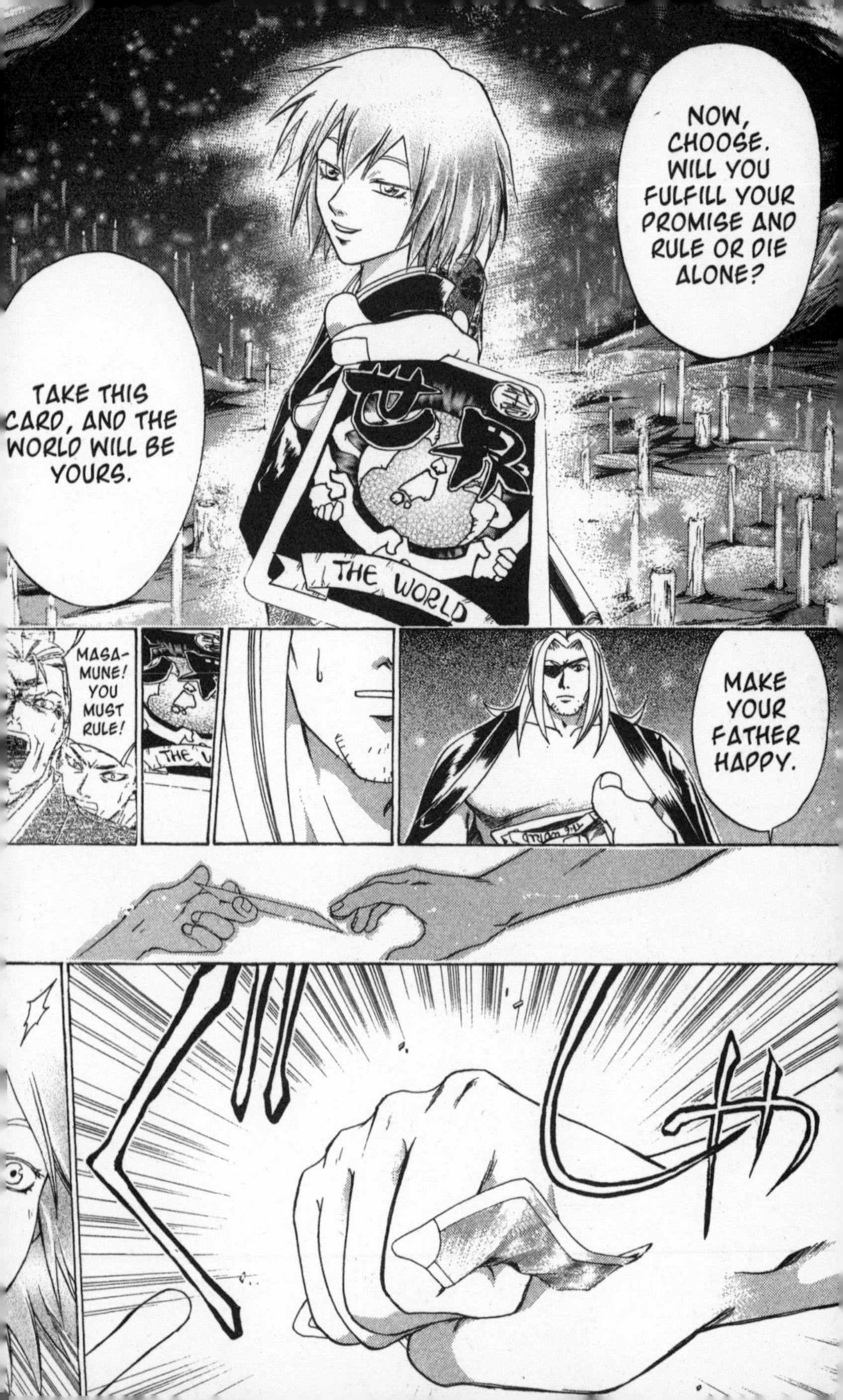
NOW, CHOOSE. WILL YOU FULFILL YOUR PROMISE AND RULE OR DIE ALONE?
TAKE THIS CARD, AND THE WORLD WILL BE YOURS.
THE WORLD
MAKE YOUR FATHER HAPPY.
MASA-MUNE! YOU MUST RULE!

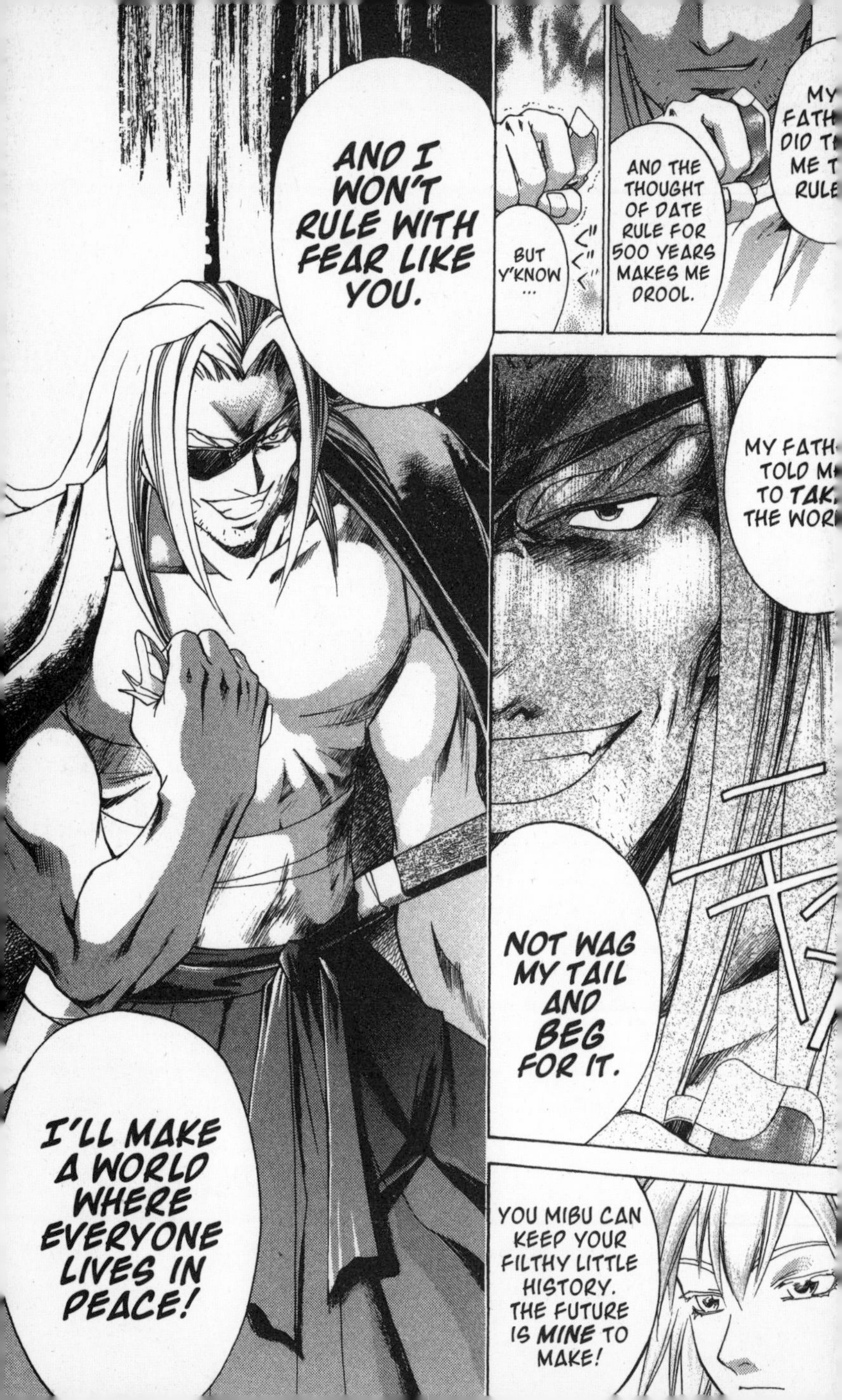

MY FATH DID T ME T RULE
AND THE THOUGHT OF DATE RULE FOR 500 YEARS MAKES ME DROOL.
BUT Y'KNOW...
MY FATH TOLD M TO TAK THE WOR
NOT WAG MY TAIL AND BEG FOR IT.
YOU MIBU CAN KEEP YOUR FILTHY LITTLE HISTORY. THE FUTURE IS MINE TO MAKE!
AND I WON'T RULE WITH FEAR LIKE YOU.
I'LL MAKE A WORLD WHERE EVERYONE LIVES IN PEACE!

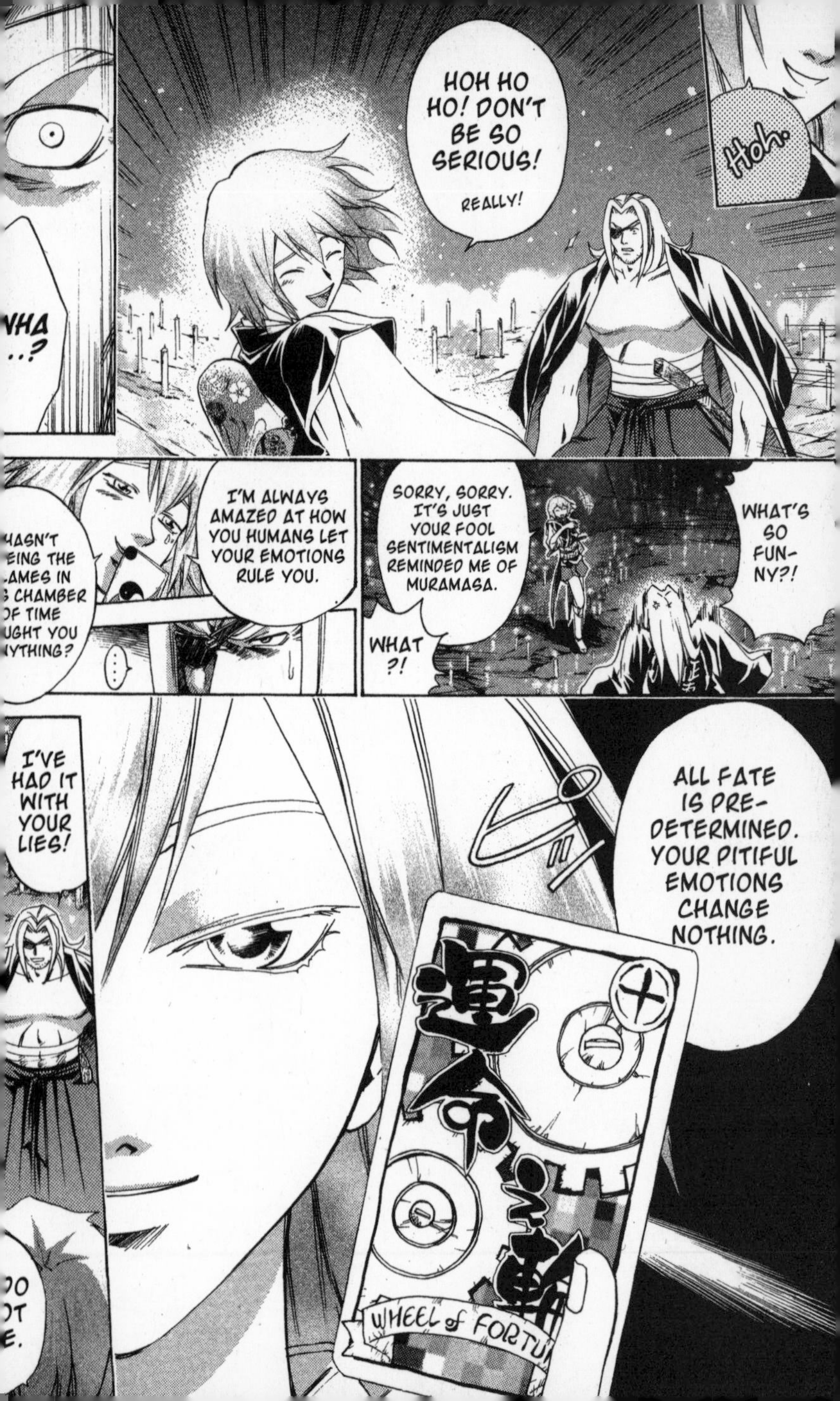
Hoh.
HOH HO HO! DON'T BE SO SERIOUS!
REALLY!
WHA ...?
WHAT'S SO FUN-NY?!
SORRY, SORRY. IT'S JUST YOUR FOOL SENTIMENTALISM REMINDED ME OF MURAMASA.
WHAT ?!
I'M ALWAYS AMAZED AT HOW YOU HUMANS LET YOUR EMOTIONS RULE YOU.
...
HASN'T EING THE AMES IN CHAMBER OF TIME UGHT YOU YTHING?
ALL FATE IS PRE-DETERMINED. YOUR PITIFUL EMOTIONS CHANGE NOTHING.
運命の車輪
WHEEL of FORTU
I'VE HAD IT WITH YOUR LIES!

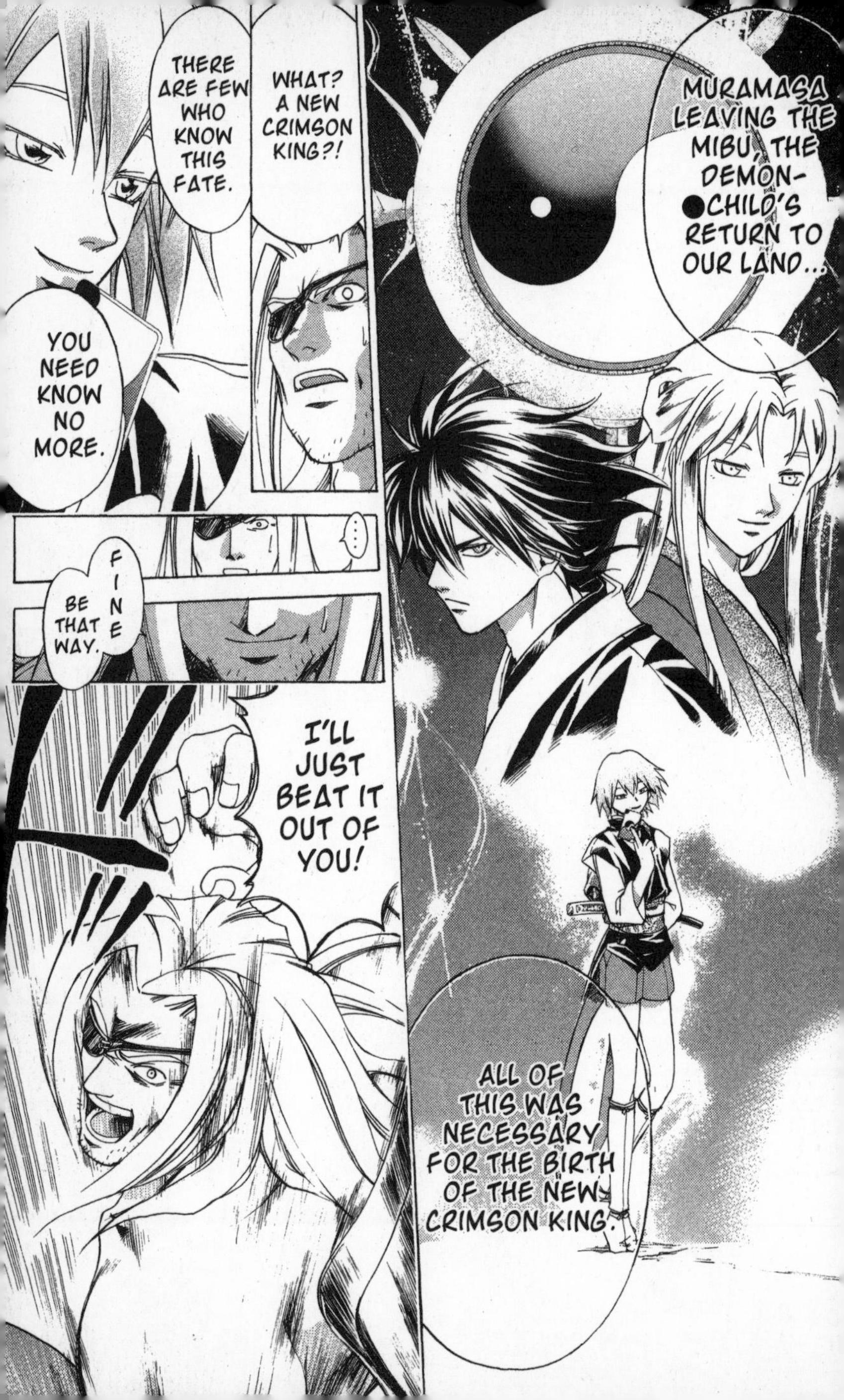
MURAMASA LEAVING THE MIBU, THE DEMON-CHILD'S RETURN TO OUR LAND...
ALL OF THIS WAS NECESSARY FOR THE BIRTH OF THE NEW CRIMSON KING.
WHAT? A NEW CRIMSON KING?!
THERE ARE FEW WHO KNOW THIS FATE.
YOU NEED KNOW NO MORE.
...
FINE
BE THAT WAY.
I'LL JUST BEAT IT OUT OF YOU!

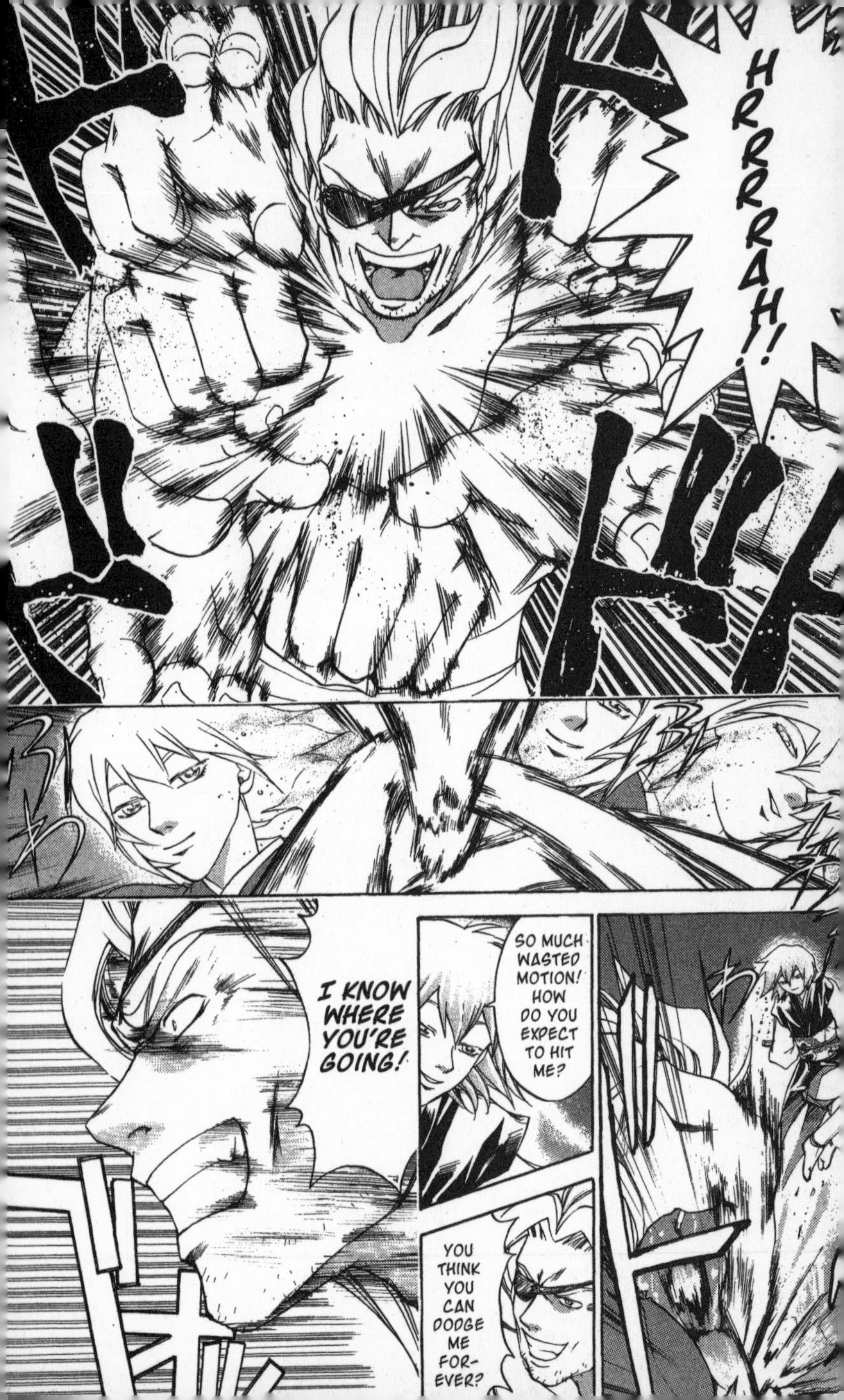
HRRRRAH!!
SO MUCH WASTED MOTION! HOW DO YOU EXPECT TO HIT ME?
YOU THINK YOU CAN DODGE ME FOR-EVER?
I KNOW WHERE YOU'RE GOING!

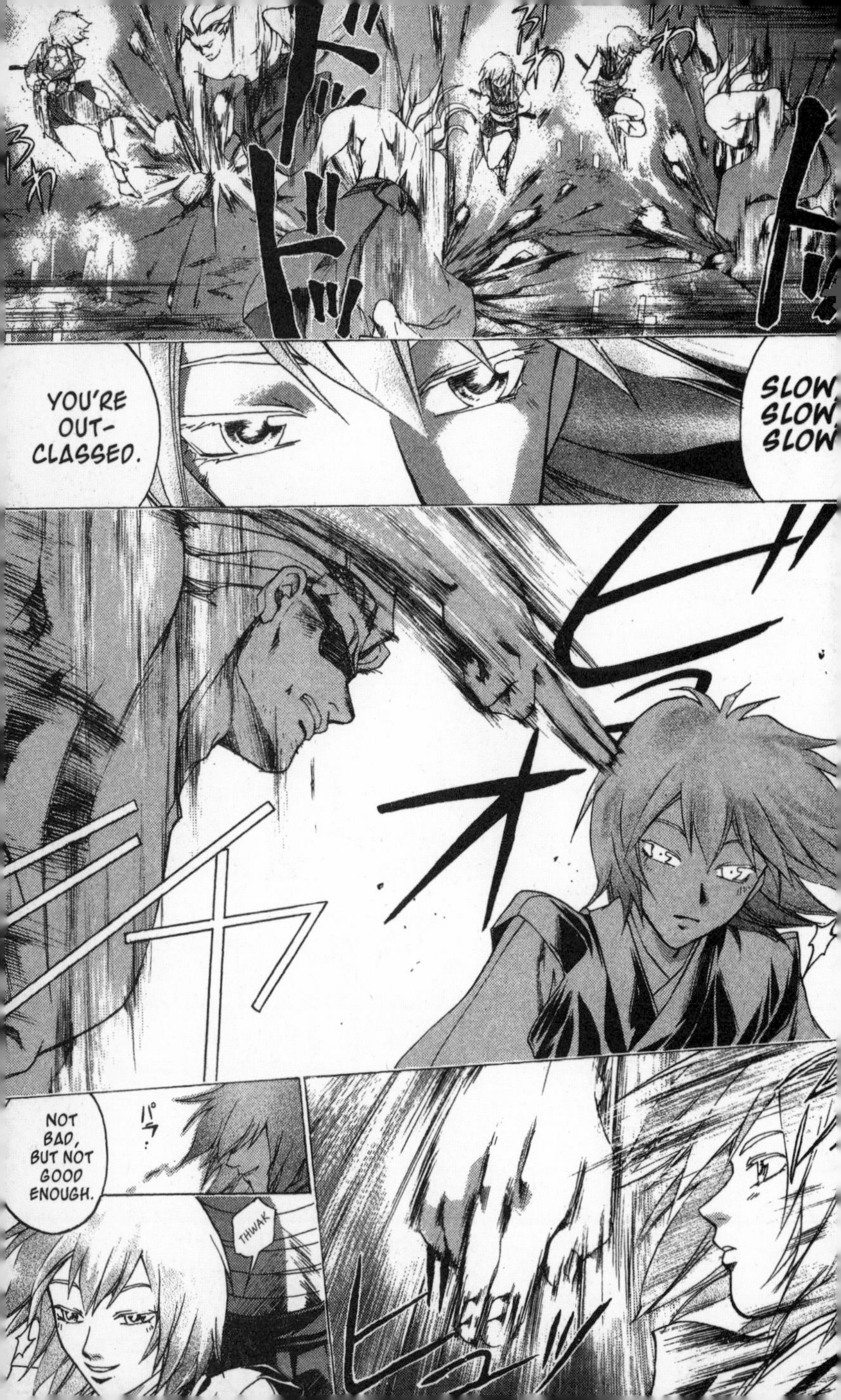

SLOW SLOW SLOW
YOU'RE OUT-CLASSED.
NOT BAD, BUT NOT GOOD ENOUGH.
THWAK

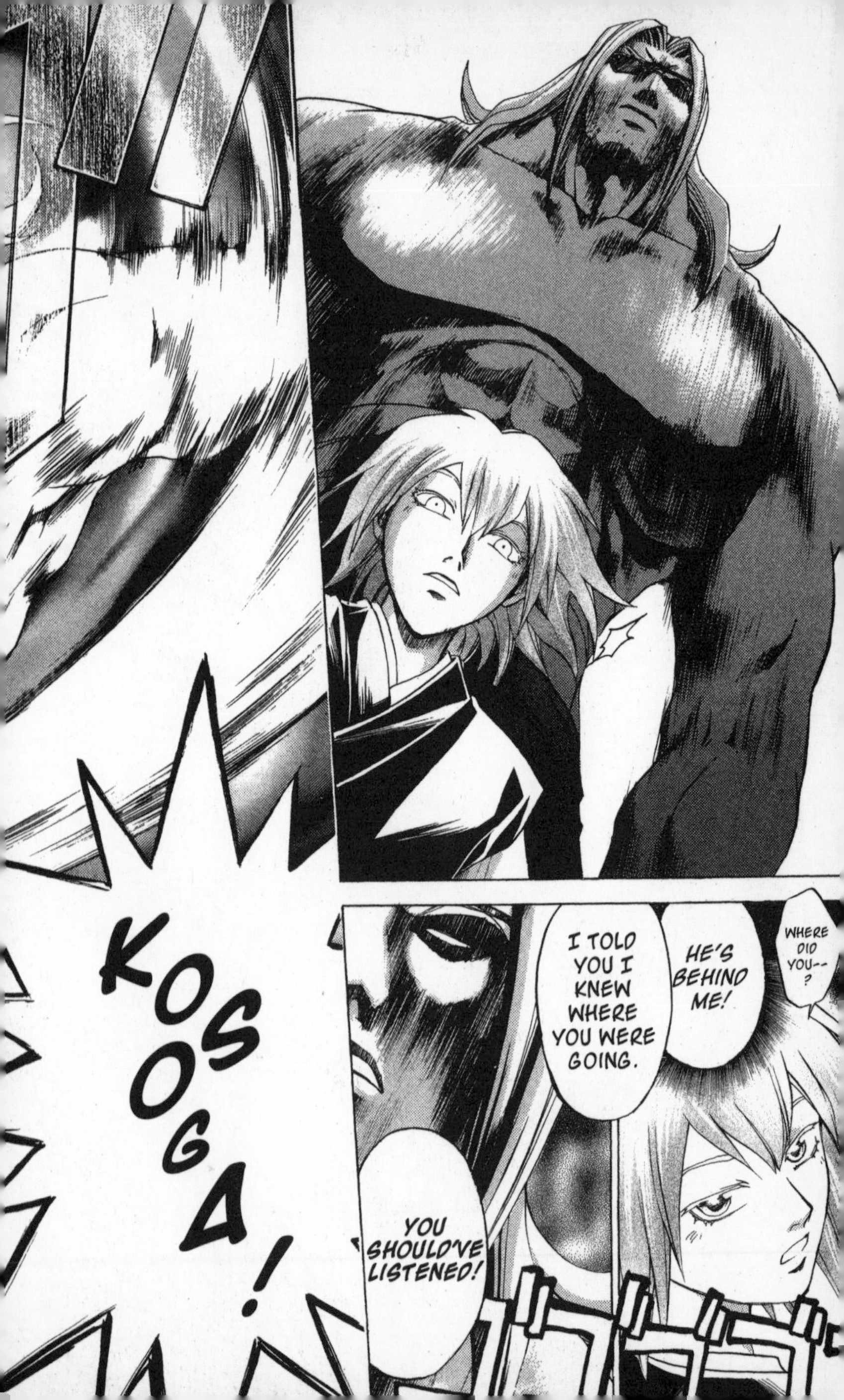
WHERE DID YOU--?
HE'S BEHIND ME!
I TOLD YOU I KNEW WHERE YOU WERE GOING.
YOU SHOULD'VE LISTENED!
KOSOGA!

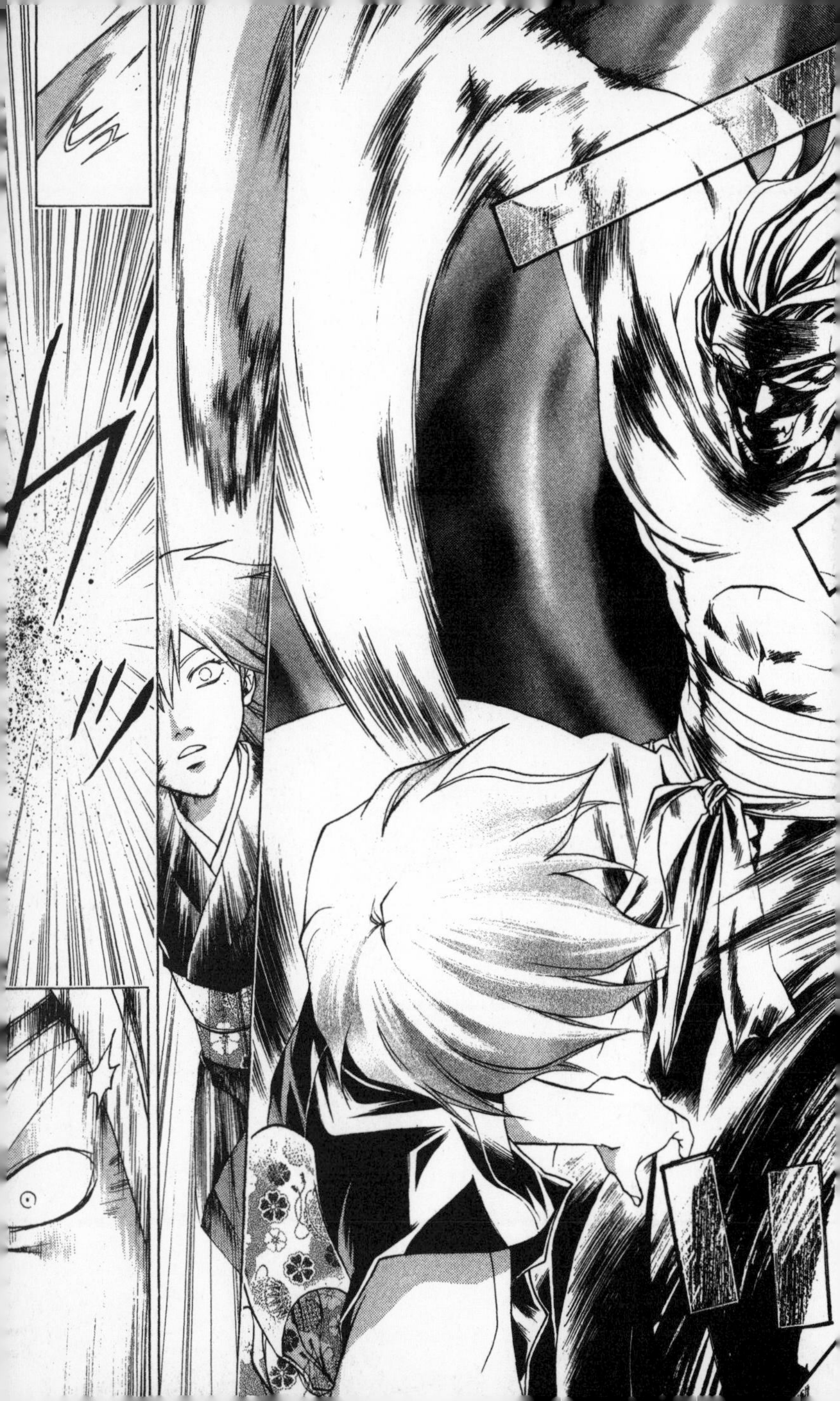
ヒュ

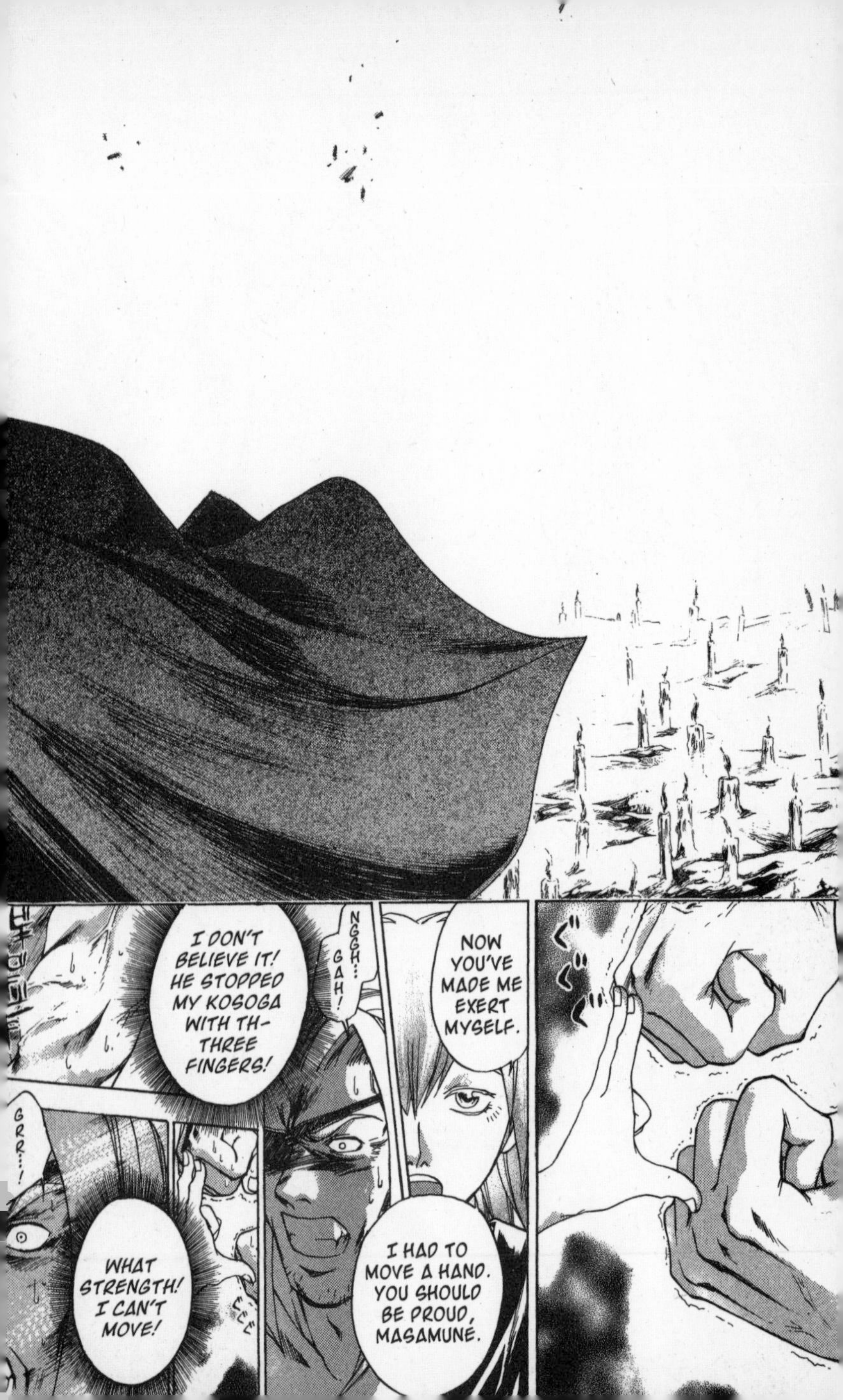
NOW YOU'VE MADE ME EXERT MYSELF.
NGGH... GAH!
I DON'T BELIEVE IT! HE STOPPED MY KOSOGA WITH TH-THREE FINGERS!
I HAD TO MOVE A HAND. YOU SHOULD BE PROUD, MASAMUNE.
GRR...!
WHAT STRENGTH! I CAN'T MOVE!

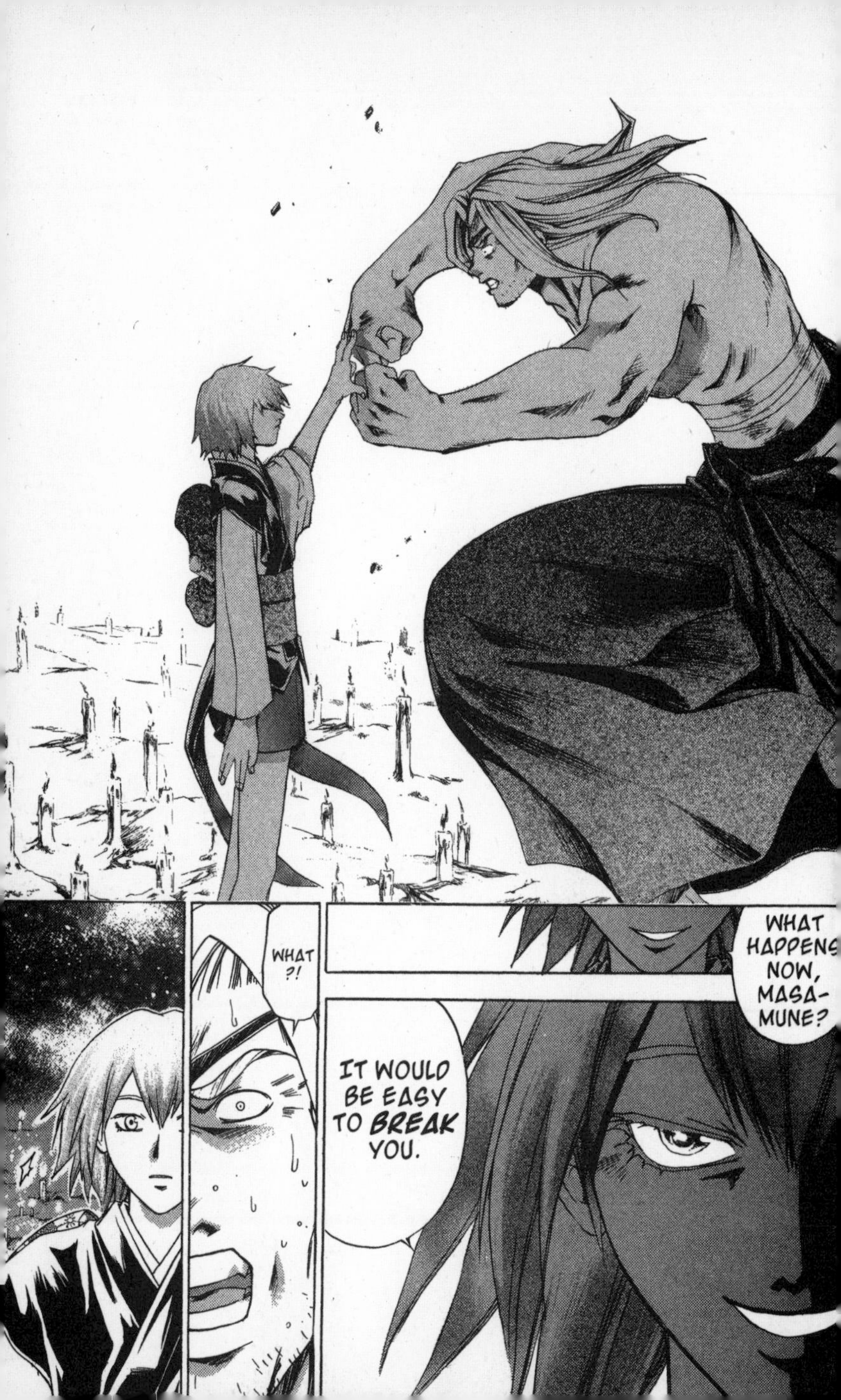
WHAT HAPPENS NOW, MASAMUNE?
IT WOULD BE EASY TO BREAK YOU.
WHAT ?!

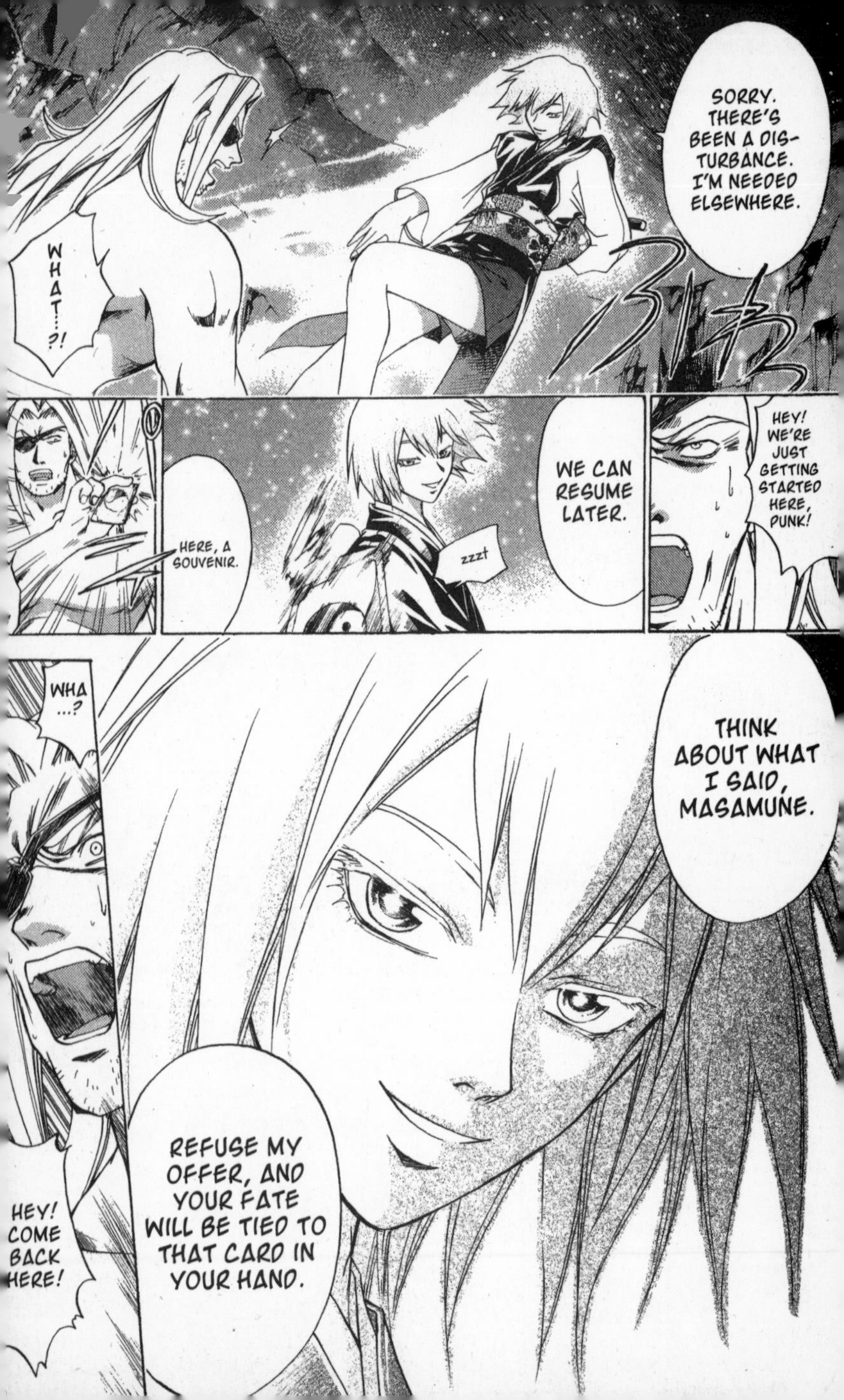
SORRY. THERE'S BEEN A DIS-TURBANCE. I'M NEEDED ELSEWHERE.
WHAT...?!
HEY! WE'RE JUST GETTING STARTED HERE, PUNK!
WE CAN RESUME LATER.
zzzt
HERE, A SOUVENIR.
THINK ABOUT WHAT I SAID, MASAMUNE.
WHA ...?
REFUSE MY OFFER, AND YOUR FATE WILL BE TIED TO THAT CARD IN YOUR HAND.
HEY! COME BACK HERE!

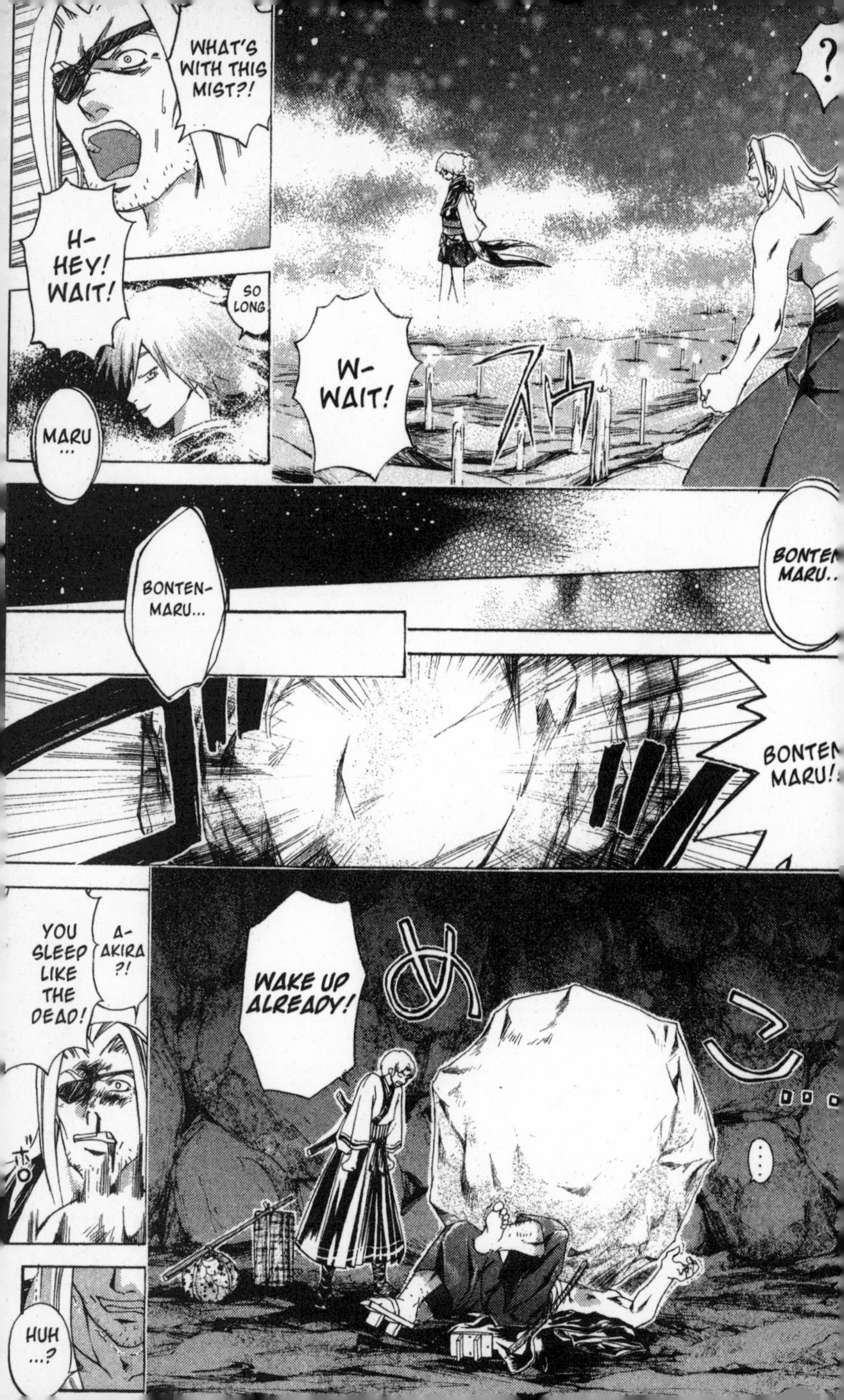
?
W-WAIT!
WHAT'S WITH THIS MIST?!
H-HEY! WAIT!
SO LONG
MARU...
BONTEN MARU..
BONTEN-MARU...
BONTEN MARU!..
...
WAKE UP ALREADY!
A-AKIRA?!
YOU SLEEP LIKE THE DEAD!
HUH...?

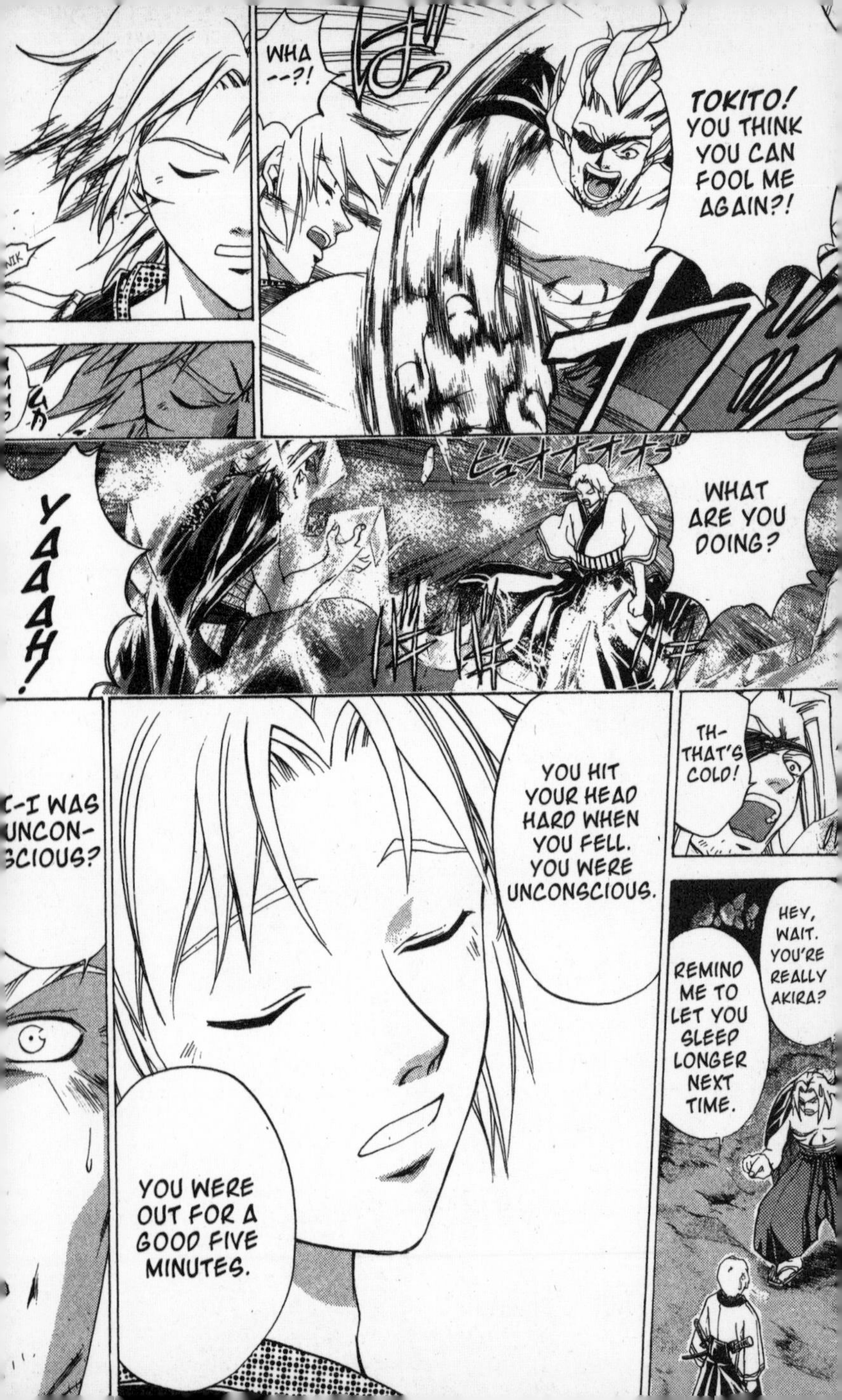

TOKITO! YOU THINK YOU CAN FOOL ME AGAIN?!
WHA --?!
NIK
WHAT ARE YOU DOING?
YAAAAH!
TH- THAT'S COLD!
HEY, WAIT. YOU'RE REALLY AKIRA?
REMIND ME TO LET YOU SLEEP LONGER NEXT TIME.
YOU HIT YOUR HEAD HARD WHEN YOU FELL. YOU WERE UNCONSCIOUS.
YOU WERE OUT FOR A GOOD FIVE MINUTES.
-I WAS UNCON- SCIOUS?

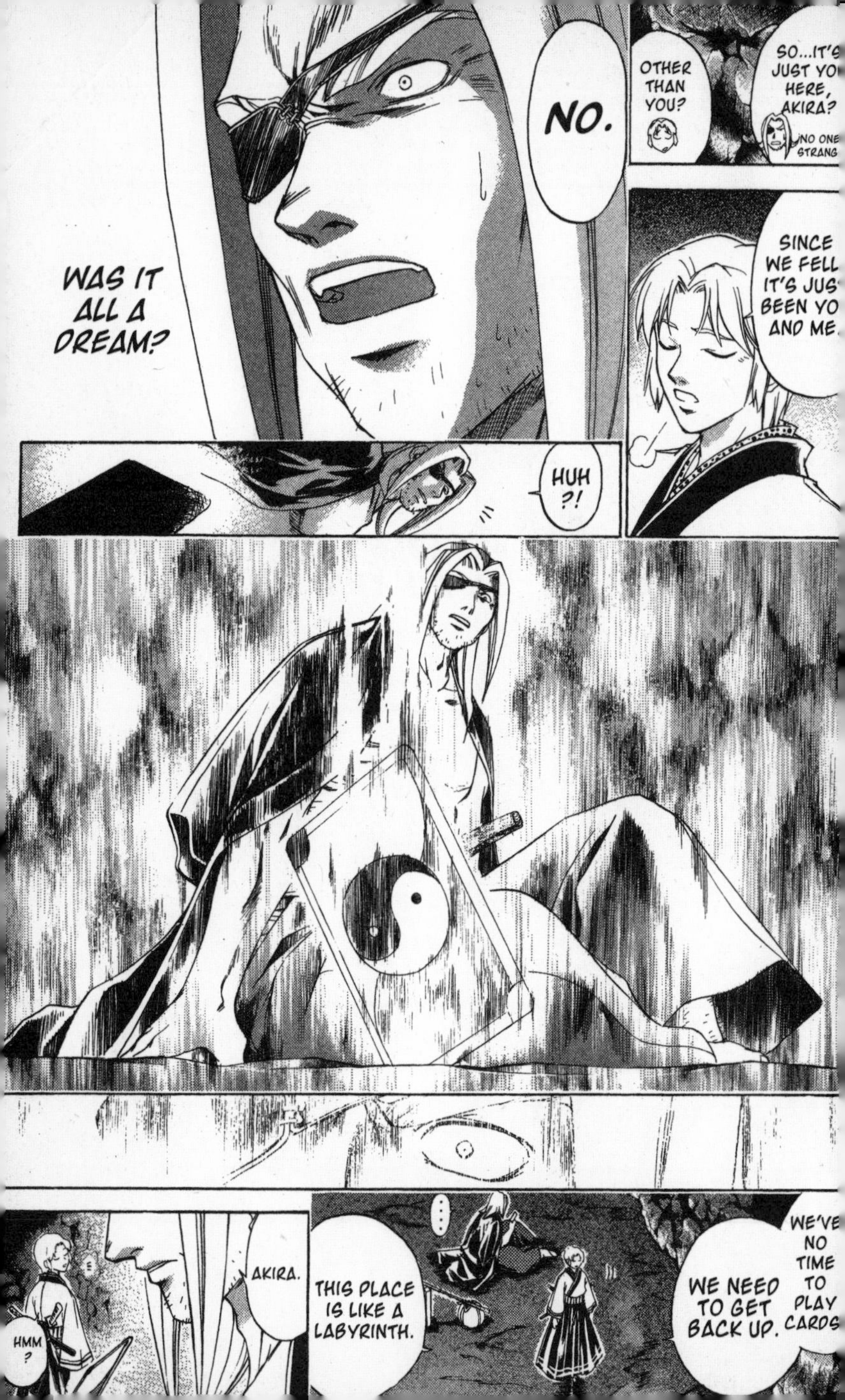
SO...IT'S JUST YO HERE, AKIRA?
NO ONE STRANG
OTHER THAN YOU?
SINCE WE FELL IT'S JUS BEEN YO AND ME.
NO.
WAS IT ALL A DREAM?
HUH ?!
WE'VE NO TIME TO PLAY CARDS
WE NEED TO GET BACK UP.
...
THIS PLACE IS LIKE A LABYRINTH.
AKIRA.
HMM ?

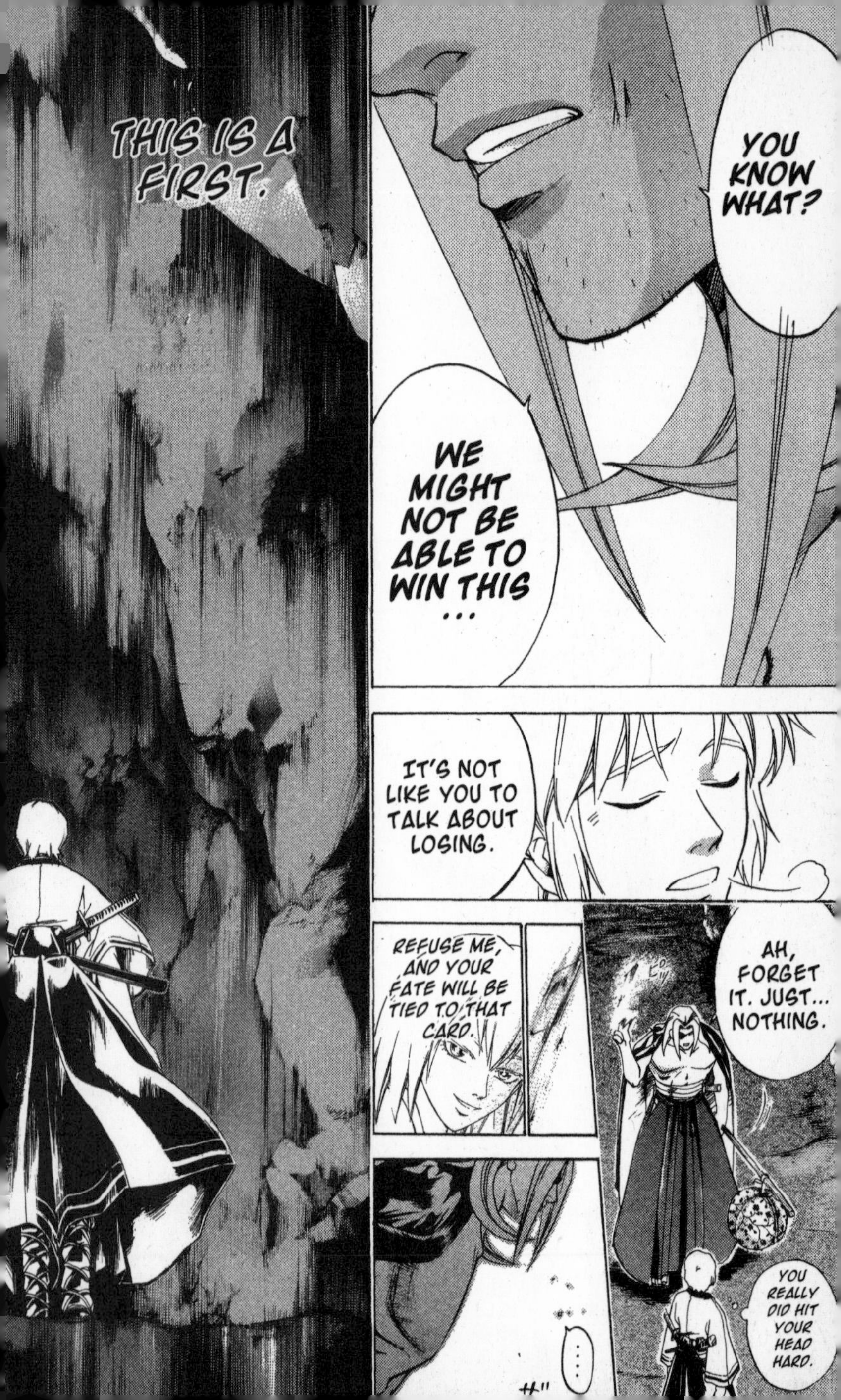
YOU KNOW WHAT?
WE MIGHT NOT BE ABLE TO WIN THIS...
IT'S NOT LIKE YOU TO TALK ABOUT LOSING.
AH, FORGET IT. JUST... NOTHING.
YOU REALLY DID HIT YOUR HEAD HARD.
REFUSE ME, AND YOUR FATE WILL BE TIED TO THAT CARD.
...
THIS IS A FIRST.

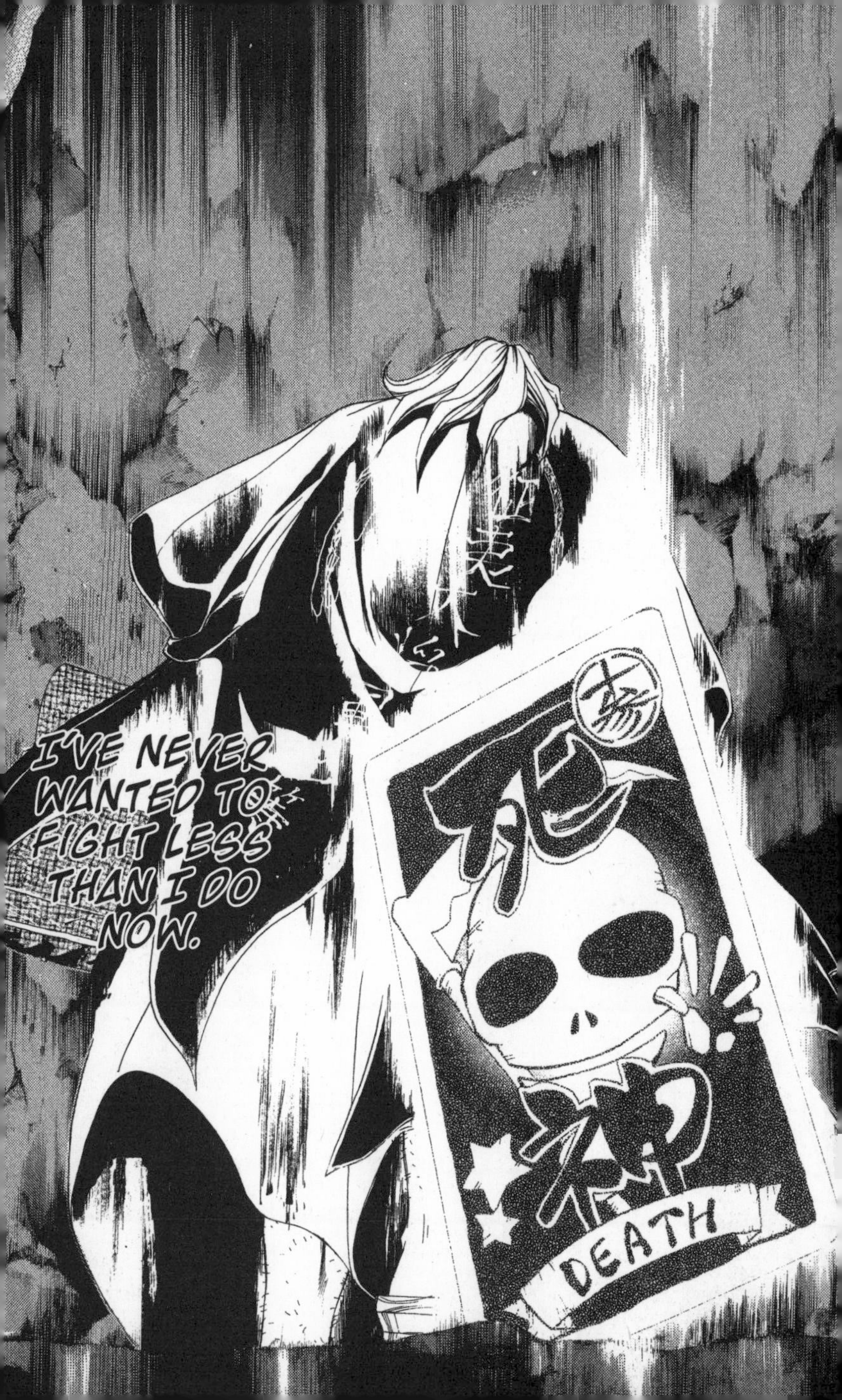
I'VE NEVER WANTED TO FIGHT LESS THAN I DO NOW.
DEATH

kamijyou ni chousen
上条(かみじょう)に挑戦(ちょうせん)!

Try to Draw Like Kamijyo Akimine!

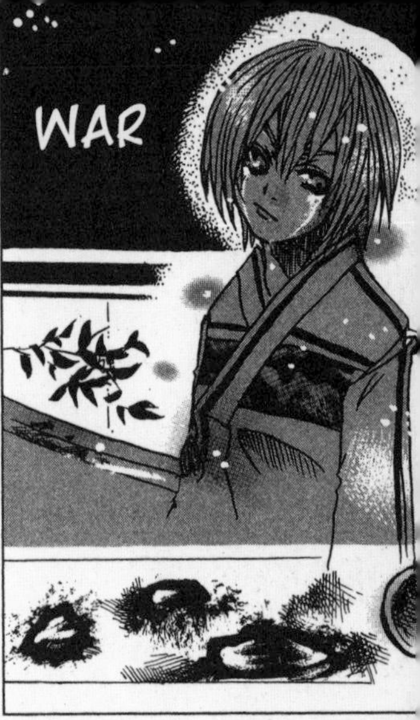
WAR

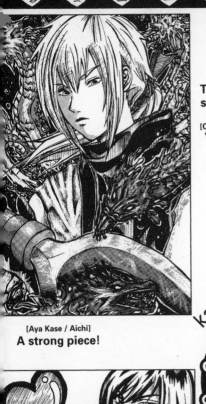

A child's tears shoot straight to the heart.

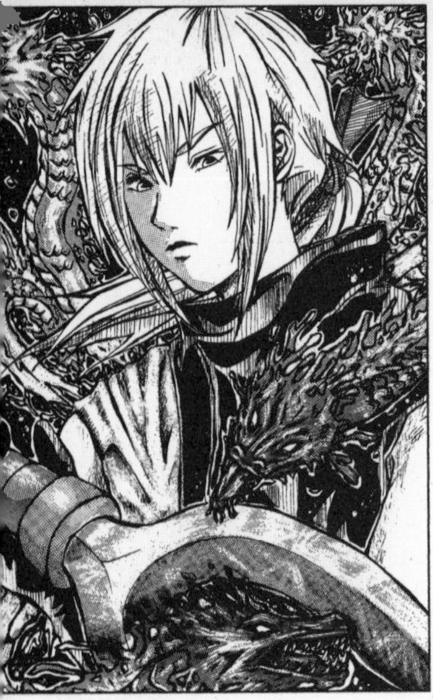

This one strikes a chord.
[Chuken Ko / Yamagata]

[Aya Kase / Aichi]
A strong piece!

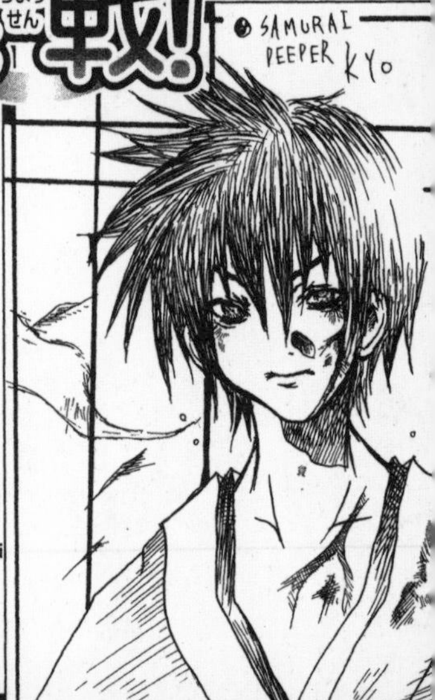
SAMURAI DEEPER KYO

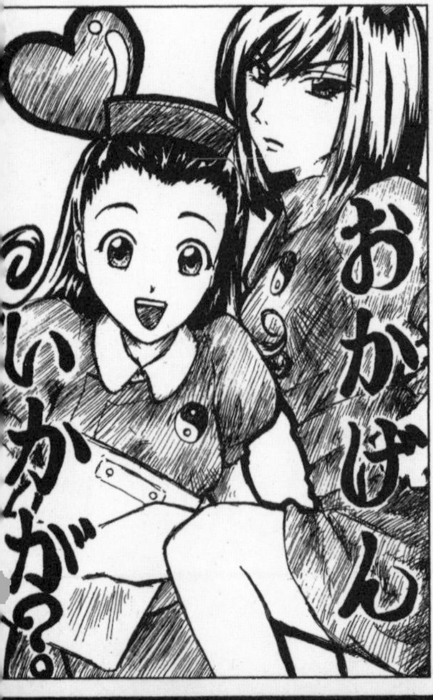
おかげんいかが?

Nice legs when bared.
[heart]
[Mao Mizogaki / Shizuoka]

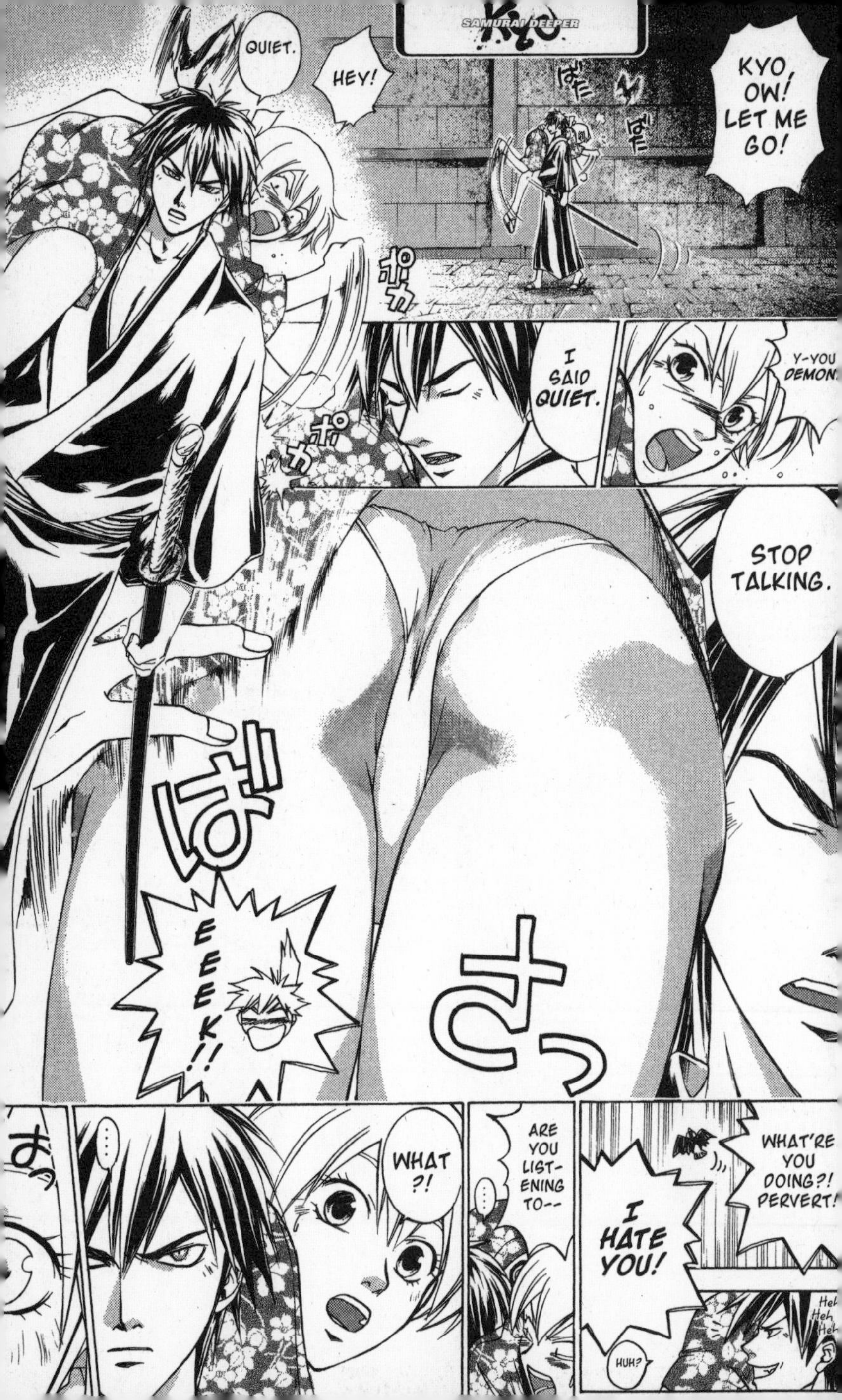
SAMURAI DEEPER KYO
KYO OW! LET ME GO!
ばた ばた
HEY!
QUIET.
ポカ
Y-YOU DEMON!
I SAID QUIET.
ポカ
STOP TALKING.
さっ
ばっ
EEEK!!
WHAT'RE YOU DOING?! PERVERT!
I HATE YOU!
Heh Heh Heh
HUH?
ARE YOU LIST-ENING TO--
...
WHAT ?!
...
おっ

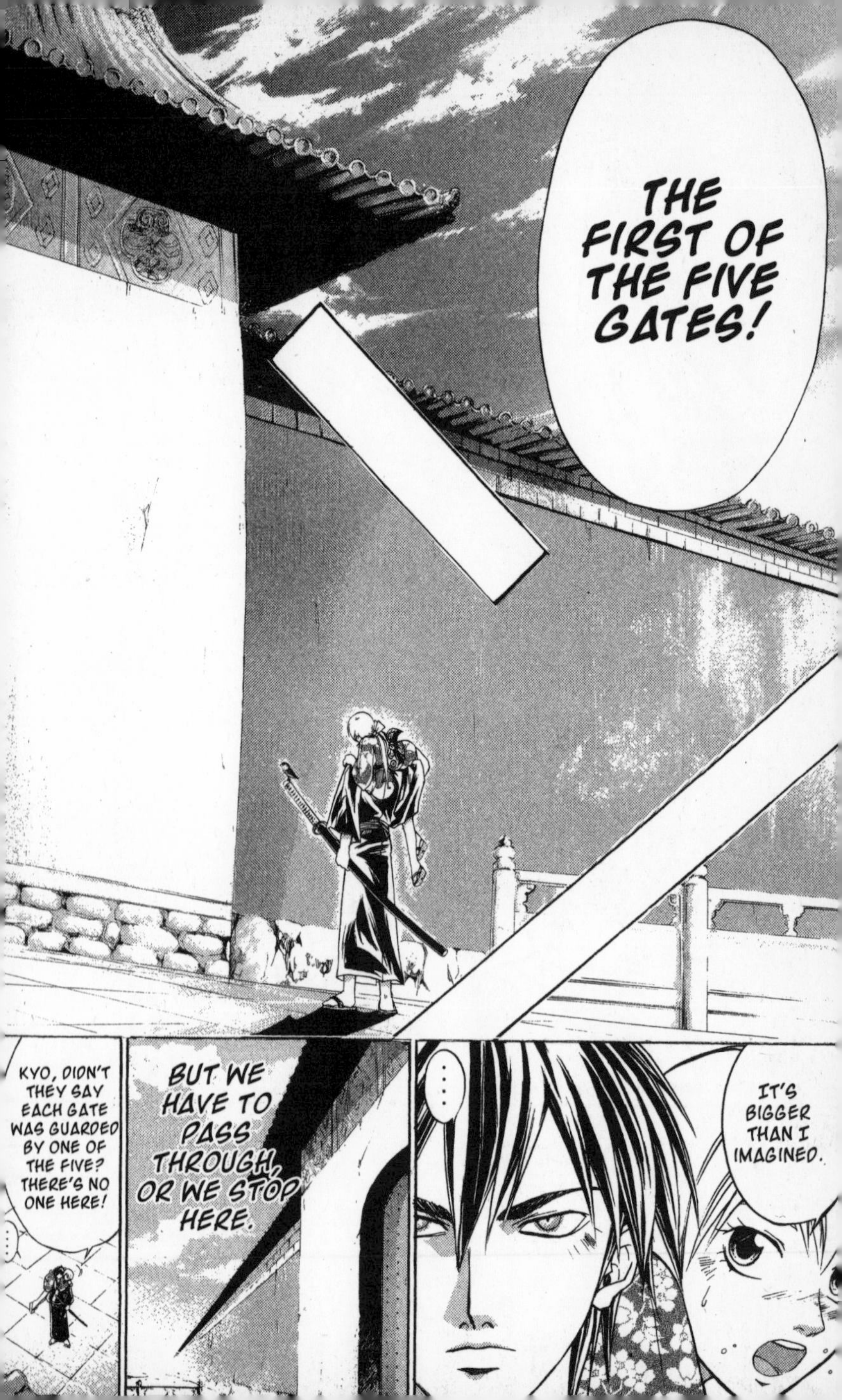
THE FIRST OF THE FIVE GATES!
IT'S BIGGER THAN I IMAGINED.
.....
BUT WE HAVE TO PASS THROUGH, OR WE STOP HERE.
KYO, DIDN'T THEY SAY EACH GATE WAS GUARDED BY ONE OF THE FIVE? THERE'S NO ONE HERE!
...

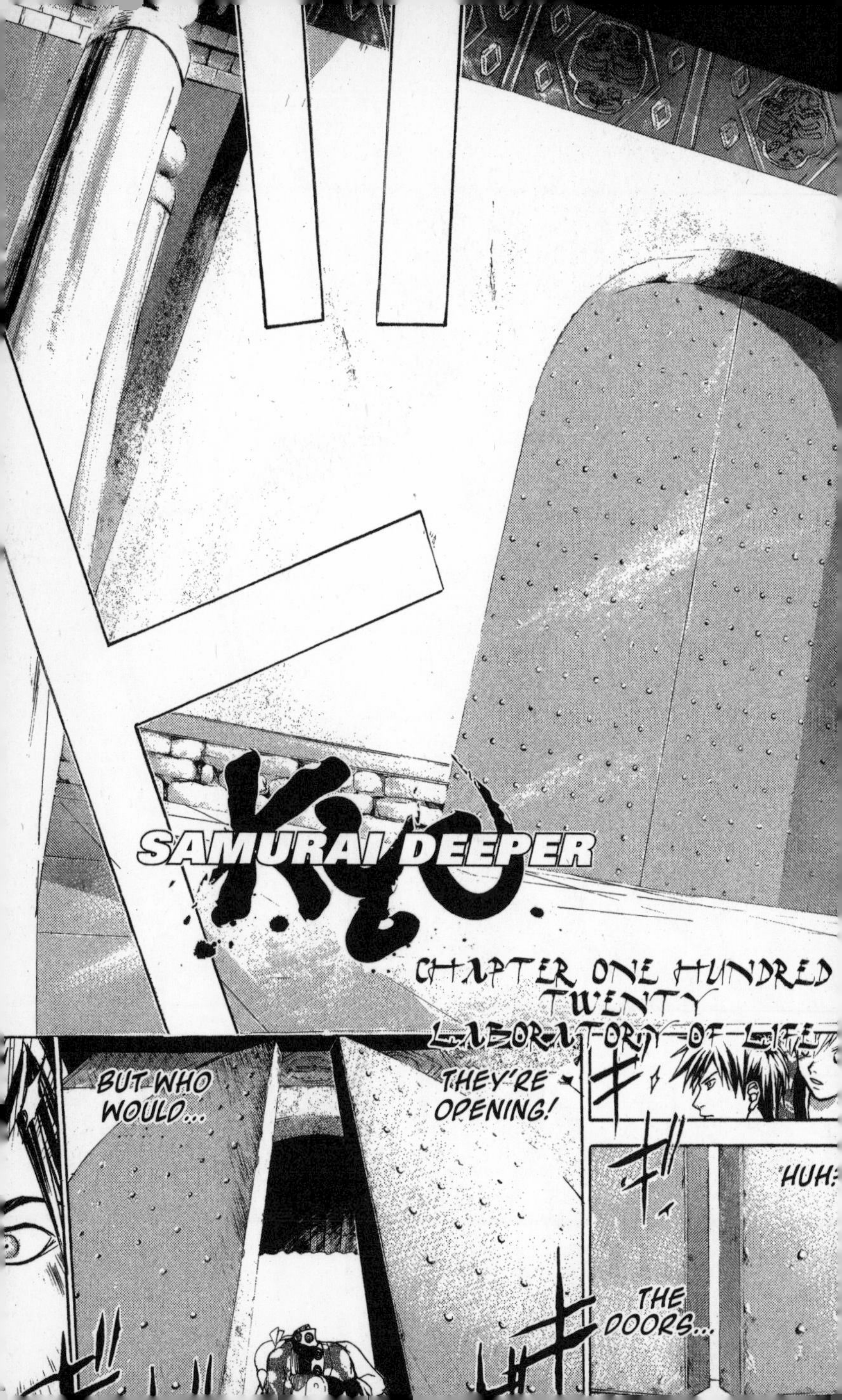
SAMURAI DEEPER KYO
CHAPTER ONE HUNDRED TWENTY
LABORATORY OF LIFE
HUH
THE DOORS...
THEY'RE OPENING!
BUT WHO WOULD...

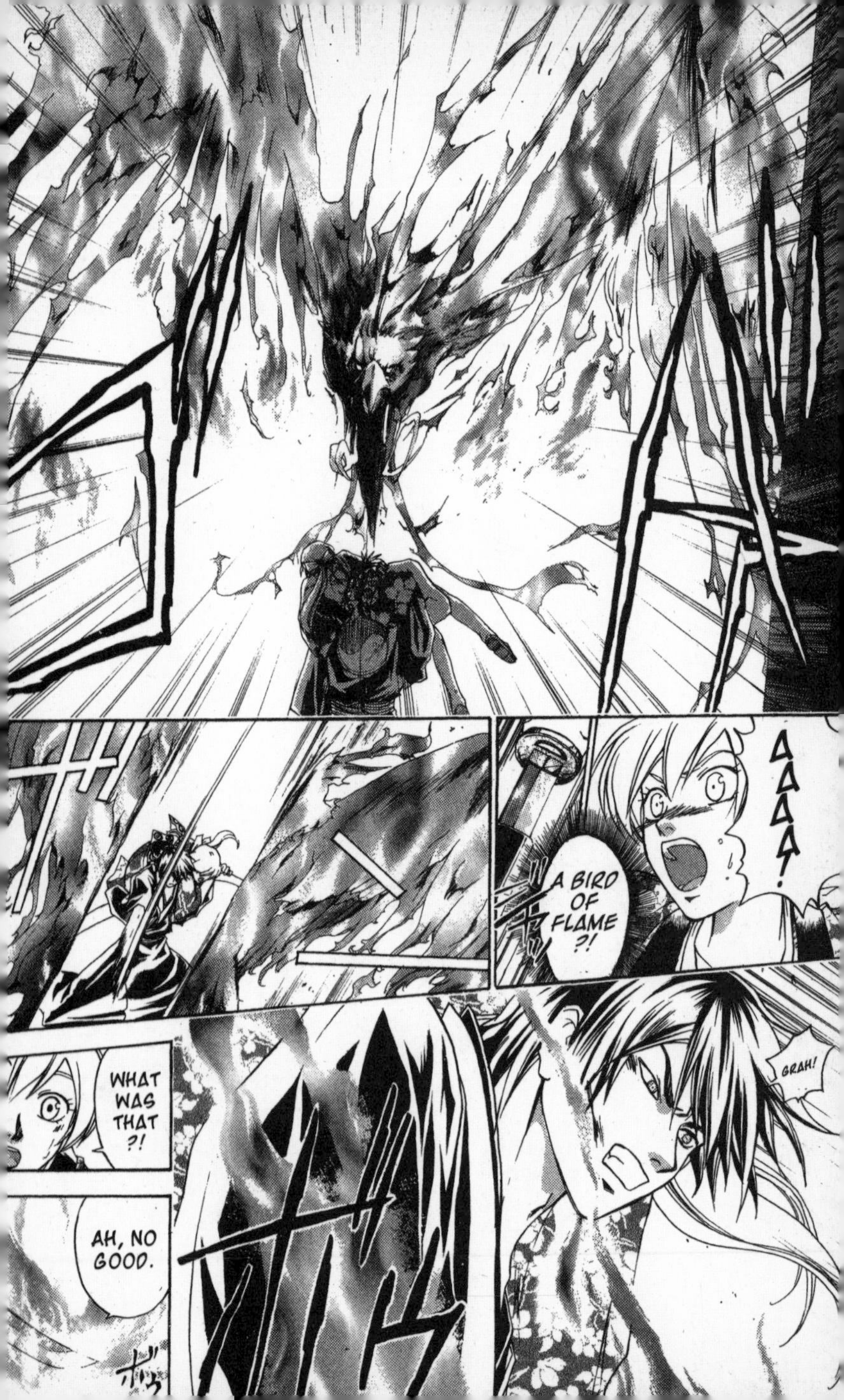
AAAA!
A BIRD OF FLAME ?!
GRAH!
WHAT WAS THAT ?!
AH, NO GOOD.

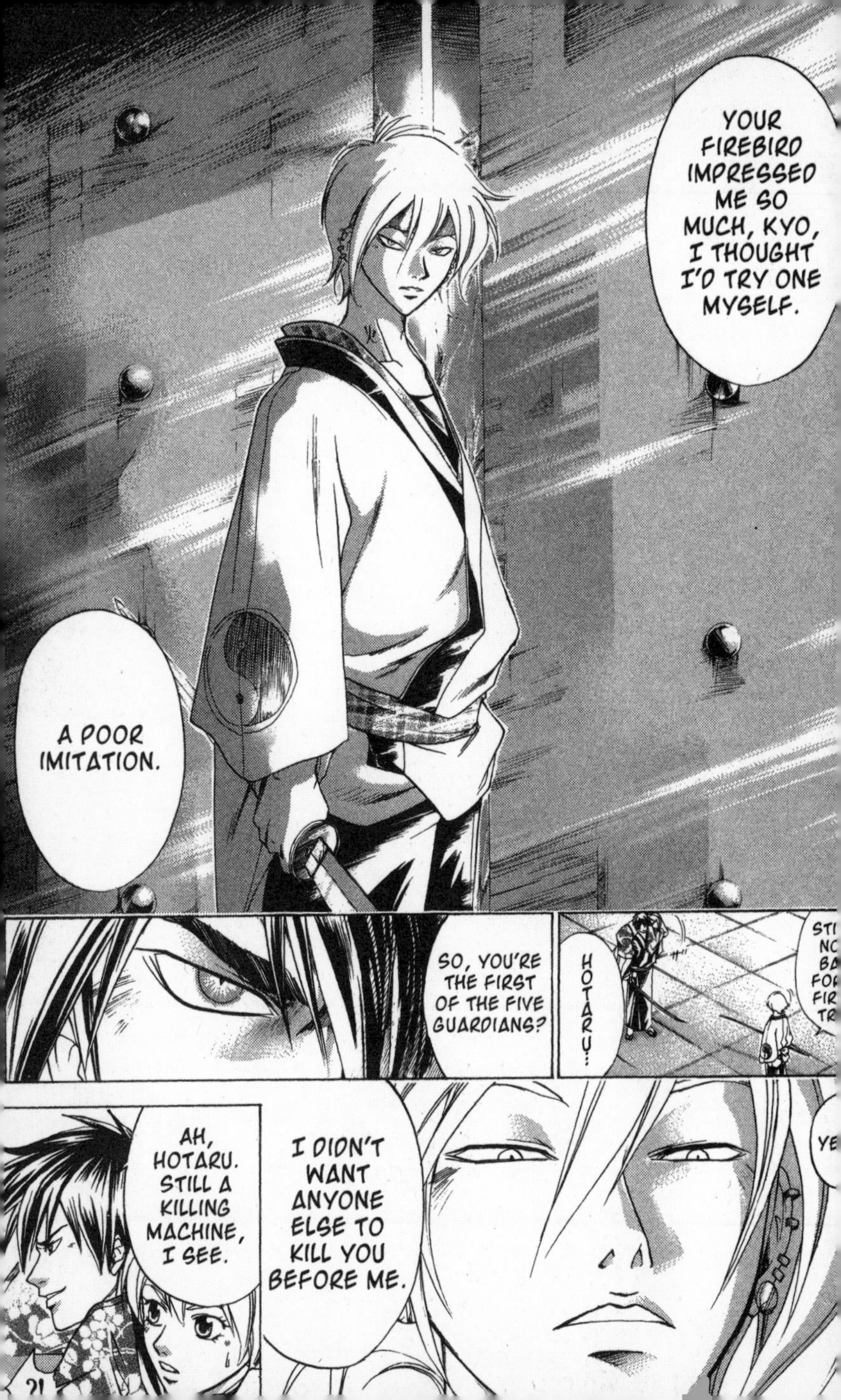
YOUR FIREBIRD IMPRESSED ME SO MUCH, KYO, I THOUGHT I'D TRY ONE MYSELF.
A POOR IMITATION.
HOTARU!
SO, YOU'RE THE FIRST OF THE FIVE GUARDIANS?
I DIDN'T WANT ANYONE ELSE TO KILL YOU BEFORE ME.
AH, HOTARU. STILL A KILLING MACHINE, I SEE.

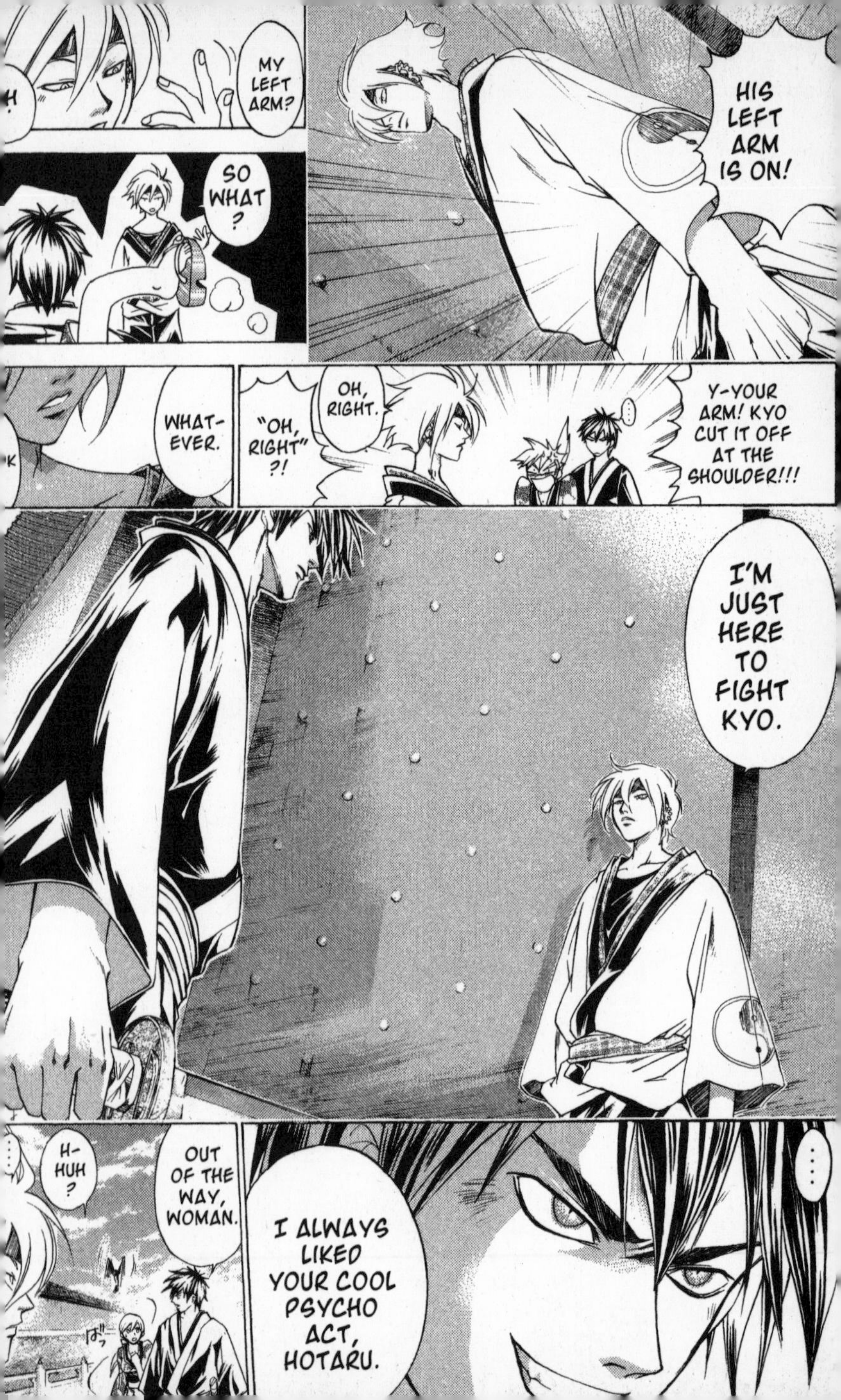
HIS LEFT ARM IS ON!
MY LEFT ARM?
SO WHAT ?
Y-YOUR ARM! KYO CUT IT OFF AT THE SHOULDER!!!
...
OH, RIGHT.
"OH, RIGHT" ?!
WHAT-EVER.
I'M JUST HERE TO FIGHT KYO.
....
I ALWAYS LIKED YOUR COOL PSYCHO ACT, HOTARU.
OUT OF THE WAY, WOMAN.
ばっ
H-HUH ?
....

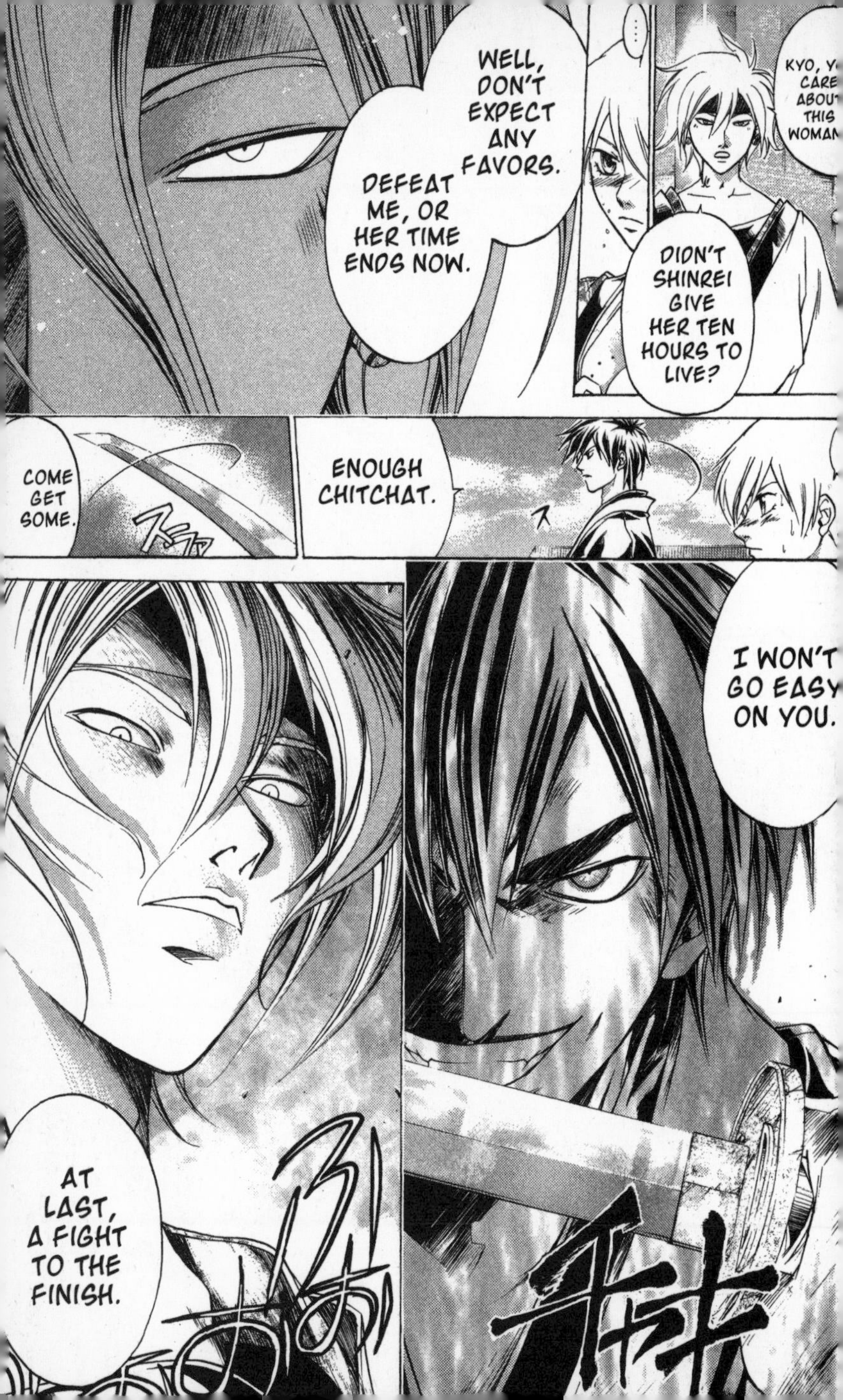

KYO, Y CARE ABOUT THIS WOMAN
DIDN'T SHINREI GIVE HER TEN HOURS TO LIVE?
...
WELL, DON'T EXPECT ANY FAVORS.
DEFEAT ME, OR HER TIME ENDS NOW.
ENOUGH CHITCHAT.
COME GET SOME.
I WON'T GO EASY ON YOU.
AT LAST, A FIGHT TO THE FINISH.

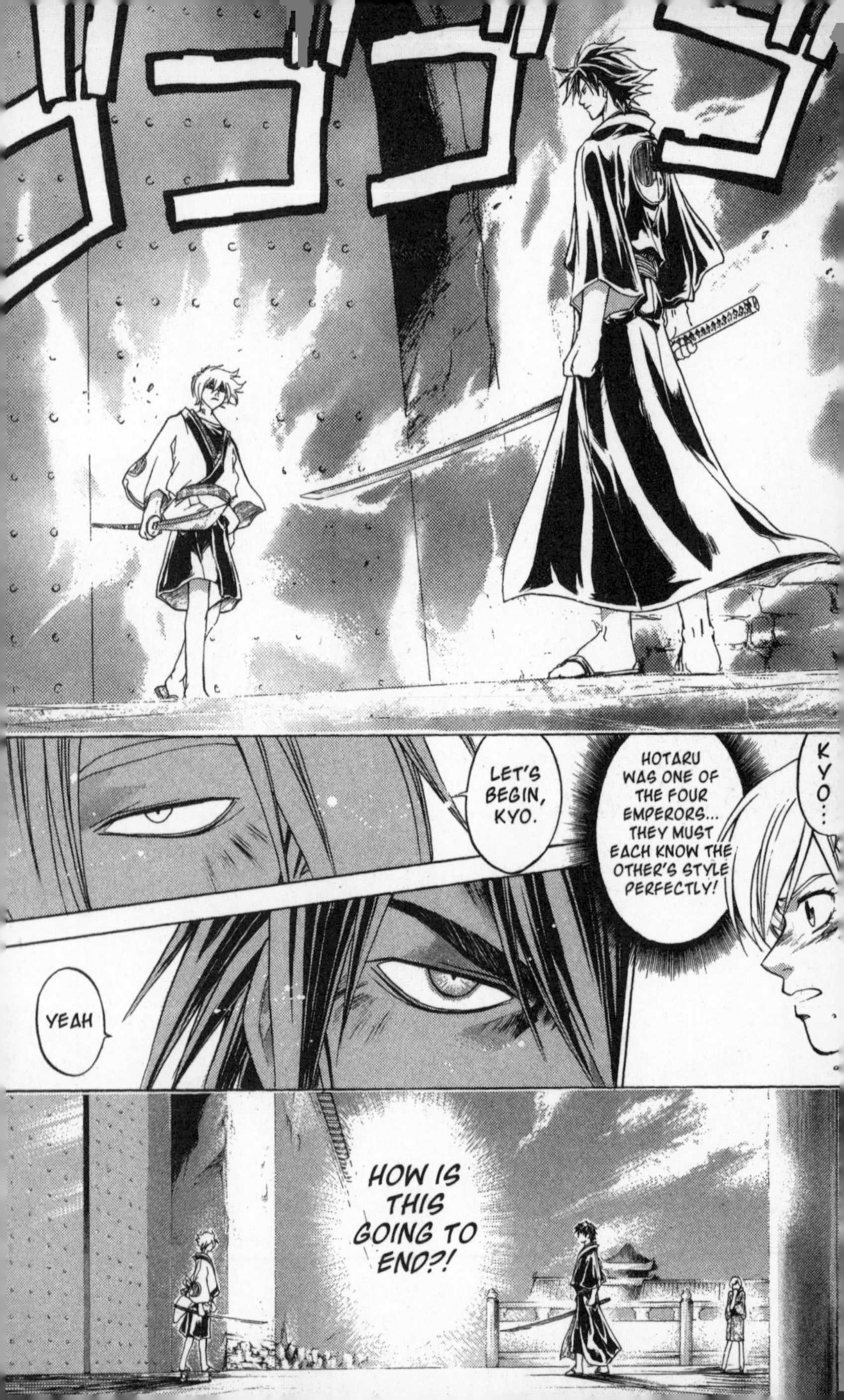
KYO...
HOTARU WAS ONE OF THE FOUR EMPERORS... THEY MUST EACH KNOW THE OTHER'S STYLE PERFECTLY!
LET'S BEGIN, KYO.
YEAH
HOW IS THIS GOING TO END?!

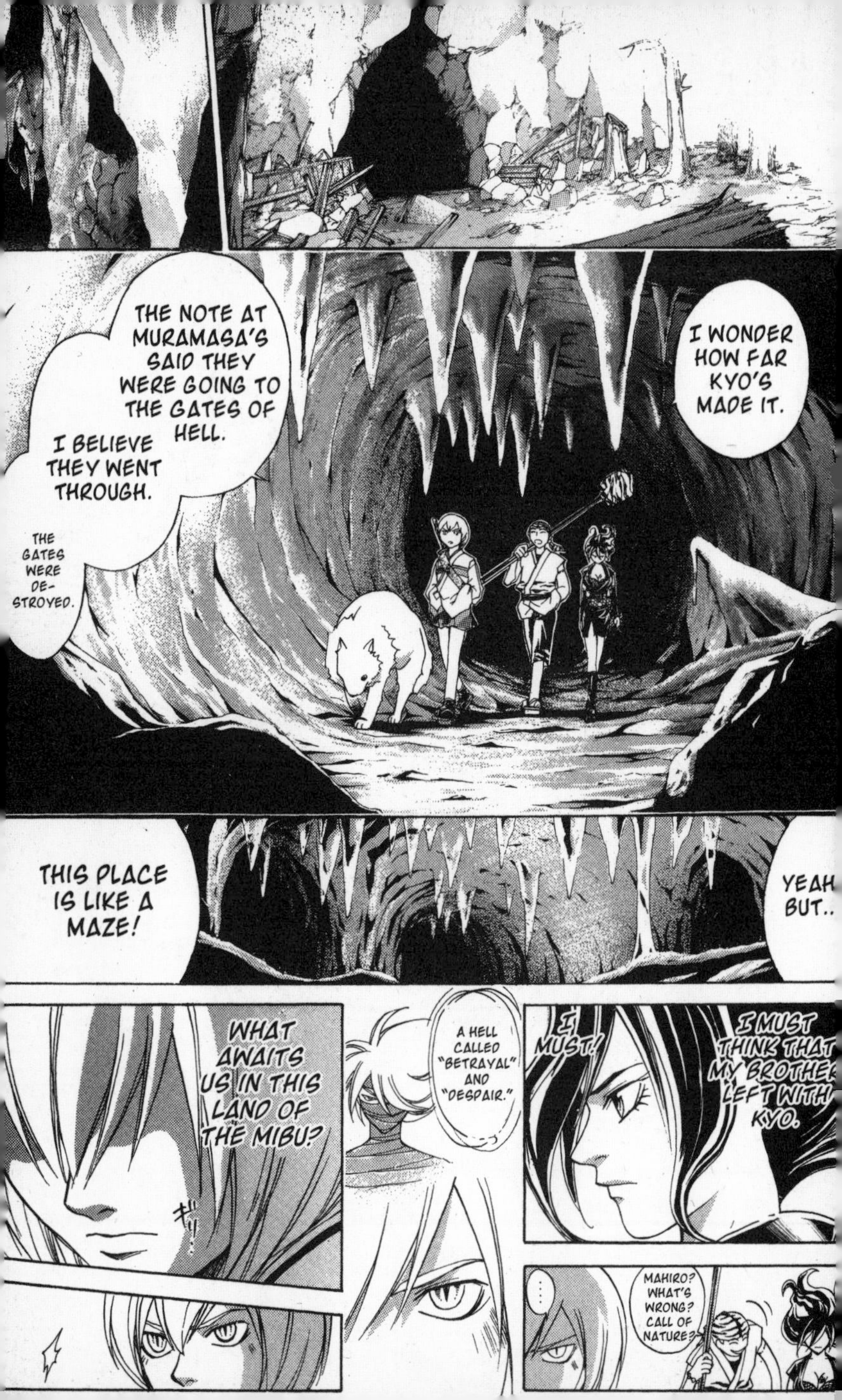

I WONDER HOW FAR KYO'S MADE IT.
THE NOTE AT MURAMASA'S SAID THEY WERE GOING TO THE GATES OF HELL.
I BELIEVE THEY WENT THROUGH.
THE GATES WERE DE-STROYED.
YEAH BUT...
THIS PLACE IS LIKE A MAZE!
I MUST THINK THAT MY BROTHE LEFT WITH KYO.
I MUST!
A HELL CALLED "BETRAYAL" AND "DESPAIR."
WHAT AWAITS US IN THIS LAND OF THE MIBU?
MAHIRO? WHAT'S WRONG? CALL OF NATURE?
....

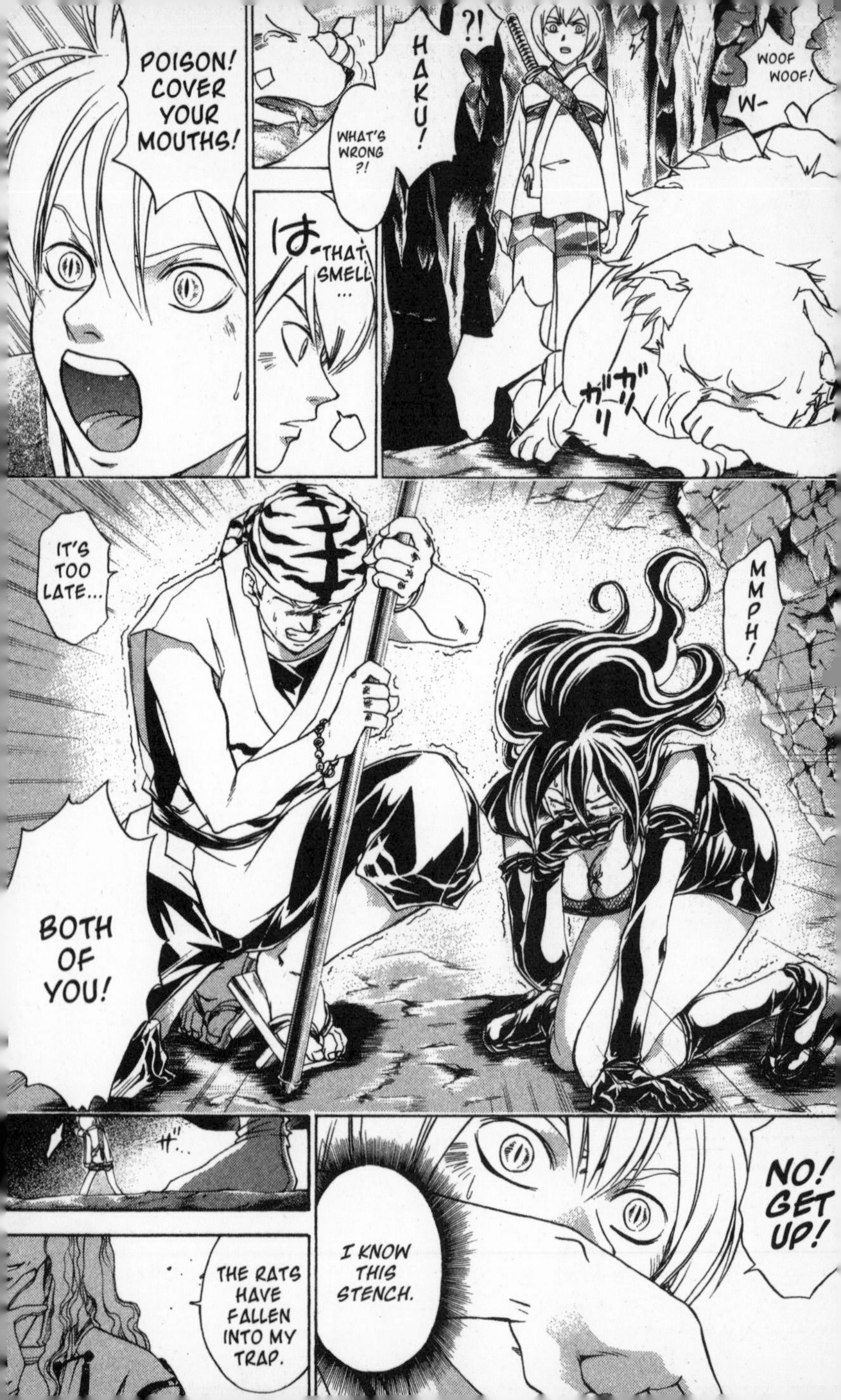
WOOF WOOF!
W-
?!
HAKU!
ガリ ガリ
WHAT'S WRONG ?!
は-
THAT SMELL ...
POISON! COVER YOUR MOUTHS!
MMPH!
IT'S TOO LATE...
BOTH OF YOU!
NO! GET UP!
I KNOW THIS STENCH.
THE RATS HAVE FALLEN INTO MY TRAP.

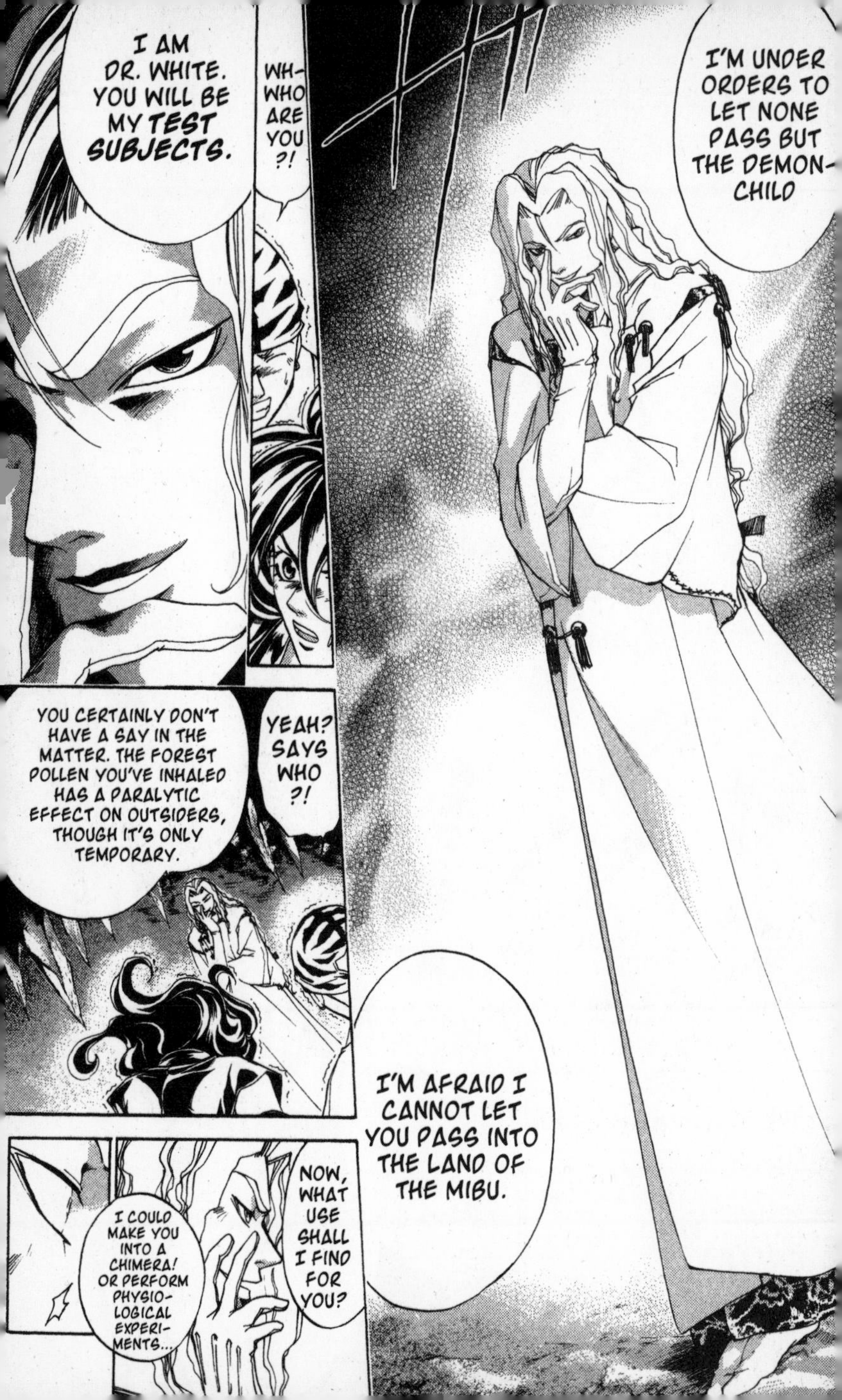
I'M UNDER ORDERS TO LET NONE PASS BUT THE DEMON-CHILD
I'M AFRAID I CANNOT LET YOU PASS INTO THE LAND OF THE MIBU.
WH-WHO ARE YOU?!
I AM DR. WHITE. YOU WILL BE MY **TEST SUBJECTS.**
YEAH? SAYS WHO?!
YOU CERTAINLY DON'T HAVE A SAY IN THE MATTER. THE FOREST POLLEN YOU'VE INHALED HAS A PARALYTIC EFFECT ON OUTSIDERS, THOUGH IT'S ONLY TEMPORARY.
NOW, WHAT USE SHALL I FIND FOR YOU?
I COULD MAKE YOU INTO A CHIMERA! OR PERFORM PHYSIO-LOGICAL EXPERI-MENTS...

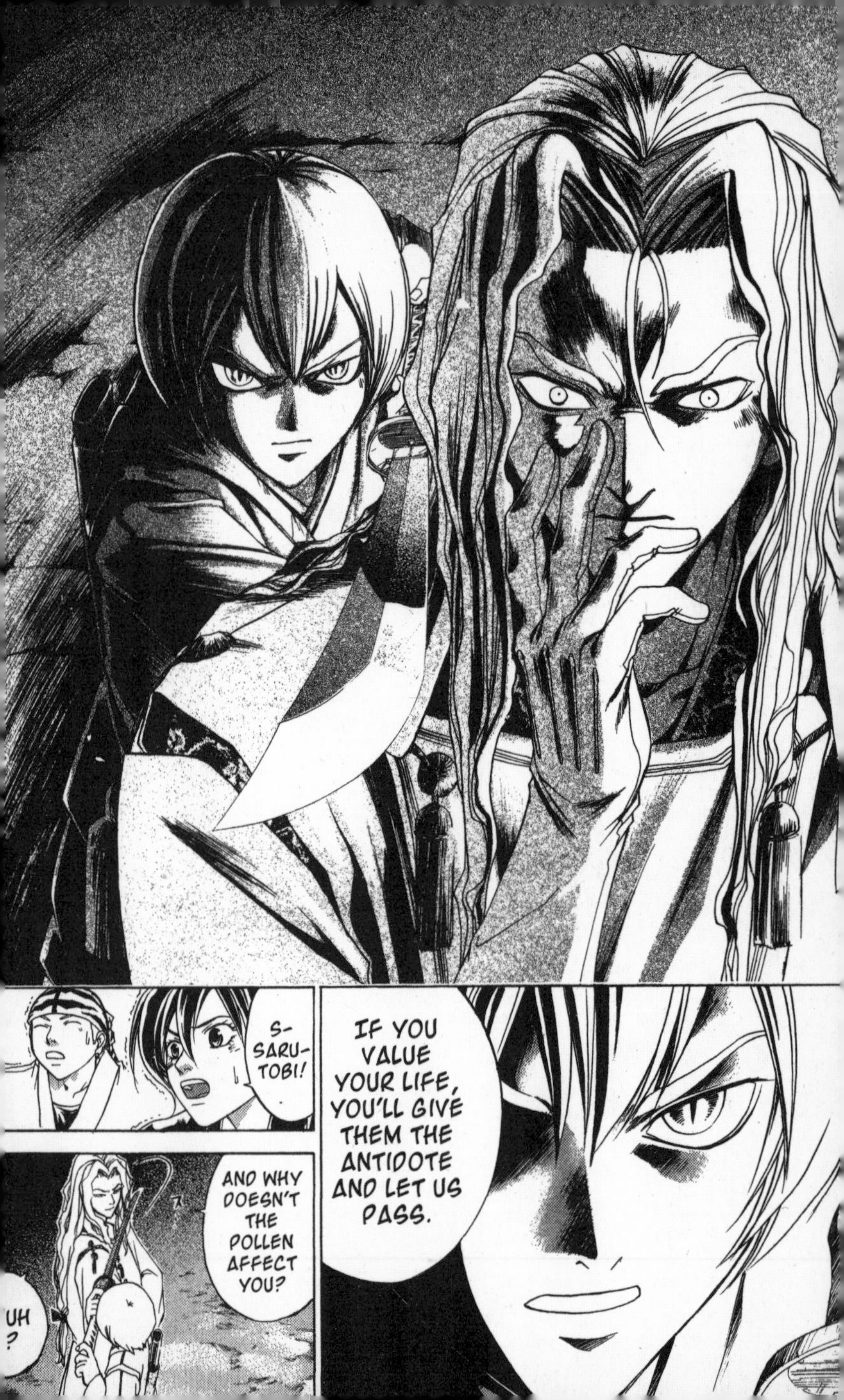
IF YOU VALUE YOUR LIFE, YOU'LL GIVE THEM THE ANTIDOTE AND LET US PASS.
S-SARUTOBI!
AND WHY DOESN'T THE POLLEN AFFECT YOU?
UH?

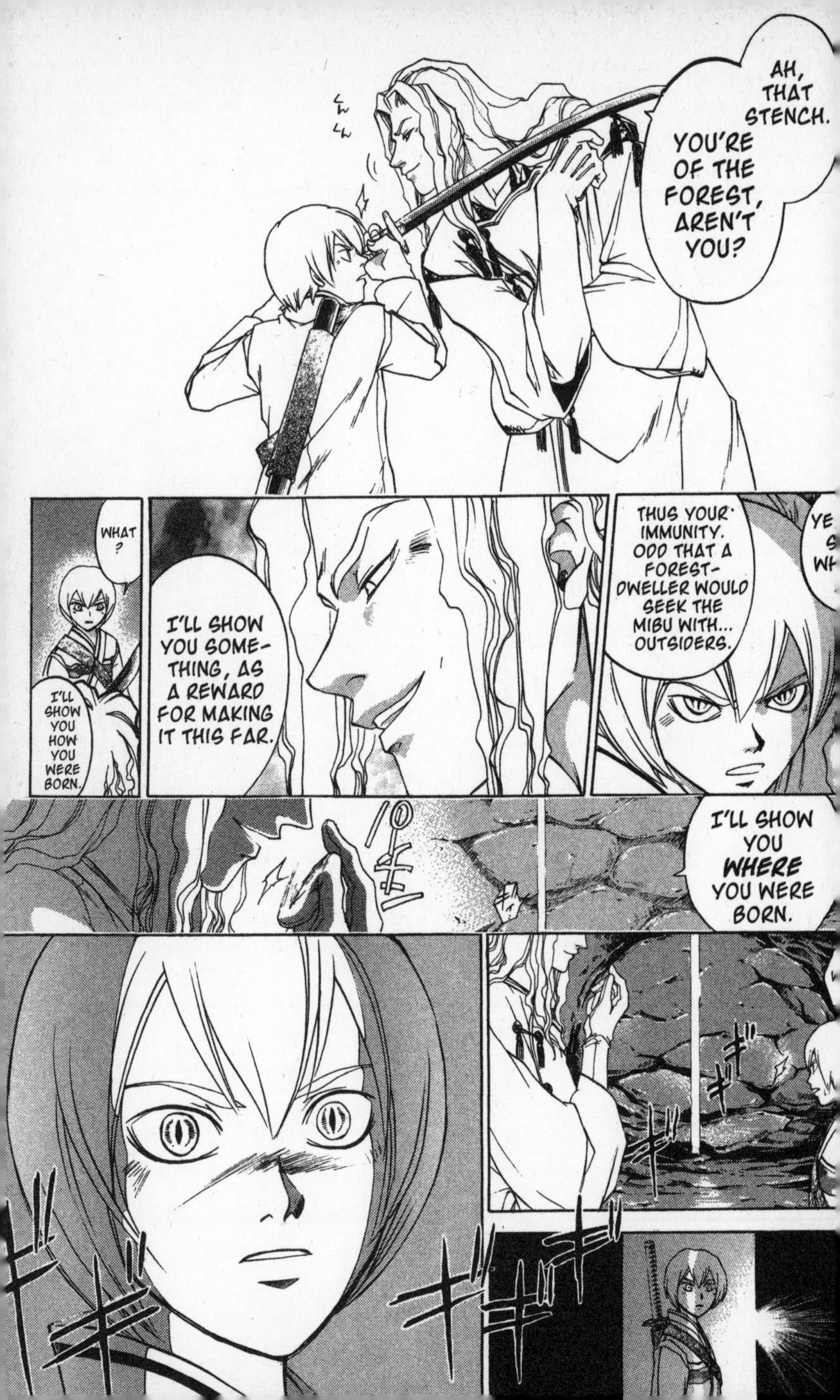
AH, THAT STENCH. YOU'RE OF THE FOREST, AREN'T YOU?
THUS YOUR IMMUNITY. ODD THAT A FOREST-DWELLER WOULD SEEK THE MIBU WITH... OUTSIDERS.
I'LL SHOW YOU SOME-THING, AS A REWARD FOR MAKING IT THIS FAR.
WHAT?
I'LL SHOW YOU HOW YOU WERE BORN.
I'LL SHOW YOU *WHERE* YOU WERE BORN.

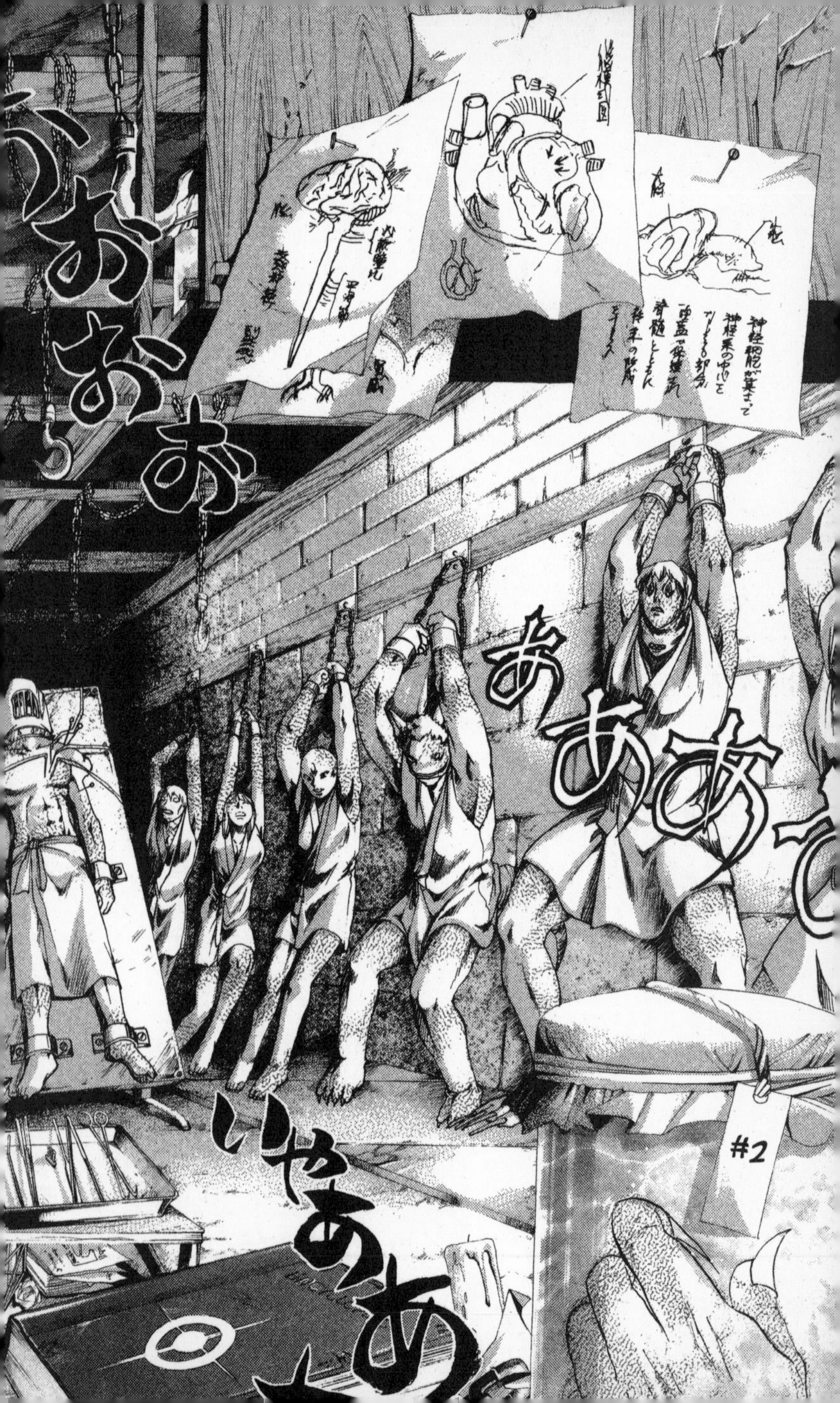

ふぉおおお
あああぁ
いやああ
#2

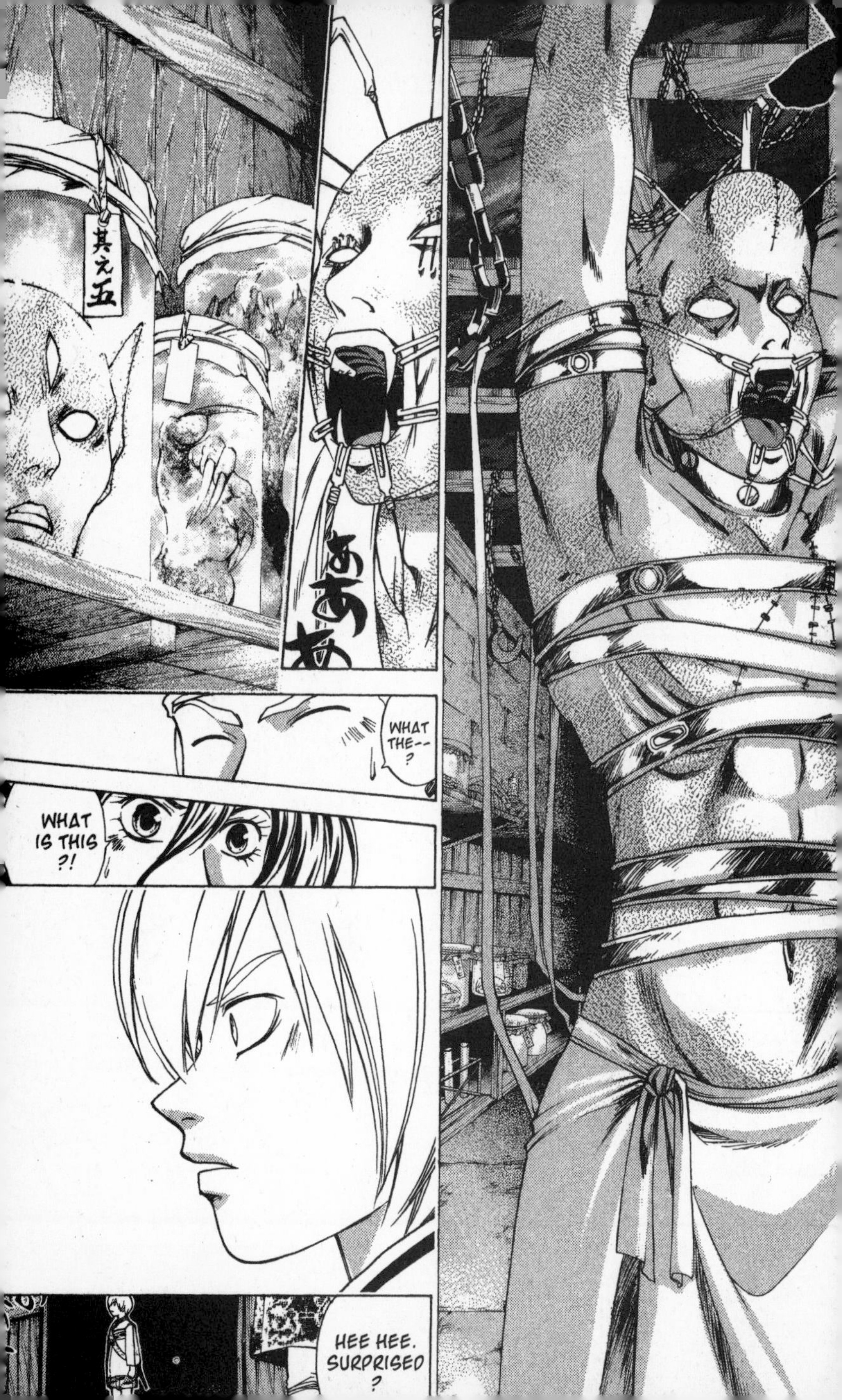
其え五
WHAT THE--?
WHAT IS THIS?!
HEE HEE. SURPRISED?

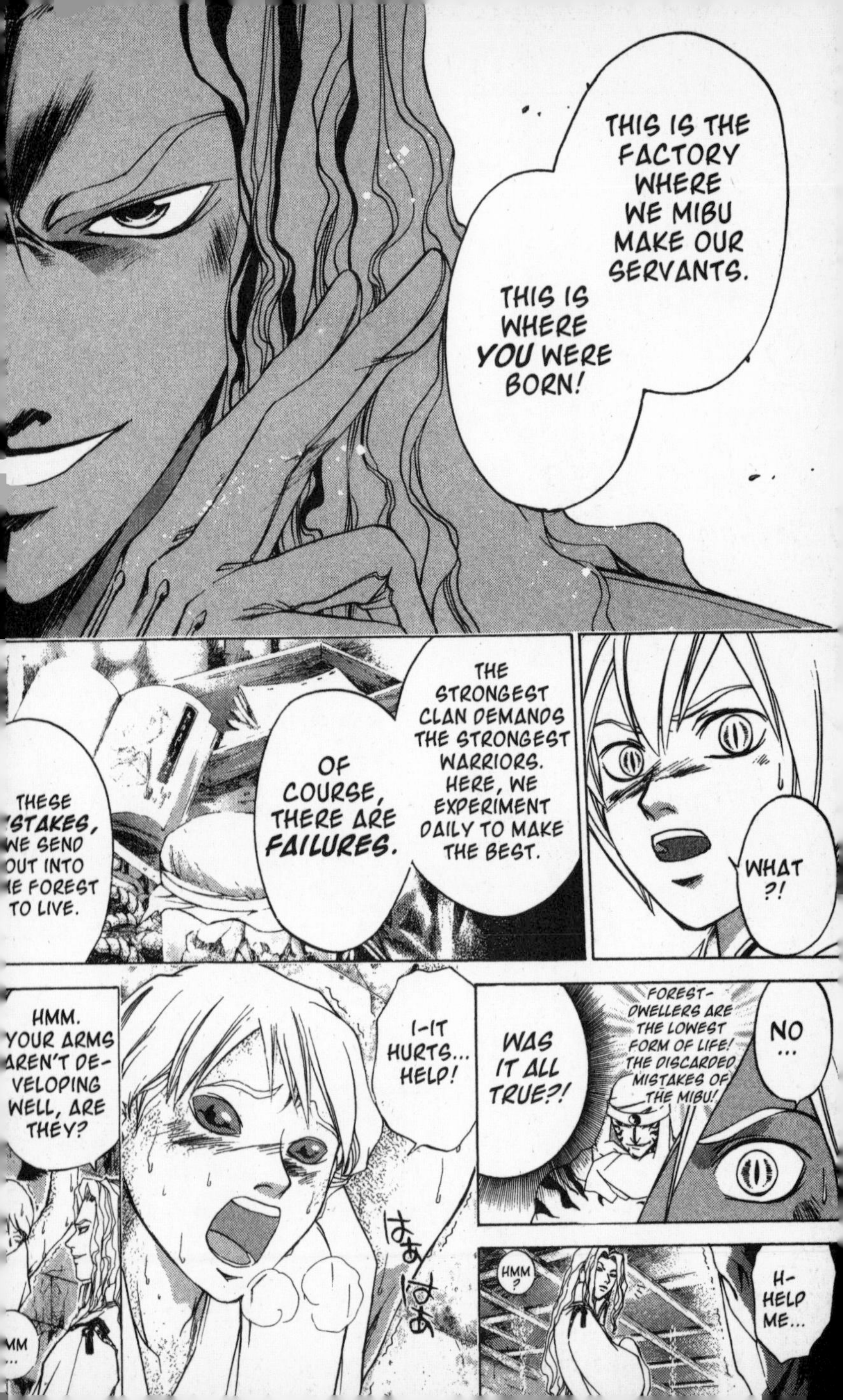
THIS IS THE FACTORY WHERE WE MIBU MAKE OUR SERVANTS.
THIS IS WHERE *YOU* WERE BORN!
WHAT ?!
THE STRONGEST CLAN DEMANDS THE STRONGEST WARRIORS. HERE, WE EXPERIMENT DAILY TO MAKE THE BEST.
OF COURSE, THERE ARE **FAILURES.**
THESE **STAKES,** WE SEND OUT INTO E FOREST TO LIVE.
NO ...
FOREST-DWELLERS ARE THE LOWEST FORM OF LIFE! THE DISCARDED MISTAKES OF THE MIBU!
WAS IT ALL TRUE?!
H-HELP ME...
HMM ?
I-IT HURTS... HELP!
はあはあ
HMM. YOUR ARMS AREN'T DE-VELOPING WELL, ARE THEY?
MM ...

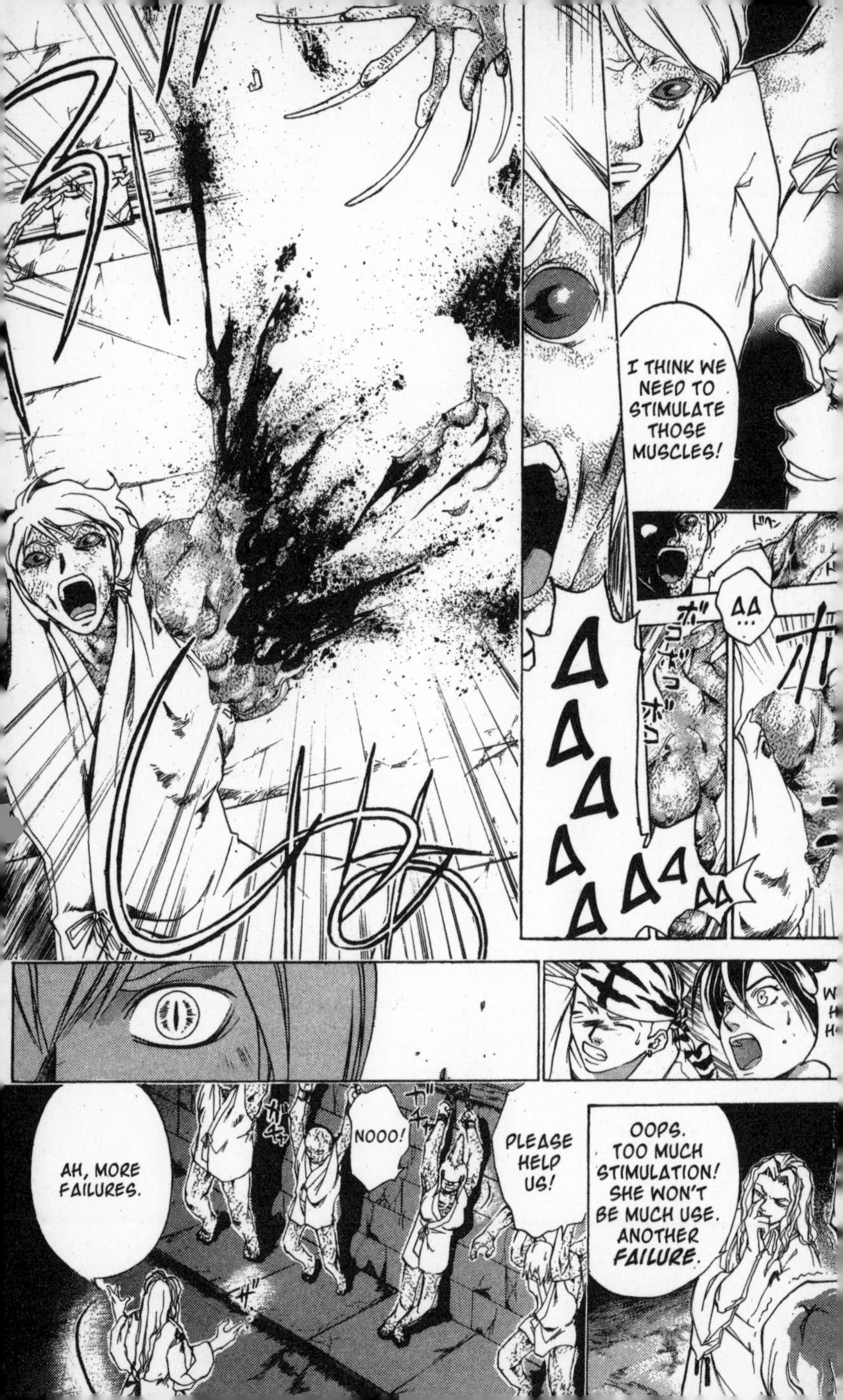
I THINK WE NEED TO STIMULATE THOSE MUSCLES!
AA...
AAAAAAAAAAA
OOPS. TOO MUCH STIMULATION! SHE WON'T BE MUCH USE. ANOTHER FAILURE.
PLEASE HELP US!
NOOO!
AH, MORE FAILURES.

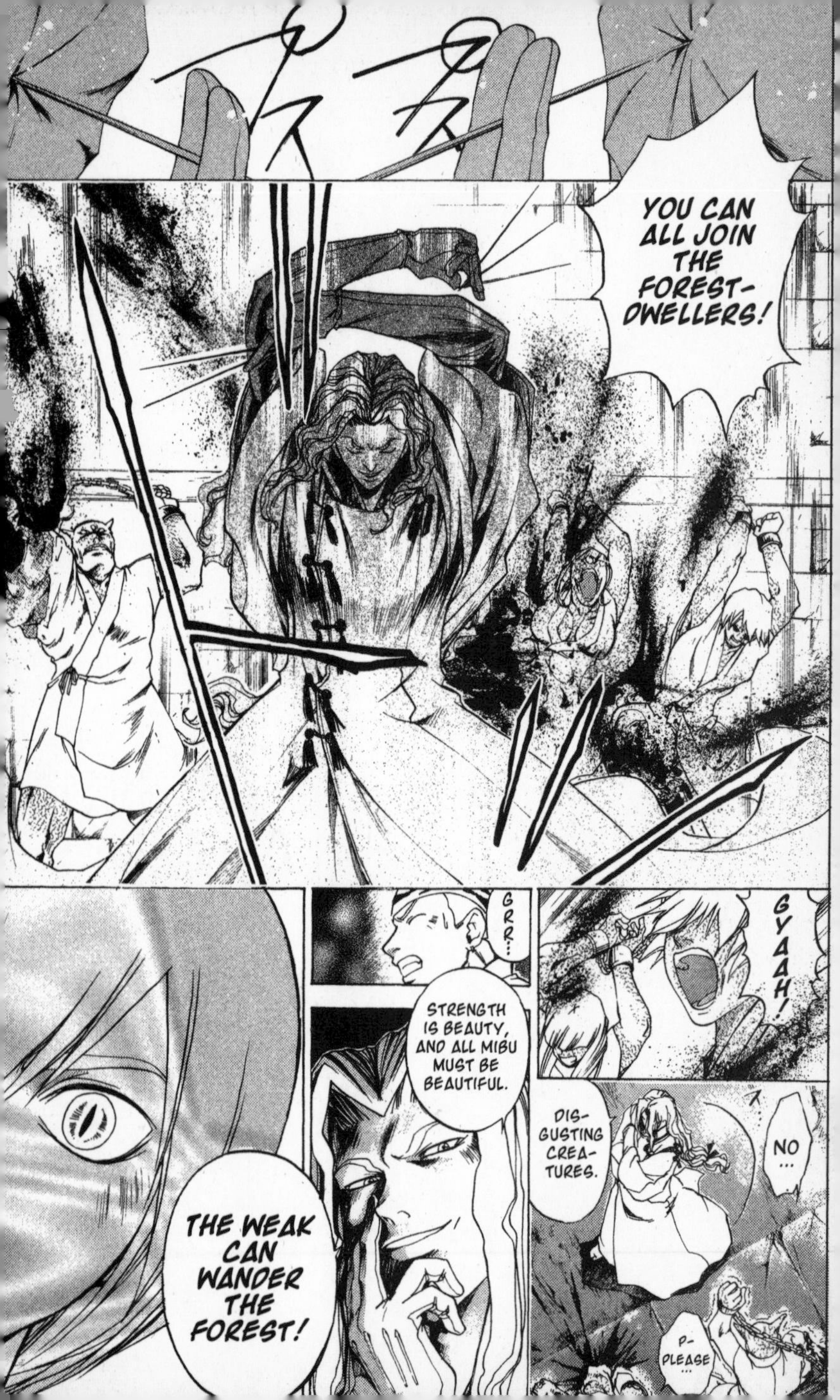
YOU CAN ALL JOIN THE FOREST-DWELLERS!
GYAAH!
NO...
DIS-GUSTING CREA-TURES.
P-PLEASE...
GRR...
STRENGTH IS BEAUTY, AND ALL MIBU MUST BE BEAUTIFUL.
THE WEAK CAN WANDER THE FOREST!

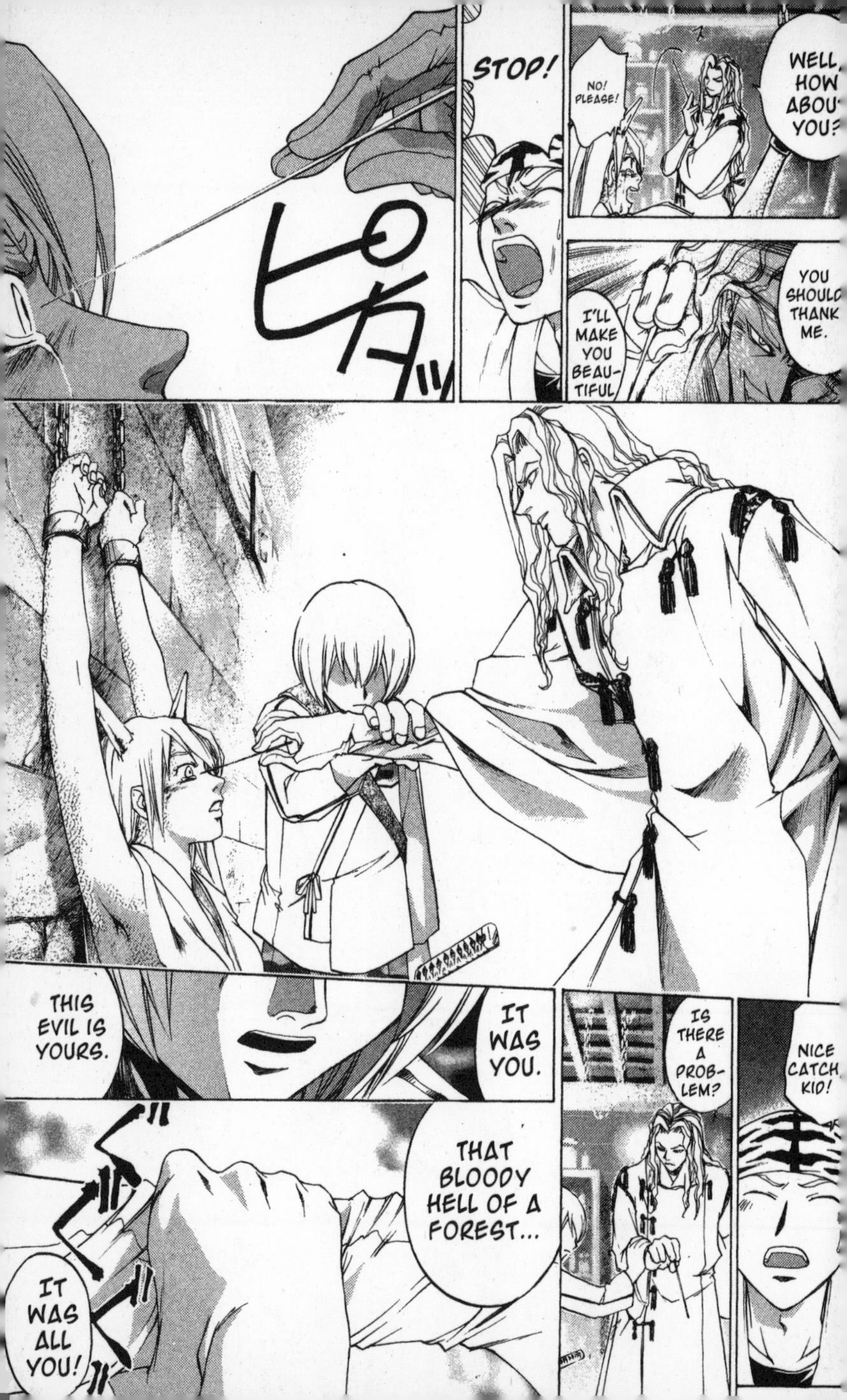
WELL, HOW ABOUT YOU?
NO! PLEASE!
YOU SHOULD THANK ME.
I'LL MAKE YOU BEAU-TIFUL
STOP!
ピカッ
NICE CATCH, KID!
IS THERE A PROB-LEM?
IT WAS YOU.
THIS EVIL IS YOURS.
THAT BLOODY HELL OF A FOREST...
IT WAS ALL YOU!

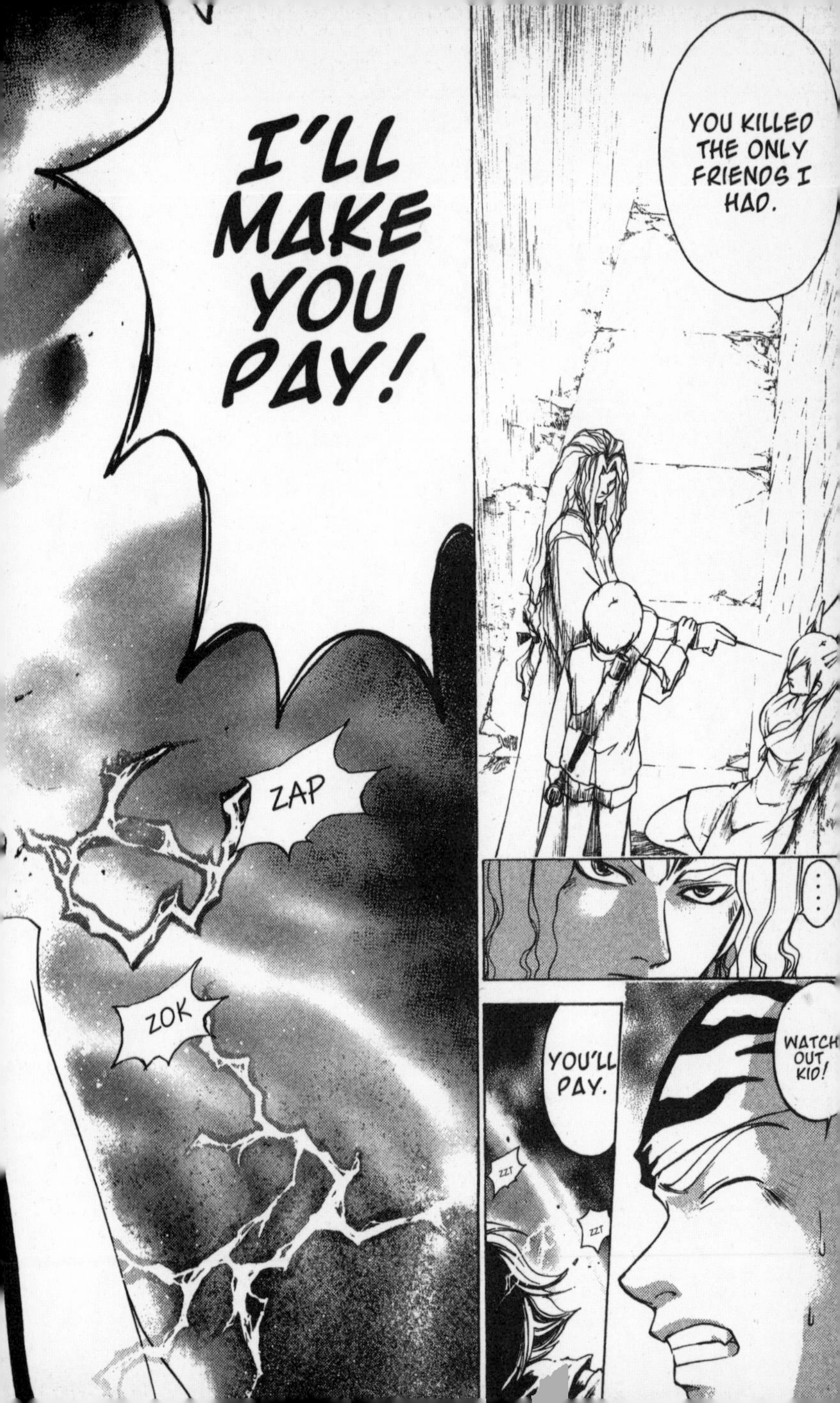
YOU KILLED THE ONLY FRIENDS I HAD.
....
WATCH OUT KID!
YOU'LL PAY.
ZZT
ZZT
I'LL MAKE YOU PAY!
ZAP
ZOK

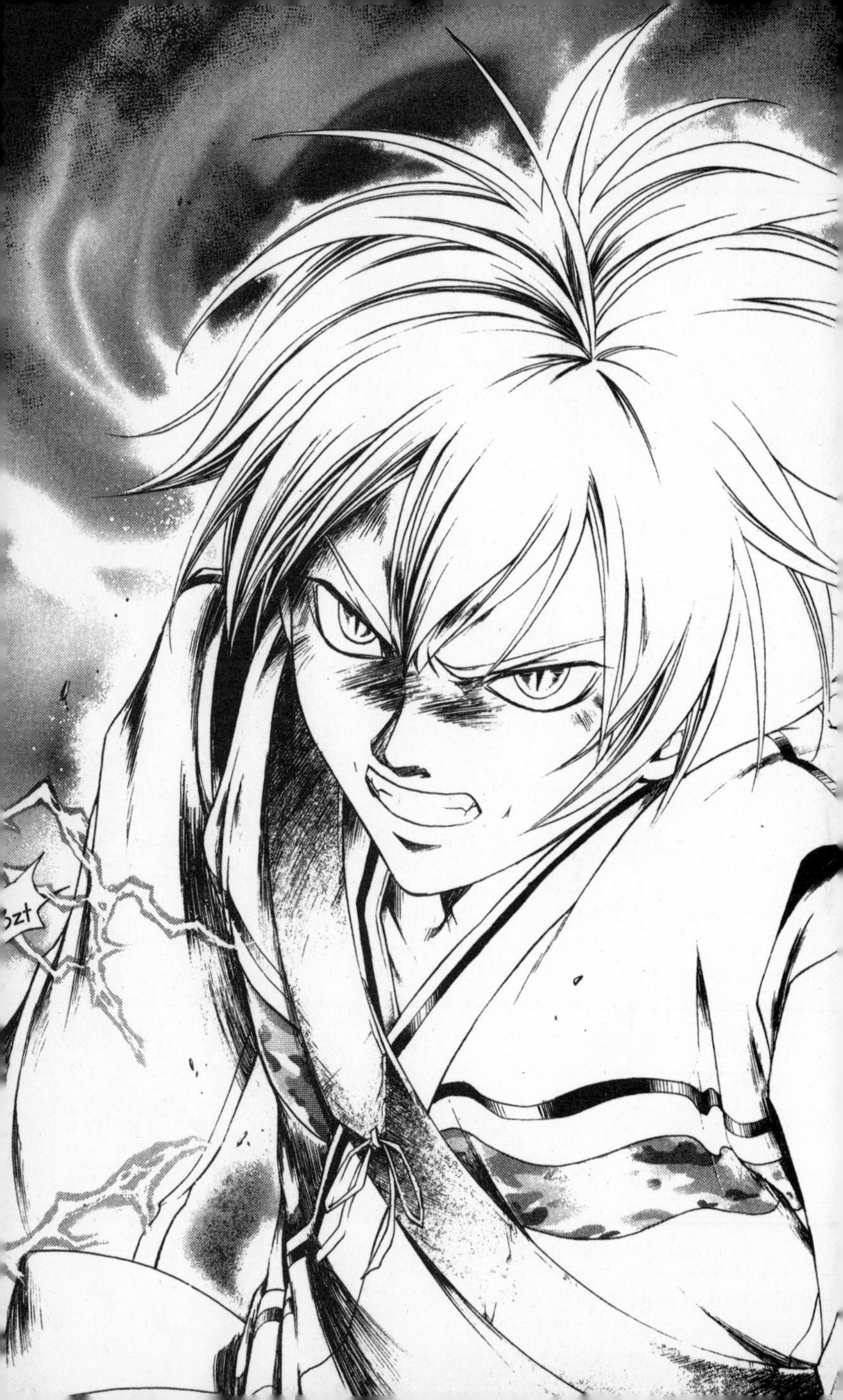

zt

YUYA SPECIAL

kamijyou ni chousen

上条(かみじょう)に挑戦(ちょうせん)!

Try to Draw Like Kamijo Akimine!

SO MANY ENTRIES!!!! (WHY?!) MORE PAGES!

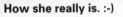

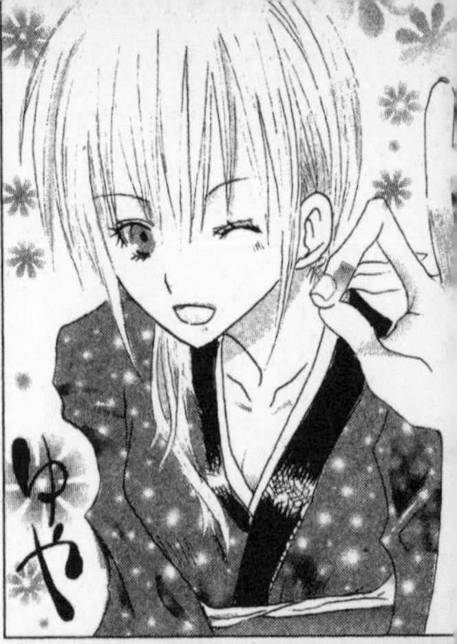
ゆや

Whatever you want. Just ask!

[Teruka Hozeki / Chiba]

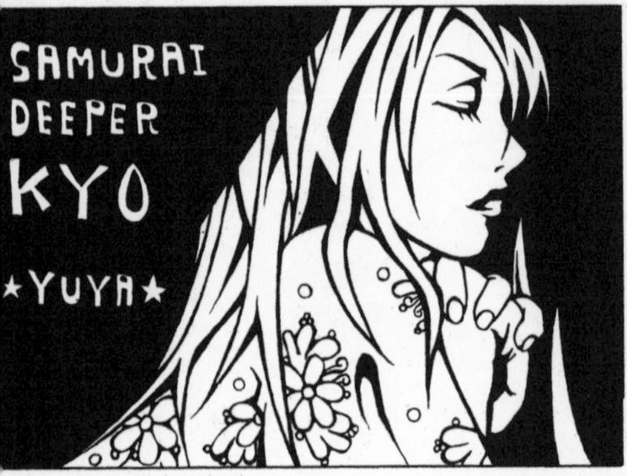
SAMURAI DEEPER KYO
★YUYA★

How she really is. :-)

[Aki Kagaya / Chiba]

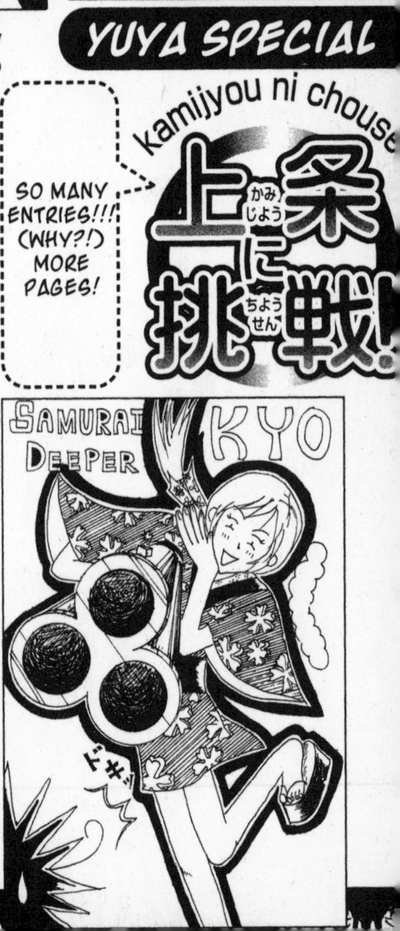
SAMURAI DEEPER KYO
ドキッ

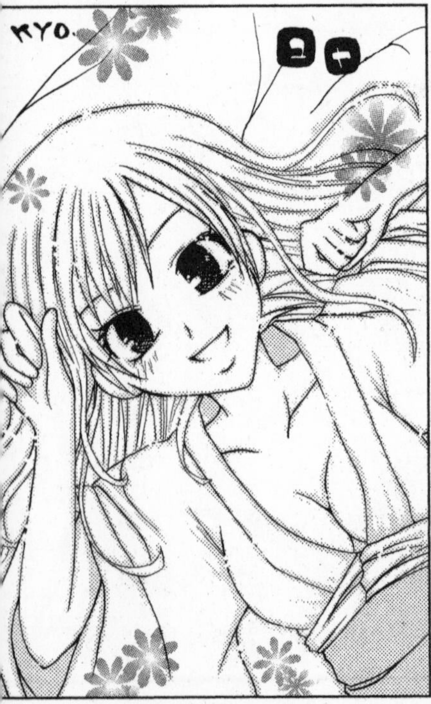
KYO.
ユヤ

I'd like to see this Yuya!

[Juran / Kagoshima]

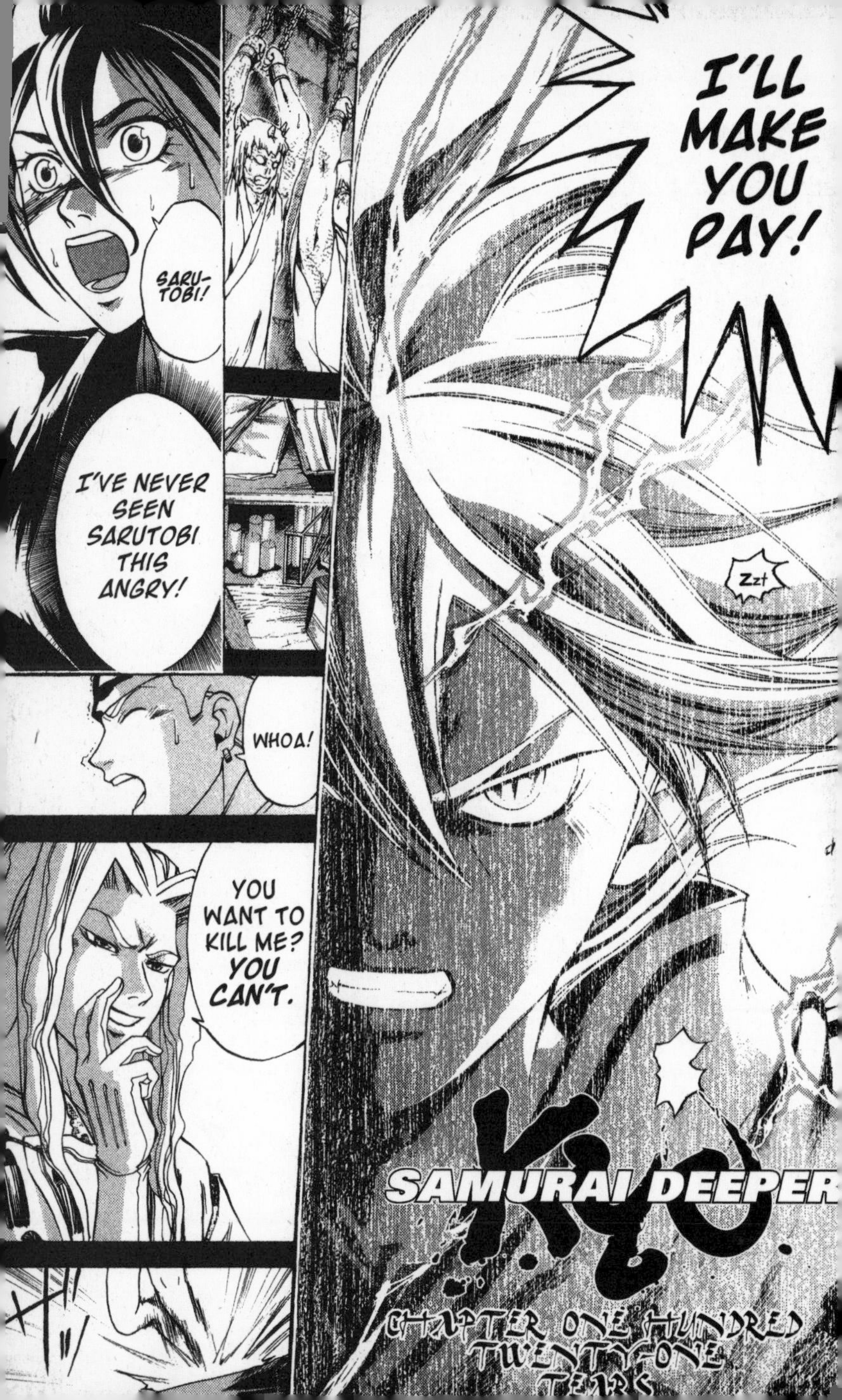
I'LL MAKE YOU PAY!
Zzt
SAMURAI DEEPER
K.Y.O.
CHAPTER ONE HUNDRED TWENTY-ONE
TEARS
SARU-TOBI!
I'VE NEVER SEEN SARUTOBI THIS ANGRY!
WHOA!
YOU WANT TO KILL ME? YOU CAN'T.

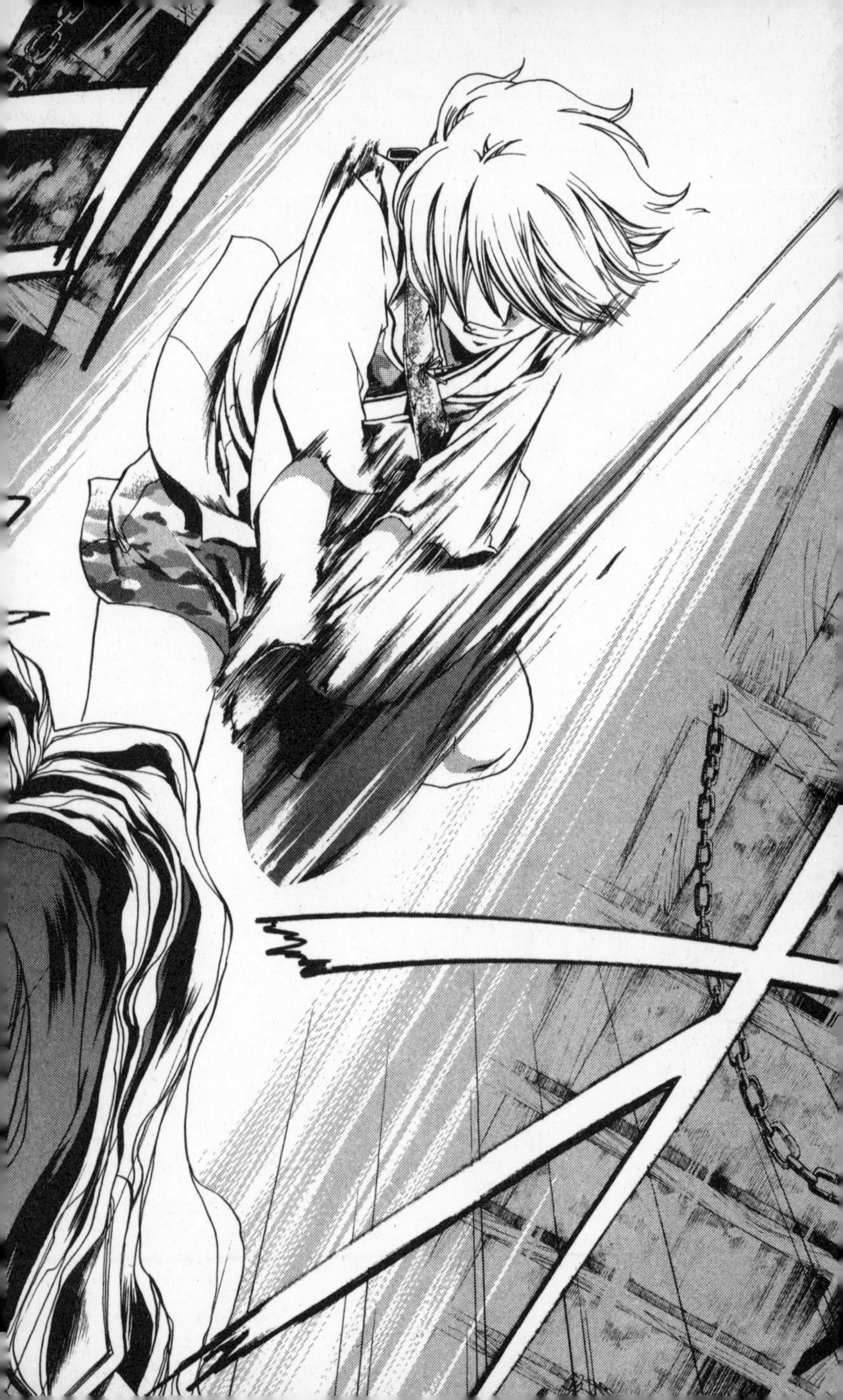

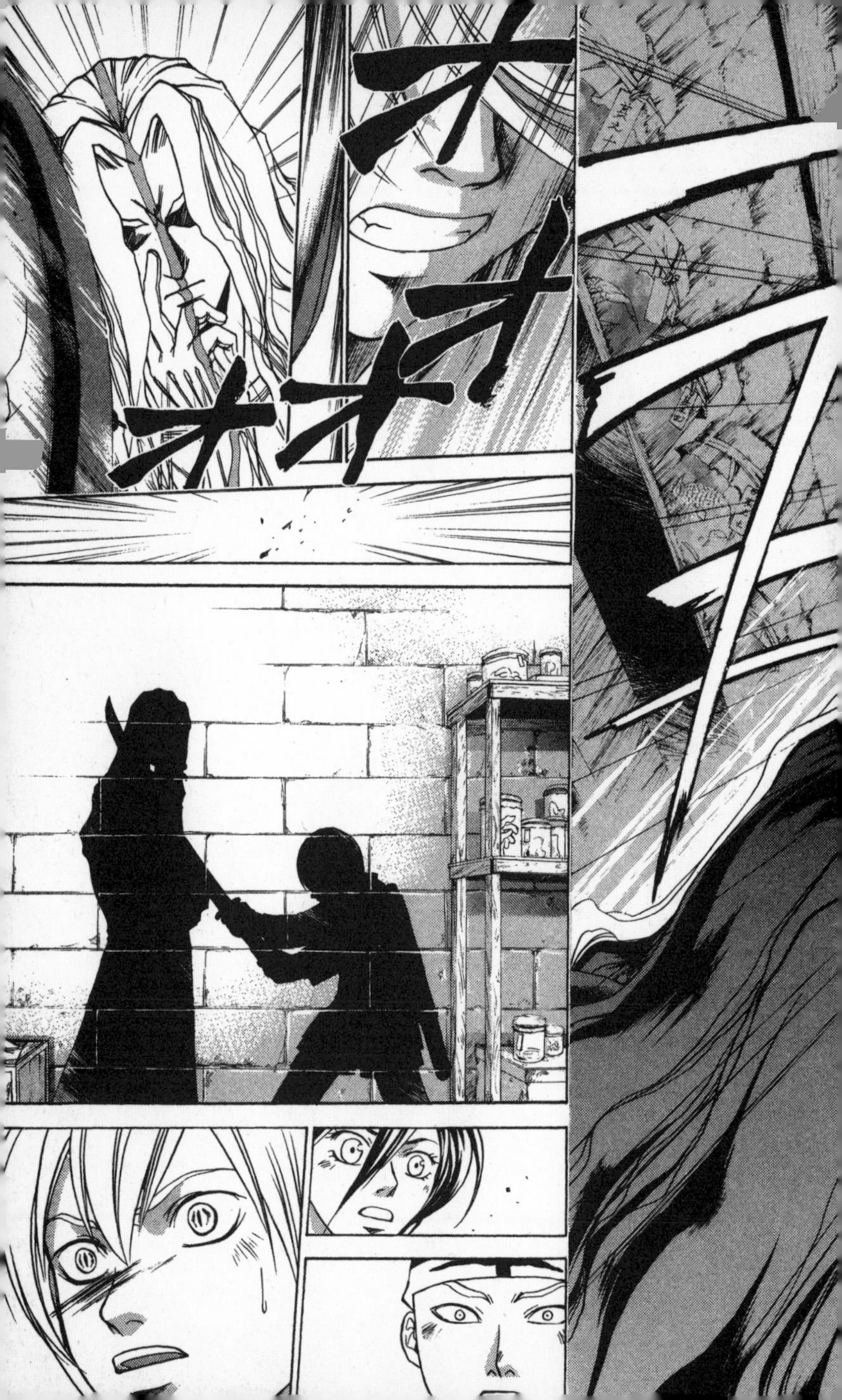
オオオオ

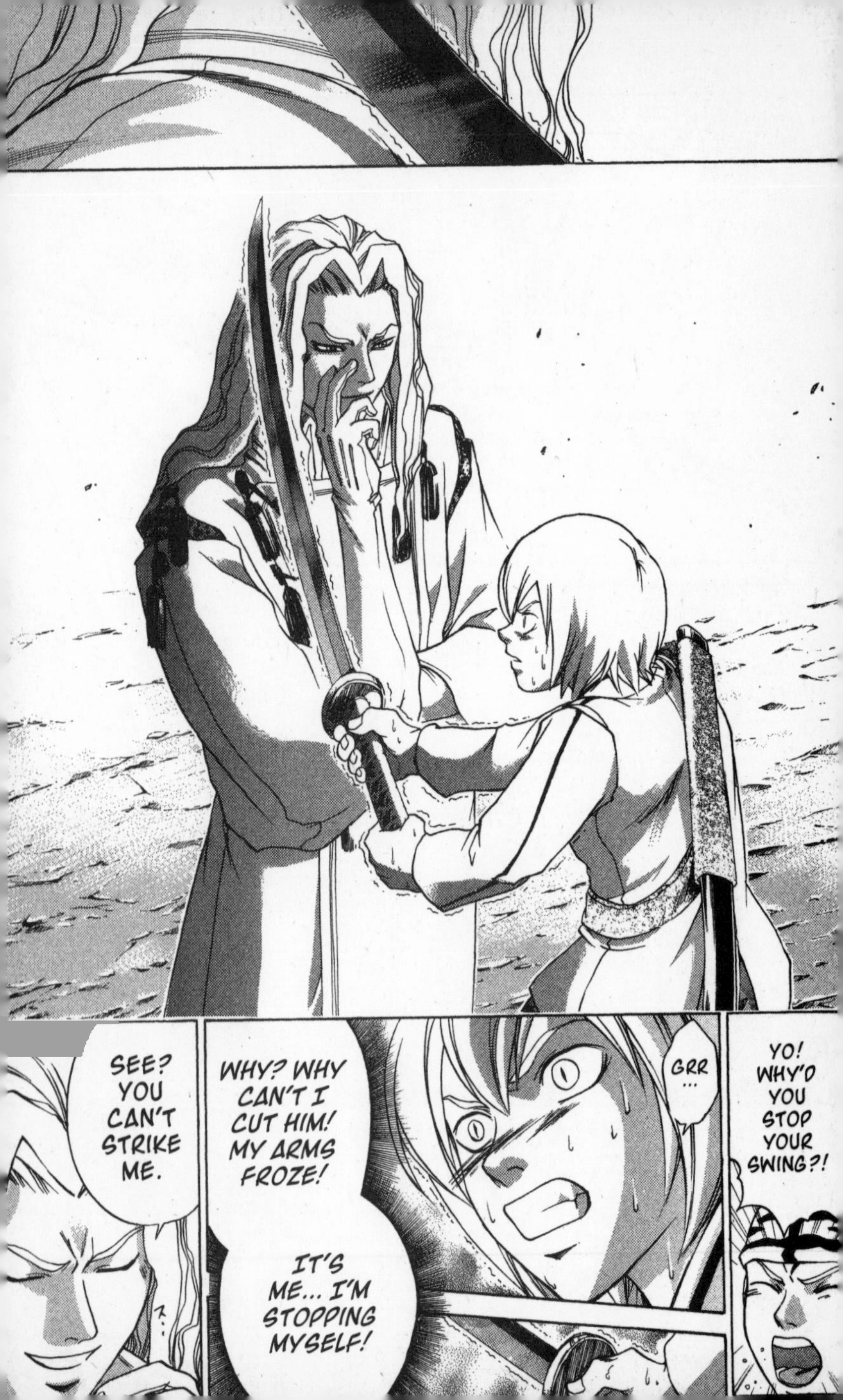
YO! WHY'D YOU STOP YOUR SWING?!
GRR...
WHY? WHY CAN'T I CUT HIM! MY ARMS FROZE!
IT'S ME... I'M STOPPING MYSELF!
SEE? YOU CAN'T STRIKE ME.

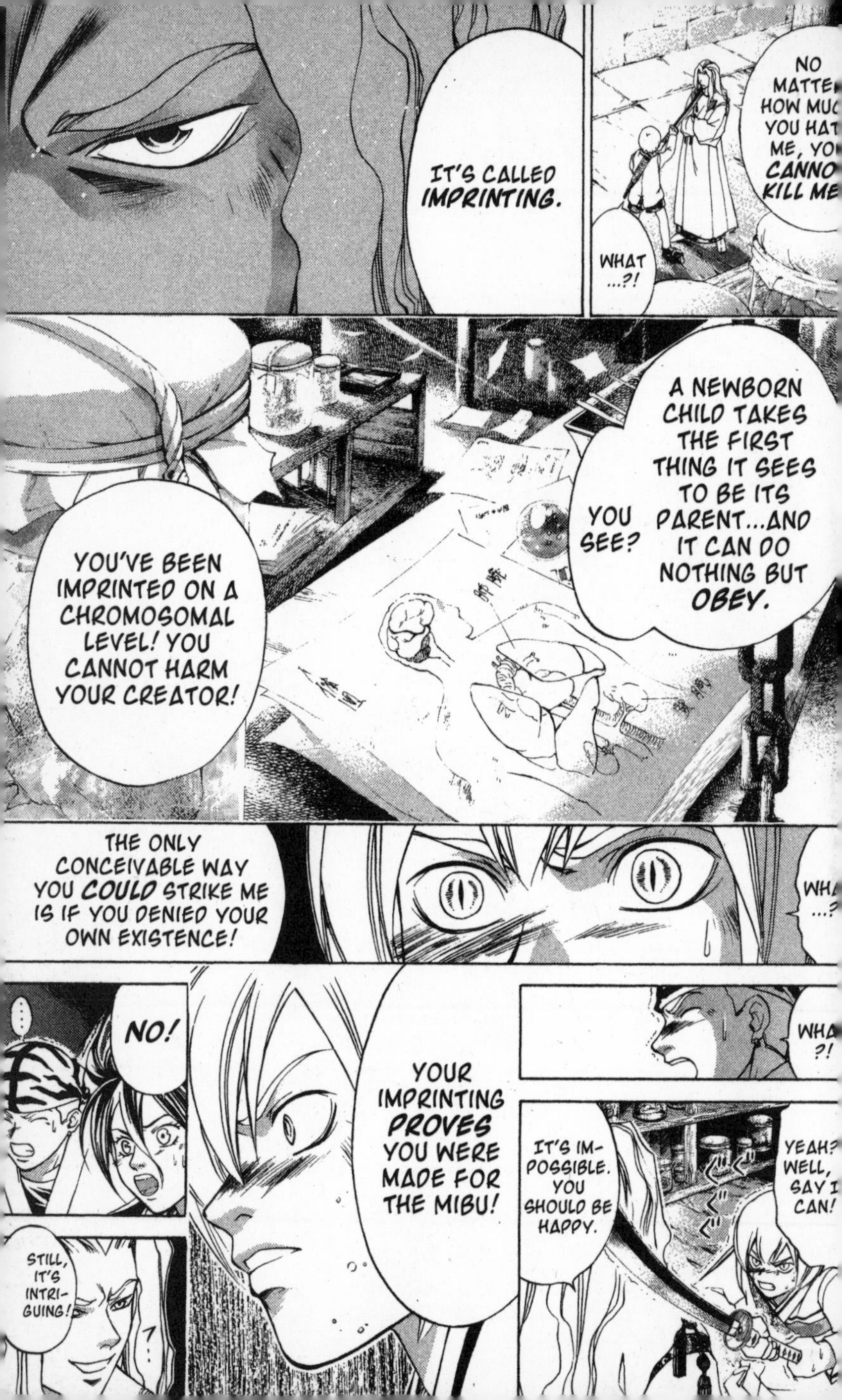
NO MATTE HOW MUC YOU HAT ME, YO CANNO KILL ME
WHAT ...?!
IT'S CALLED IMPRINTING.
A NEWBORN CHILD TAKES THE FIRST THING IT SEES TO BE ITS PARENT...AND IT CAN DO NOTHING BUT OBEY.
YOU SEE?
YOU'VE BEEN IMPRINTED ON A CHROMOSOMAL LEVEL! YOU CANNOT HARM YOUR CREATOR!
WHA ...?
THE ONLY CONCEIVABLE WAY YOU COULD STRIKE ME IS IF YOU DENIED YOUR OWN EXISTENCE!
WHA ?!
YEAH? WELL, SAY I CAN!
IT'S IM-POSSIBLE. YOU SHOULD BE HAPPY.
YOUR IMPRINTING PROVES YOU WERE MADE FOR THE MIBU!
NO!
...
STILL, IT'S INTRI-GUING!

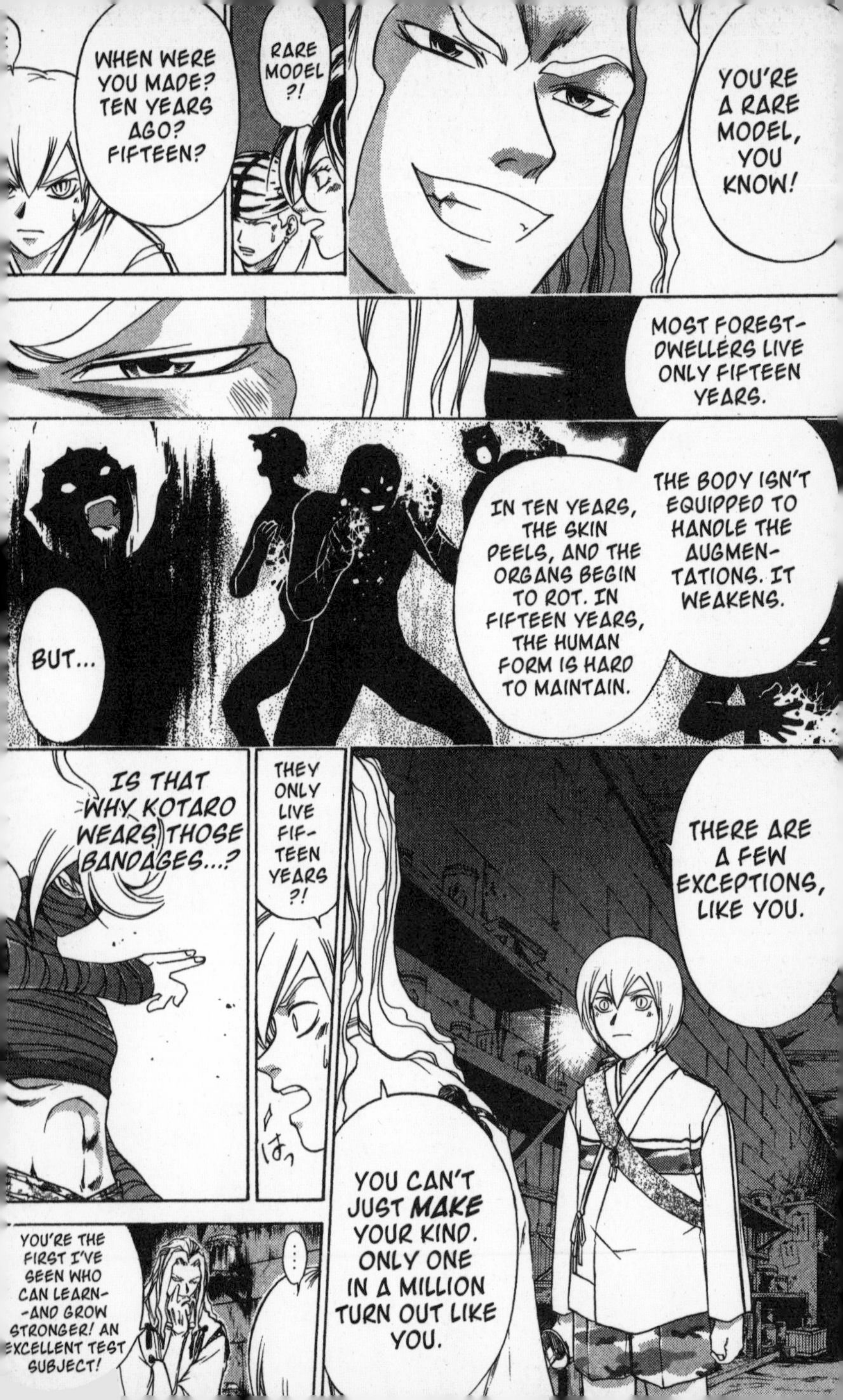
YOU'RE A RARE MODEL, YOU KNOW!
RARE MODEL ?!
WHEN WERE YOU MADE? TEN YEARS AGO? FIFTEEN?
MOST FOREST-DWELLERS LIVE ONLY FIFTEEN YEARS.
THE BODY ISN'T EQUIPPED TO HANDLE THE AUGMENTATIONS. IT WEAKENS.
IN TEN YEARS, THE SKIN PEELS, AND THE ORGANS BEGIN TO ROT. IN FIFTEEN YEARS, THE HUMAN FORM IS HARD TO MAINTAIN.
BUT...
THERE ARE A FEW EXCEPTIONS, LIKE YOU.
YOU CAN'T JUST **MAKE** YOUR KIND. ONLY ONE IN A MILLION TURN OUT LIKE YOU.
THEY ONLY LIVE FIFTEEN YEARS ?!
はっ
IS THAT WHY KOTARO WEARS THOSE BANDAGES...?
....
YOU'RE THE FIRST I'VE SEEN WHO CAN LEARN--AND GROW STRONGER! AN EXCELLENT TEST SUBJECT!

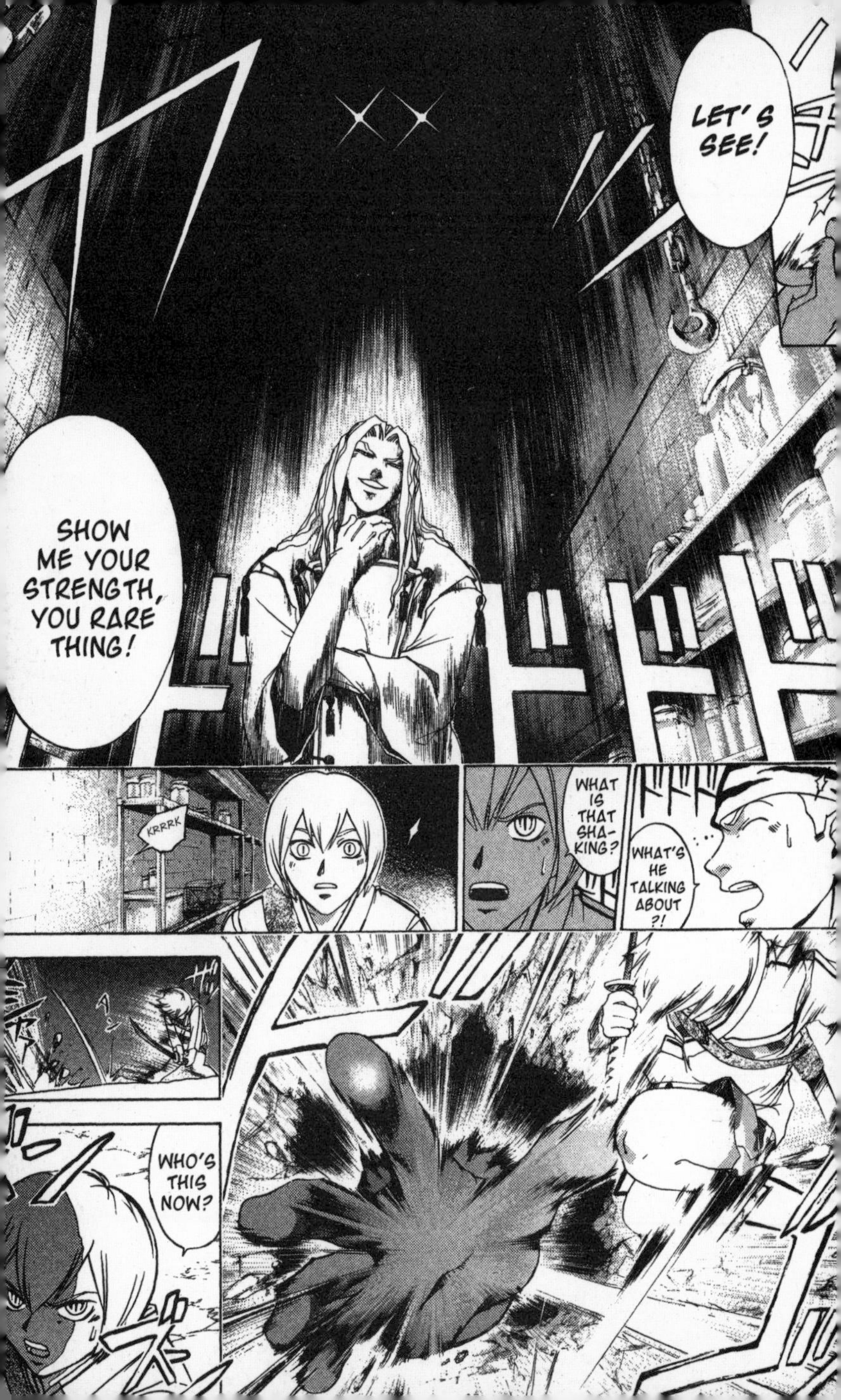
LET'S SEE!
SHOW ME YOUR STRENGTH, YOU RARE THING!
WHAT'S HE TALKING ABOUT?!
WHAT IS THAT SHAKING?
KRRRK
WHO'S THIS NOW?

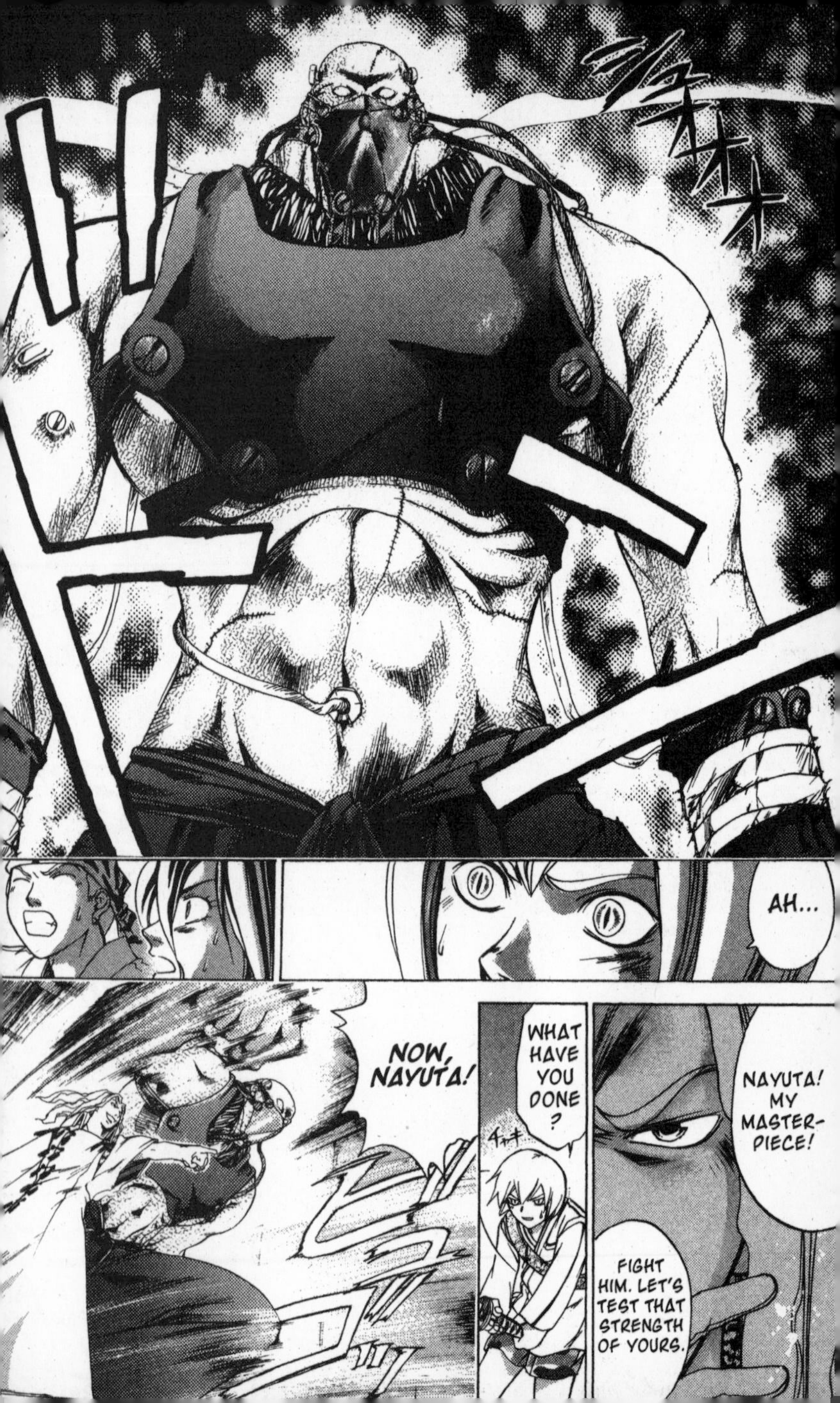
AH...
NAYUTA! MY MASTER-PIECE!
FIGHT HIM. LET'S TEST THAT STRENGTH OF YOURS.
WHAT HAVE YOU DONE?
NOW, NAYUTA!

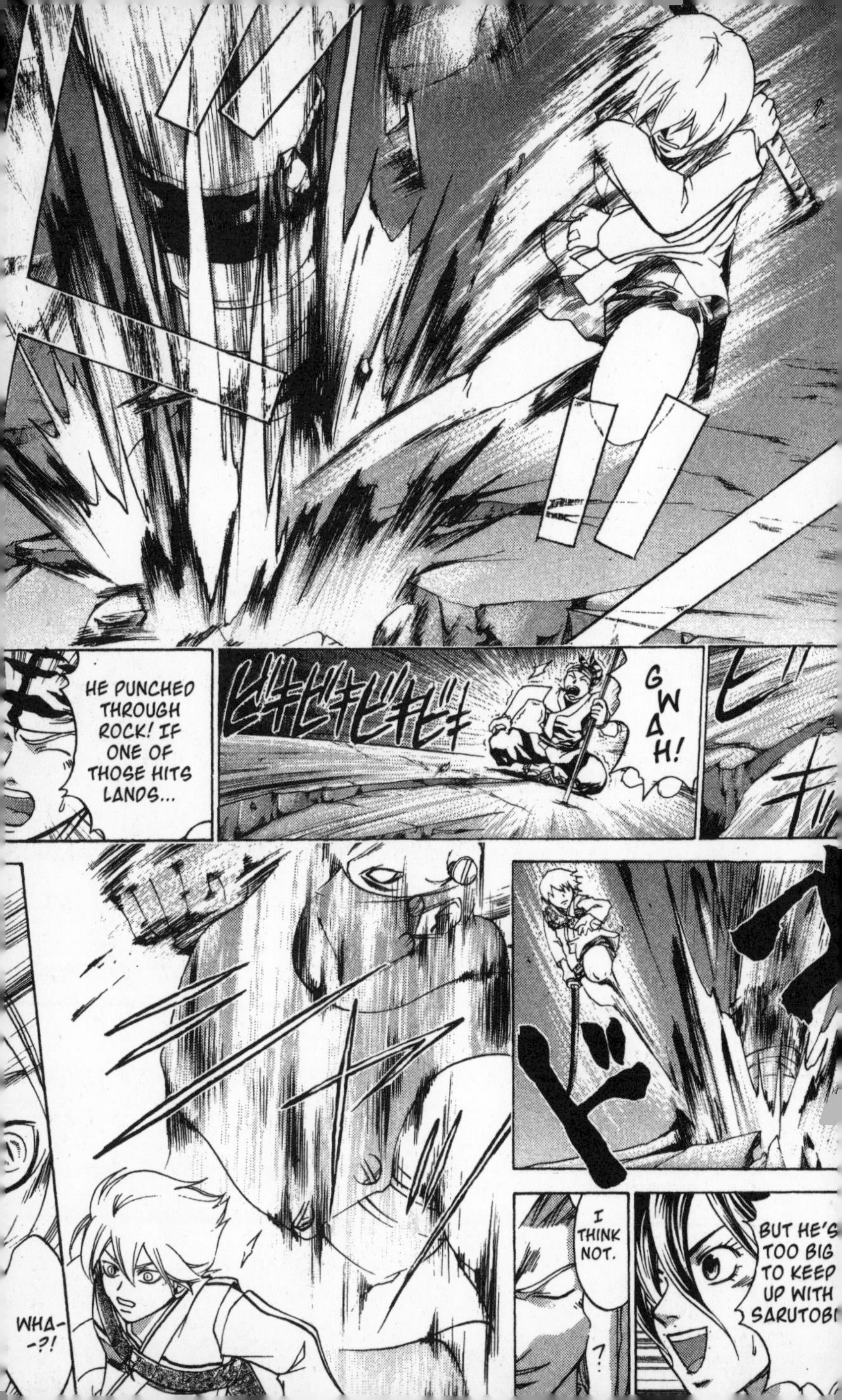
GWAH!
HE PUNCHED THROUGH ROCK! IF ONE OF THOSE HITS LANDS...
BUT HE'S TOO BIG TO KEEP UP WITH SARUTOBI
I THINK NOT.
?
WHA--?!

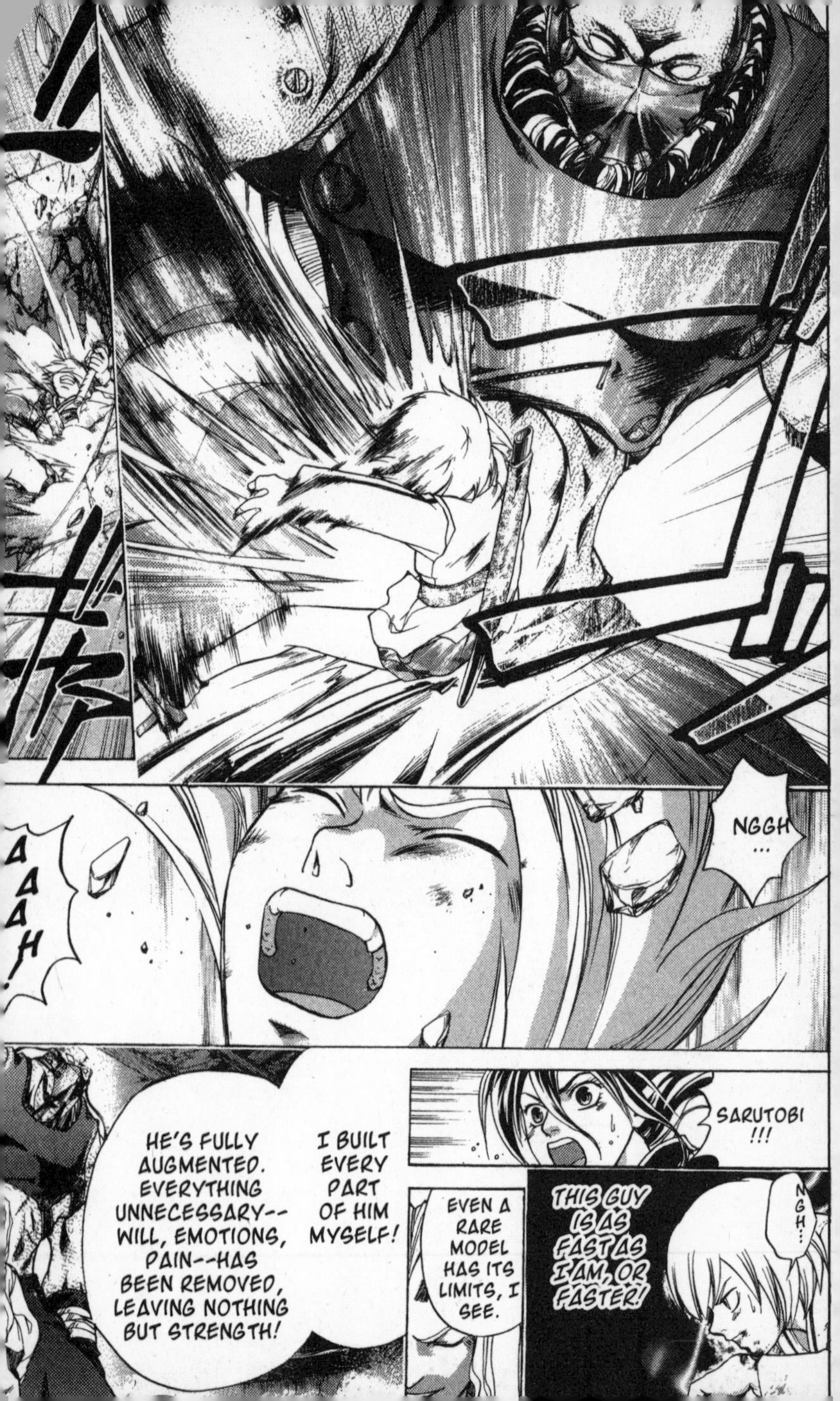
NGGH ...
AAAAH!
SARUTOBI !!!
NGH...
THIS GUY IS AS FAST AS I AM, OR FASTER!
EVEN A RARE MODEL HAS ITS LIMITS, I SEE.
HE'S FULLY AUGMENTED. EVERYTHING UNNECESSARY--WILL, EMOTIONS, PAIN--HAS BEEN REMOVED, LEAVING NOTHING BUT STRENGTH!
I BUILT EVERY PART OF HIM MYSELF!

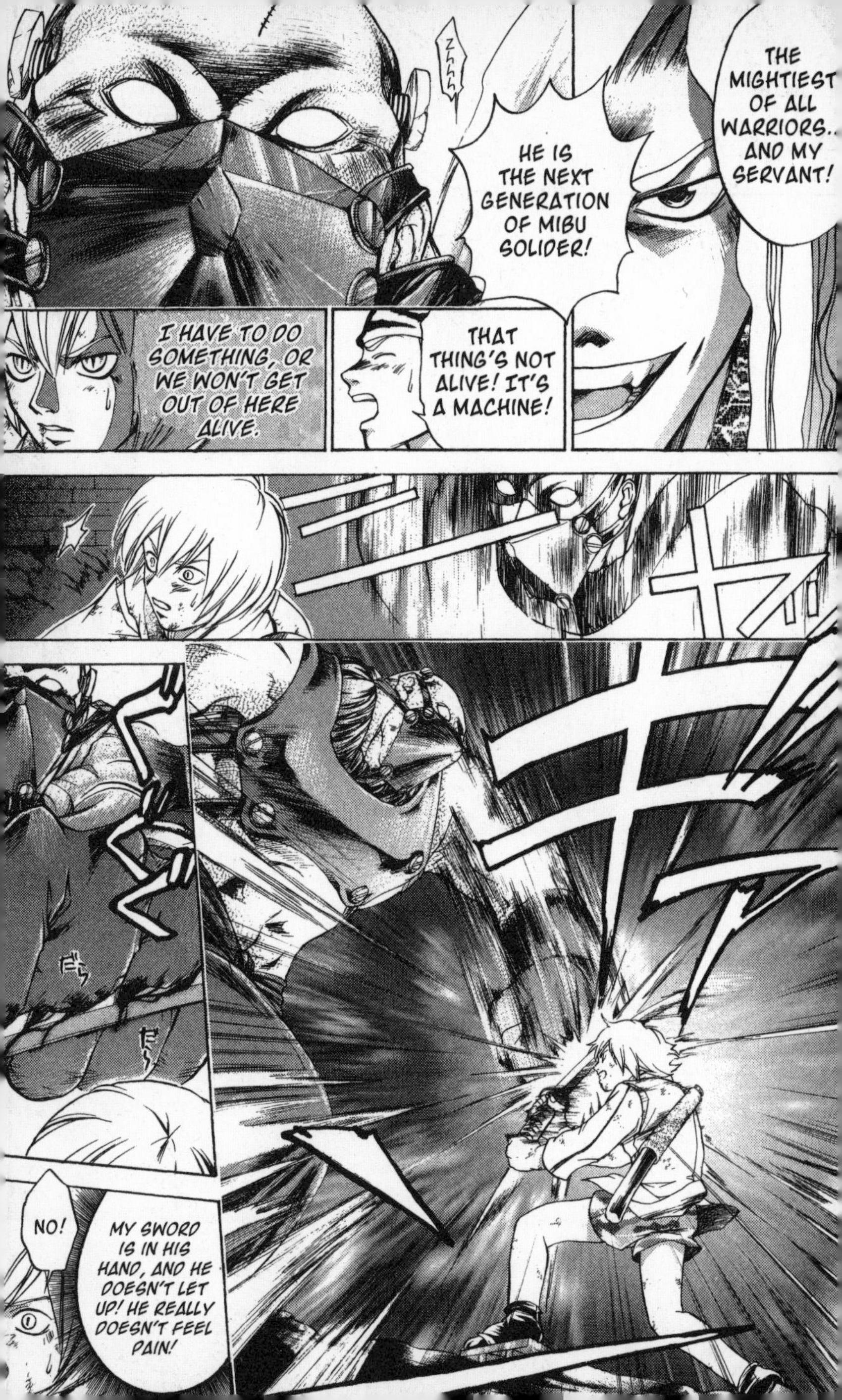
THE MIGHTIEST OF ALL WARRIORS.. AND MY SERVANT!
HE IS THE NEXT GENERATION OF MIBU SOLIDER!
THAT THING'S NOT ALIVE! IT'S A MACHINE!
I HAVE TO DO SOMETHING, OR WE WON'T GET OUT OF HERE ALIVE.
MY SWORD IS IN HIS HAND, AND HE DOESN'T LET UP! HE REALLY DOESN'T FEEL PAIN!
NO!

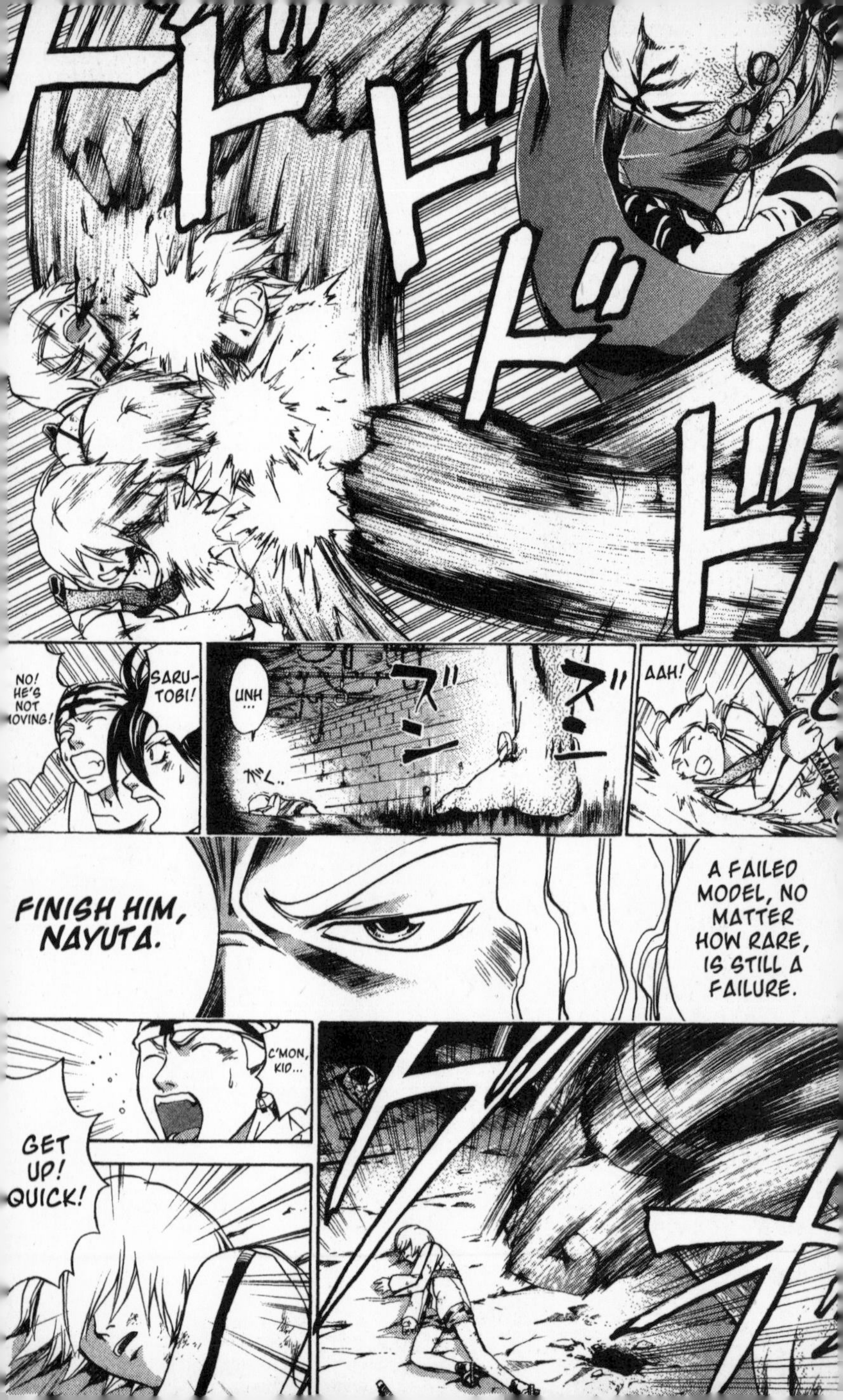

AAH!
UNH...
SARU-TOBI!
NO! HE'S NOT MOVING!
A FAILED MODEL, NO MATTER HOW RARE, IS STILL A FAILURE.
FINISH HIM, NAYUTA.
C'MON, KID...
GET UP! QUICK!

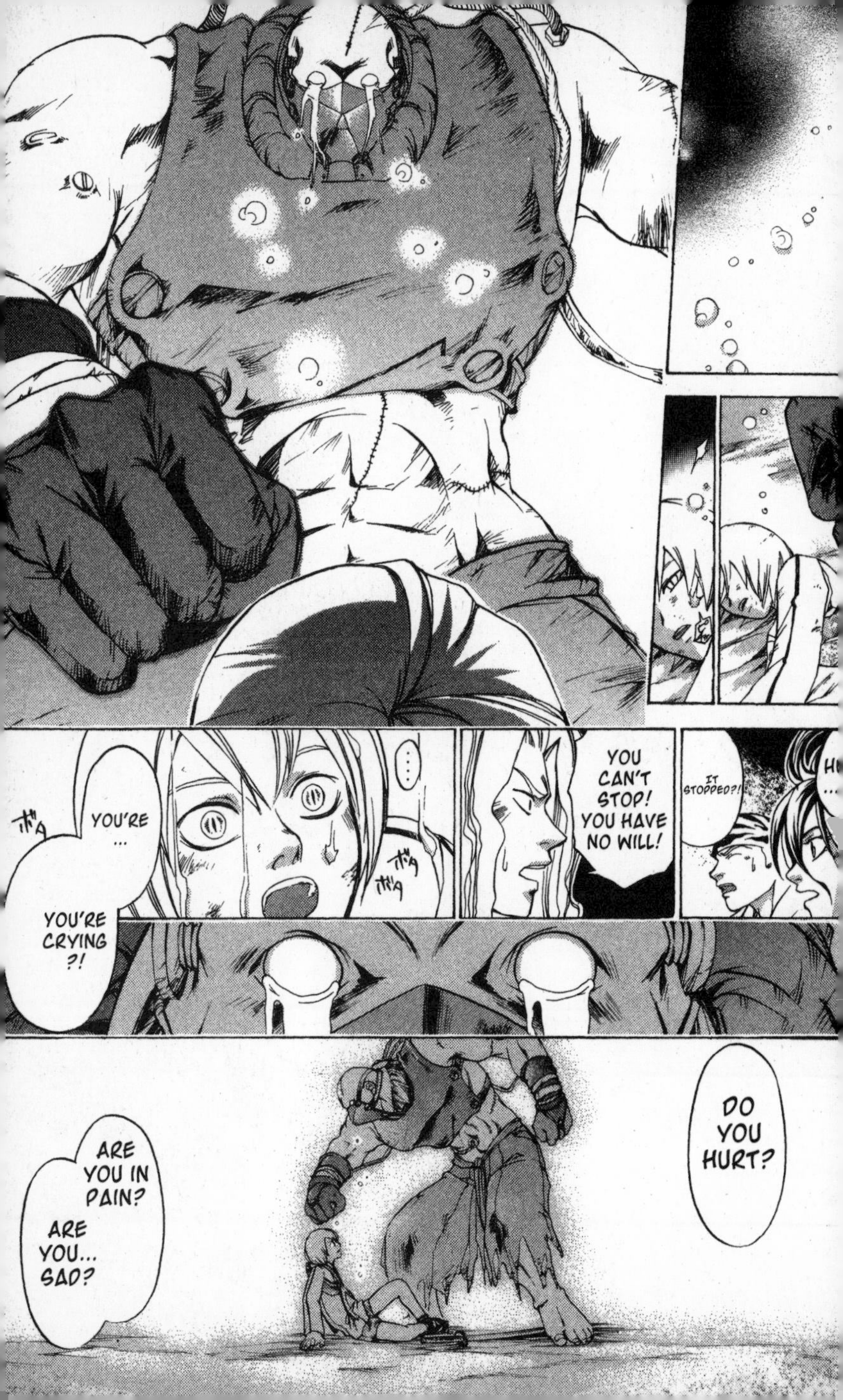
IT STOPPED?!
YOU CAN'T STOP! YOU HAVE NO WILL!
....
YOU'RE ...
YOU'RE CRYING ?!
DO YOU HURT?
ARE YOU IN PAIN?
ARE YOU... SAD?

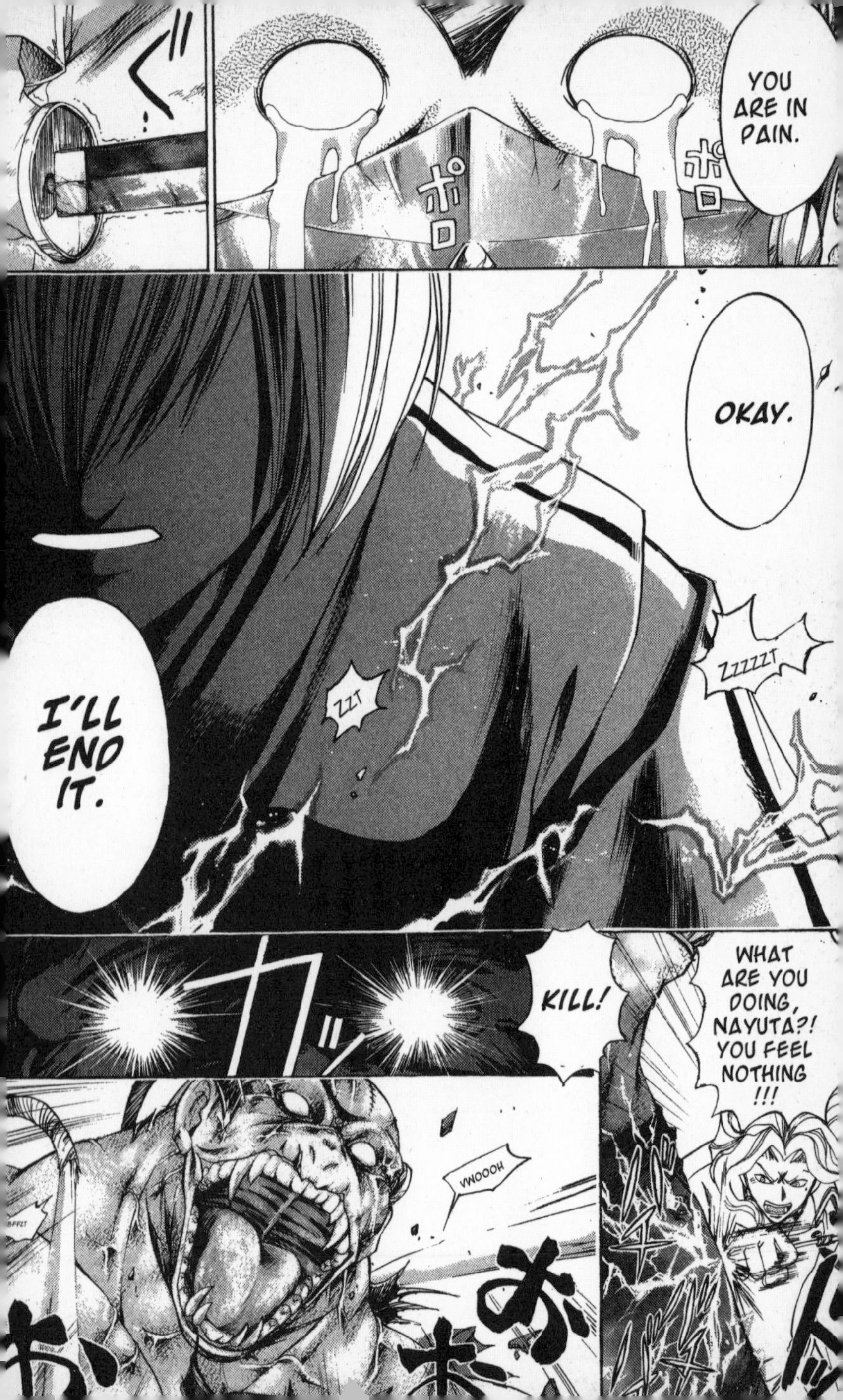
YOU ARE IN PAIN.
ポロ
ポロ
OKAY.
ZZZZZT
ZZT
I'LL END IT.
WHAT ARE YOU DOING, NAYUTA?! YOU FEEL NOTHING!!!
KILL!
VWOOOH

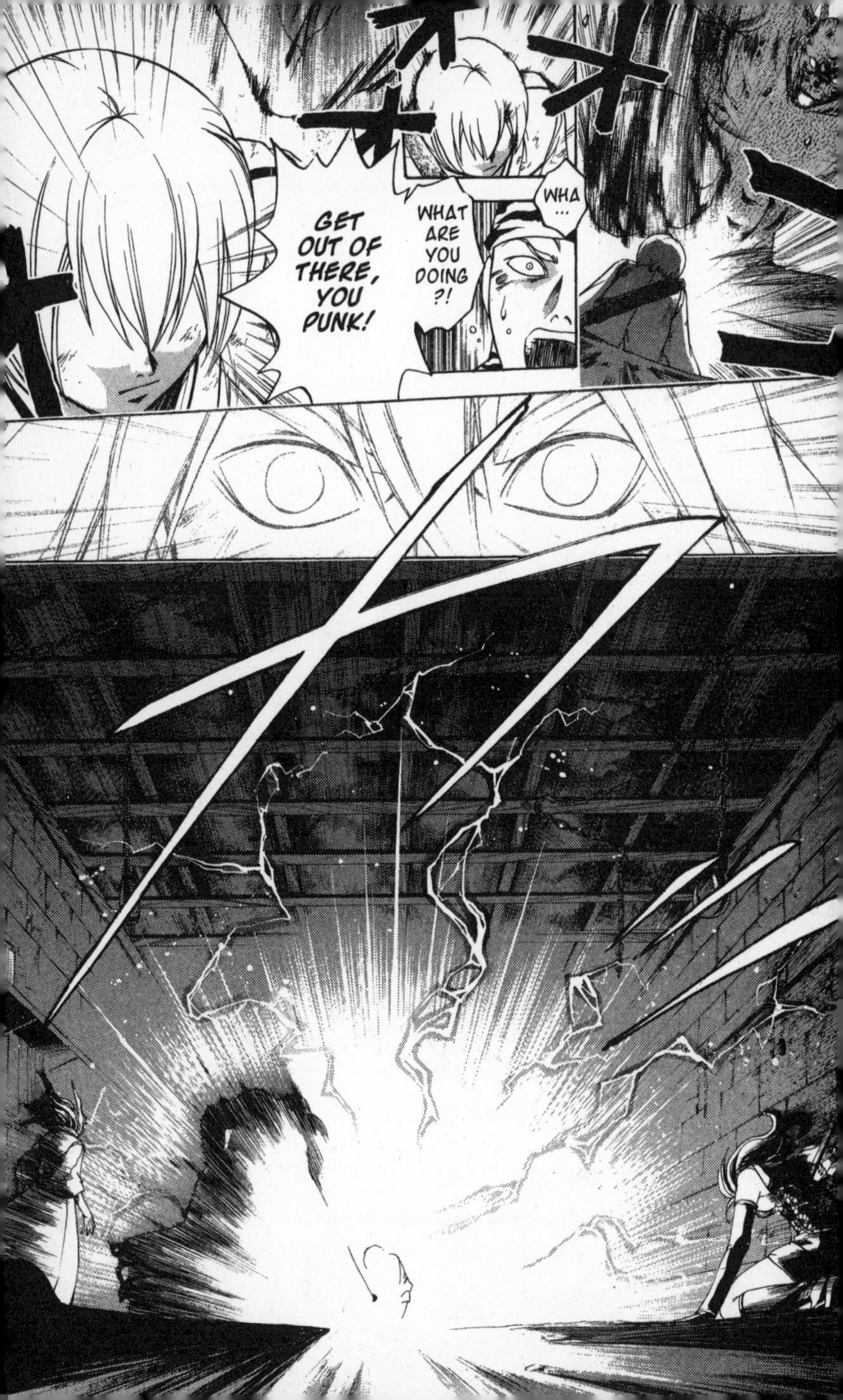
WHA...
WHAT ARE YOU DOING?!
GET OUT OF THERE, YOU PUNK!

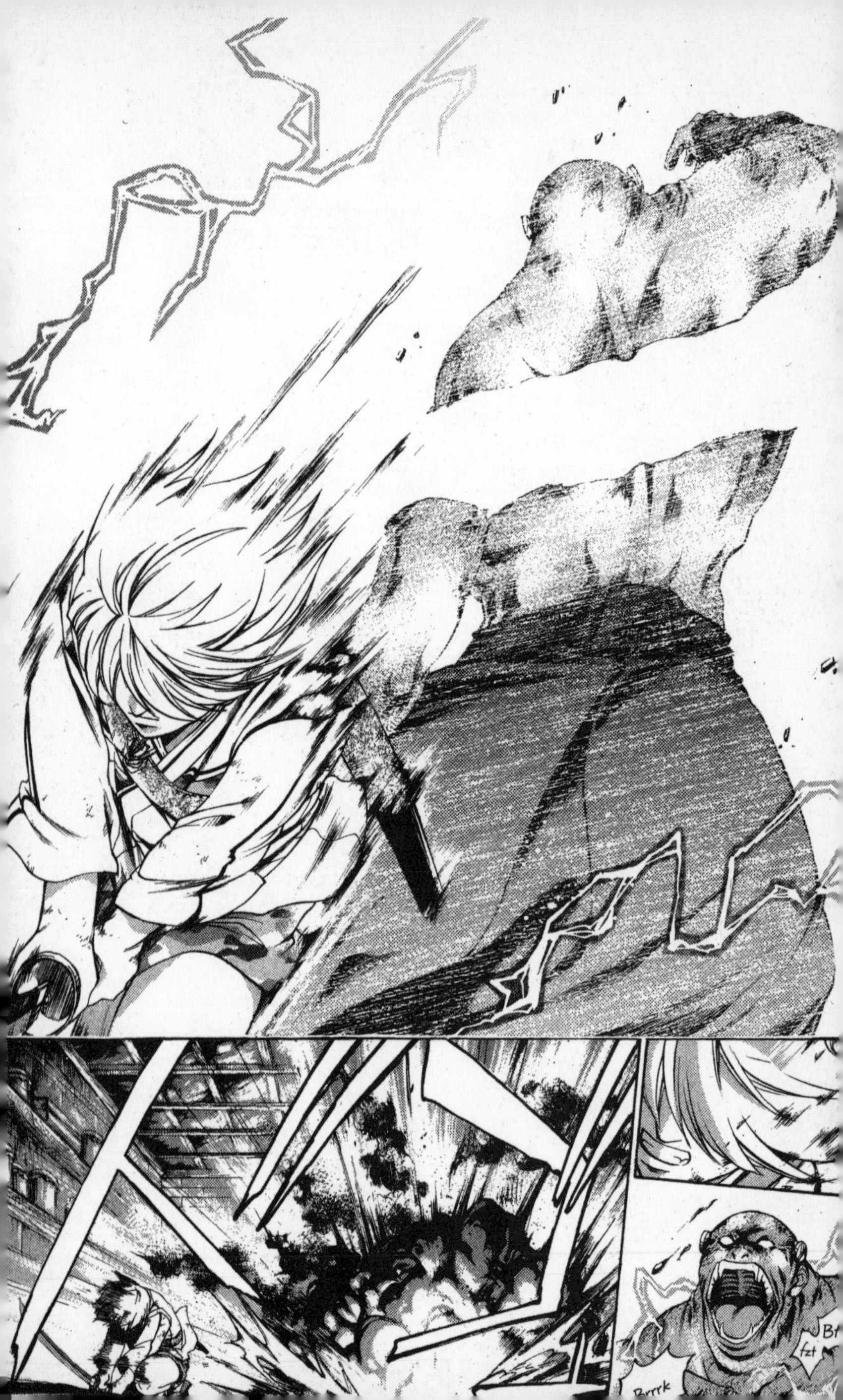
fzt
Brrrk

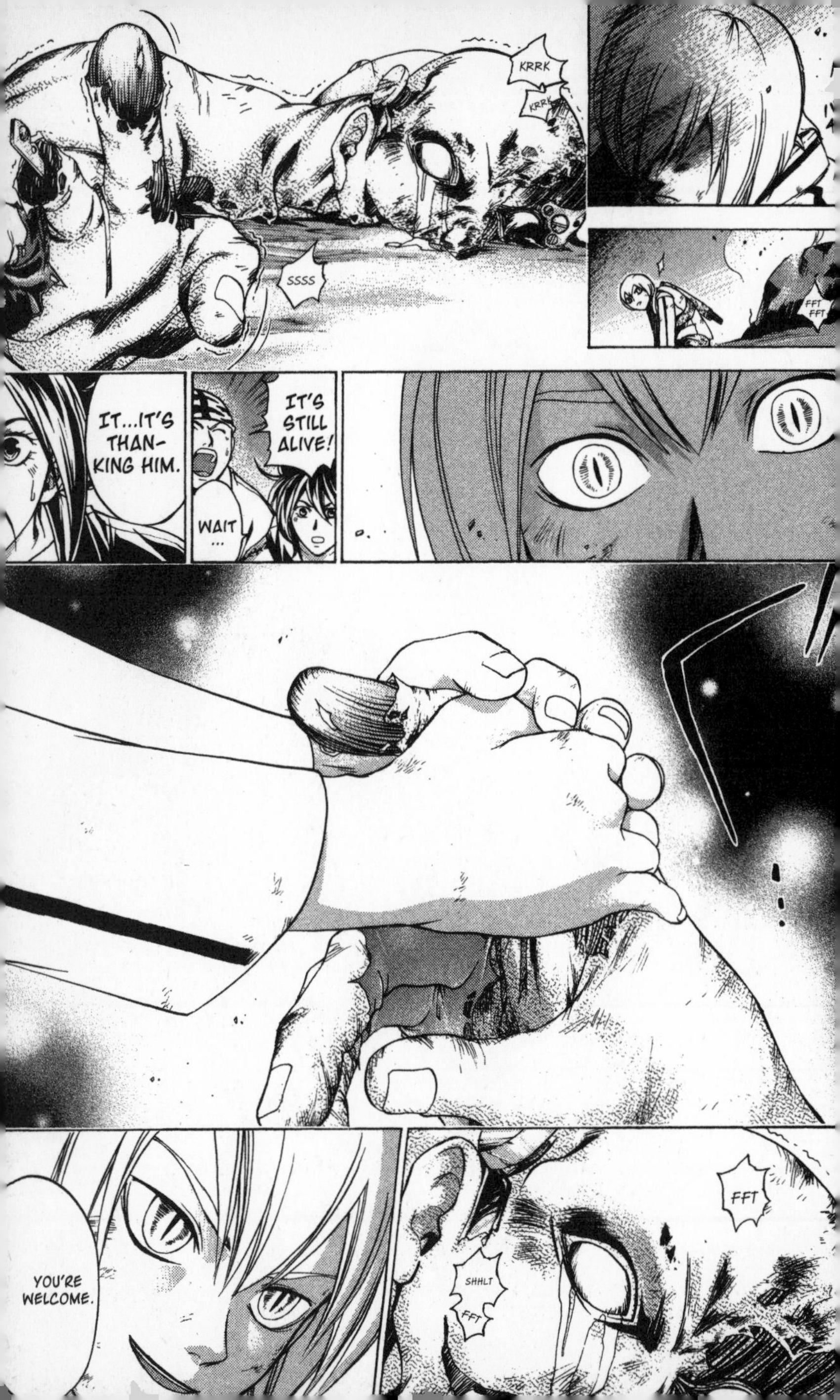
FFT FFT
KRRK
KRRK
SSSS
..
IT'S STILL ALIVE!
WAIT ...
IT...IT'S THAN-KING HIM.
...
FFT
SHHLT
FFT
YOU'RE WELCOME.

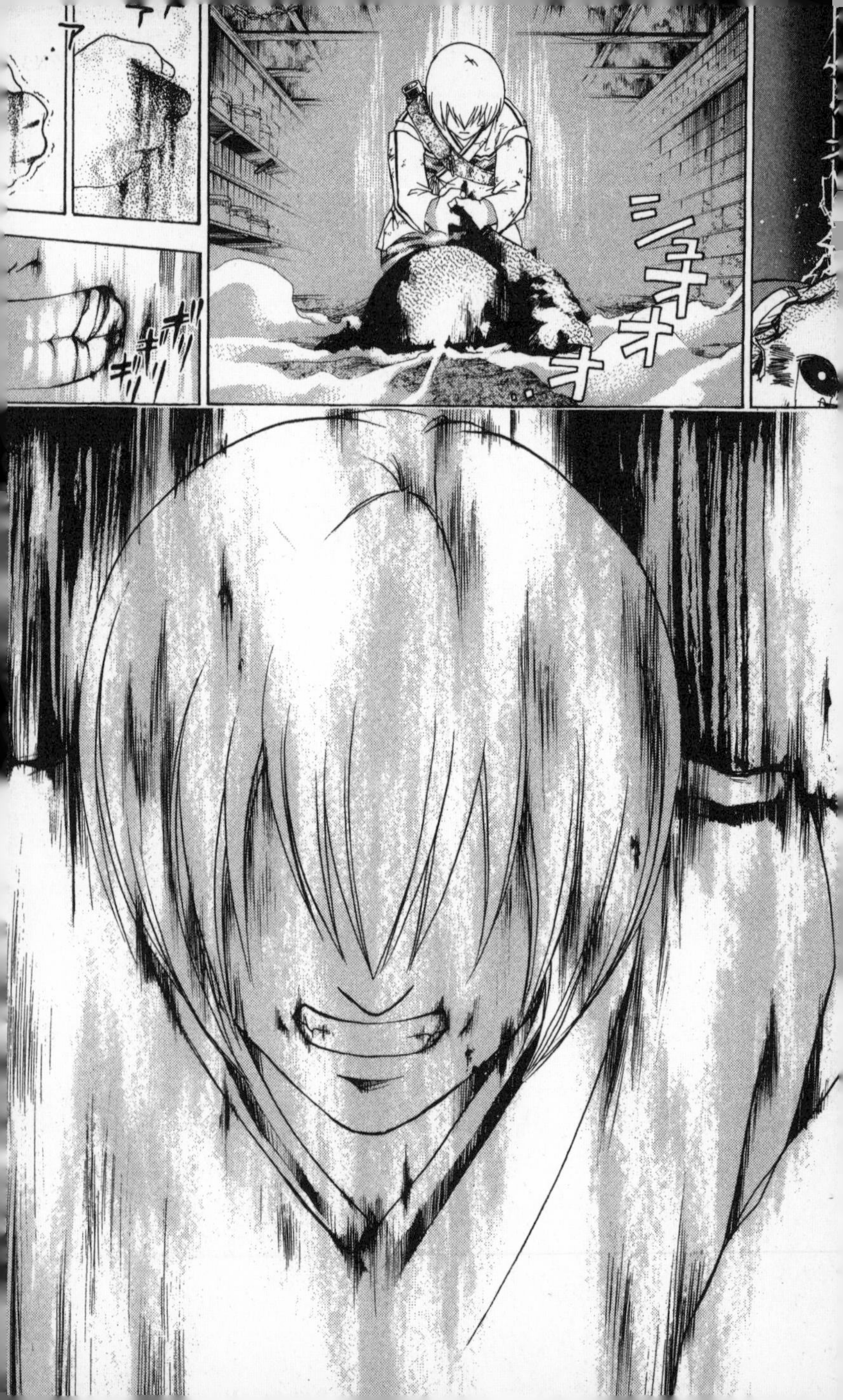
シュオオオオ
ア' ア…
ギッギッギッ

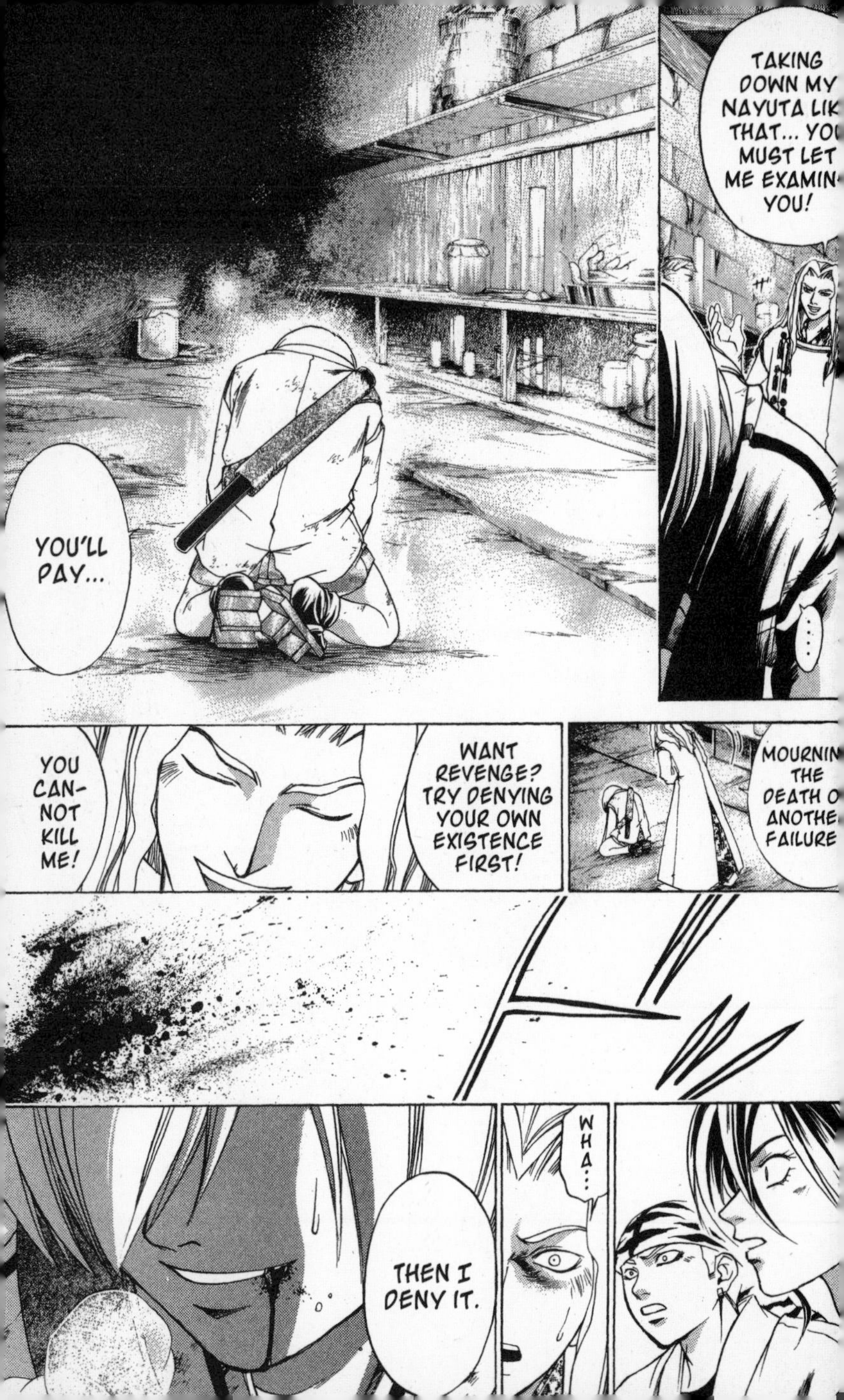
TAKING DOWN MY NAYUTA LIK THAT... YOU MUST LET ME EXAMIN YOU!
...
YOU'LL PAY...
MOURNIN THE DEATH O ANOTHE FAILURE
WANT REVENGE? TRY DENYING YOUR OWN EXISTENCE FIRST!
YOU CAN-NOT KILL ME!
WHA...
THEN I DENY IT.

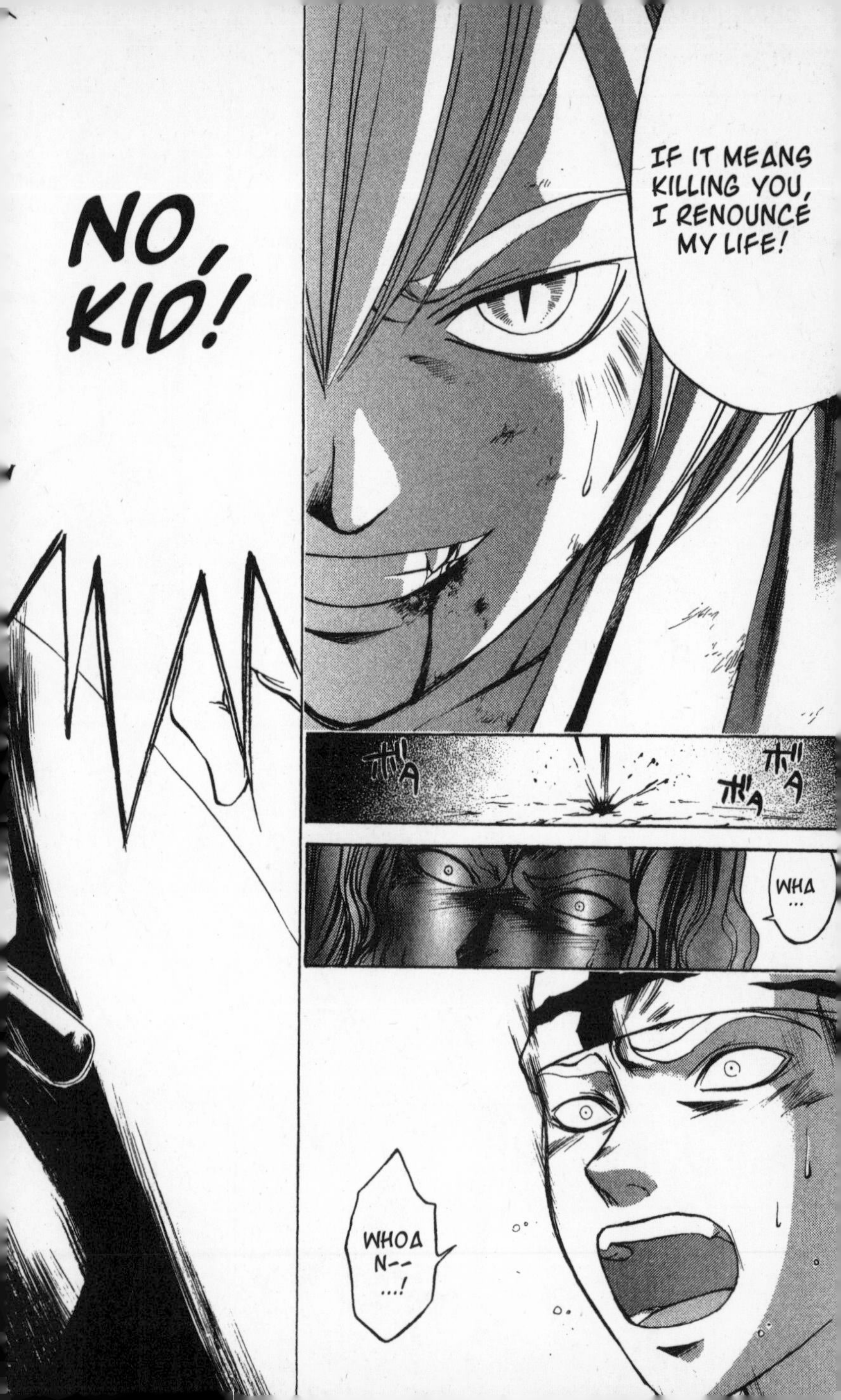
IF IT MEANS KILLING YOU, I RENOUNCE MY LIFE!
ボA
ボA
ボA
WHA ...
WHOA N-- ...!
NO, KID!

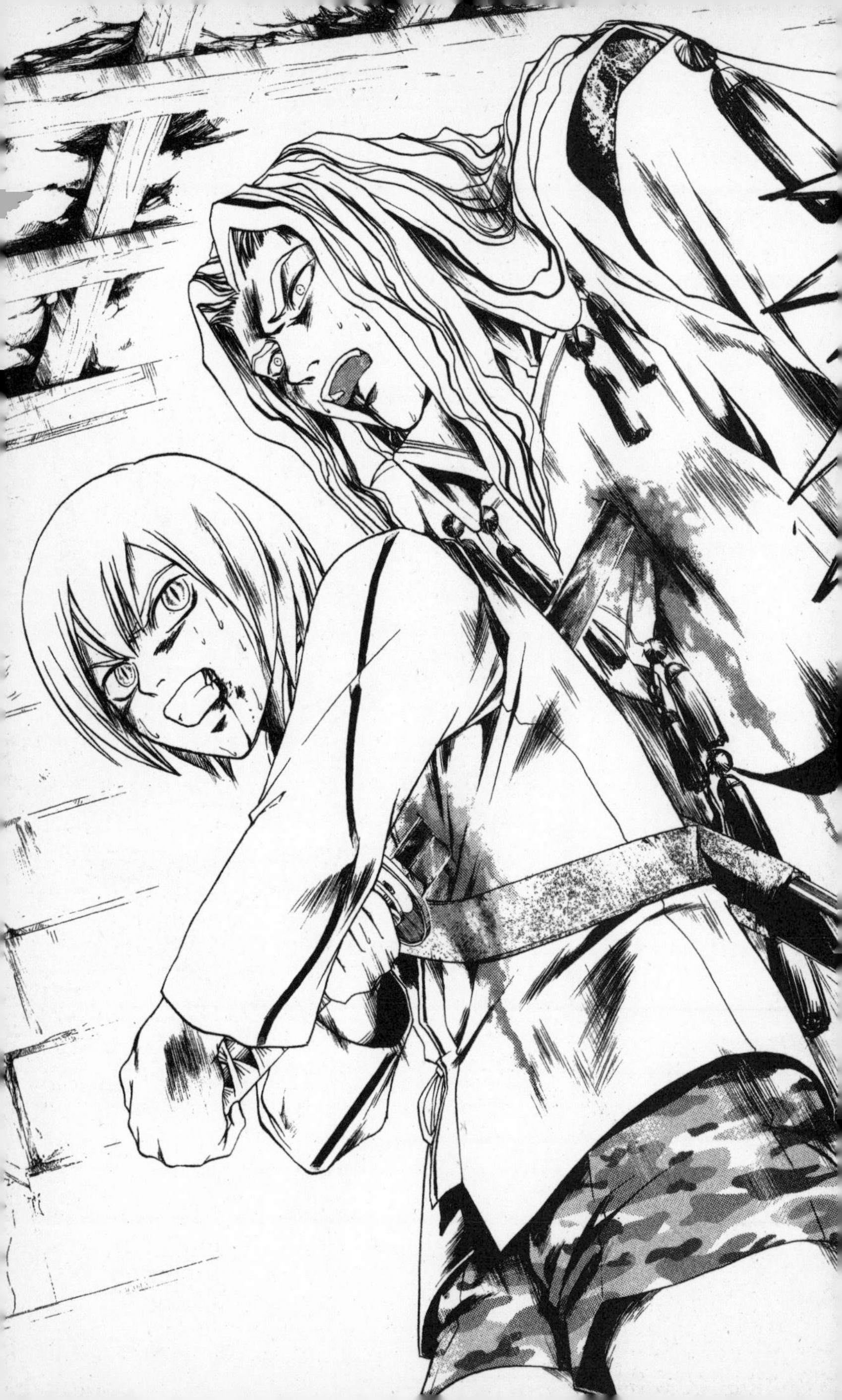

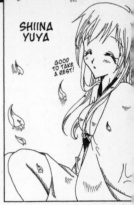

SHIINA YUYA
GOOD TO TAKE A REST!

She does need to rest more! Really!
[Urana / Nara]

A MESSAGE FROM KAMIJO

NEXT VOLUME: BENITORA SPECIAL! NOW ACCEPTING SUBMISSIONS FOR THE LONG AWAITED (?) YUKIMURA!

I'd hate to have to pay her cell phone bill! Y'know?!
[Asami Fuchiue / Osaka]

kamijyo ni chou...

上条(かみじょう)に挑戦(ちょうせん)

TWO GIRLS IN HIGH SCHOOL
TRY TO DRAW LIKE KAMIJYO AKIMINE!
+ EXTRAS! :)
I LOVE MIYABI-SAN FROM VOL. 6!
YUYA ♡
I LOVE NATSUKI FROM VOL. 5!
WHY AM I ALL OFF TO THE SIDE?!
I BET THESE TWO WOULD REALLY GET ALONG! (I LOVE YUYA-CHAN AND MIZUKI-CHAN!!)
NOW, NOW...

The purest smile!
[Sakiko Ono / Miyagi]

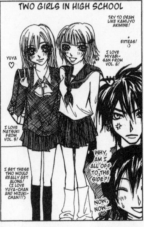

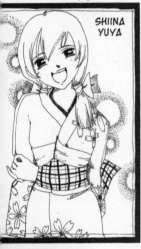

SHIINA YUYA

yuya
SAMURAI DEEPER KY
KISS ME...

Wha--?! Y-you're sure it's okay?!
[Yuki / Nagano]

Fan Art Info

...bmission Info

How to submit:
1) Send your work via regular mail (NOT e-mail) to:
SAMURAI DEEPER KYO FAN MAIL
C/O TOKYOPOP
5900 WILSHIRE BLVD., SUITE 2000
LOS ANGELES, CA 90036
2) All work should be in black-and-white and no larger than 8.5"x11".(And try not to fold it too many times!) 3) Anything you send will not be returned. If you want to keep your original, it's fine to send us a copy. 4) Please include your full name, age, city and state for us to print with your work. If you'd rather us use a pen name, please include that too. 5) IMPORTANT: If you're under the age of 18, you must have your parent's permission in order for us to print your work. Any submissions without a signed note of parental consent will not be used. 6) For full details, please check out
http://www.tokyopop.com/aboutus/fanart.php

...mer: Anything you send to us becomes the property of TOKYOPOP Inc. and will not be returned to you. We will have the right to ...roduce, distribute or modify the artwork for use in future volumes of Samurai Deeper Kyo or on the Web without payment to you.

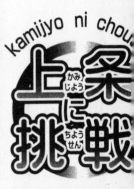

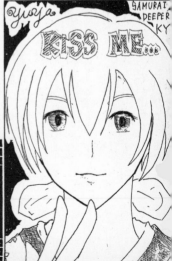

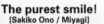

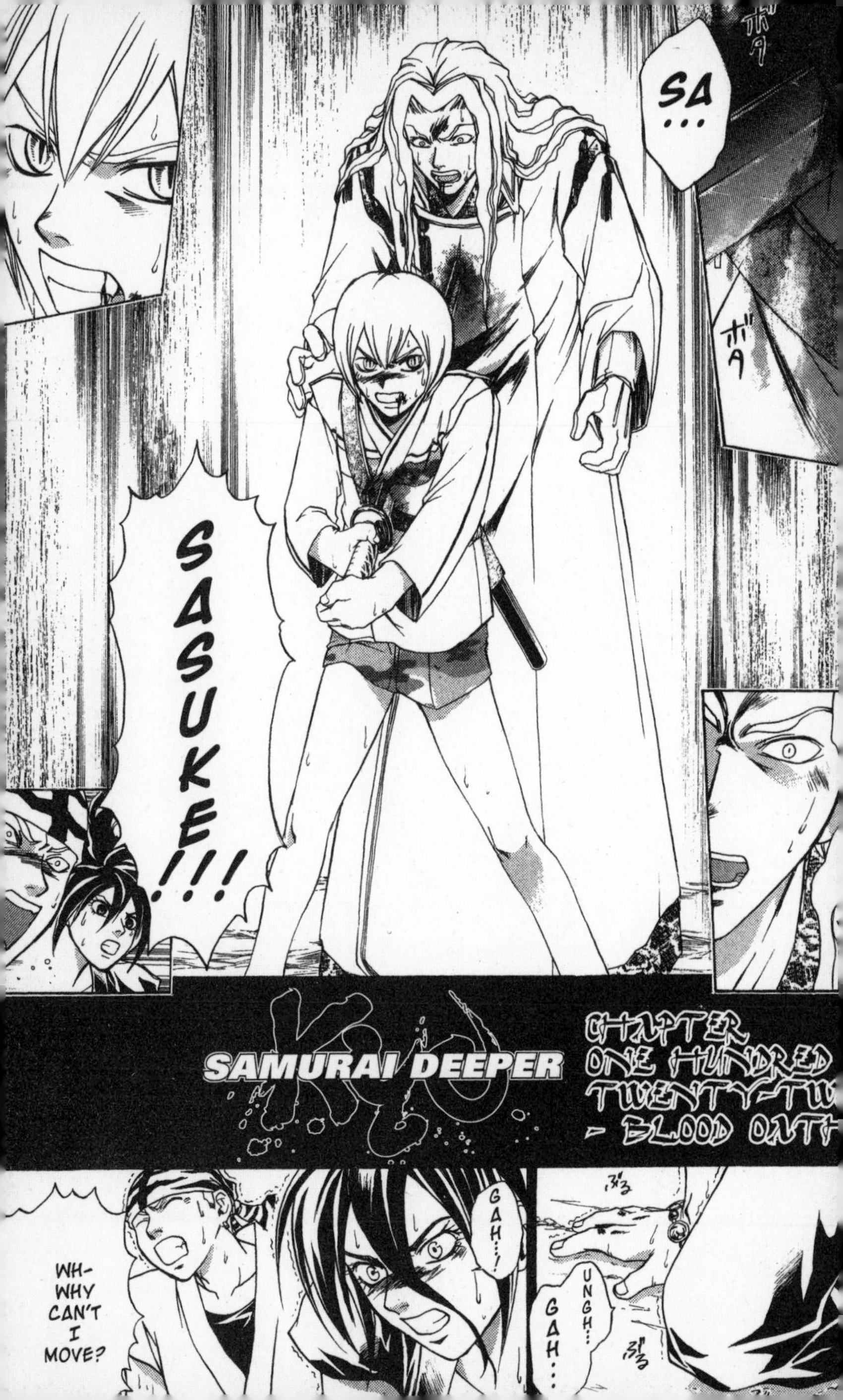
ボタ
SA...
ボタ
SASUKE!!!
SAMURAI DEEPER KYO
CHAPTER ONE HUNDRED TWENTY-TW
- BLOOD OATH
ぶる
UNGH...
GAH...
ぶる
GAH...!
WH-WHY CAN'T I MOVE?

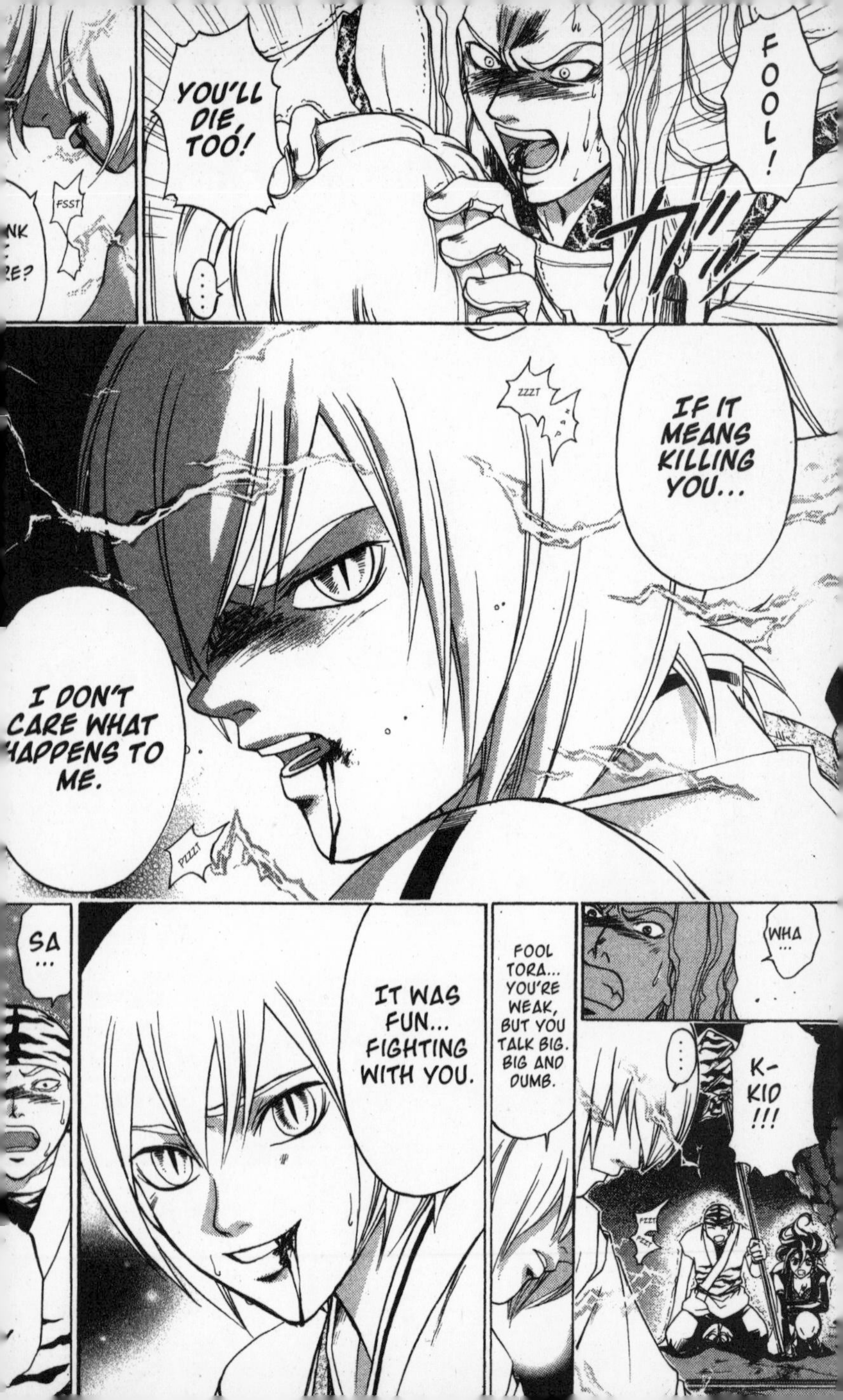
FOOL!
YOU'LL DIE, TOO!
...
FSST
IF IT MEANS KILLING YOU...
ZZZT
I DON'T CARE WHAT HAPPENS TO ME.
PZZZT
WHA ...
K-KID!!!
...
FZZT
FZZT
FOOL TORA... YOU'RE WEAK, BUT YOU TALK BIG. BIG AND DUMB.
IT WAS FUN... FIGHTING WITH YOU.
SA ...

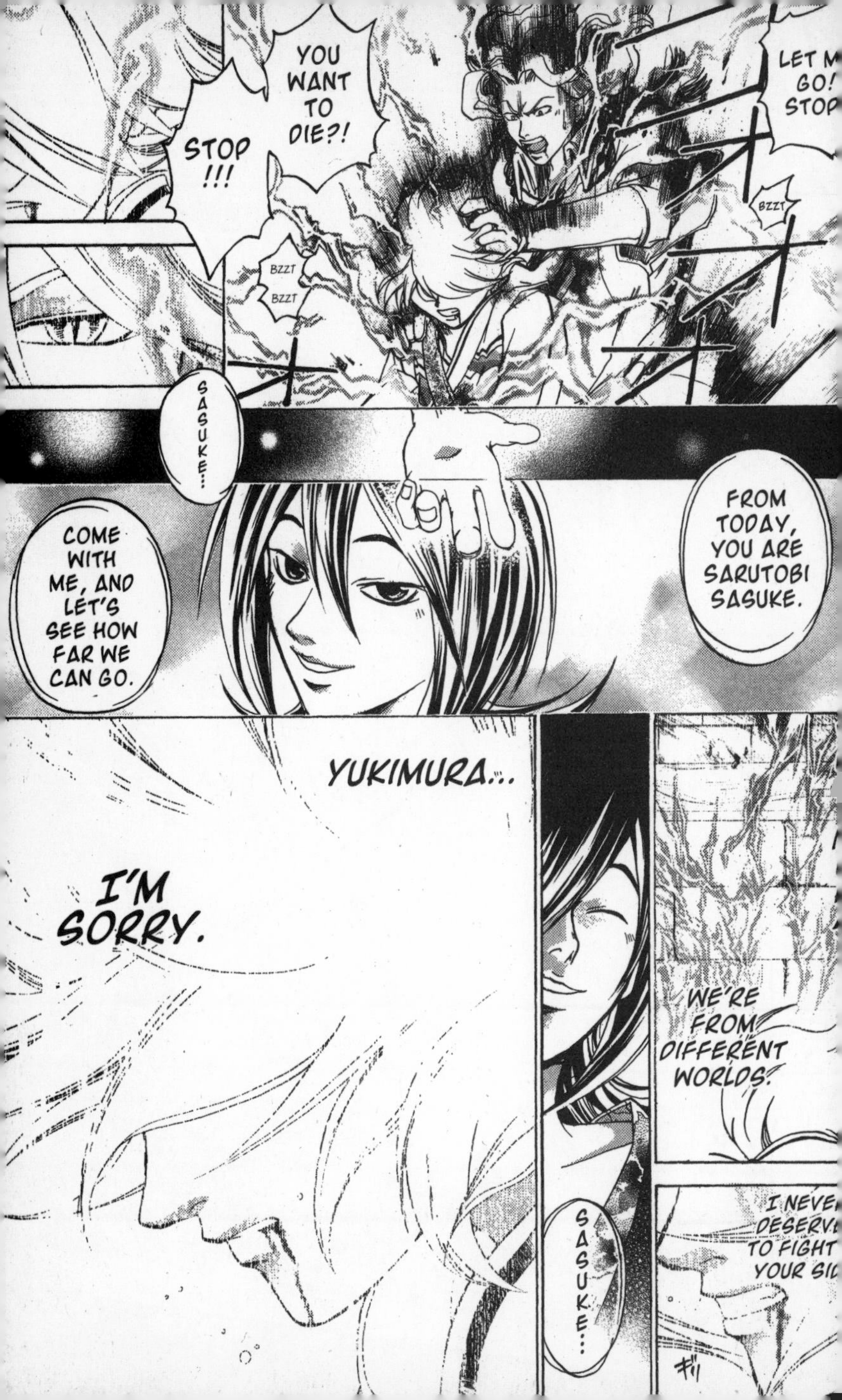

LET M GO! STOP
BZZT
YOU WANT TO DIE?!
BZZT BZZT
STOP !!!
SASUKE...
FROM TODAY, YOU ARE SARUTOBI SASUKE.
COME WITH ME, AND LET'S SEE HOW FAR WE CAN GO.
WE'RE FROM DIFFERENT WORLDS.
I NEVE DESERV TO FIGHT YOUR SI
SASUKE...
YUKIMURA...
I'M SORRY.

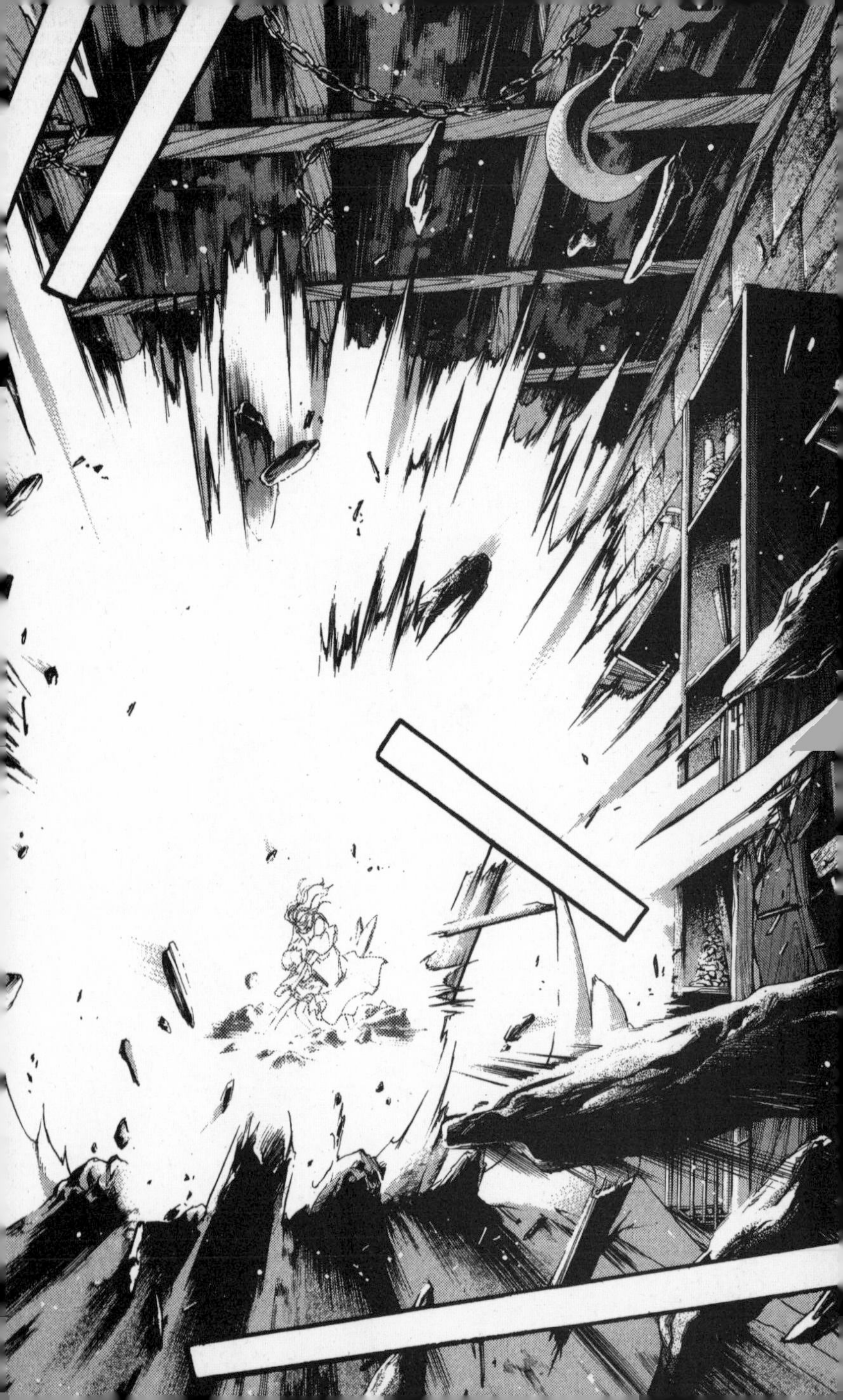

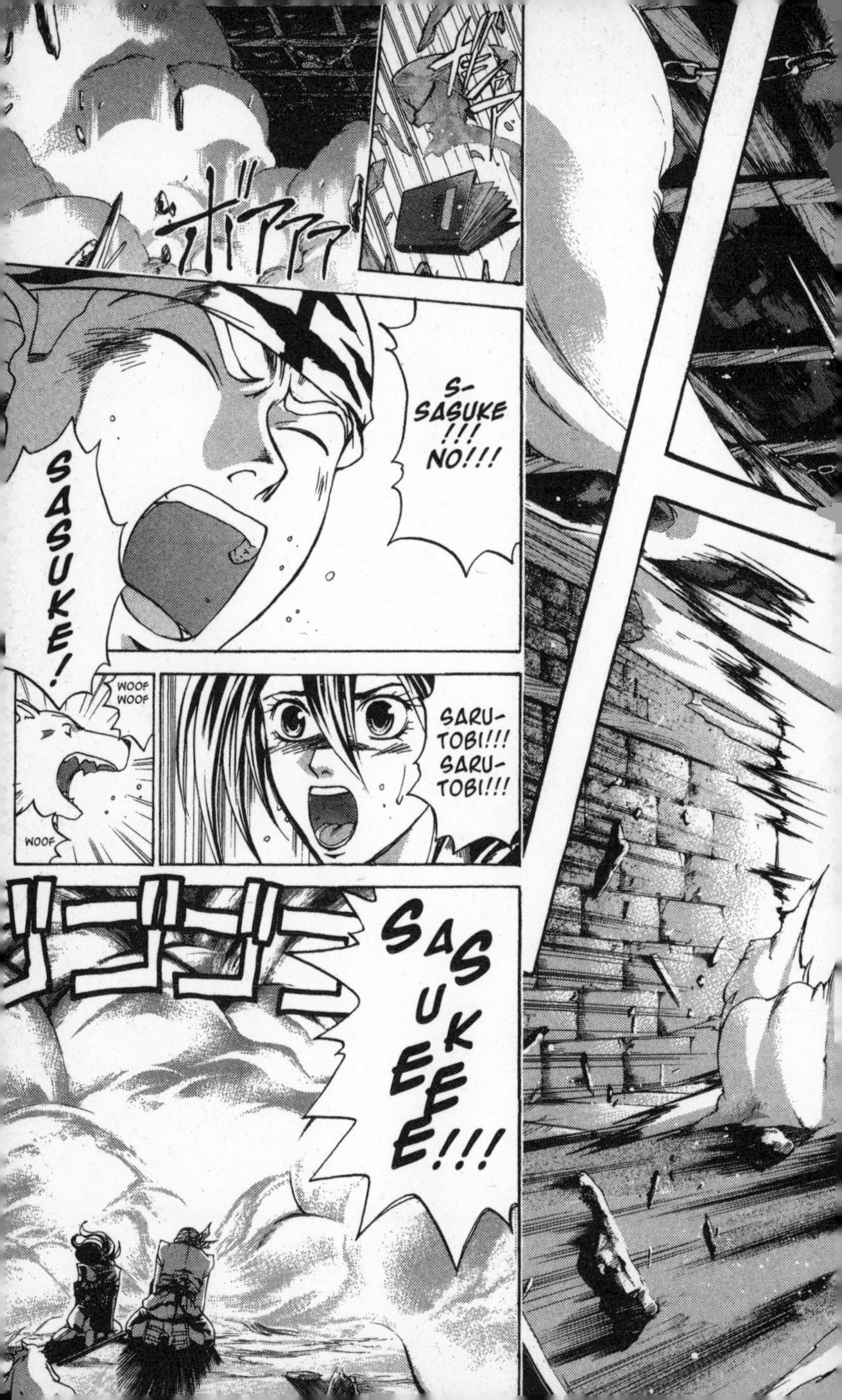
ボアアア
S-SASUKE!!! NO!!!
SASUKE!
SARU-TOBI!!! SARU-TOBI!!!
WOOF WOOF
WOOF
SASUKEEEE!!!

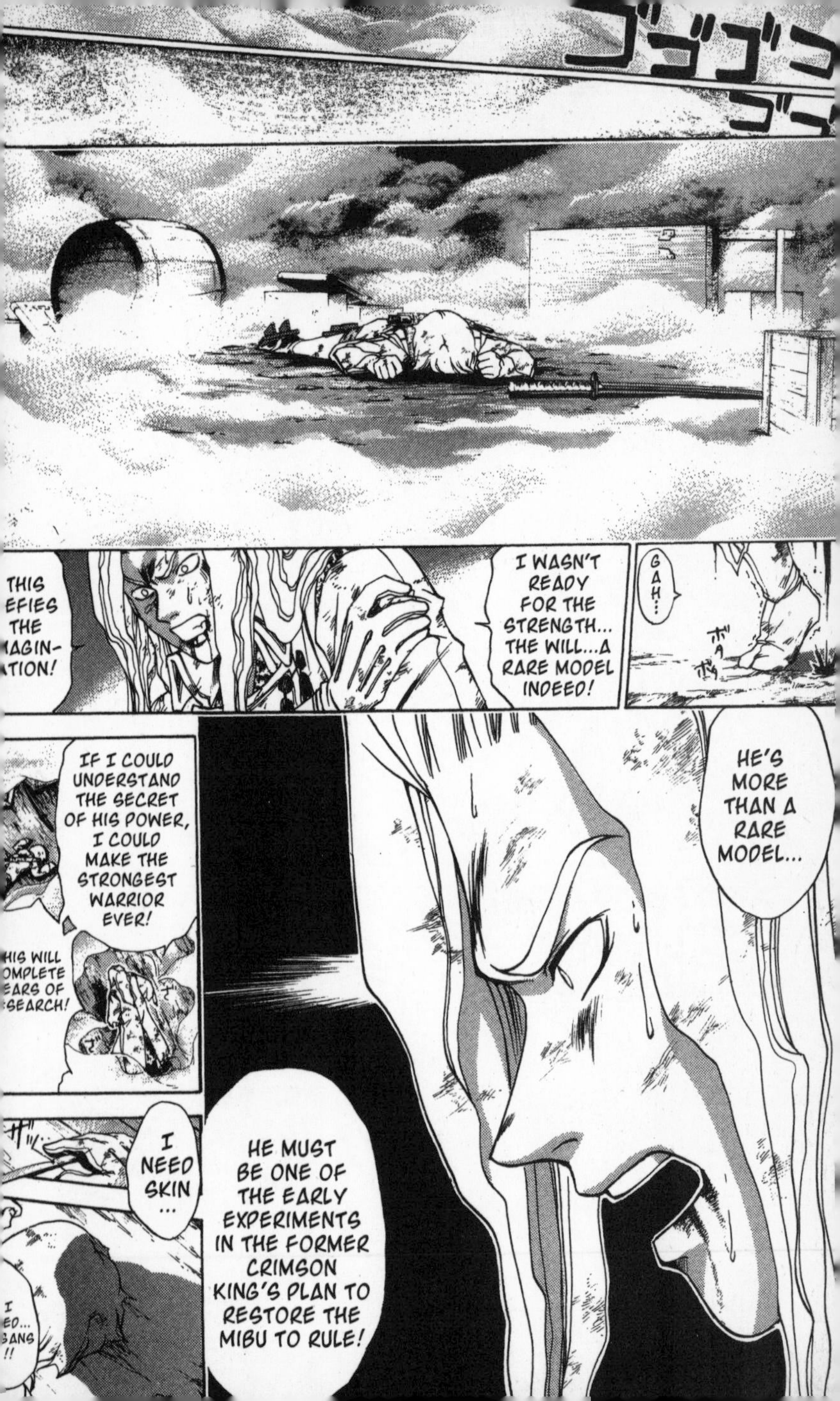
ゴゴゴ
GAH...
ボタ ボタ
I WASN'T READY FOR THE STRENGTH... THE WILL...A RARE MODEL INDEED!
THIS EFIES THE MAGIN- ATION!
HE'S MORE THAN A RARE MODEL...
HE MUST BE ONE OF THE EARLY EXPERIMENTS IN THE FORMER CRIMSON KING'S PLAN TO RESTORE THE MIBU TO RULE!
IF I COULD UNDERSTAND THE SECRET OF HIS POWER, I COULD MAKE THE STRONGEST WARRIOR EVER!
HIS WILL OMPLETE EARS OF SEARCH!
I NEED SKIN...
I ED... GANS !!

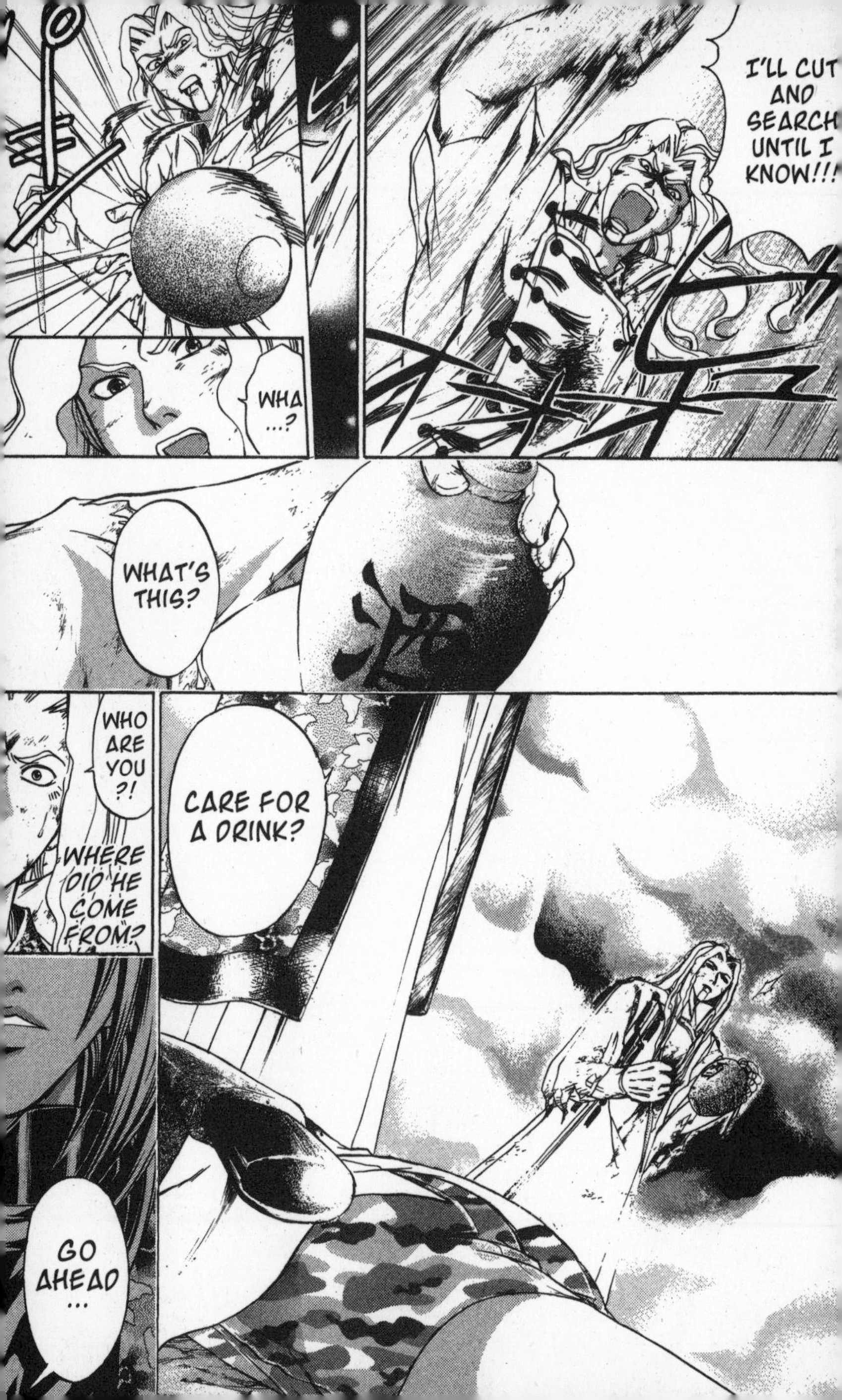
I'LL CUT AND SEARCH UNTIL I KNOW!!!
WHA ...?
WHAT'S THIS?
酒
CARE FOR A DRINK?
WHO ARE YOU ?!
WHERE DID HE COME FROM?
GO AHEAD ...

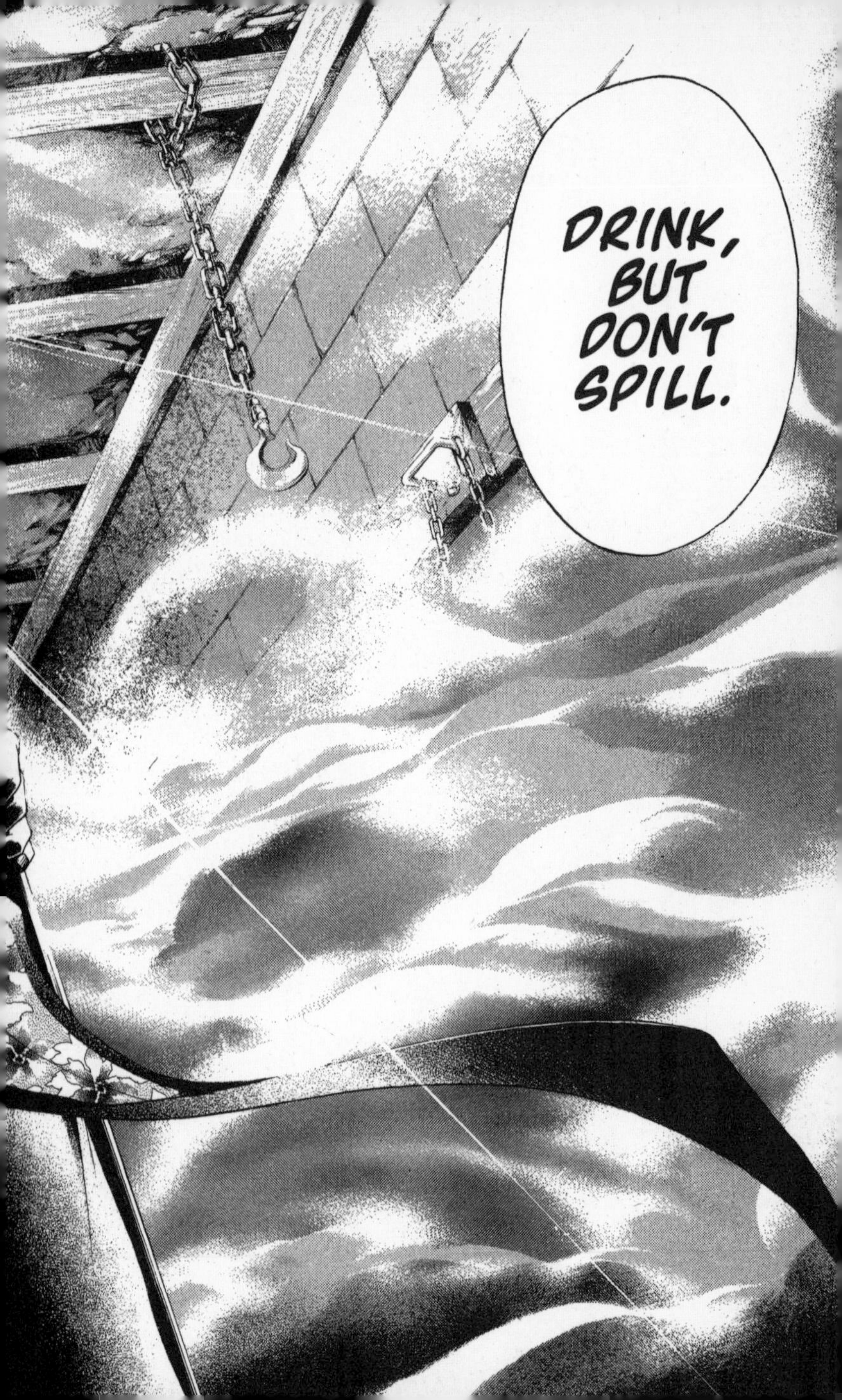
DRINK, BUT DON'T SPILL.

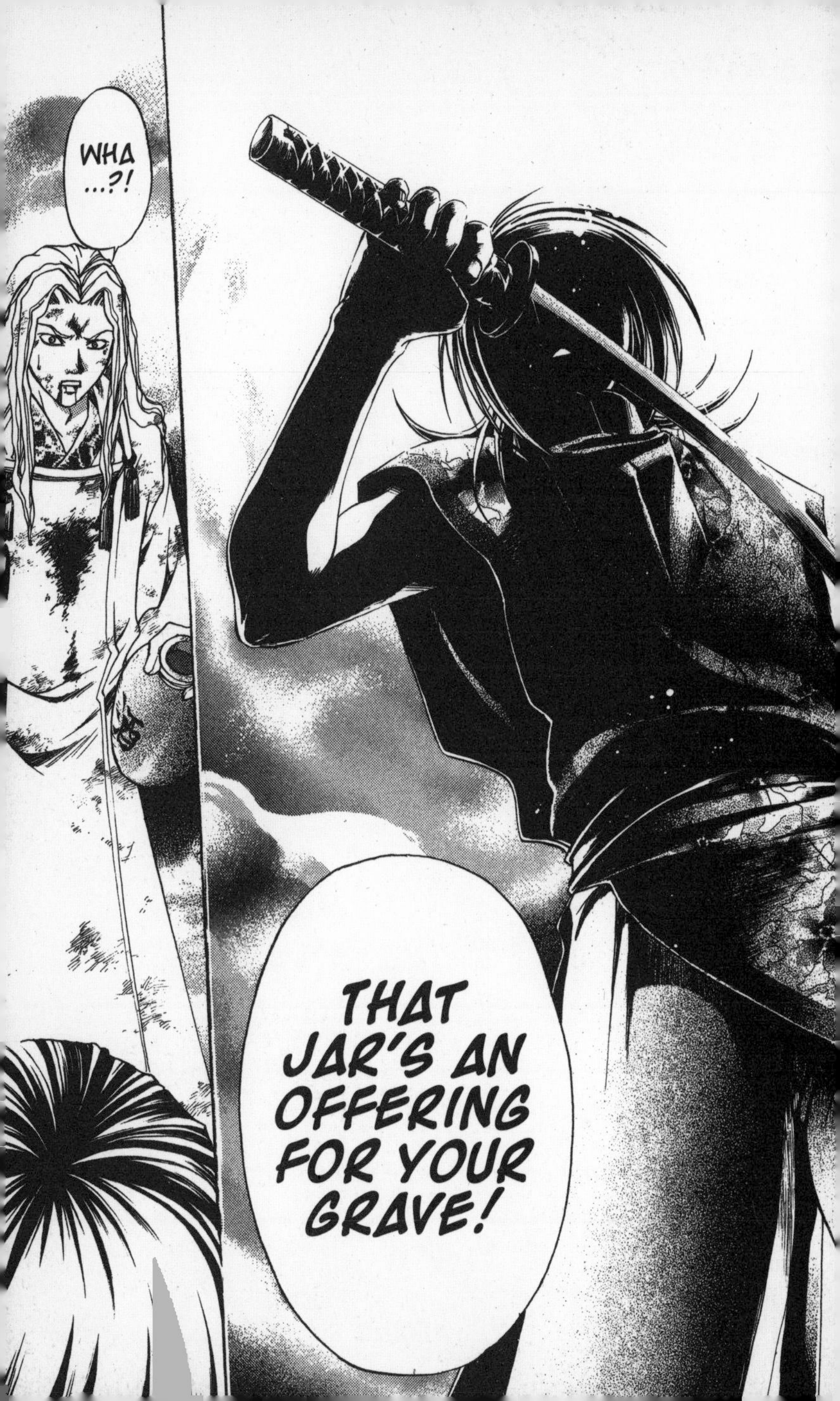
THAT JAR'S AN OFFERING FOR YOUR GRAVE!
WHA ...?!

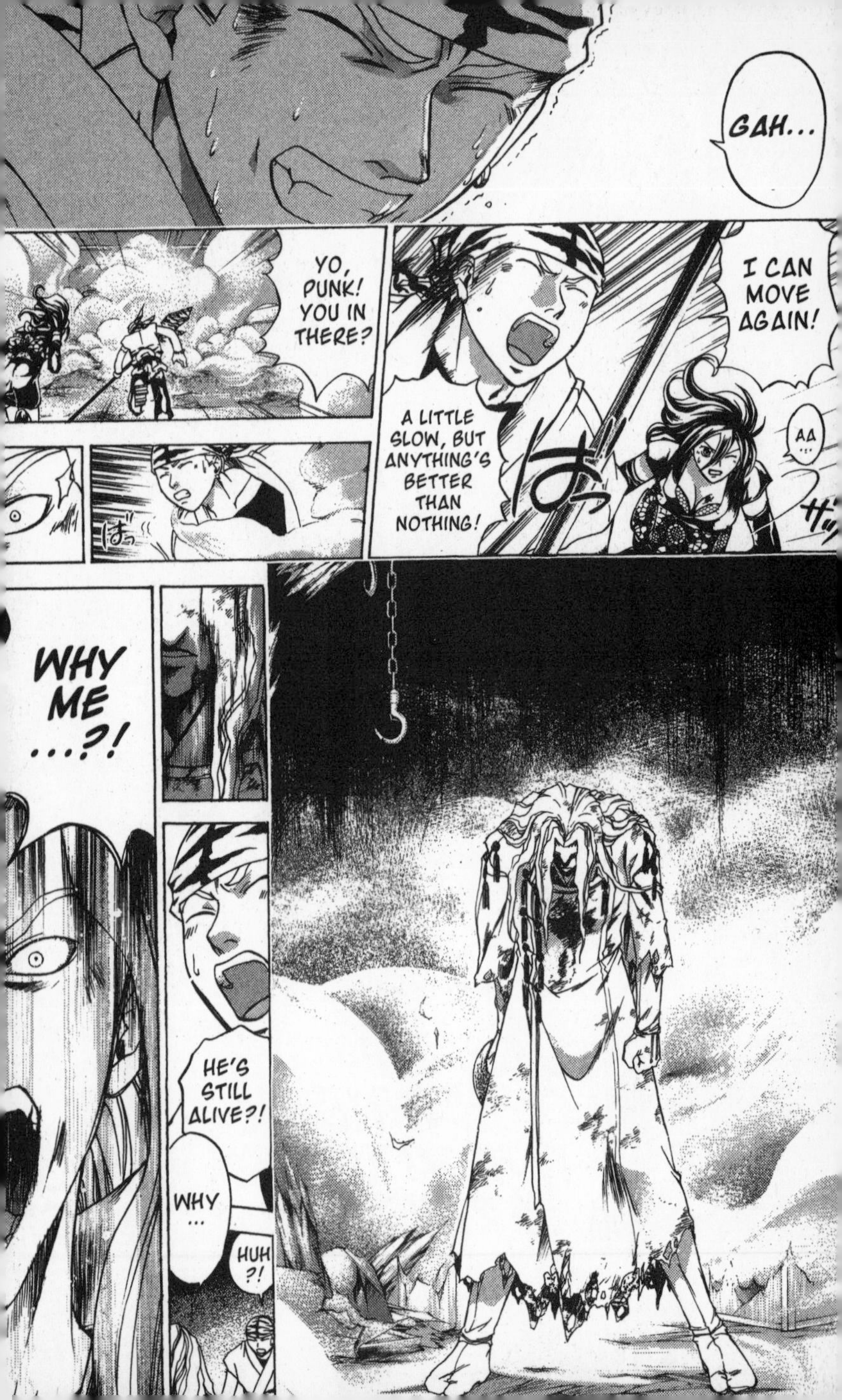
GAH...
I CAN MOVE AGAIN!
AA ...
A LITTLE SLOW, BUT ANYTHING'S BETTER THAN NOTHING!
YO, PUNK! YOU IN THERE?
HE'S STILL ALIVE?!
WHY ...
HUH ?!
WHY ME ...?!

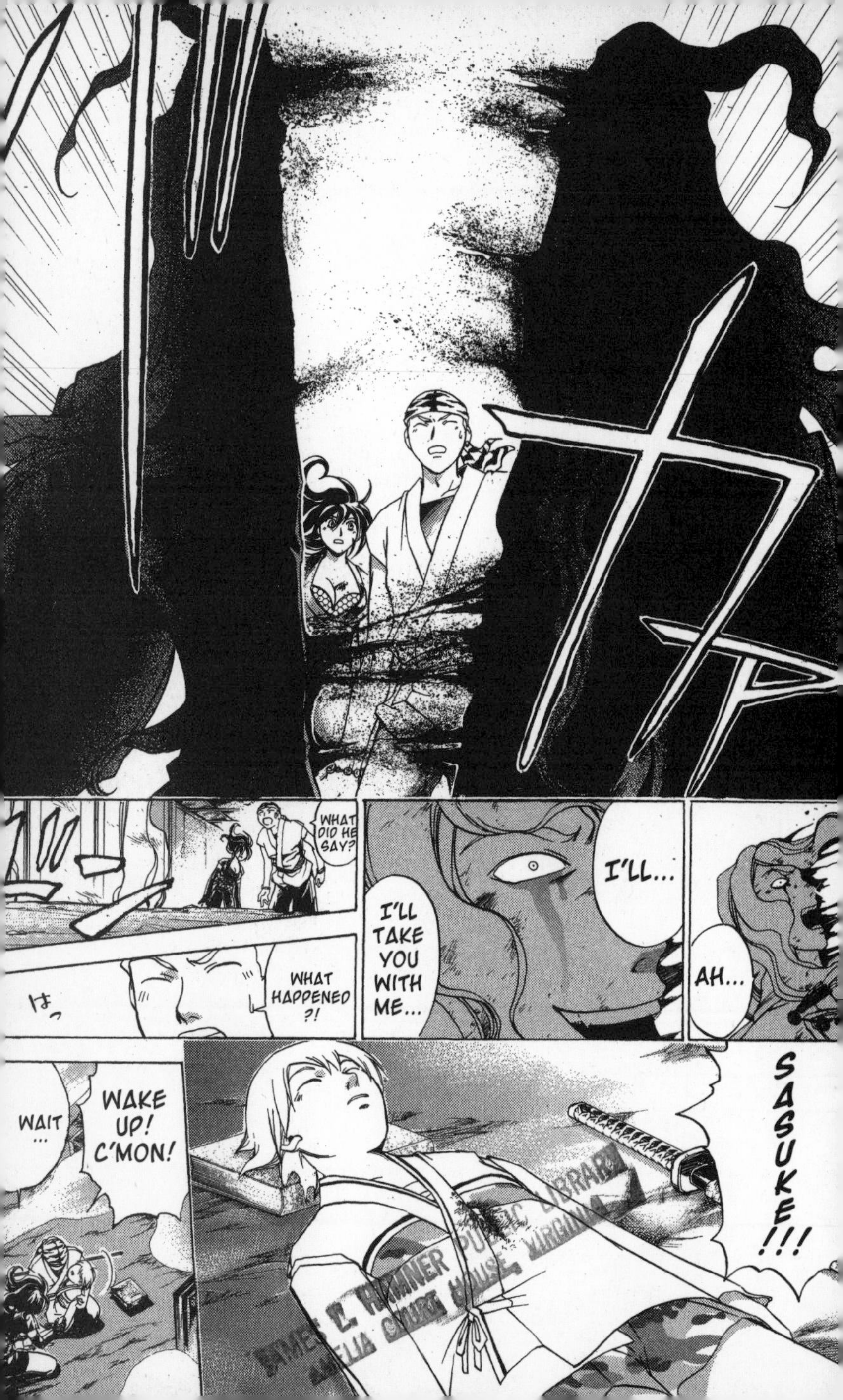
AH...
I'LL...
I'LL TAKE YOU WITH ME...
WHAT DID HE SAY?
WHAT HAPPENED ?!
はっ
SASUKE!!!
WAKE UP! C'MON!
WAIT ...

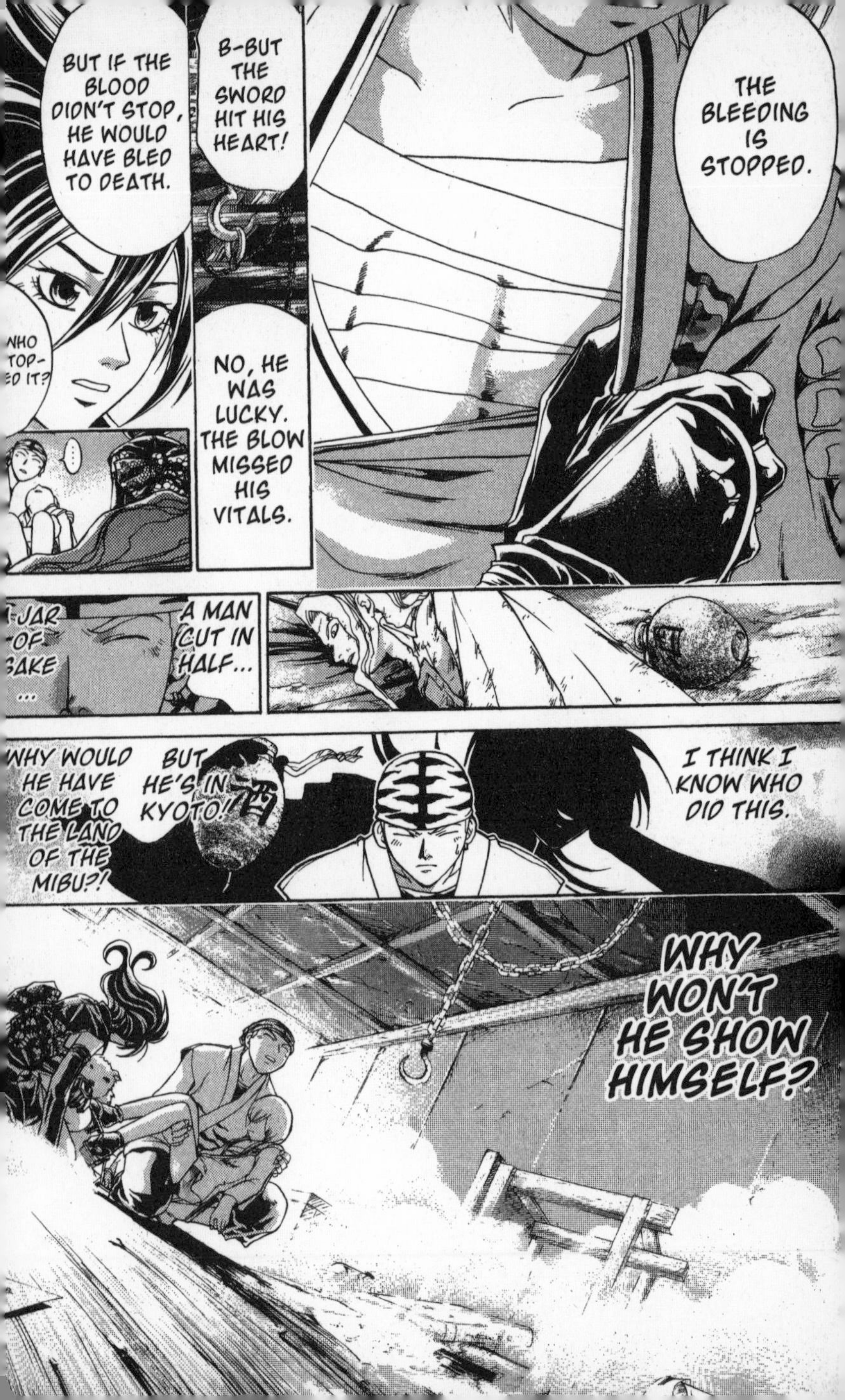
THE BLEEDING IS STOPPED.
B-BUT THE SWORD HIT HIS HEART!
NO, HE WAS LUCKY. THE BLOW MISSED HIS VITALS.
BUT IF THE BLOOD DIDN'T STOP, HE WOULD HAVE BLED TO DEATH.
HO TOP- ED IT?
...
A MAN CUT IN HALF...
JAR OF SAKE ...
I THINK I KNOW WHO DID THIS.
BUT HE'S IN KYOTO!
WHY WOULD HE HAVE COME TO THE LAND OF THE MIBU?!
WHY WON'T HE SHOW HIMSELF?

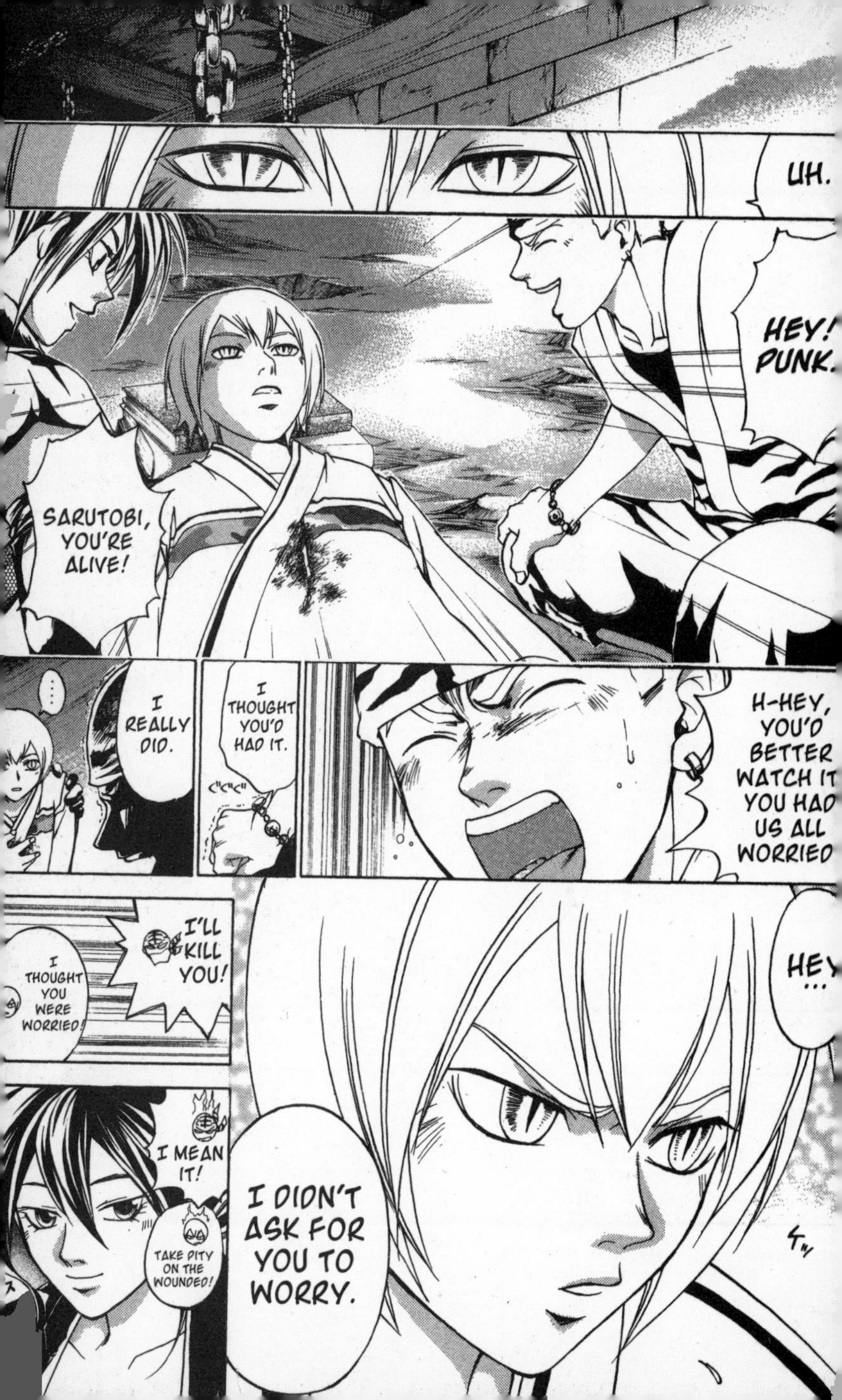
UH.
HEY! PUNK.
SARUTOBI, YOU'RE ALIVE!
H-HEY, YOU'D BETTER WATCH IT YOU HAD US ALL WORRIED
I THOUGHT YOU'D HAD IT.
I REALLY DID.
...
HEY...
I DIDN'T ASK FOR YOU TO WORRY.
I'LL KILL YOU!
I THOUGHT YOU WERE WORRIED!
I MEAN IT!
TAKE PITY ON THE WOUNDED!

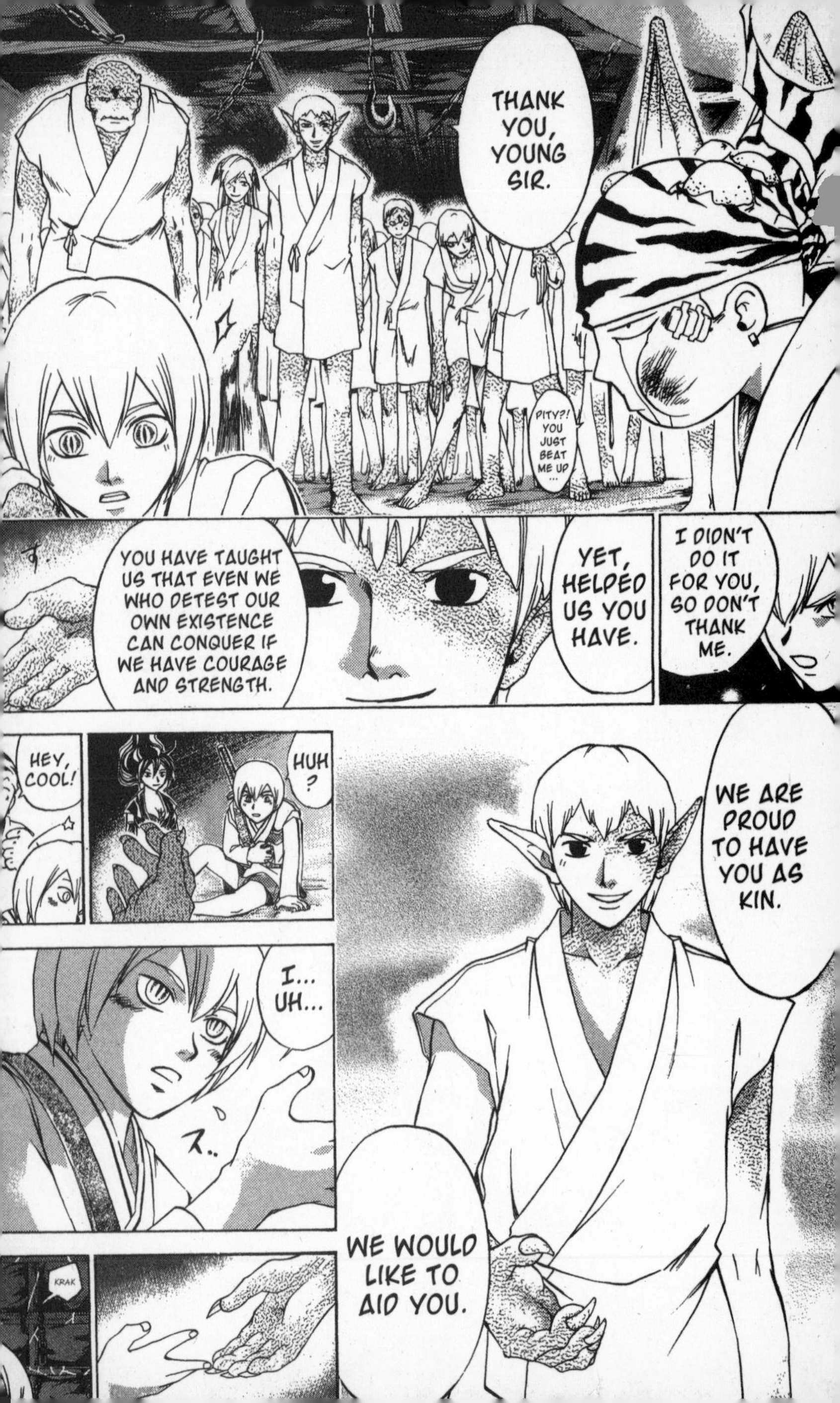
THANK YOU, YOUNG SIR.
PITY?! YOU JUST BEAT ME UP...
I DIDN'T DO IT FOR YOU, SO DON'T THANK ME.
YET, HELPED US YOU HAVE.
YOU HAVE TAUGHT US THAT EVEN WE WHO DETEST OUR OWN EXISTENCE CAN CONQUER IF WE HAVE COURAGE AND STRENGTH.
WE ARE PROUD TO HAVE YOU AS KIN.
WE WOULD LIKE TO AID YOU.
HUH?
HEY, COOL!
I... UH...
KRAK

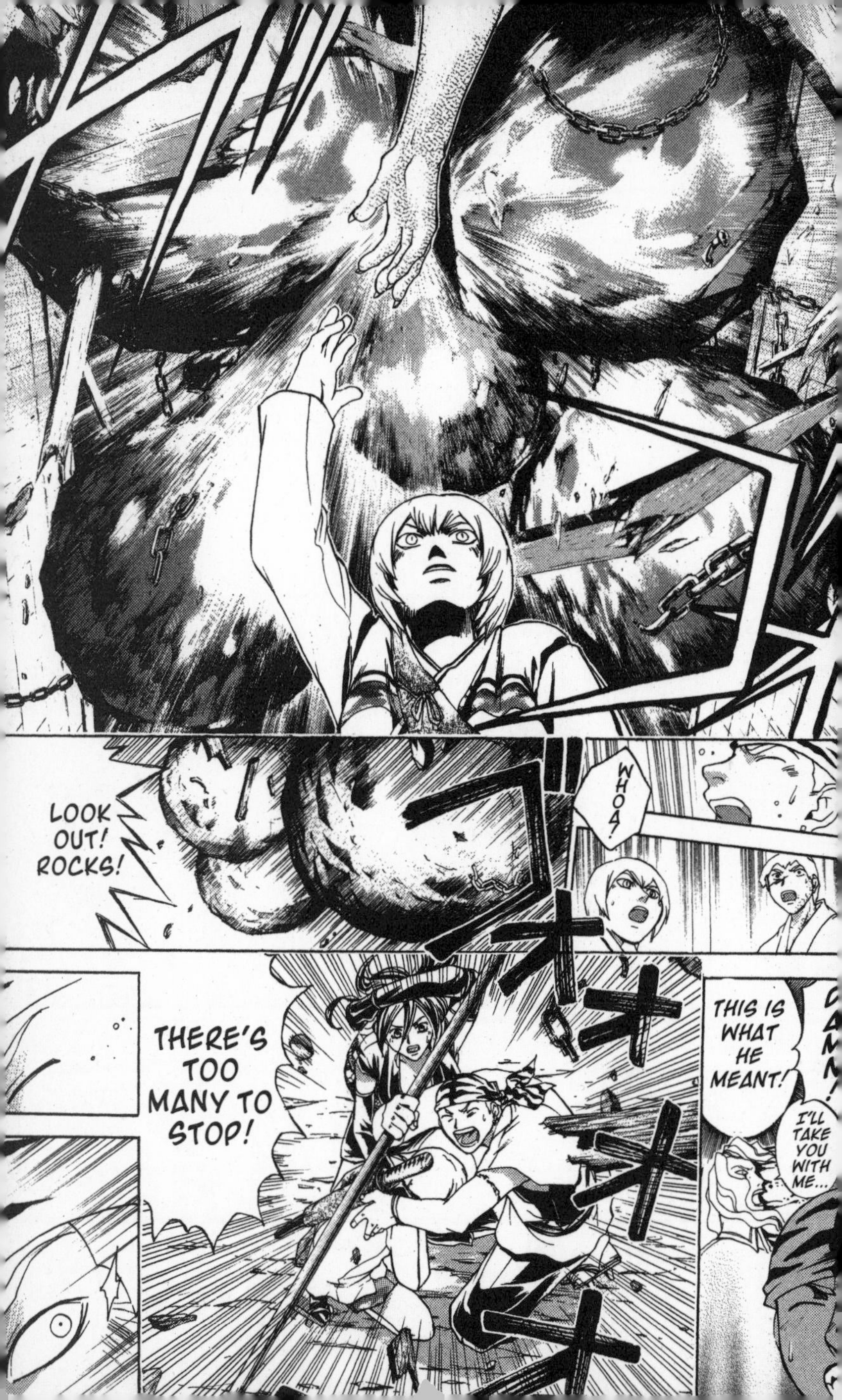

WHOA!
LOOK OUT! ROCKS!
DAMN!
THIS IS WHAT HE MEANT!
I'LL TAKE YOU WITH ME...
THERE'S TOO MANY TO STOP!

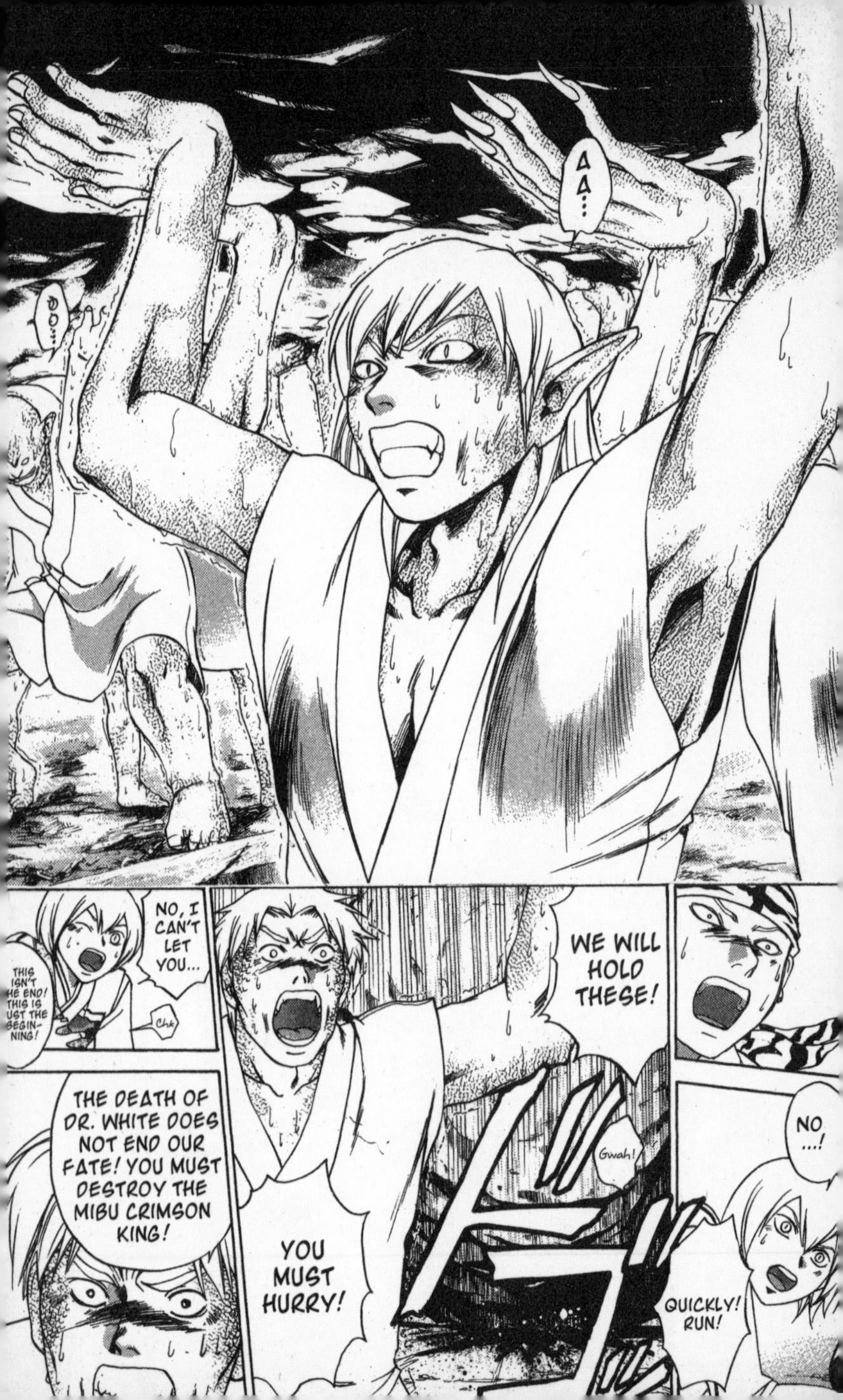
AA...
OO...
QUICKLY! RUN!
NO ...!
WE WILL HOLD THESE!
Gwah!
YOU MUST HURRY!
NO, I CAN'T LET YOU...
Chk
THIS ISN'T HE END! THIS IS UST THE BEGIN-NING!
THE DEATH OF DR. WHITE DOES NOT END OUR FATE! YOU MUST DESTROY THE MIBU CRIMSON KING!

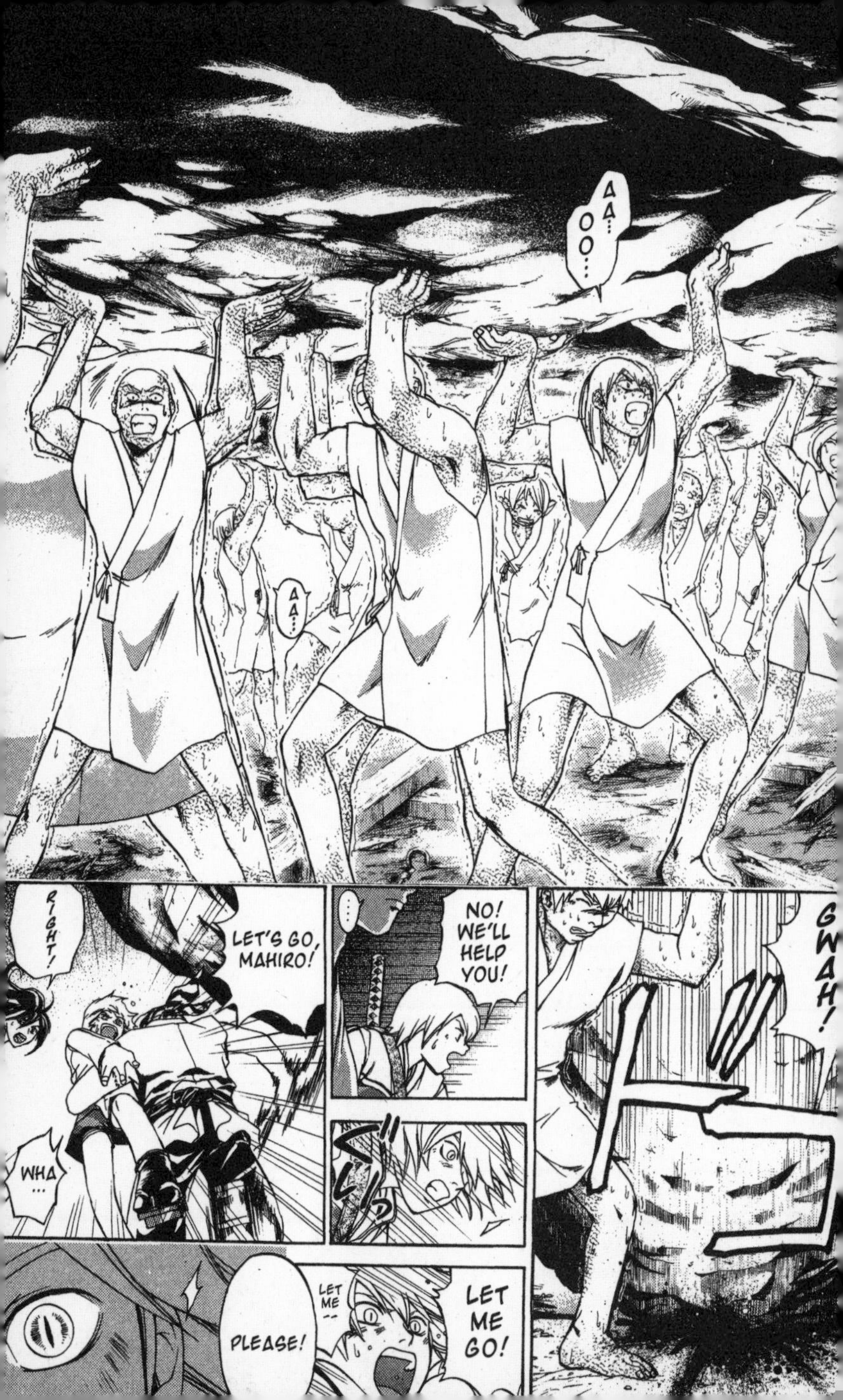
AA... OO...
AA...
GWAH!
NO! WE'LL HELP YOU!
...
LET'S GO, MAHIRO!
RIGHT!
WHA ...
LET ME GO!
LET ME --
PLEASE!

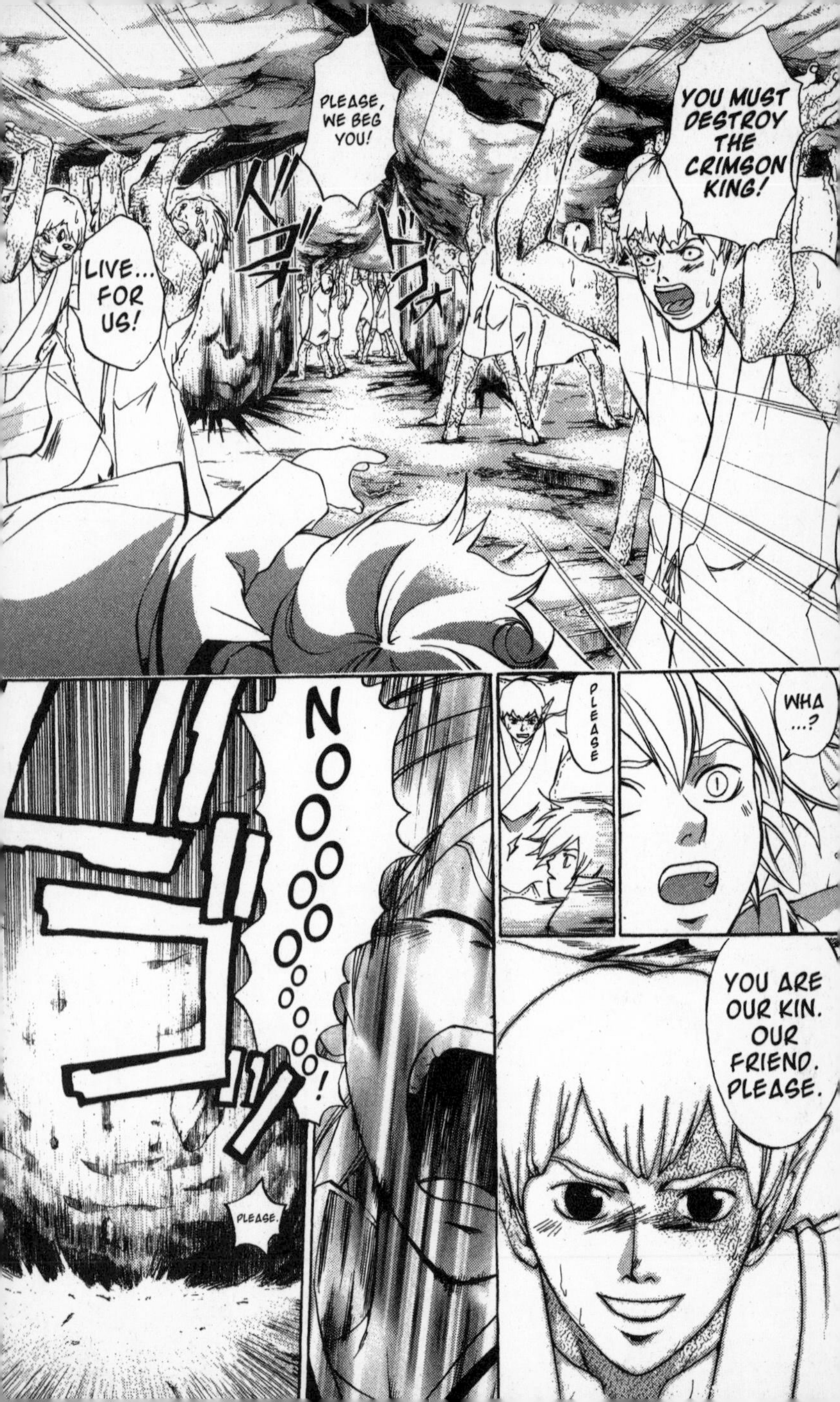
YOU MUST DESTROY THE CRIMSON KING!
PLEASE, WE BEG YOU!
LIVE... FOR US!
WHA ...?
PLEASE
YOU ARE OUR KIN. OUR FRIEND. PLEASE.
NOOOOOOOOOOOOOO!
PLEASE.

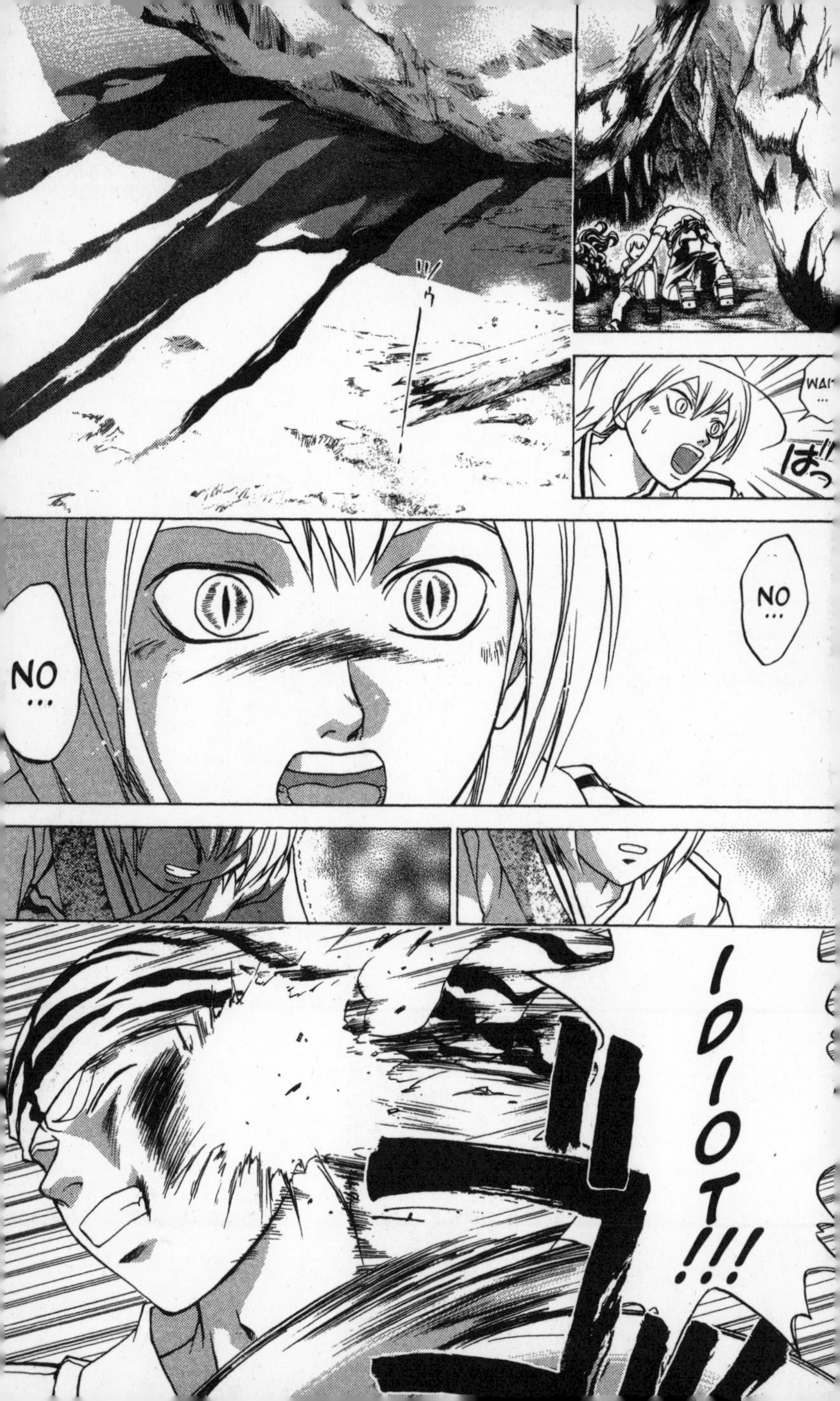
WAI ...
ばっ
ヅウー
NO ...
NO ...
IDIOT!!!

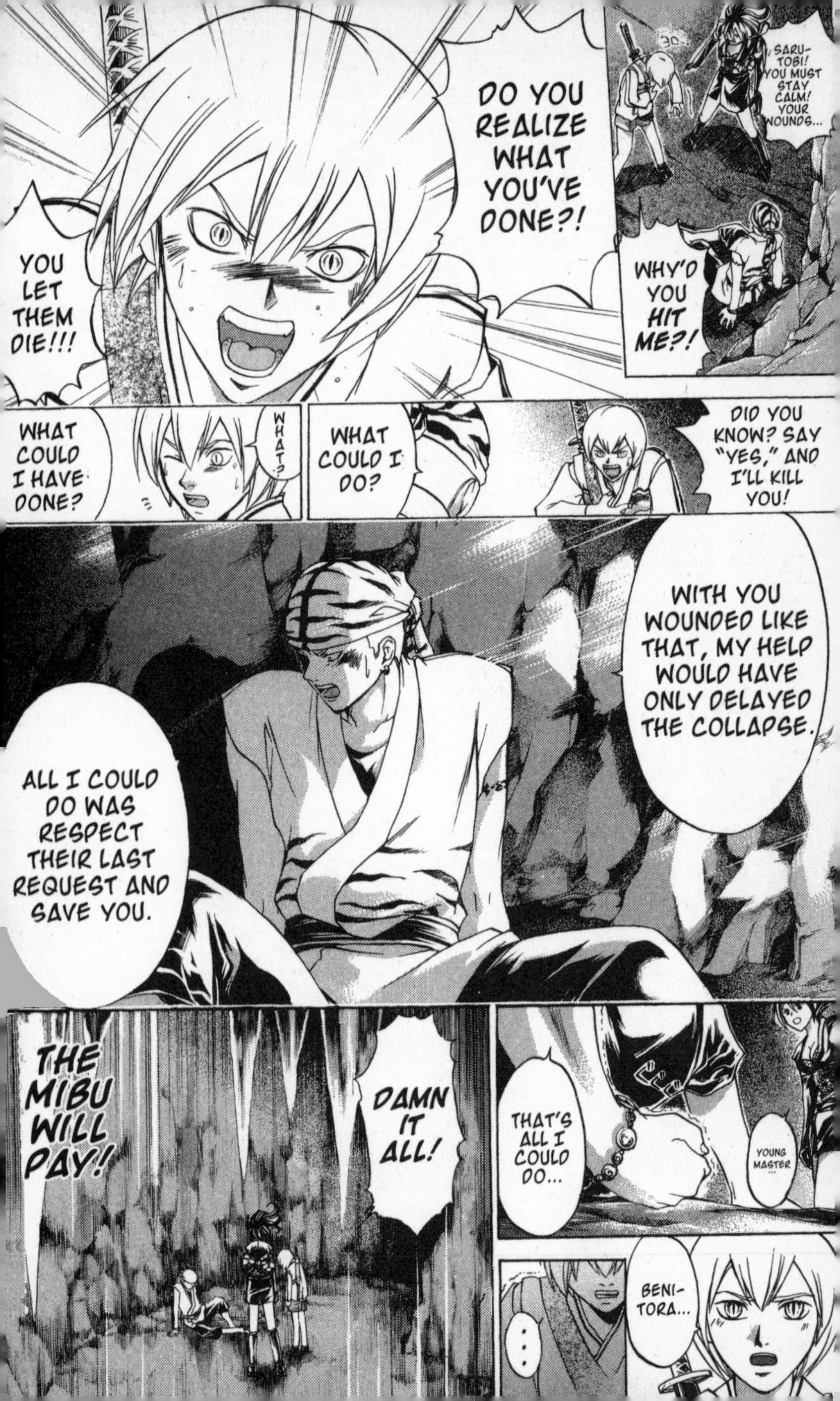
SARU-TOBI! YOU MUST STAY CALM! YOUR WOUNDS...
WHY'D YOU HIT ME?!
DO YOU REALIZE WHAT YOU'VE DONE?!
YOU LET THEM DIE!!!
DID YOU KNOW? SAY "YES," AND I'LL KILL YOU!
WHAT COULD I DO?
WHAT?!
WHAT COULD I HAVE DONE?
WITH YOU WOUNDED LIKE THAT, MY HELP WOULD HAVE ONLY DELAYED THE COLLAPSE.
ALL I COULD DO WAS RESPECT THEIR LAST REQUEST AND SAVE YOU.
YOUNG MASTER...
THAT'S ALL I COULD DO...
BENI-TORA...
...
DAMN IT ALL!
THE MIBU WILL PAY!

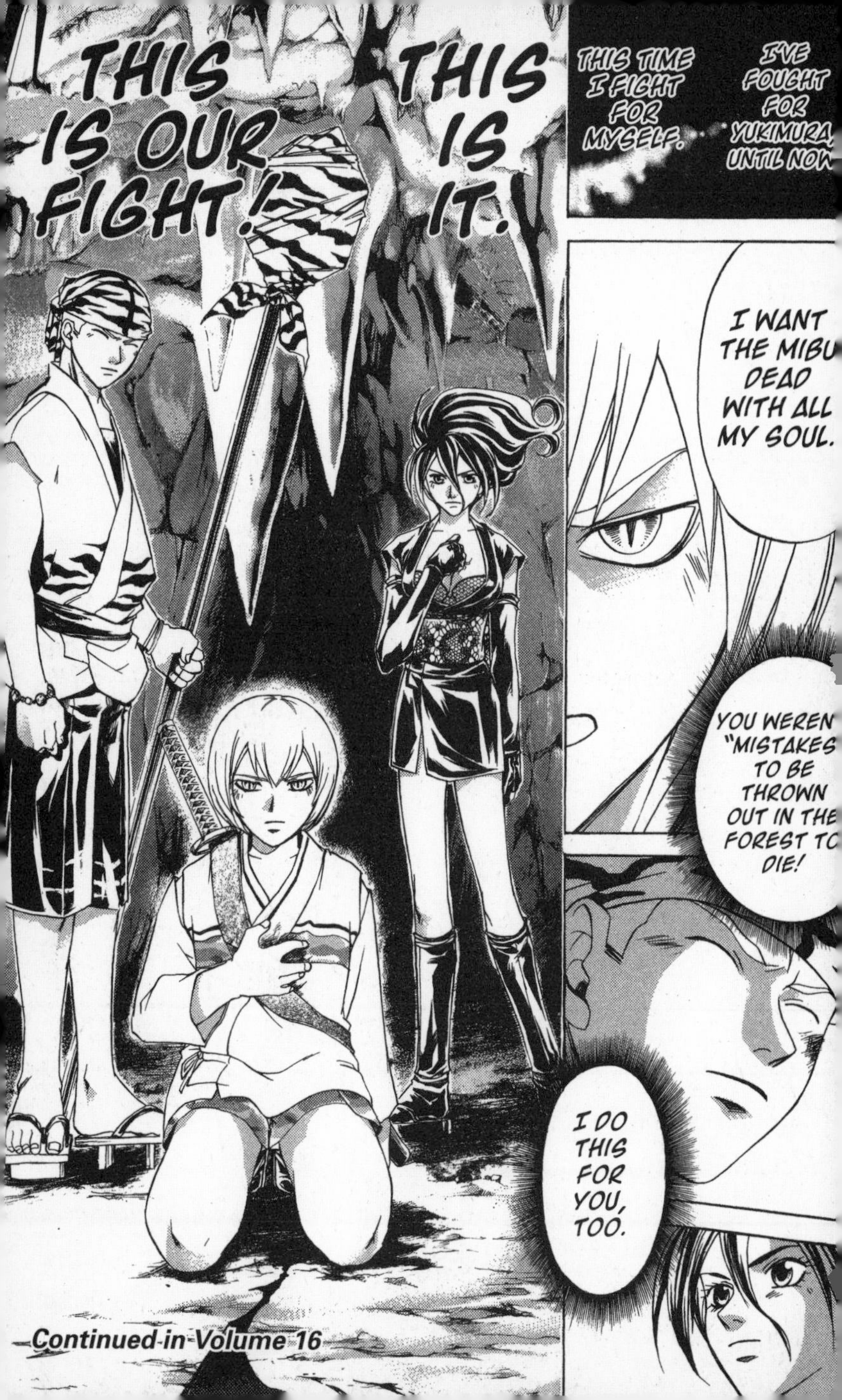
I'VE FOUGHT FOR YUKIMURA, UNTIL NOW
THIS TIME I FIGHT FOR MYSELF.
I WANT THE MIBU DEAD WITH ALL MY SOUL.
YOU WEREN "MISTAKES TO BE THROWN OUT IN THE FOREST TO DIE!
I DO THIS FOR YOU, TOO.
THIS IS IT.
THIS IS OUR FIGHT!
Continued in Volume 16

2002年 THE 2002 VALENTINES WAR

I GOT EVEN MORE CHOCOLATE AND PRESENTS THIS YEAR THAN LAST! THANKS! [SMALL]
I SHARED WITH THE STAFF!
ALL THAT LOVE IS GOING RIGHT INTO THE CHARACTERS!!!
HERE ARE THIS YEAR'S RESULTS ON THE BIG PAGE!!!

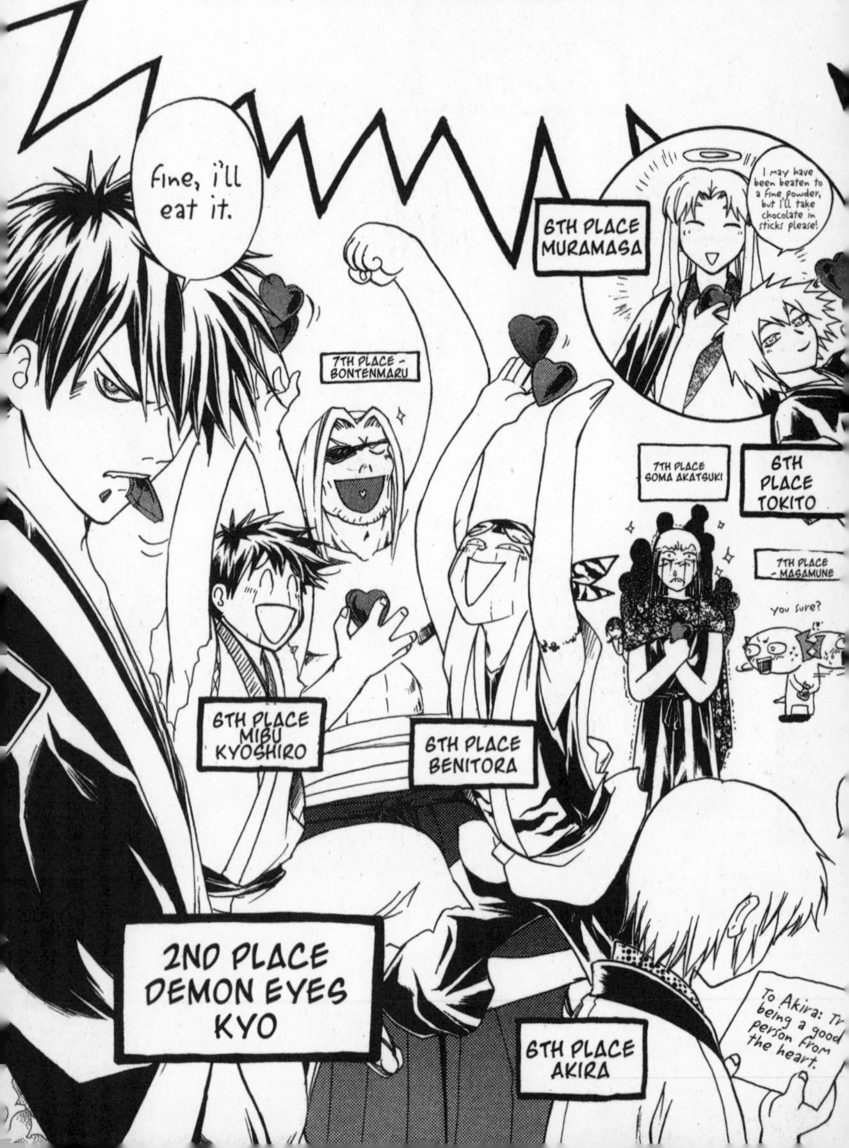

I may have been beaten to a fine powder, but I'll take chocolate in sticks please!
6TH PLACE MURAMASA
fine, i'll eat it.
6TH PLACE TOKITO
7TH PLACE SOMA AKATSUKI
7TH PLACE - MASAMUNE
You sure?
7TH PLACE - BONTENMARU
6TH PLACE BENITORA
6TH PLACE MIBU KYOSHIRO
To Akira: Tr being a good person from the heart.
6TH PLACE AKIRA
2ND PLACE DEMON EYES KYO

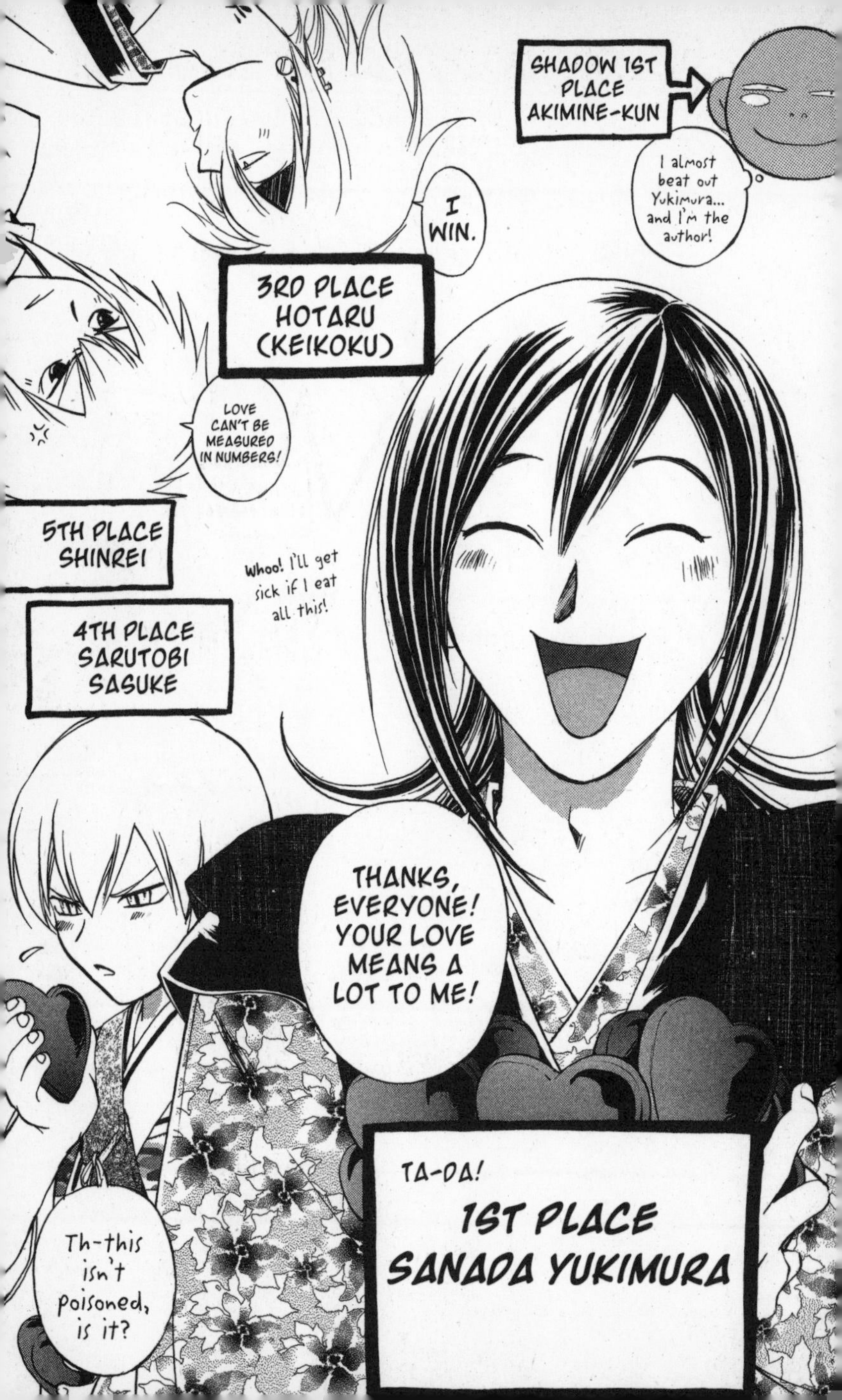
SHADOW 1ST PLACE AKIMINE-KUN
I almost beat out Yukimura... and I'm the author!
I WIN.
3RD PLACE HOTARU (KEIKOKU)
LOVE CAN'T BE MEASURED IN NUMBERS!
Whoo! I'll get sick if I eat all this!
5TH PLACE SHINREI
4TH PLACE SARUTOBI SASUKE
THANKS, EVERYONE! YOUR LOVE MEANS A LOT TO ME!
TA-DA!
1ST PLACE SANADA YUKIMURA
Th-this isn't poisoned, is it?

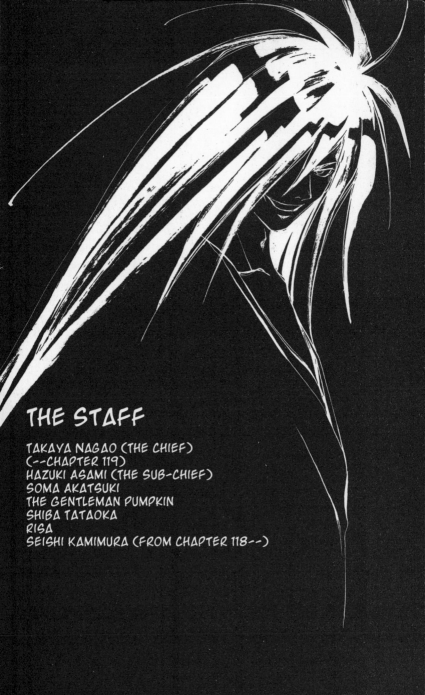

THE STAFF

TAKAYA NAGAO (THE CHIEF)
(--CHAPTER 119)
HAZUKI ASAMI (THE SUB-CHIEF)
SOMA AKATSUKI
THE GENTLEMAN PUMPKIN
SHIBA TATAOKA
RISA
SEISHI KAMIMURA (FROM CHAPTER 118--)

SAMURAI DEEPER KYO NEXT

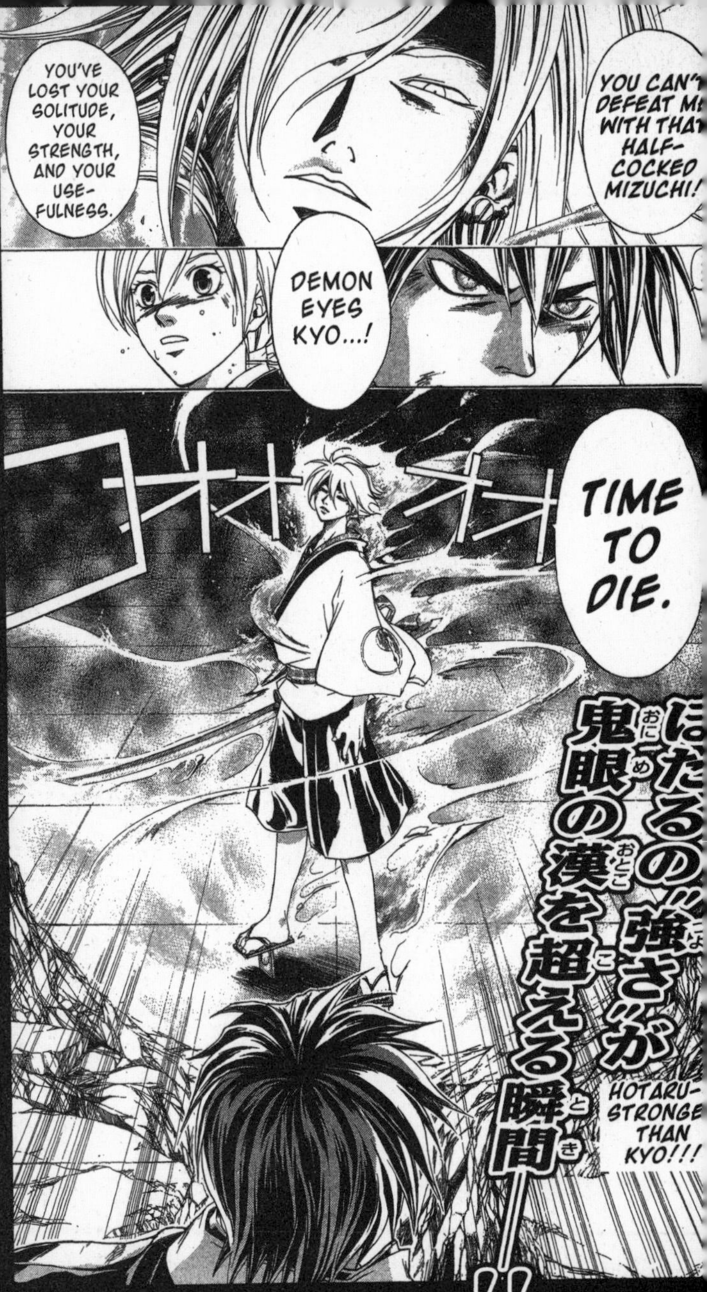
YOU CAN'T DEFEAT ME WITH THAT HALF-COCKED MIZUCHI!
YOU'VE LOST YOUR SOLITUDE, YOUR STRENGTH, AND YOUR USE-FULNESS.
DEMON EYES KYO...!
TIME TO DIE.
コオオオオ
たるの強さが
鬼眼の漢を超える瞬間!!
HOTARU-STRONGE THAN KYO!!!

BACKS AGAINST THE WALL IN SDK VOLUME 16, ON SALE SOON!!!

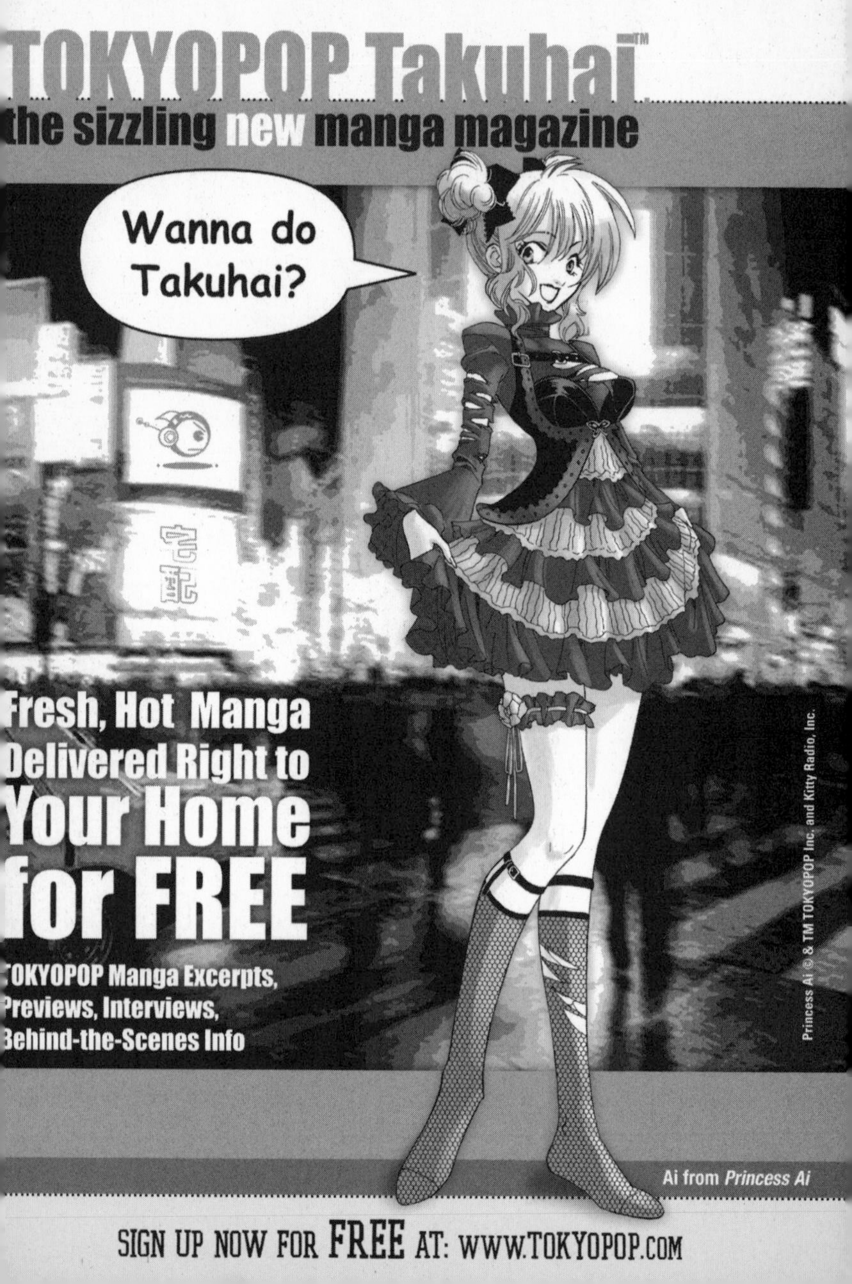
TOKYOPOP Takuhai™
the sizzling new manga magazine
Wanna do Takuhai?
宅配
Fresh, Hot Manga Delivered Right to Your Home for FREE
TOKYOPOP Manga Excerpts, Previews, Interviews, Behind-the-Scenes Info
Princess Ai © & TM TOKYOPOP Inc. and Kitty Radio, Inc.
Ai from Princess Ai
SIGN UP NOW FOR FREE AT: WWW.TOKYOPOP.COM

TOKYOPOP SHOP

WWW.TOKYOPOP.COM/SHOP

HOT NEWS!
Check out the
TOKYOPOP SHOP!
The world's best
collection of manga in
English is now available
online in one place!

SAIYUKI RELOAD

.HACK NOVEL

BIZENGHAST

Bizenghast
and other hot
titles are
available at
the store that
never closes!

- LOOK FOR SPECIAL OFFERS
- PRE-ORDER UPCOMING RELEASES
- COMPLETE YOUR COLLECTIONS

OT
OLDER TEEN
AGE 16+

In the deep South, an ancient voodoo curse unleashes the War on Flesh—a hellish plague of voracious Ew Chott hornets that raises an army of the walking dead. This undead army spreads the plague by ripping the hearts out of living creatures to make room for a Black Heart hive, all in preparation for the most awesome incarnation of evil ever imagined… An unlikely group of five mismatched individuals have to put their differences aside to try to destroy the onslaught of evil before it's too late.

VOODOO MAKES A MAN NASTY!

WAR ON FLESH

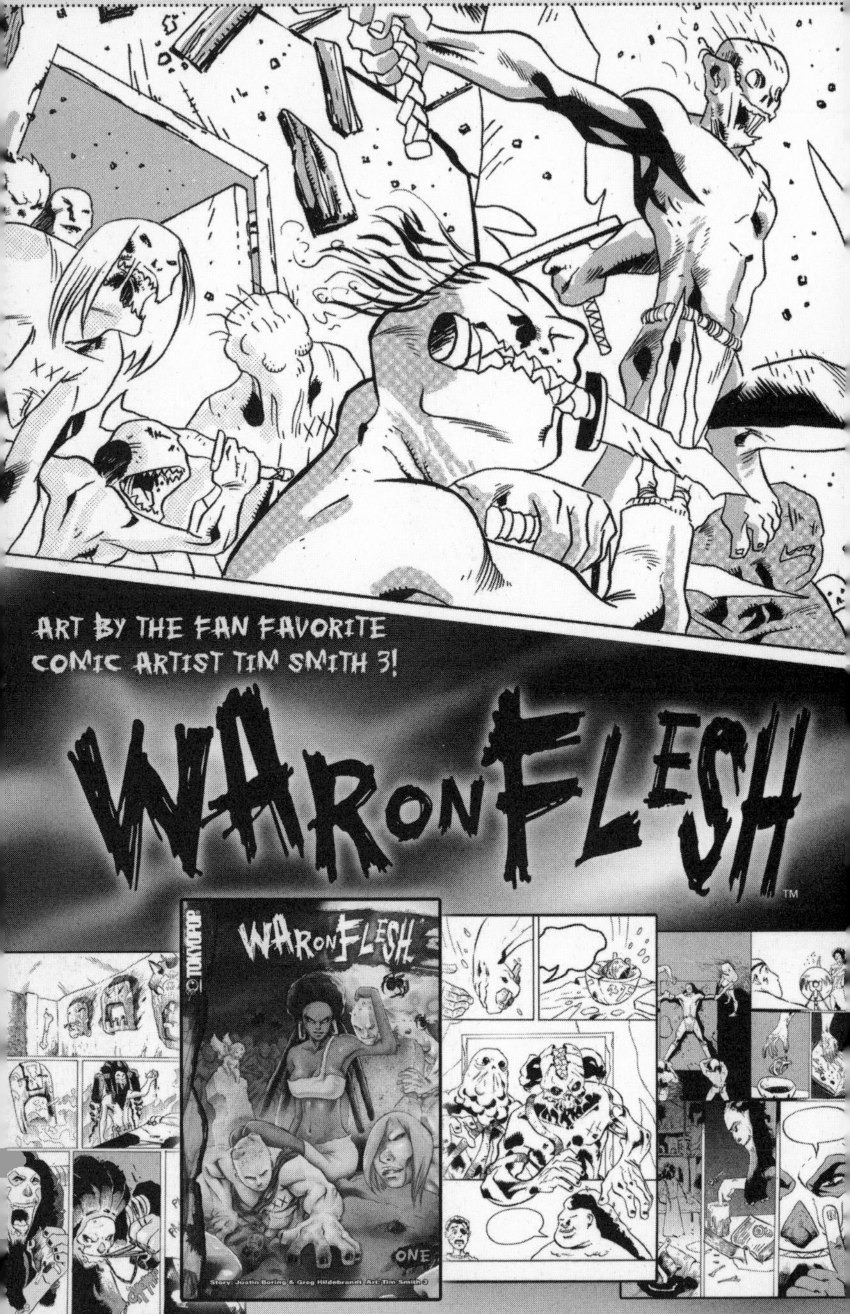
ART BY THE FAN FAVORITE
COMIC ARTIST TIM SMITH 3!
WAR ON FLESH™
WAR ON FLESH
TOKYOPOP
ONE
Story: Justin Boring & Greg Hildebrandt Art: Tim Smith 3

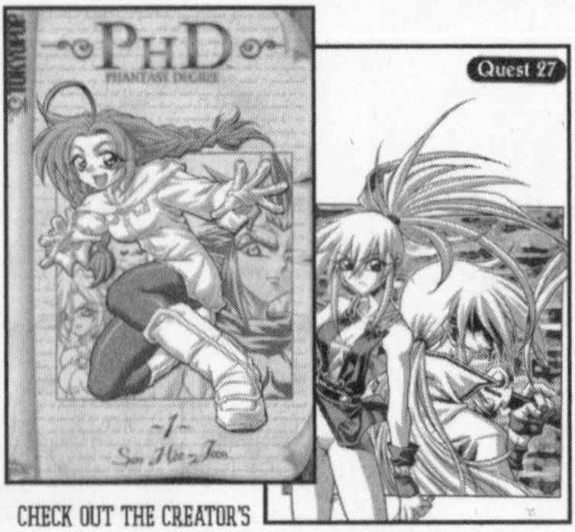
PhD
PHANTASY DEGREE
Quest 27

CHECK OUT THE CREATOR'S *iD_eNTITY*

BY SON HEE-JOON

PhD: PHANTASY DEGREE

So you think you've got it rough at *your* school? Try attending classes at Demon School Hades! When sassy, young Sang makes her monster matriculation to this arcane academy, all hell breaks loose—literally! But what would you expect when the graduating class consists of a werewolf, a mummy and demons by the score? Son Hee-Joon's underworld adventure is pure escapist fun. Always packed with action and often silly in the best sense, *PhD* never takes itself too seriously or lets the reader stop to catch his breath.

~Bryce P. Coleman, Editor

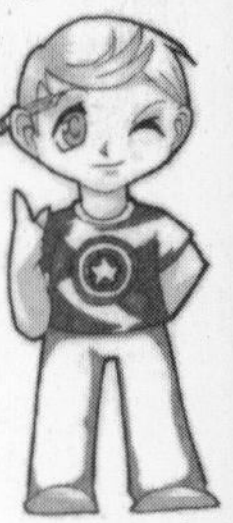

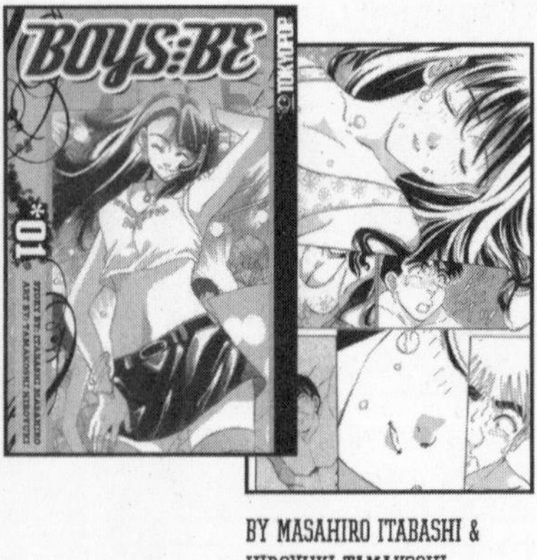
BOYS:BE
10

BY MASAHIRO ITABASHI & HIROYUKI TAMAKOSHI

BOYS BE...

Boys Be... is a series of short stories. But although the hero's name changes from tale to tale, he remains Everyboy—that dorky high school guy who'll do anything to score with the girl of his dreams. You know him. Perhaps you *are* him. He is a dirty mind with the soul of a poet, a stumblebum with a heart of sterling. We follow this guy on quest after quest to woo his lady loves. We savor his victory; we reel with his defeat...and the experience is touching, funny and above all human.

Still not convinced? I have two words for you: fan service.

~Carol Fox, Editor

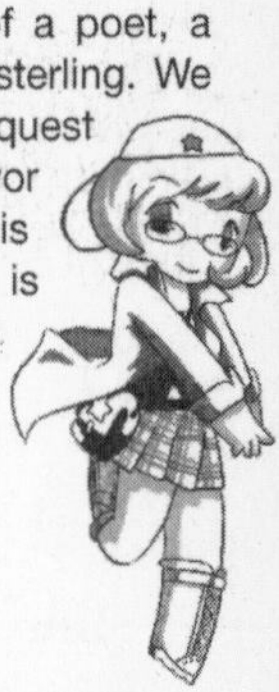

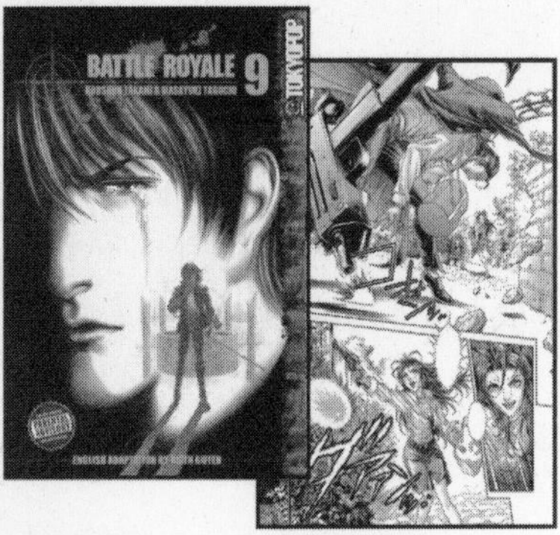
BATTLE ROYALE 9
TOKYOPOP

BY KOUSHUN TAKAMI & MASAYUKI TAGUCHI

BATTLE ROYALE

As far as cautionary tales go, you couldn't get any timelier than *Battle Royale*. Telling the bleak story of a class of middle school students who are forced to fight one another to the death on national television, Koushun Takami and Masayuki Taguchi have created a dark satire that's sickening, yet undeniably exciting as well. And if we have that reaction reading it, it becomes alarmingly clear how the students could be so easily swayed into *doing* it.

~Tim Beedle, Editor

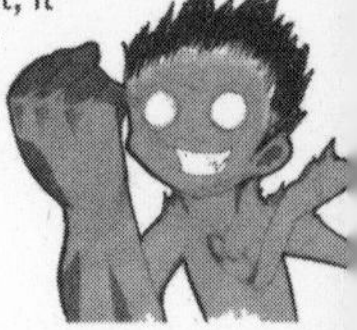

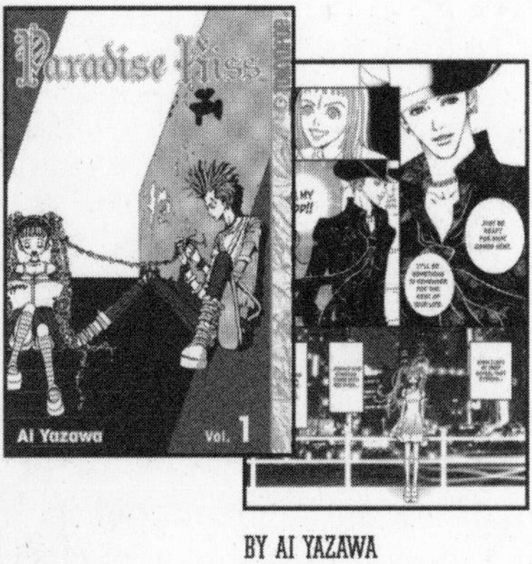
Paradise Kiss
TOKYOPOP
Ai Yazawa
Vol. 1

BY AI YAZAWA

PARADISE KISS

The clothes! The romance! The clothes! The intrigue! And did I mention the clothes?! *Paradise Kiss* is the best fashion manga ever written, from one of the hottest shojo artists in Japan. Ai Yazawa is the coolest. Not only did she create the character designs for *Princess Ai*, which were amazing, but she also produced five fab volumes of *Paradise Kiss*, a manga series bursting with fashion and passion. Read it and be inspired.

~Julie Taylor, Sr. Editor

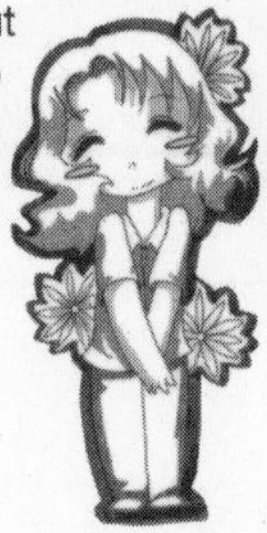

STOP!

This is the back of the book.
You wouldn't want to spoil a great ending!

This book is printed "manga-style," in the authentic Japanese right-to-left format. Since none of the artwork has been flipped or altered, readers get to experience the story just as the creator intended. You've been asking for it, so TOKYOPOP® delivered: authentic, hot-off-the-press, and far more fun!

DIRECTIONS

If this is your first time reading manga-style, here's a quick guide to help you understand how it works.

It's easy... just start in the top right panel and follow the numbers. Have fun, and look for more 100% authentic manga from TOKYOPOP®!